always up to date

The law changes, but Nolo is on top of it! We offer several
ways to make sure you and your Nolo products are up to date:

1 **Nolo's Legal Updater**
We'll send you an email whenever a new edition of this book
is published! Sign up at **www.nolo.com/legalupdater**.

2 **Updates @ Nolo.com**
Check www.nolo.com/update to find recent changes
in the law that affect the current edition of your book.

3 **Nolo Customer Service**
To make sure that this edition of the book is the most
recent one, call us at **800-728-3555** and ask one of
our friendly customer service representatives.
Or find out at **www.nolo.com**.

5th Edition

Your Limited Liability Company

An Operating Manual

By Attorney Anthony Mancuso

FIFTH EDITION	JULY 2007
Editor	CATHERINE CAPUTO
Proofreader	PAUL TYLER
CD-ROM Preparation	ELLEN BITTER
Index	MEDEA MINNICH
Printing	DELTA PRINTING SOLUTIONS, INC.

Mancuso, Anthony.
  Your limited liability company : an operating manual / Anthony Mancuso. -- 5th ed.
    p. cm.
  ISBN-13: 978-1-4133-0651-4 (pbk.)
  ISBN-10: 1-4133-0651-9 (pbk.)
   1. Private companies--United States--Popular works. I. Title.
  KF1380.Z9M3643 2007
  346.73'0668--dc22

2007002245

Quantity sales: For information on bulk purchases or corporate premium sales, please contact the Special Sales Department. For academic sales or textbook adoptions, ask for Academic Sales. Call 800-955-4775 or write to Nolo, 950 Parker Street, Berkeley, CA 94710.

Acknowledgments

Many thanks to Cathy Caputo for her invaluable assistance in organizing and editing this edition of this book. Thanks also to Jaleh Doane and all of Nolo's Production Department for their great design and layout work and to André Zivkovich and Ellen Bitter in Nolo's Applications Development Department for making all the forms accessible on the CD-ROM.

About the Author

Anthony Mancuso is a corporations and limited liability company expert. He graduated from Hastings College of Law in San Francisco and is an active member of the California State Bar. He performs research, writes books, and programs software in the fields of corporate and LLC law, and studies advanced business taxation at Golden Gate University in San Francisco. He also has been a consultant for Silicon Valley EDA (Electronic Design Automation) companies working on C++ software documentation automation.

Tony is also the author of Nolo's bestselling titles on forming and operating corporations (both profit and nonprofit) and limited liability companies, including *Incorporate Your Business*, *How to Form a Nonprofit Corporation* (national and California editions), *Form Your Own Limited Liability Company*, *The Corporate Records Handbook*, and *LLC or Corporation*? He researched, wrote and programmed *LLCMaker* and *Incorporator Pro* software programs, published by Nolo, which generate state-by-state articles and other forms for organizing corporations and LLCs. His books and software have shown over a quarter of a million businesses and organizations how to form an LLC or corporation. He also is a licensed helicopter pilot and performs as a guitarist in various musical idioms, including jazz and blues.

Table of Contents

Preparing for LLC Meetings

Meeting Summary Sheet

Meeting Participant List

Notice of Meeting

Acknowledgment of Receipt of Notice of Meeting

Membership Voting Proxy

Certification of Mailing of Notice

LLC Minutes and Written Consents

Minutes of LLC Meeting

Waiver of Notice of Meeting

Approval of LLC Minutes

Cover Letter for Approval of Minutes of LLC Meeting

Written Consent to Action Without Meeting

Standard LLC Business Resolutions

Authorization of Treasurer to Open and Use LLC Accounts

Authorization of Treasurer to Open and Use Specific LLC Account(s)

Authorization of LLC Account and Designation of Authorized Signers

Authorization of Rental of Safe Deposit Box

Adoption of Assumed LLC Name

Approval of Contract

Approval of Lease of Premises by LLC

Purchase of Real Property by LLC

Authorization of Sale of Real Property by LLC

Delegation of LLC Authority

Ratification of Contract or Transaction

Rescission of Authority

Certification of LLC Resolution

Affidavit of LLC Resolution

Acknowledgment

LLC Tax Resolutions

LLC Election of Corporate Tax Treatment

Approval of Independent Audit of LLC Financial Records

Approval of LLC Tax Year

Resolutions to Amend the LLC Articles and Operating Agreement

Approval of Amendment to Articles of Organization

Approval of Restatement of Articles of Organization

Amendment of Articles Form

Amendment of LLC Operating Agreement

Membership Resolutions

Approval of LLC Distribution

Approval of Additional Contributions of Capital by Members

Admission of New Member

Approval of Transfer of Membership

Approval of LLC Purchase of Interest of Withdrawing Member

LLC Hiring and Compensation Resolutions

Approval of LLC Hiring

Approval of Bonuses and Salary Increases

Approval of Independent Contractor Services

Appointment of LLC Officers

Authorization of Payment for Attending LLC Meetings

Annual Stipend for Attendance at LLC Meetings

LLC Indemnification and Insurance

Loans to the LLC

Authorization of Loan to LLC at Specific Terms

Authorization of Maximum Loan Amount to LLC

Authorization of LLC Representative to Borrow Funds on Behalf of LLC as Needed

Authorization of Loan Terms Secured by LLC Property

Authorization of Line of Credit

Authorization of Line of Credit With Cap on Each Transaction

Loans by the LLC

Self-Interested Business Dealings Between the LLC and Its Members or Managers

Index

Your LLC Companion

Congratulations—you've formed a limited liability company (LLC)! Running your business as an LLC gives you limited liability for business debts (like a corporation) but allows you to avoid some of the legal formalities and tax rules that apply to corporations. It's one of the most flexible—and efficient—ways small business owners can structure their business.

To get your LLC up and running, you've already had to complete some essential start-up tasks: preparing and filing articles of organization (called a "certificate of organization" in some states) and preparing and signing an LLC operating agreement. Once these documents are completed and the initial membership interests are sold to the founders and initial investors, you may be tempted to forego any further formalities and get back to doing what you do best—running the day-to-day business.

You can't simply keep running your business exactly as you did before you formed an LLC, however. There are a few new formalities and paperwork requirements you should observe to keep proper records of important LLC decisions, transactions, and meetings. This will protect your LLC status and keep members, managers, and others apprised of the LLC's activities.

This book will help you take care of these formalities, quickly and easily. It provides all of the forms and advice you'll need to:

- hold and document LLC managers' and members' meetings
- document actions taken by managers and members without having met, and
- approve common ongoing LLC legal, tax, and business decisions.

Why You Should Record Key LLC Decisions

If you don't take the time to properly memorialize important decisions and meetings, you could run into trouble. You can lose crucial tax benefits if you fail to properly document and support important tax decisions and elections. Even worse, ignoring the legal technicalities of running your LLC may jeopardize its legal existence as a separate business entity, which means that you could be held personally liable for LLC debts. And, of course, as time passes and memories fade, the reasons important LLC decisions were made, and the extent of each member's or manager's participation in these decisions, may be forgotten. This can lead to controversy and dissension, even in the ranks of a closely held LLC, unless you use written minutes, consent forms, and resolutions to keep track of all important LLC decisions and votes.

Here are some reasons why you should record important LLC decisions:

- Annual LLC meetings may be required under your state law. If you fail to pay at least minimal attention to this and other ongoing legal formalities, you may lose the protection of your LLC limited liability status. If this happens, LLC members can be held personally liable for the debts of the LLC.

- The paperwork you create will provide a record of important LLC transactions. This "paper trail" can be important if disputes arise. It will show your managers, members, creditors, and suppliers, as well as the IRS and the courts, that you acted appropriately and in compliance with legal requirements.

- Formally documenting key LLC actions is a sure-fire way to keep all members informed of major LLC decisions, particularly those who don't manage the business day to day.

- Owners of small LLCs commonly approve business transactions in which they have personal, material, or financial interests. Your minutes or consent forms can help prevent legal problems by proving that these "self-interested" decisions were arrived at fairly, after careful consideration of the issues and full disclosure to the disinterested owners.

- Institutions like banks, trust companies, escrow companies, title companies, and property management companies may refuse to do business with your LLC unless you submit a copy of a manager or membership resolution approving the transaction in question. If you want to take out a loan or purchase or rent property, for example, you may have to provide a resolution authorizing the transaction.

You don't need to document routine business decisions—only those that require formal manager or membership approval. In other words, you don't have to clutter up your LLC records binder (see Chapter 1) with records of decisions to purchase supplies or products, maintain or improve services or products, or other day-to-day issues.

However, key legal, tax, and financial decisions absolutely should be acted on and recorded by your managers and/or members. For example, you'll want to keep records of:

- the proceedings of annual meetings of managers and/or members

- the admission of a new member by the LLC

- the buyback of an existing membership interest by the LLC

- the purchase of real estate

- the authorization of a significant loan or substantial line of credit, and

- important federal or state tax elections.

These and other important decisions should be made by your managers and/or members and backed with legal paperwork. That way, you'll have solid documentation if key decisions are questioned or reviewed later by managers, members, creditors, the courts, or the IRS.

Who Should Use This Book

Although all LLCs should formally record important decisions, some may need more help than this book provides. This book is for smaller LLCs—those that are privately owned and have a manageable number of members (up to about 35) and employees (up to about 50)—whose members and managers can work together without a great deal of controversy. A typical example is a family-owned LLC or an LLC that is owned by several people.

If your LLC is larger and/or sells membership interests to the public, you will have to contend with a wider variety of viewpoints—and may not be able to count on the cooperation of all members in making or documenting decisions. Similarly, if a significant number of your LLC's members don't participate in the day-to-day management of the business, you'll need to use procedures that keep these members informed of LLC actions. The procedures described in this book won't be sufficient for LLCs that have to contend with a lot of disagreement among members or have to spend significant time and energy apprising far-flung, uninvolved members of the LLC's activities.

Managers and Members in a Small LLC

In every business, someone must be responsible for managing the day-to-day affairs of the company, and the LLC is no exception. There are two types of LLC management structures. In a member-managed LLC, all members are responsible for managing the business; most small LLCs take this form. In a manager-managed LLC, the business is managed by just some (not all) of its members, or is managed by one or more managers who is not an LLC member.

This book refers to "managers' meetings" and "members' meetings." However, if your LLC is member-managed, then you don't have to hold separate managers' meetings to approve LLC decisions—a members' meeting will do. If your LLC is manager-managed, then you should hold separate managers' and members' meetings to approve important LLC decisions. After all, you want to make sure that all owners (all members) agree with the important decisions made by the management team.

How to Use This Book

This book explains, step by step, how to document important LLC decisions, votes, and transactions. You'll learn how to hold meetings and create the minutes, written consent forms, resolutions, and promissory notes necessary to record LLC business.

You can handle most of this routine paperwork yourself, using the forms and instructions in this book. And, as explained in Chapter 2, LLC owners don't necessarily have to get together in person every time you have to make an important decision—you may also be able to approve LLC business through written consents or minutes. (The methods you can use depend on your state's law—see Appendix B for state-by-state LLC rules.) The information in this book will help you decide which approval method to use and how to prepare the necessary records.

The paperwork you'll need to complete consists of minutes and written consent forms for members and managers, together with resolution forms that are inserted into the minutes or consent forms to show approval of various types of LLC actions. To help you complete these forms, you'll find detailed instructions and samples in each chapter. All of the forms are included in Appendix C and on the CD-ROM accompanying this book.

However, you won't have to read the whole book cover to cover to get the information and forms you need. Start by reading Chapters 1 and 2, which explain some basics about LLCs and the options you have for making decisions. Armed with this information, you can decide whether to document the particular decision you're facing by (1) holding an actual meeting of your members and/or managers, (2) preparing minutes for a meeting that doesn't actually occur (called a "paper meeting"), or

(3) obtaining the written consent of your members and/or managers to the action or decision at hand.

- If you decide to hold a real meeting of your managers and/or members, follow the steps covered in Chapters 3 and 4 to prepare for and hold the meeting. Then prepare the appropriate minutes form to document the decisions taken at the meeting, following the step-by-step instructions in Chapter 5.

- If you opt for a "paper" meeting—one that occurs on paper only but reflects the real decisions of your managers and members— follow the instructions for creating minutes for a paper meeting in Chapter 6.

- To document a particular decision by preparing written consent forms to be signed by the managers and/or members, follow the instructions in Chapter 7.

- If a business deal or transaction should be approved—and is covered by—a resolution included in this book (Chapters 8 through 15), fill in the resolution form following the instructions contained in the appropriate chapter, then place or paste the completed resolution into your minutes or consent form. (See the beginning of Appendix C for a list of resolution forms included with this book, with a cross-reference to the chapter and section of the book that contains instructions for preparing each resolution.)

When to Consult a Professional

Small, privately held LLCs routinely hold LLC meetings and prepare standard resolutions and other legal paperwork. However, you may occasionally face a more complicated decision that has important legal, tax, or financial ramifications—and in this situation, you should get some professional advice.

Please see a tax or legal specialist before using the forms in this book if:

- the decision you are facing is complex

- you anticipate any complications or objections, or

- you simply have questions and need more information.

A consultation of this sort will be far more cost-effective than making the wrong decision and having to fix it later. For information on choosing and using a legal or tax professional, see Chapter 16. ●

LLC Documents

This book explains how to create the documents you need to record important LLC decisions and transactions. But these minutes, consents, and resolutions aren't the only written records your LLC must keep—you'll also need to have other basic documents, such as your articles of organization, operating agreement, and membership paperwork. This chapter explains how to organize and store these important documents, what their purpose is, and how they work—together with the laws of your state—to provide the legal framework for your LLC's operations.

Organize Your LLC Records

Anyone who sets up an LLC needs to be able to quickly locate key organizational documents. These are your LLC articles of organization (sometimes called a "certificate of formation" or a "certificate of organization") and operating agreement. Because these are the founding documents—like the charter—of your LLC, you'll refer to them again and again. When using this book to produce LLC minutes and consent forms, you'll often have to consult your LLC's organizational documents.

If you have not already done so, you should set up an LLC records binder that contains all of your important LLC documents. You can do this on your own, using a simple three-ring binder.

Your LLC records binder should contain the following items, each of which is discussed in "Basic LLC Documents," below:

- articles of organization
- operating agreement
- membership certificates and stubs (if your LLC decides to issue certificates to members)

- membership register that lists the names and addresses of your members
- membership transfer ledger, showing the dates of any transfers of membership interests by a member, and
- minutes of LLC meetings and written consent forms.

If you formed your LLC with the help of a professional, such as a lawyer, accountant, paralegal, or financial planner, you probably received originals or copies of these documents. However, some lawyers attempt to hold on to LLC records in the hope that you will ask them to take care of all ongoing technicalities. If so, you will need to request the originals or copies of all the LLC documents in your client file. (In California, you are entitled to the original LLC documents, although the lawyer can keep copies, made at the lawyer's expense.) These documents are your property, so don't take "No" for an answer.

If you can't find the original or a copy of your articles, write your secretary of state's LLC filing office and request a certified or file-stamped copy of your articles. (Appendix B lists state LLC filing offices and their addresses and phone numbers.) It's a good idea to call first so that you can also send the correct copying fee, which should be just a few dollars.

Basic LLC Documents

The LLC documents you are required to have on hand depend on your state's LLC act—the law regulating the operations of LLCs in your state. Many states require LLCs to maintain specified records and/or make them available for inspection by members and managers. Examples of documents you might have to make available include membership lists, articles of organization, your LLC's operating agreement, tax returns and financial records, and records of each member's contribution of money, property, or services—or promise to provide the same—to the LLC.

How to Find Your State's LLC Act

In Appendix B you'll find information on each state's LLC rules, including a citation to each state's LLC act. These laws govern the operation of LLCs in every state. Although Appendix B summarizes key state rules, you may need more information—or simply want to read the law yourself.

Here are three easy ways to find your state's LLC act:

1. Check your state LLC office's website. Most states provide an online version of their LLC act. Appendix B provides the URLs for each state's LLC office, along with instructions for linking to the LLC act, if it's available on the Web.

2. Ask at your state LLC office. Many will provide a copy of the LLC act free, or for a small charge. Or, the office may refer you to a commercial publisher that sells a volume containing the state's LLC act.

3. Visit a local law library, a law school library that is open to the public, or a large public library with a substantial business collection. Ask the research librarian to show you where the business material is shelved, then look up the law using the citation in Appendix B.

Even if your state doesn't require you to keep these documents, it's still a very good idea. Because your operating agreement and articles of organization dictate how your LLC will be run, you will have to refer to them often for day-to-day issues. Records on members and managers—and their contributions and

obligations to the LLC—will be equally useful. And, as explained in the Introduction to this book, you will want to have records of important LLC decisions and transactions, in the form of minutes, consent forms, and resolutions.

Articles of Organization

The document that formally creates an LLC is its articles of organization (in some states, this document is called a certificate of organization or certificate of formation). An LLC comes into existence when its articles of organization are filed with the state LLC filing office. The articles usually contain fundamental structural information about the company, such as:

- the name of the LLC
- whether the LLC is managed by all of its members or by specially selected managers (most smaller LLCs are member-managed)
- the names and addresses of its members and/or managers and its registered agent, and
- the agent's office address (this is the registered office of the LLC to which the state can send documents and people can serve legal papers on the LLC).

For the majority of small LLCs, no additional information is required in this document. However, larger LLCs sometimes add optional articles containing special provisions if they wish to set up a more complex structure for their LLC.

RESOURCE

If you have not yet formed your LLC, Nolo publishes *Form Your Own Limited Liability Company*, also by Anthony Mancuso. This book shows you how to prepare and file articles of organization with your state's LLC filing office. It also takes you through the other LLC formation steps, including the preparation of an LLC operating agreement. This book is good in all states, with state-by-state rules included in Appendix B. In addition, *Nolo's LLC Maker* software creates articles of organization and operating agreements for every state.

Do Your Articles Limit the Term of Your LLC?

Early state LLC statutes required LLCs to limit their own duration in their articles—for example, to a term of 30 years. Once the term expired, the LLC would automatically dissolve. This term-limit requirement was tied to old federal tax classification rules requiring LLCs to limit their lifespan in order to be treated as a partnership for tax purposes (the tax treatment most LLC owners desire for their LLC). Under the current IRS rules, however, an LLC is automatically treated as a partnership for tax purposes, so most states have eliminated this "limited term" requirement.

If your LLC articles limit the term of your LLC, and your state no longer requires this limitation, you have two options:

1. File an amendment to your articles deleting the term limit—just retype your articles, omitting the provision that limits the term of your LLC—and file the amended articles with the state LLC filing office.

2. Do nothing for now, but make a note in your LLC records to file the amendment to the articles later, before the end of the term stated in your articles.

Operating Agreement

The operating agreement is an LLC's second-most important document. You don't have to file the operating agreement with the state—it is an internal document, much like corporate bylaws or a partnership agreement.

The operating agreement lists the capital, profits, and voting interests of current LLC members, and may include other operating rules for your business. For example, the operating agreement may specify how often regular meetings of managers and members will be held and the call, notice, quorum, and voting rules for each type of meeting. Or it may not deal with these issues, leaving these details to the LLC managers and members to decide later. Typically, the operating agreement also includes state requirements for approving special matters, such as any state-mandated manager and member voting requirements for admitting new members or for approving the sale of a membership interest.

 CAUTION

Do your voting rules need an update? Many states have changed their voting rules for LLCs. For example, state rules used to require a majority vote of all members to continue the legal existence of the LLC after a member dies, withdraws, or otherwise gives up his or her membership interest. This rule was intended to help LLCs qualify for partnership classification with the IRS. Because LLCs are now automatically treated as partnerships for tax purposes by the IRS and most states, however, this rule is no longer necessary—and many states have eliminated it. If your operating agreement includes this outdated rule, you might want to take it out. On the other hand, you may want to continue following it, even though you are no longer legally required to do so. After all, it shouldn't be difficult to get all members to approve the continuance of the LLC after a member withdraws. (And if it is, this is a good sign that you should resolve the disagreement before getting on with the business of your LLC.)

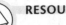 **RESOURCE**

Need help drafting an operating agreement? If you formed your LLC in a hurry, you may have filed articles of organization and done nothing more. If so, you need to take the extra step of preparing a basic operating agreement for your LLC. You can use Nolo's *Form Your Own Limited Liability Company* or *LLC Maker* to prepare your agreement.

Membership Certificates and Stubs

Your LLC is not legally required to issue membership certificates to members. However, some LLC owners like this additional formality.

If you wish to issue certificates, there is no required format. Most certificates include the name of the LLC, the name of the member, and the date the certificate was issued. Certificates are signed by one or more LLC officers (the LLC president and secretary, typically). A certificate usually does not show the exact capital, profits, or voting interests of a member; instead, it simply recites that the member is entitled to the rights and subject to the responsibilities of membership, as set out in the articles of organization and operating agreement of the LLC. After the certificate is issued to a member, the LLC's secretary should fill out the certificate stub, listing the certificate number and the date it was issued. These stubs should be kept in the LLC records binder. The stubs usually include a transfer section, to be filled in if the member transfers the membership back to the LLC or to another person.

Membership Register

State laws generally require LLCs to keep an alphabetical list of the names and addresses of all current members. This list must be available for inspection by members during regular business hours of the LLC. It should also be made available to all members at any membership meeting. The LLC secretary will use this list to prepare and mail notice of meetings to members. If the LLC is managed by specially selected managers, the LLC should also have a separate list of the managers' names and addresses.

Membership Transfer Ledger

You should keep a record of the date and details of any transfers of membership in your LLC. Typically, a membership transfer ledger shows:

- the name of the transferring member (the transferor)
- the date of the transfer of membership, and
- the name of the transferee (the person or entity to whom the membership is transferred—if a membership is redeemed (bought back) by the LLC itself, the transferee is the LLC).

If the transferring member was originally issued a membership certificate, the certificate should be returned to the LLC, marked "canceled" by the LLC secretary, and attached to the transfer ledger. If your LLC issues membership certificates with stubs that contain a transfer section for supplying transfer information, the retained certificate stubs can serve as your membership transfer ledger.

Minutes of LLC Meetings and Written Consent Forms

If your LLC has been in existence for some time, you may already have prepared minutes of LLC manager or member meetings or written consent forms. This is especially likely if a lawyer helped you form your LLC. Contact your attorney to get copies of previously prepared minutes and written consents, and place them in your LLC records binder.

If you have not prepared minutes or written consent forms, this book shows you how to prepare them (in Chapter 5 and Chapter 7).

You will add these items to your LLC records binder on an ongoing basis.

Other State Laws May Affect Your LLC's Operations

Your state's LLC act is the basic law governing the operation of LLCs in your state. However, additional state laws regulate special areas of LLC activity. These laws include:

- **Securities ("Blue Sky") laws.** These laws establish each state's rules and procedures for offering, issuing, or selling securities. In many states, LLC membership interests are considered securities, just like stock interests in a corporation or ownership interests in limited partnerships. Therefore, they must be registered with the state, or must qualify for a state exemption from registration, before being issued to members. Many states offer streamlined procedures for smaller businesses issuing shares to a limited number of people.

- **Tax laws.** Each state's tax or revenue code (or similar law) regulates the taxation of business profits. In most states, LLC profits pass through to the members and are reported on their individual state income tax return (if the state imposes an individual state income tax). In some states, LLCs must pay a separate entity-level income or franchise tax like a corporation. You can find the Web address of your state's tax or revenue office in Appendix B. That website should link you to state tax publications and LLC-related tax statutes.

- **Commercial laws.** Your state's commercial code contains the rules for entering into and enforcing commercial contracts, promissory notes, and other standard commercial documents.

- **Other state and local laws.** Various laws may affect the activities and operations of all businesses, whether operated as LLCs or otherwise. For example, you might have to follow building codes, professional licensing laws, and/or zoning rules as you go about your daily business.

Using Meetings, Minutes, and Written Consents

This chapter explains the three basic ways LLCs members and managers make and formally document important decisions:

- by calling meetings of managers or members and documenting these meetings with formal minutes

- by holding a paper meeting—reaching agreement on LLC actions, then documenting those decisions with formal minutes, as if the decisions had been made at a face-to-face meeting, and

- having managers or members prepare and sign written approval paperwork (called "written consents") without convening a formal meeting.

This chapter compares these three procedures and answers common questions about their use. Once you finish this material, you should be able to decide when you need to hold formal LLC meetings and when you can document LLC decisions without a meeting.

Three Ways to Make and Document Formal LLC Decisions

There are three basic ways to make and document formal LLC decisions. They are:

- real managers' or members' meetings with minutes

- "paper" meetings with minutes, and

- actions by written consent.

Legally, it makes no difference which way—or ways—you choose. All are equally valid and will provide adequate documentation of important LLC decisions. However, each method is particularly useful in some circumstances and less useful in others. You'll find information on how to choose between these methods for a particular decision in the "Questions and Answers" section below.

Real Meeting With Minutes

Your managers or members and all interested parties can get together in person to discuss and vote on items of LLC business. During or after the meeting, written minutes should be prepared that show:

- the date, time, place, and purpose of the meeting, and

- the decisions (resolutions) approved by the managers or members.

Paper Meeting With Minutes

Here, there is no actual meeting where the managers or members come together as a group. Instead, the managers and members informally agree to a specific LLC action (to reelect the current managers or to approve the purchase of real estate, for example). Minutes are then prepared as though the decision had been approved at a real meeting of managers or members. I call these "paper" meetings, because they take place on paper only. Paper meetings are often used when LLC members don't want to go to the trouble of holding a real meeting, but do want to keep a record of important decisions with traditional formal minutes. Although state LLC acts don't specifically provide for paper meetings, they are a common method of making and documenting LLC decisions. You shouldn't have any problems as long as the decisions reflected in the minutes of the paper meeting accurately reflect the actual decisions reached by your managers or members. This procedure is quite similar to taking action by written consent (discussed below) with one key difference: Formal minutes are prepared for "paper" decisions, but not for decisions reached by written consent.

Action by Written Consent

This is the quickest way of taking formal LLC action. The managers or members approve of a decision or action by signing written consent forms specifying the items under consideration. No minutes are prepared. The written consent forms are kept in the LLC records binder, to indicate that managers and members approved the decisions.

TIP

Schedule a meeting with yourself. If you have a single-member LLC that you manage yourself, you will probably document your decisions by paper meetings (see Chapter 6) or written consents (see Chapter 7). However, a single-member or single-manager LLC can always hold a real meeting, with yourself as the lone attendee. You may also want to hold a real meeting with other people in some circumstances, such as to gather staff, officers, lawyers, and tax advisers together to hear reports and build consensus.

How Your Management Structure Affects Decision-Making Requirements

The management structure you've chosen for your LLC affects how you must make certain decisions—and who should be involved in making them.

There are two basic LLC management structures: member-managed and manager-managed:

- **A member-managed LLC** is run by all of its members. Most state statutes provide that an LLC is member-managed unless its articles say otherwise, and most small LLCs adopt this management structure.

- **A manager-managed LLC** is managed by one or more persons who are specifically designated as "managers" (the appointment of just one manager is typical). Managers may be members, officers, or anyone else (even independent contractors, or others who are not members of the LLC). To elect manager-management, the articles might say, "This LLC is managed by one or more managers, whose names and addresses are as follows: [name(s) and address(es) of manager(s)]."

In a member-managed LLC, the members make all decisions, either by holding real meetings and recording the decisions in written minutes, or by simply preparing written minutes of a paper meeting or written consents for the members to sign. But in a manager-managed LLC, where one or more persons (who may be members or nonmembers) are selected to manage the LLC, members must make certain decisions, while managers are responsible for others.

RESOURCE

Finding your state's default rules for voting. Most state LLC acts include a section titled "Management," which sets out the rules for reelection of managers and recites the duties and responsibilities of managers. (In a member-managed LLC, the members act in the place of managers and are subject to the same rights and responsibilities as those set out for managers in a manager-managed LLC.) You can find each state's voting rules—including how managers are reelected, which decisions members must make (and by what percentage of the membership), and how these decisions can be made—in Appendix B. Most of these rules are default rules, which means that they apply only if you haven't adopted different rules in your LLC articles or operating agreement.

In a manager-managed LLC, *members* typically must make these decisions:

- reelecting managers and electing new managers
- amending the LLC's articles or operating agreement
- issuing a new membership
- admitting a transferee as a member
- continuing the LLC after a member withdraws, and
- dissolving the LLC.

It is also a very good idea (though not generally required under state LLC acts) to have all members participate in decisions that significantly affect the LLC's profitability or that involve the personal financial interests of one or more managers. After all, if a course of LLC action will reduce or gamble LLC profits, obtaining the advance approval of all members can help avoid membership complaints later if the LLC loses money on the decision or deal. And if an action may benefit one or more managers personally—such as a hefty pay raise for a manager (who also works as an LLC officer and receives an officer salary) or a manager's sale of property to the LLC—asking members to approve it is just fair play and common sense. If, after full disclosure, the members approve a deal that benefits a manager personally, it's less likely that a member will complain (or sue) later. (Self-interested transactions are covered in Chapter 15.)

So how do you figure out which decisions should be approved by members and which can be made by managers? Generally, you should treat nonmanaging members in a manager-managed LLC just as you would any outside investor in a business: You don't need to involve them in basic managerial decisions, such as hiring minor employees or approving a sales contract (and they probably won't want to be bothered with these day-to-day issues). But you will want to get their advance approval for decisions that may affect their pocketbook or make them feel blindsided if they learn of the decisions later.

Questions and Answers About LLC Meetings, Minutes, and Written Consents

The questions and answers below illustrate the advantages and disadvantages of each of the three LLC decision-making methods. Which method you should use for a particular decision depends on:

- the nature of your business
- the type of decision involved, and
- the amount of time available to make and document the decision.

Should You Hold a Real or a Paper Meeting?

You should hold either a real or a paper meeting when you want to document decisions formally, using written minutes. The benefit of holding a real meeting is that it allows the participants to meet face to face and arrive at decisions that require the give-and-take of conversation, argument, or persuasion. A paper meeting does not require the time and effort necessary to gather everyone together for a meeting, but it still results in the same formal paperwork that would come out of a real meeting.

Sometimes it will be clear that you really do need to hold a formal meeting to hash out the details or discuss the pros and cons of an important decision. If all members are already in agreement, however, it may be a waste of time to actually get together. You can use whichever method works best under the circumstances.

 SKIP AHEAD

If you have a one-member LLC that you manage yourself. In practice, member meetings for a one-member LLC and manager meetings for a one-manager LLC are often held on paper only, to formally record decisions that the sole member or manager wishes to document. If you are in this situation, turn to Chapter 6, which explains how to prepare minutes for this type of "paper meeting." You may also record decisions by written consents (see Chapter 7) or hold a real one-person meeting (you can talk to yourself if you wish).

Is an LLC Required to Hold Formal Meetings?

LLC operating agreements sometimes require annual meetings of members and, in manager-managed LLCs, annual meetings of managers. In manager-managed LLCs, the annual members' meeting is held first, in order to elect the managers for the upcoming year. After the members' meeting (and usually on the same day), the annual managers' meeting is held. At this meeting, the managers accept their positions for the upcoming year and tend to any pending business and LLC planning.

All other meetings of managers or members are special meetings, which may be called (requested) anytime during the year, according to rules contained in the operating agreement. Special meetings may be called to discuss urgent items of business or to approve legal or tax formalities that arise from time to time. For example, a special meeting might be called to approve:

- the adoption of a new LLC tax year recommended by the LLC's accountant

- the conditions of a loan made by the LLC to an officer, or

- a bank loan or real estate transaction.

Why Bother to Document LLC Decisions With Minutes or Written Consent Forms?

LLC minutes and consent forms serve a dual role: They not only show that important LLC decisions were reached with the proper notice and vote of your managers or members, but they also allow you to set out the reasons for these decisions. This can be crucial if an LLC decision is later examined by the IRS as part of a tax audit or scrutinized by a court as evidence in a lawsuit. In other words, minutes serve to document and substantiate important LLC decisions.

Likewise, you can use your minutes to document LLC strategies or decisions to incur expenses that might give rise to controversy or even lawsuits. (Lawsuits may arise among the members and managers themselves, as well as from creditors making claims against the LLC because of a negligent or wrongheaded LLC decision.) Examples include:

- settling a claim against a disgruntled employee

- setting the price to buy back the membership interest of a departing member, or

- deciding to implement safeguards in a hazardous location or line of LLC activity (for instance, paying for measures to protect pedestrians at a construction site or implementing manufacturing controls in producing a consumer product).

Even if your managers or members don't need to actually meet to reach a decision, it's a good idea to prepare regular minutes or consent forms. If, for example, you later sell your business, a formal record-keeping system can make your business look more organized and official. Minutes and consent forms can be important, in themselves, to show that you respect and are entitled to the benefits that arise from the separate legal status of your LLC.

EXAMPLE:

In preparation for a lawsuit against the LLC by an unpaid creditor, the creditor's attorney requests copies of minutes of all annual and special meetings of your members and managers. If your LLC record binder is bare, or contains minutes for just a few meetings over the life of your LLC, the plaintiff will stand a better chance of convincing the judge that the members didn't treat the LLC as a separate legal entity, and should therefore be personally liable for the debt just as if they had never formed an LLC.

What Paperwork Should an LLC Prepare?

Here's my recommendation for creating your paper trail: At a minimum, prepare written minutes (for either real or paper meetings) for any annual meetings scheduled in your operating agreement. Typically, this means preparing minutes for an annual members' meeting. Manager-managed LLCs should also prepare minutes for the annual managers' meeting that follows.

Also prepare formal LLC documentation for all important legal, tax, financial, or business decisions reached by the managers or members during the year. This documentation can be in the form of minutes for special meetings—either real or on paper—or written consent forms signed by your managers or members.

By preparing this simple paperwork, you will have made a record of important LLC decisions, which should give your LLC records

binder enough girth to help satisfy courts, the IRS, and others that you have attended to the necessary legal and tax niceties.

When Can Written Consents Be Used?

Legally, written consents work just as well as written minutes of meetings to document manager or member decisions. They are the quickest way to approve and document a formal decision by an LLC's managers or members, because they do not require the time and effort needed to hold a meeting and prepare minutes (or document a paper meeting). Managers or members simply sign consent forms that recite the action or business approved. The written consent forms are then placed in the LLC records binder as proof of the decision.

But written consents do have a downside. For managers or members who do not directly work in the business, a request to sign a written consent form may come as a surprise. After all, they may not know anything about the LLC action or decision at hand, nor the reasons it should be approved. As explained in "How Should Meetings Be Held for LLCs With Inactive Members," below, a real meeting generally works best to let outsiders know the reasons for important LLC decisions.

This being said, there is still a role for the written consent procedure in many circumstances, including:

- Decisions by one- or two-person LLCs. Written consent forms are particularly useful if one person owns and manages the LLC as its only member. The consent form procedure allows the sole LLC manager-member to formally approve LLC decisions without going to the trouble of preparing minutes for a pretend meeting. The same holds true for a member-managed LLC in which two people who work closely are the only persons active in the business.

- Noncontroversial or time-sensitive decisions in larger LLCs. Particularly if time is of the essence and a face-to-face meeting of managers or members is not necessary, it may make sense to take action by written consent.

EXAMPLE 1:

Better Mousetraps, LLC, a member-managed LLC, is advised by its accountant to pass a resolution approving a change in tax year. After discussing this issue briefly, the LLC president asks the secretary to prepare a written consent form for the members to sign that shows their approval of the tax election. They see no need to meet in person to approve the decision or to prepare paper minutes for a fictitious meeting. In this situation, either of these procedures seems like overkill for this simple—and uncontroversial—tax formality.

EXAMPLE 2:

The treasurer of Best Business Bureaus, Ltd. Liability Co., a commercial furniture supplier organized as a manager-managed LLC, decides to ask the managers to approve a 401(k) profit-sharing plan for the LLC's employees. A special meeting of managers is scheduled to discuss whether the LLC will make matching contributions for employees and to hear from various LLC personnel, including the chairperson of the Employee Benefits Committee, who wish to present their opinions on the advisability of adopting a plan and the level of contributions the LLC should make.

At this meeting, comments and feedback are exchanged before the managers reach a decision on options available under the plan. This gives the managers a chance to discuss the financial implications and pros and cons of this important piece of LLC business. Because of the complexity of the issues involved, a real face-to-face meeting is more appropriate here than paper minutes or written consents.

What's the Best Way to Hold Meetings for Closely Held LLCs?

A small, "closely held" LLC—one owned and operated by a close-knit group of friends, family, and/or business associates—has only a few members, who are usually all active in the business. The typical closely held LLC is member-managed.

In a closely held LLC, the annual meeting of members is typically a paper meeting with minutes. These minutes show the members' approval of the prior year's business and of plans for undertaking business in the new year. In a small, manager-managed LLC, the paper meeting is a joint managers'/members' meeting. The members reelect the current managers to another term, and the reelected managers accept their positions by approving the minutes of a paper meeting.

EXAMPLE:

Windows, Drapes, Sofas, and Ottomans, LLC, is a closely held LLC owned by members Saul and Barbara, a married couple. Barbara is the designated manager of the manager-managed LLC (Saul stays in the background as an investor in the business). At the end of each LLC fiscal year, Saul and Barbara approve minutes of a paper meeting showing that they both vote to reelect Barbara as manager, and that Barbara accepts her manager role for another year. (The meeting is a joint managers'/members' meeting.) If any important decisions need to be reached for the upcoming fiscal year, these decisions are also noted in the minutes.

Special meetings of the managers and members of closely held LLCs follow a similar pattern. If the resolution or business at hand is a tax or legal formality that everyone agrees on, special meetings are often held on paper, not in person. But if the issue under consideration requires discussion (such as the approval of competing bids for the remodeling of LLC headquarters), then the members or managers often decide to get together for a real meeting. At the meeting, they can discuss the pros and cons of the proposed course of action before making a decision and preparing minutes.

How Should Meetings Be Held for LLCs With Inactive Members?

LLCs that have at least one member who doesn't work actively in the business—that is, (1) a member-managed LLC with one or more nonmanaging members or (2) a manager-managed LLC—often find it best to hold annual and special meetings in person. Even if the business conducted is routine, this gives the passive members a chance to ask questions and get up to speed before voting on the decisions at hand.

It's particularly important to meet in person for the annual meeting of manager-managed LLCs. Even if the election of the managers is a formality, holding a joint annual managers'/members' meeting allows outside members a chance to catch up on LLC business. Hopefully, they will leave satisfied that their investment is in safe, capable hands. In other words, a face-to-face annual meeting can serve the same purpose as the annual report sent to shareholders by large, publicly held LLCs:

It informs members about, and sells them on, past and future LLC operations. Even for smaller LLCs, a little soft-pitch self-promotion to members can help prevent future investor disputes.

EXAMPLE:

Flexible Fliers, Ltd., a round-the-clock, go-anywhere charter airline, is organized as a manager-managed LLC. Three members own a majority interest in the company and act as its only managers. Two outside members, having put up a portion of the capital necessary to get the business off the ground, own minority interests in the LLC.

Each year, the LLC puts out the red carpet for its outside investors, inviting them to an annual managers'/members' meeting, where the annual financial and business reports of the LLC are presented by the LLC secretary and president, followed by nominations and a vote for next year's managers.

Although the three managers obviously have the power to reelect themselves each year (if they vote as a group) and make other important LLC decisions, they go out of their way to include the outside members in this decision-making process. Not only does this give the outside members a feeling that they are taken seriously, but it also gives the LLC a chance to showcase its operations and plans for future expansion. The LLC could simply prepare paper minutes for a fictional annual meeting and circulate this document (or a written consent form with election and acceptance information) to the investor-members for approval. But a real meeting seems like a friendlier way to interact with the investors and foster a long-term relationship. Besides, the LLC may need to ask for additional capital in the future.

Do You Need to Hold Meetings or Prepare Minutes for All LLC Decisions?

Not every decision has to be documented. People who are actively involved in LLC businesses hold many scheduled and impromptu meetings throughout the year to discuss and resolve items of ongoing business. In a small LLC, managers and members who also work for the LLC are likely to attend these meetings in their capacity as regular LLC employees—they don't need to don their manager or member hats.

You don't need to prepare LLC minutes or consent forms to document a garden-variety business or staff meeting decision. However, if what starts out as a routine matter of LLC business takes on important legal or tax overtones, you should record those decisions by preparing LLC minutes or consent forms. (The types of decisions customarily made at formal managers' and members' meetings are discussed below.)

EXAMPLE:

Software Works Limited Liability Company, a small software publisher, does not need to prepare minutes for its weekly product development or sales meetings. But if important legal or tax decisions come up at these weekly meetings, they should be considered either at a real managers' or members' meeting or (if all managers or members agree) by use of consent forms signed by the managers or members.

What Decisions Should the Members and Managers Make?

The management of the LLC (the managing members in a member-managed LLC or the managers of a manager-managed LLC) should approve important legal, tax, and financial matters or those affecting the overall management of the LLC. Typical management decisions that are later formally approved by the membership at meetings or by written consent include:

- setting officer and key employee compensation
- amending the LLC articles of organization or operating agreement
- admitting a new member
- dissolving the LLC
- approving the construction, lease, purchase, or sale of real estate, and
- approving the terms of a loan to or from members, managers, officers, banks, or other outsiders.

 TIP

Ready-made resolutions help you approve specific items of business at meetings. Chapters 8 through 15 include fill-in-the-blank resolutions, as well as instructions on preparing them, for these and other common types of ongoing LLC business. (See the beginning of Appendix C for a list of resolution forms included with this book, with a cross-reference to the section of the book that contains instructions for preparing each resolution.) After preparing them, you should insert these resolutions into your minutes or written consents, as explained in Chapters 5 to 7.

What Decisions Must Be Made (or Ratified) by Members?

State law may require membership approval for certain decisions, even in manager-managed LLCs. The most common issues that require a membership vote involve structural changes to the LLC, such as:

- an amendment to the LLC's articles or operating agreement
- the admission of new members
- the transfer of membership interests by a current member, or

- the dissolution or merger of the LLC with another company (subject to membership approval in most states).

Your LLC operating agreement should list the decisions that must always be approved by all or a majority of LLC members.

Options for Members Who Don't Want to Manage

What if you want to have a member-managed LLC but some members don't want to have a management role? LLCs can accomplish this by granting voting power (that is, management authority) only to the members who are active in the business. The remaining members, who wish to assume a passive, investor role in the LLC, are issued nonvoting memberships. Although this type of LLC is officially "member-managed," it operates much like a manager-managed LLC, with a few differences:

1. In a manager-managed LLC, a nonmember may be elected a manager, with voting rights; in a member-managed LLC, only members can vote.

2. In a member-managed LLC, a nonvoting member may not have a right to vote at all, even on important structural changes such as amendments to articles or the approval of new members (unless state law says otherwise— voting rules for important LLC decisions are covered in Appendix B). In a manager-managed LLC, all members typically have voting rights (unless the operating agreement says otherwise).

3. In a member-managed LLC, all members, including any nonvoting members, are normally considered "agents" of the LLC under state law. This means any member can generally bind the LLC to a contract or transaction. In a manager-managed LLC, usually only managers are legally considered agents of the LLC under state law.

Given these differences, the most sensible course of action is to elect manager-management when one or more members will not be active in the LLC. The active members can be the managers, and the nonmanaging members can be regular voting members, with the right to vote on special matters brought before the membership. On the other hand, if all members will be active and will participate in management, then member-management makes sense (with all members getting full voting rights).

Steps to Take Before Holding a Meeting

If you're planning to hold a real, in-person LLC meeting, you'll need to do a few things ahead of time. Someone will have to call (request) the meeting and provide notice of the meeting, according to any rules contained in your LLC operating agreement and your state's LLC statutes. (You should provide notice even if your operating agreement and state law don't require you to do so—giving notice ensures that all potential participants know about the upcoming meeting and the nature of the business to be presented and discussed there.)

This chapter explains how to handle premeeting formalities and paperwork. It also covers practical measures that will help you get the most out of the meeting process. These include preparing an agenda, sending participants any necessary background information, arranging for the presentation of reports, and making arrangements to keep good minutes. To help you handle these premeeting tasks, this chapter includes forms you can use to:

- create meeting summaries
- call meetings
- draft meeting participant lists
- provide notice of meetings
- acknowledge receipt of notice, and
- grant proxies to other members.

All of these forms are included in Appendix C and on the CD-ROM at the back of this book. You'll find instructions for completing the forms in this chapter.

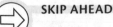

SKIP AHEAD

If you don't plan to meet in person, you can skip this chapter. This chapter explains formalities you'll have to take care of before an actual in-person meeting. Skip to Chapter 6 if you're planning to hold a paper meeting instead of a face-to-face meeting. If you want to take action by written consent, skip to Chapter 7.

SKIP AHEAD

If you're the sole member or manager of your LLC, you probably won't want to hold a formal meeting. Usually, the sole member or manager of a one-member or one-manager LLC won't want to go to the trouble of providing notice of—and attending—a real meeting, unless others will attend (for example, you might want a staff member to brief you on important LLC business or an accountant to present financial information). In most cases, a paper meeting or written consent is much more practical. Go directly to Chapters 6 and 7 to learn how to record your official LLC decisions with a paper meeting or written consents.

Types of LLC Meetings

Before you dive into the mechanics of preparing for your LLC meetings, you'll need to understand what kinds of meetings an LLC can hold. The type of meeting you're planning will determine how you prepare for it.

Members' and Managers' Meetings

If your LLC is member-managed, all of your meetings will be members' meetings—even if some members don't play an active role in managing the LLC. If your LLC is manager-managed, however, it can have three types of meetings:

- **Managers' meetings.** If the LLC has more than one manager, managers' meetings should be held to discuss and approve major management decisions. If the LLC has only one manager, the manager may wish to prepare written minutes of a manager meeting to create a record of the reasons for an important decision, which the members can refer to later if they have any questions about the decision. (Of course, the sole manager may choose to have a paper meeting, as explained in Chapter 6, or use a written consent form to record his or her decision, as explained in Chapter 7.)

- **Joint managers'/members' meetings.** If a decision is important enough, the managers may invite members to the meeting so that they can listen to reports and join in the discussion, prior to a vote on the matter by the managers.

- **Members' meetings.** If the articles or operating agreement calls for the periodic election of managers, regular (annual or semiannual) members' meetings are usually scheduled in the operating agreement for this purpose. Special members' meetings can also be called by the managers or members to make decisions that only the members are entitled to make under state law, the articles, or the operating agreement. Examples of decisions that are usually reserved to the members include:

  - amending the articles or operating agreement

  - issuing a new membership

  - admitting a transferee (a person who is sold a membership interest by a departing member)

  - continuing the LLC, or

  - dissolving the LLC after a membership interest is terminated (for example, on the death or departure of a member).

Regular and Special LLC Meetings

Your LLC meeting will be either a *regular* or a *special* meeting. A regular meeting is one that is held at set intervals—for example, once a year or once every three months. A special meeting is called if the need arises to discuss a particular item of business.

Regular Meetings

Regular meetings are usually scheduled in the LLC's operating agreement and are held at certain intervals. For example, the operating agreement of a manager-managed LLC may call for annual members' meetings to elect managers (if managers are elected for a fixed term). In a member-managed LLC, your operating agreement may call for semiannual meetings of members, where LLC officers report on the business and members review and plan operations for the next six months.

A few states require manager-managed LLCs to hold regular members' meetings to elect managers, if managers serve for one year or for some other fixed length of time. In most states, however, managers are elected for indefinite terms, so no annual meeting is legally required. (See the heading "Manager Election" in Appendix B to find out your state's rules.) In these states, your operating agreement does not have to provide for annual or other regular meetings.

Even if your state law and/or operating agreement don't require regular members' meetings, however, it's a good idea to hold them. Meeting regularly can help keep members current on LLC business operations—and provide written proof that each member received regular reports and information on the LLC's activities. This proof might be important later, if a member challenges an LLC action.

Special Meetings

Special meetings are held when called for by a member, manager, LLC officer, or anyone else who is authorized to call meetings under the operating agreement or state law. (See Step 3 under "Steps to Prepare for a Meeting," below, for more information on who may call special meetings.) Special meetings may be called to discuss urgent items of business or approve legal or tax formalities that arise from time to time. For example, a special meeting might be called to approve:

- adopting a new LLC tax year
- the conditions of a loan from the LLC to an officer, or
- a bank loan or real estate transaction.

State laws don't require LLCs to hold special meetings—by definition, these are called only if and when the need arises.

How to Find the Rules for Holding LLC Meetings

Your operating agreement establishes the rules and procedures for calling, providing notice of, and holding formal meetings. If your agreement doesn't address these issues (or you haven't yet prepared an operating agreement for your LLC), check the heading "Meeting Requirements" for your state in Appendix B; it lists the basic meeting rules that apply under your state's LLC act. You can look up these laws yourself online or at the library (see "Basic LLC Documents" in Chapter 1 for information on finding your state's LLC law).

Most states let you call, provide notice of, and hold members' and managers' meetings as you see fit; only rarely does a state impose specific rules that must be followed. And these rules usually apply only if you do not provide otherwise in your operating agreement. For example, your state LLC act may require an annual meeting of members "unless otherwise provided in your operating agreement." If your operating agreement says that members' meetings of members will be held only when called by one or more members, you don't have to hold an annual members' meeting.

Steps to Prepare for a Meeting

Before you begin preparing for your LLC meeting, it's helpful to know where you're headed—that is, how the LLC meeting process works. Here are the typical steps involved in holding an LLC meeting:

- The meeting is called (requested) by someone authorized under the operating agreement or state law to do so. (See Step 3, below.)
- An LLC officer (usually the secretary) gives notice of the time, place, and purpose of the meeting, together with any necessary meeting materials, to all potential meeting participants. (See Steps 5 and 6, below.)
- The meeting is held—business is discussed and proposed actions are approved or voted down. (See Chapter 4.)
- Minutes of the meeting are prepared, signed, and placed in the LLC records binder. (See Chapter 5.)

The legal formalities associated with the first two procedures—calling the meeting and providing notice and other materials ahead of time—are discussed below. You'll also find commonsense compliance tips designed to help you meet (or exceed) any state law requirements for preparing for meetings (for example, how to prepare meeting summary sheets and meeting participant lists prior to the meeting). Finally, I've made a number of practical suggestions for making your meeting a productive one—a goal that's easy to lose sight of if you become too focused on the legal rules.

If you run your LLC formally, or if your LLC has more than 30 or so members, you will probably want to follow all of the procedures discussed in this section. If not, you may decide to skip some of the preliminaries covered below.

After reading through the material, use your own judgment in deciding whether it makes sense to take any shortcuts.

> **SKIP AHEAD**
>
> **One-person or family-run LLCs can usually skip the preliminaries.** LLCs owned and operated by one person or one family probably don't need to pay particular attention to preliminary meeting steps and can usually forego calling and providing notice for LLC meetings. (Again, skip to Chapter 6 if you want to prepare minutes for a paper meeting.)

Step 1. Prepare a Meeting Folder

You may be surprised at the number of forms and other paperwork that even the most routine meeting can generate. To avoid misplacing any of them, you should set aside a blank file folder for each upcoming meeting. Write the date and type of meeting on the tab for the folder (for example, "Annual LLC Meeting, July 6, 2010" or "Special LLC Meeting, March 15, 2010") and keep the folder handy.

As you create each document for your meeting, place it in this file folder. After the meeting takes place and you have prepared and completed the written minutes and any other paperwork, you can transfer the entire contents of the file folder into the minutes section of your LLC records binder.

If you're using a computer to generate documents for your meetings, another way to keep your materials organized is to place all copies of computer files associated with a given meeting in one folder on your hard disk. For example, a computer user may wish to create a folder named "ANNMTG10" on the hard disk to hold all computer files generated for the annual LLC meeting in 2010.

Step 2. Prepare Meeting Summary Sheets

When you are planning and preparing for an LLC meeting, paperwork and tasks can mount up fast. To help you keep track of key dates and times, including when important notices should be sent, use the Meeting Summary Sheet in Appendix C and on the enclosed disc. This form contains spaces where you can enter information about what needs to be done to prepare for the meeting and check items off the list as you complete them. Use your summary sheet as both a scheduler and a reminder for upcoming meetings. If any questions are raised later, the summary sheet also serves as an excellent record that your LLC actually had meetings, and that they were called, noticed, and held correctly.

You'll need a separate summary sheet for each meeting. Start by having your LLC secretary prepare summary sheets for any annual (or other regular) meetings required in your operating agreement. Note that the form includes space for the secretary to insert information on the basic call and notice requirements for each meeting—this will help the secretary handle these premeeting requirements on time. The secretary should keep the summary sheets handy and use them to:

- keep track—and provide timely notice—of upcoming meetings
- make revisions to existing sheets (for example, when meetings are postponed or adjourned), and
- add sheets as necessary.

When a manager, an officer, a member, or another authorized person calls for a special managers' or members' meeting, the secretary should create a new sheet, filling in all relevant information for the meeting.

TIP

Meeting summary sheets help if you are audited. Summary sheets can come in handy if you later need to show members, managers, a court, or others, that you paid serious attention to LLC formalities. Members and managers sometimes ask to see a record of LLC meetings to track the legal and tax history of the company. Summaries of this sort are also prepared by lawyers prior to a lawsuit, to have a clear record of key LLC decisions—particularly if the suit involves a decision made at an LLC meeting. Preparing your own meeting summary forms in advance may save you time and money later.

CD-ROM

Below is a sample of the Meeting Summary Sheet included on the CD-ROM and as a tearout form in Appendix C. (See Appendix A for information on selecting and using the CD-ROM files.) Fill in the form following the special instructions provided below.

Special Instructions

❶ Check the type of meeting—whether it is a regularly scheduled meeting (either an annual or other periodic meeting) or a special meeting.

❷ Indicate whether it is a managers' or members' meeting (if both, check both boxes).

❸ If you know the meeting date and time, fill that in. If you expect to hold a special meeting but are not sure of the exact date, make a note of the possible meeting date as a reminder.

❹ Show the location of the meeting. Most meetings will be held at the principal office of the LLC.

Location of Meetings Held in Cyberspace

Some companies use technology to help them get together by holding a meeting in "cyberspace." You can do this via a conference telephone call, a video conference hookup, or even a conference using audio/video conferencing software with a webcam hookup. If you use any of these alternate meeting methods, make sure to specify the location and method on the meeting summary sheet—for example, "a video conference located at the following video conference sites: [name the sites]." Most state statutes are not high-tech enough to specifically authorize electronic meetings, but the few states that do chime in on this issue say that meetings can be held electronically as long as all members can hear each other and can simultaneously have their own voices heard. I'll leave it to you to decide whether your electronic meeting satisfies these conditions. Generally, it's probably fine to meet electronically as long as all of the following are true:

- your participants are technologically savvy and equipped

- you can verify that each participant is in attendance and is heard from on all decisions

- you don't expect anyone to object later to your method of holding an electronic meeting ("I didn't have an Internet account," "I couldn't get my modem to work"), and

- you can keep a complete record of the electronic meeting (a text-file log of a bulletin board or intranet session, a video tape of a video conference, or an audio tape of a conference call) to place in your LLC records binder.

Meeting Summary Sheet

Name of LLC:

[insert name of LLC]
_____

Year of Meeting: [insert year]
_____

Type of Meeting: ☐ Regular or ☐ Special ❶

Meeting of: ☐ Managers and/or ☐ Members ❷

Date: _____ Time: _____:_____ _____.M. ❸

Place: _____ ❹

Meeting Called by: _____ ❺

Purpose: _____[insert purpose of meeting]_____ ❻

_____

Committee or Other Reports or Presentations: _____ ❼

Other Reminders or Notes: _____ ❽

Notice: ☐ Written ☐ Verbal ☐ None ❾

Notice Must Be Given by Date: _____ ❿

Notice of Meeting Given to:

Name	Type of Notice*	Date Notice Given	How and Where Communicated	Date of Acknowledgment
				⓫

*Types of Notice: Written (mailed, hand-delivered); Verbal (in person, telephone conversation, answering machine, voice mail); Email; Fax.

❺ Generally, no one has to call regular managers' and/or members' meetings, as they are usually already scheduled in the operating agreement. If so, just insert "operating agreement" in this blank. Special meetings of the members or managers are called by those authorized to do so under the operating agreement. Insert the name of the person who called the meeting here. (See Step 3, below, for more information.)

❻ Set forth a brief statement of the purpose of the upcoming meeting. The purpose of a regular members' meeting in a manager-managed LLC will usually include "the election of managers of the LLC for another term." The purpose of other regular LLC meetings is typically "to hear reports from LLC officers, review past LLC business, and to plan upcoming LLC business and the transaction of any other business that may be brought before the meeting." Special meetings are called for a particular purpose, such as:

- "to vote on the purchase of real property by the LLC"

- "to vote on the admission of a new member"

- "to consider whether members will be required to make an additional capital contribution to the LLC"

- "to decide whether to authorize a distribution of cash to LLC members"

- "to vote on whether to purchase the membership interest of a departing member and the terms of the purchase," or

- "to vote on the continuance of the LLC, as required by law, following the departure of a member of the LLC."

CROSS REFERENCE

Use resolution forms to approve particular actions. Chapters 8 through 15 provide resolutions that you can use to handle many of the most common special and recurring items of business that occur during the life of the LLC. (For a list of these resolutions, see the first page of Appendix C.) You'll be able to use these resolution forms at your special meetings to approve most of the objectives listed above.

❼ Indicate any LLC committee or officer reports you wish to have presented at the meeting, for example:

- financial report by treasurer

- operations report by president

- report by compensation committee appointed by managers on proposed salary increases to LLC officers, or

- report by building committee on projected cost of site improvements to LLC headquarters.

❽ The LLC secretary should insert any necessary reminders to help make arrangements for the upcoming meeting (for example, "Reserve video conference facility by January 10," "Have John in MIS verify each member's ability to log on to company intranet by February 15").

❾ Check your operating agreement for the type of meeting notice that must be provided—written or verbal. If no notice is required—for example, if your operating agreement specifically dispenses with notice for annual managers' meetings—*and* you decide not to send notice (even though I recommend it in "Prepare Notice of the Meeting," below)—check "None."

❿ Enter the date by which you need to send out or personally provide notice to the meeting participants. If notice is not required under your operating agreement, and you do not plan to give any, write "no notice given" in the blank.

⓫ After notice is actually given, fill in this portion of the form to indicate who received notice prior to a meeting. Insert the name of the person who was given notice, the type of notice (written or verbal), and the date the notice was given (mailed or communicated). Next, state how and where the notice was communicated—for example, "first-class mail to LLC address," "faxed to 555-5555," "in person at LLC office," "email to person@place. com," "phone conversation at 555-5555," "phone message left on answering machine at 555-5555," "voice mail left at 555-5555." Finally, if you receive documentation from the participant showing receipt or acknowledgment of notice (see the Acknowledgment of Receipt form in Step 7, below), list the date of the receipt or acknowledgment on the summary sheet. Place the receipt or acknowledgment in the meeting folder or the meetings section of your LLC records binder.

Step 3. Call the Meeting

Technically, no one has to call a regular meeting (one scheduled in your operating agreement, such as an annual meeting of members). The LLC secretary is expected to remember when to start making arrangements for these prescheduled meetings. This is one of the purposes of the meeting summary sheet: to remind the secretary to make arrangements for each upcoming regular meeting scheduled in the operating agreement.

To call a special LLC meeting, someone within the LLC asks that a meeting be scheduled. Usually, this request is made to the LLC secretary. Your operating agreement or state law may authorize particular individuals to call meetings. Typically, LLC operating agreements allow the LLC president, any member (or a specified number or percentage of members), or one or more managers of a manager-managed LLC to call LLC meetings.

Most states let you call managers' and/or members' meetings as you like, but some states have a default rule that applies if you don't address the issue in your operating agreement. Typically, state LLC acts allow a manager or the LLC president to call a managers' or members' meeting (in a manager-managed LLC), and a specified number or percentage of members, such as 10%, to call members' meetings (in both manager- and member-managed LLCs). For state rules on calling meetings, see "Meeting Requirements" for your state in Appendix B.

How and When to Call LLC Meetings

Usually, neither state law nor an LLC's operating agreement imposes any requirements on the time and manner of calling a meeting (but check yours, just to make sure). Absent specific requirements, a meeting can be called verbally or in writing by any LLC officer (I suggest the LLC secretary). The secretary should call the meeting far enough in advance to:

- provide meeting participants with ample notice of the meeting—usually a minimum of ten days prior to the meeting date, but two to three weeks is generally considered more appropriate, particularly for important LLC meetings (see Step 5, below), and

- allow enough time to prepare any necessary background material and other materials for the meeting—this can (and often does) take more than ten days, particularly if important financial or business reports or presentations are to be made at the meeting.

In smaller LLCs where members (or managers) are in close contact and work well together, a meeting can be called orally, a day or two ahead of time. However, in larger LLCs, especially those with nonmanaging members, and for any meeting at which a hot topic will be discussed, the meeting should be called in writing, at least ten days (or more) ahead of time, to document that all members had ample notice of the meeting.

EXAMPLE 1:

Pants de Lyon, LLC, a Miami clothing boutique, is a small, member-managed LLC, owned and operated by Stephanie, Claude, and their spouses. Stephanie has been working hard to set up a 401(k) retirement plan for the members/employees of the LLC. At long last, she is ready to discuss and approve investment options and get the plan up and running. Stephanie, the president, asks Claude, the secretary, to arrange for a special members' meeting in one week to approve the 401(k) plan. Stephanie and Claude tell their spouses about the meeting; no formal notice is sent out.

EXAMPLE 2:

Home Redux Limited Co., a home-remodeling and furnishing company organized as a manager-managed LLC, is owned and run by two manager/employees, Kevin and Gale, who are also members. Five other people hold nonmanaging memberships in the LLC. The operating agreement allows any manager, the LLC president, or members owning at least 10% of the LLC to call a meeting of managers or members.

Gale wants to increase the LLC's line of credit with the local bank. Also, the LLC's accountant suggests that the managers approve a change in the company's accounting method. Gale and Kevin are in complete agreement on these issues, which are traditionally left to the managers—members don't have to vote on these day-to-day concerns. Because the managers' meeting to document these decisions will be a mere formality, Gale feels that an in-person call and five days' written notice is sufficient. At the meeting, Gale notes for the record that the increased credit line is necessary to meet increased costs of doing business, which

she specifies. Kevin reads the accountant's recommendation and reasons for proposing a change in the accounting method used by the LLC. The minutes of the meeting are placed in the LLC records binder, which can be inspected by any of the nonmanaging members at any time (as required under state law and the LLC's operating agreement), should they wish to later examine Kevin and Gale's managerial track record.

EXAMPLE 3:

Grand Plans, Ltd. is a medium-sized building contractor with five managers and seven members. Two managers feel that the business needs more capital and want to raise it by selling an additional membership. The LLC's operating agreement and state law require all members to approve the issuance of a new membership. The president prepares a written call for a special joint managers' and members' meeting, where the managers will present a proposal to seek out and admit an additional member and the full membership will vote on it. Six weeks before the proposed date of the meeting, the president gives a written call of meeting form to the secretary, who mails written notice to all meeting participants.

How to Prepare a Call of Meeting Form

A written call of meeting form should specify:

- the type of meeting (members' and/or managers')
- the date, time, and place of the meeting
- the purpose of the meeting, and
- how much advance notice participants should be given of the upcoming meeting.

The secretary will use this form as a guideline for sending out notice, as explained below.

CD-ROM

Below is a sample of the Call of Meeting form included on the CD-ROM and as a tearout form in Appendix C. (See Appendix A for information on using CD-ROM files.) Complete the form following the special instructions provided below.

Special Instructions

❶ Insert the name of the LLC secretary (to whom the call will be given), the name of the LLC, and the LLC address (where the call will be delivered or mailed).

Measuring Membership Interests in the LLC

State laws and LLC operating agreements sometimes tie the right to call meetings (as well as other LLC membership rights) to a member's capital, profits, or capital and profits interests in the LLC. Here's what these terms mean:

- **Capital interests.** A member's current capital interest is the capital he or she has contributed to the LLC, as a percentage of the total capital contributions made by all members. For example, if one member in a two-member LLC contributes $10,000 in cash and the second pays $20,000 in property, the first member has a one-third (33%) capital interest in the LLC, and the second has a two-thirds (67%) capital interest. These numbers should be adjusted if members make additional contributions (raising the members' capital account balances) or the LLC distributes cash or property to members (reducing members' capital account balances). This is why some statutes speak in terms of a member's current capital account balance with the LLC, rather than each member's initial capital contribution to the LLC.

- **Profits interests.** LLC members are entitled to receive a percentage of the profits (and losses) of the LLC. Generally, unless the operating agreement calls for "special allocations" of profits and losses, each member is entitled to the same percentage of LLC profits and losses as the member's capital interest. (Check your operating agreement to be sure.) So a member with a 10% capital interest usually also has a 10% profits interest in the LLC. But some LLCs make special (disproportionate) allocations of profits and losses, perhaps giving a 20% profits interest to a member who paid 10% of the capital in cash, to recognize that the cash payment provides more liquidity for the LLC. Your operating agreement should specify the profits interests of all members. Many simply say that profits (and loss) interests follow the capital interests of the members.

- **Capital and profits interests.** Many state statutes specify membership rights in terms of the capital and profits interests of each member. In other words, you must average each member's share of total capital and total profits interests in the LLC. For example, if Sam has a 10% capital interest and a 20% profits interest in his LLC, he has a 15% capital and profits interest. In most LLCs, profits interests follow capital interests, so capital interests, profits interests, and capital and profits interests are all the same. For example, Jerry has a 10% capital interest and a 10% profits interest, for an average capital and profits interest of 10%.

Call of Meeting

Secretary: _____[insert name of LLC secretary]_____ ❶

Name of LLC: _____[insert name of LLC]_____

LLC Address: _____[insert address of principal office]_____

The following person(s):

Name	Title	Membership Interest (if any) ❷
_____	_____	_____
_____	_____	_____
_____	_____	_____

authorized under provisions of the operating agreement of the LLC and/or provisions of state law, hereby make(s) a call and request to hold a meeting of ["members" and/or "managers"] ❸ of the LLC for the purpose(s) of: ❹

_____[describe purpose(s) of meeting]_____

The requested date and time of the meeting is: _[state preferred date and time for holding meeting]_ . ❺

The requested location for the meeting is: _[the principal office of the LLC, or other location]_ ❻
_____ .

The following LLC officers and other individuals are expected to attend to present reports or otherwise contribute to the meeting, and, in addition to managers and/or members, should be included in those who receive notice of the meeting:

Name	Address
[list any other individuals who will be asked to attend] ❼	_____
_____	_____
_____	_____

The secretary is requested to provide all proper notices as required by the operating agreement of the LLC and state law to all persons entitled or asked to attend the meeting, and to include with the notice any other materials necessary or helpful to the holding of the upcoming meeting. If possible, the secretary is requested to provide at least _[if appropriate, specify requested notice period]_ notice of the meeting to all meeting participants. ❽

Date: _____ ❾

Signed:_____

Signed:_____

❷ List the name of each person calling the meeting. In the columns to the right of the name, indicate whether the person is a member, manager, or officer of the LLC. If your operating agreement allows only members who hold at least a certain ownership interest to call a meeting, list the percentage of ownership interest the member currently holds in the LLC. You should list the ownership interest in the form required by the operating agreement—for example, as a percentage of capital ownership, profits interests, or capital and profits interest. For more information, see "Measuring Membership Interests in the LLC," above.

If your operating agreement allows any member to call a meeting, or allows a specified number of members to call a meeting regardless of their percentage of ownership in the LLC (or if it doesn't address this issue), you can leave the "Membership Interest" item blank.

❸ Fill in the type of meeting being called. In a member-managed LLC, all meetings will be meetings of members. In a manager-managed LLC, meetings can be meetings of managers, meetings of members, or joint meetings of managers and members.

❹ In the space provided, briefly state the purpose of the meeting. You can copy this from the meeting summary sheet. If you haven't filled out a summary sheet, refer to Step 2 (item #6), above, for a list of common meeting purposes. Here are some suggestions:

- For an annual meeting of members in a manager-managed LLC whose managers have one-year terms: "electing the managers of the LLC."

- For an annual (or other regular) meeting of members (in member-managed LLCs) or managers (in manager-managed LLCs): "review of the prior year's business, discussion of LLC operations for the upcoming year, acceptance by the managers of

reelection by members for another term of office [if appropriate], and transaction of any other business that may properly come before the meeting."

- For special meetings, state the reason the meeting was called, for example, "approval of amendments to the articles of organization and the operating agreement of the LLC."

❺ For an annual or other regular meeting, specify the time and date of the meeting, as stated in the operating agreement. For a special meeting, state the specific date or general time frame when you want to hold the meeting, such as "January 15, 2010, at 10:00 a.m.," "latter half of the month of October," or "first Monday in June."

❻ Specify the address where the meeting is to be held. Meetings are usually held at the main office of the LLC, but you may wish to specify another location if it's convenient for all participants (and if your operating agreement allows alternate locations for LLC meetings).

❼ If you know in advance, specify any LLC officers, staff, consultants, or outsiders who will be asked to present reports or otherwise participate in the meeting. Listing their names (and addresses for any outsiders who do not work at the LLC) ensures that they receive notice of the upcoming meeting.

❽ If the person making the call feels that a minimum period of notice should be given to meeting participants, specify it here. If the caller has no preference for a notice period, insert "N/A." As long as the period requested meets or exceeds any minimum notice requirements set by the operating agreement or state law, the secretary should comply with this notice request. (You should give at least ten days' advance notice of all meetings to make sure you comply with any state law requirements—see Step 5, below.)

EXAMPLE:

The LLC president calls for a members' meeting to discuss the LLC's purchase of the interest of a departing member. Included with the notice are the LLC's financial statements, including balance sheets, for the past three years. The president feels that members should have notice of the meeting at least one month in advance to give them time to review their personal finances and the LLC's financial statements before discussing the valuation and purchase of the departing member's interest. The president inserts "30 days" as the requested notice period in this blank on the form. Because the operating agreement requires only 14 days' written notice for a members' meeting, the secretary will comply with the one-month notice of meeting request.

❾ Date the form and have each person making the call sign below the date line.

When you've completed the form, give a copy to the LLC secretary, who should place it in the folder for the upcoming meeting or in the meetings section of the LLC records binder.

Step 4. Prepare a Meeting Participant List

Everyone who is legally entitled to be notified of an upcoming meeting should receive such notice. You can also invite others, such as an accountant or lawyer. By preparing a Meeting Participant List, you'll make sure that you don't overlook anyone when you mail or otherwise provide notice (as part of Step 5, below). The list will also come in handy when a member or manager wishes to plan for an upcoming meeting and wants to know who will attend (to assess voting strength and interests, for example).

The participant list is usually sorted alphabetically by last name. It includes the name and address of all LLC members and managers, plus the voting interests of each member. It also includes the names and addresses of anyone else, such as an LLC officer or consultant, who will be asked to attend the meeting.

If you decide not to produce a participant list for every meeting, perhaps because your LLC is small or the same people are invited to every meeting, make sure that you have a list of all LLC members and managers (many states require you to make such a list available to members). You can use your membership and manager lists from your LLC records binder. These lists should include the names, addresses, and interests of all LLC members (and for manager-managed LLCs, the names and addresses of all managers).

CD-ROM

Below is a sample of the Meeting Participant List included on the CD-ROM and as a tear-out form in Appendix C. (See Appendix A for information on selecting and using CD-ROM files.) Complete the form following the special instructions provided below.

Your Meeting Participant List Should Be Available at the Meeting

To help members and managers vote at a meeting, particularly a large meeting with many participants or for a meeting where a controversial issue will be proposed, bring along a copy of the participant list for everyone who attends. If you did not prepare a participant list, bring along a copy of the membership and management lists from your LLC records binder. These lists will help members and managers track votes—and assess voting power—at the meeting.

Meeting Participant List

Name of LLC: _____[insert name of LLC]_____

Type of Meeting: ☐ Regular (_____) or ☐ Special ❶
Meeting of: ☐ Managers and/or ☐ Members ❷

Date: _____ Time: _____:_____ ___.M. ❸

Meeting Participants (*list names in alphabetical order*): ❹

Name: _____

Address: _____

Telephone: _____

☐ Manager: _____

☐ Member: Number or Percentage of Voting Power [per capita or according to percentage of capital, profits, or capital and profits interests as specified in operating agreement]: ❺

_____

_____

☐ Officer: Title _____

☐ Other (position and reason for attendance): _____

Name: _____

Address: _____

Telephone: _____

☐ Manager: _____

☐ Member: Number or Percentage of Voting Power [per capita or according to percentage of capital, profits, or capital and profits interests as specified in operating agreement]:

_____

☐ Officer: Title _____

☐ Other (position and reason for attendance): _____

Special Instructions

❶ Check the box to indicate whether the meeting is regular (either an annual or other periodic meeting) or special. If regular, fill in the blank to show the period for holding the meeting, such as "annual," "semiannual" (twice a year), "monthly," or "biennial" (every two years).

❷ Indicate whether it is a managers' and/or members' meeting (if both, check both boxes).

❸ Fill in the date and time of the upcoming meeting.

❹ List, in alphabetical order, the names, addresses, and phone numbers of:

- all managers and/or members asked to participate at the upcoming meeting, and

- others who may attend, such as officers who will present reports at the meeting. If you prepared a written call of meeting (see Step 3, above), include the additional people listed on that form.

If you need space to fill in more names than the form allows, make additional copies of the paragraphs providing information about meeting participants. After each name, check whether the person is an LLC member, a manager, an officer (check all that apply), or an outsider (by checking "other"), and supply the additional information requested.

Here are some guidelines to follow when deciding whom to include on your list:

- For a manager meeting in a manager-managed LLC, you should list all managers—all are generally entitled to vote on management decisions. There is a rare exception, however: If your operating agreement creates different classes of managers, each managing a separate area of LLC operations, you should list only the managers from the class entitled to vote on the decisions to be made at the meeting.

- For a meeting of members, you should list all members, unless your articles or operating agreement establishes nonvoting memberships or special classes of memberships with separate decision-making authority over different areas of LLC operation. For most member-managed LLCs, all members are entitled to attend all members' meetings and vote on the matters presented there. Check your articles or operating agreement if you have any doubts about the voting power of memberships issued by your LLC.

- For a joint managers'/members' meeting, the same guidelines apply. All managers and members should participate in the meeting unless your LLC has established separate nonvoting memberships, or classes of membership or management not entitled to vote on the matters to be presented at the meeting. However, if you are asking members to attend a meeting not just to vote their interests but also to participate in discussions, you probably will want to invite your entire membership to the meeting, even if some members don't have the right to vote on the issue.

EXAMPLE:

Dog Days Pet Boutique Franchises, LLC, is a manager-managed LLC with two classes of membership: Class A voting and Class B nonvoting memberships. The Class A members serve as managers of the LLC. They make all management decisions and also attend and vote at members' meetings when a full membership vote (unanimous membership approval) is needed to meet state legal requirements and provisions of the LLC operating agreement.

The operating agreement requires an annual managers'/members' meeting to review the past year's business and discuss future plans, to present year-end financial and business reports, and to provide a forum for members to assess management performance and review the current value of their investment in the LLC. Because managers serve for indefinite terms, the annual meeting is not called to solicit any particular membership votes. In effect, the annual meeting serves as a red carpet, rolled out yearly to facilitate communication and goodwill between management and the full membership (like a yearly corporate stockholders' meeting, only without the voting of shares). In this situation, it is important that all members—including those who hold nonvoting memberships— are asked to attend the joint managers'/ members' meeting.

❺ Specify each member's voting power according to the provisions of your operating agreement. (If your agreement doesn't address how members will vote, see the "Meeting Requirements" heading for your state in Appendix B for your state's default membership voting rule.) For example:

- If your operating agreement says that members vote per capita, then each member gets one vote, and you should insert "one vote" as each member's voting power.

- If your agreement says that members vote according to their capital interest or current capital account balance, list each member's percentage of capital ownership (that is, the proportion of the member's current capital account balance in the LLC relative to the total current capital account balance). For example, a member who has contributed 25% of the capital to the LLC will exercise 25% of the voting power (assuming there have been no adjustments to the capital accounts due to additional contributions by, or distributions to, members).

- If your agreement gives members voting power according to their profits interests in the LLC, list each member's percentage of profits interest as the member's percentage of voting power.

- If your agreement specifies membership voting power in terms of members' average percentage of both capital and profits interests in the LLC, show this combined percentage as the voting power of the member. For more information, see "Measuring Membership Interests in the LLC" in Step 3, above.

Note that a manager's voting power is not specified because, under most operating agreements, managers are given one vote each on any matter brought before the managers.

When you've completed the form, place it in the folder for the upcoming meeting or in your LLC records binder.

Step 5. Prepare Notice of the Meeting

Your next step is to provide everyone who may attend the upcoming meeting with notice of the time and date, and usually the purpose as well. In doing so, you'll want to meet any notice requirements set out in your operating agreement. If your operating agreement says nothing, take a look under the heading "Meeting Requirements" for your state in Appendix B to learn of any state default rules for providing notice. (In most states, notice rules set by the state LLC act apply only if you don't adopt a different provision in your operating agreement.) If neither your state law nor your operating agreement specifies notice requirements, you should do two things: First, give enough notice so that all participants have plenty of time to make arrangements to attend. Second, comply with the most stringent notice requirements required under any state's law.

Provide Notice Well in Advance

Always give all members and/or managers, as well as anyone else asked to attend an LLC meeting, plenty of advance notice of an upcoming meeting. After all, if an issue or decision is important enough to warrant holding a meeting, it's worth giving everyone a chance to get there. And, of course, it's particularly important to provide notice when members or managers are likely to disagree on the matter at hand. The last thing you want is for a member or manager to try to set aside a key decision because he or she didn't receive sufficient notice of the meeting.

To make sure you meet legal notice requirements, simply follow these rules:

- Provide written notice of all meetings. Your operating agreement may not require notice for regular meetings of members or managers—these are the annual or other periodic meetings scheduled in your operating agreement—but you should provide it anyway. After all, members and/or managers might not remember exactly when these meetings are to be held.

- Provide notice at least ten, and no more than 50, calendar days prior to all meetings, unless your operating agreement requires a longer notice period. The few states that specify mandatory notice periods usually use this range of days as the outside time limits for providing notice, so following this rule will ensure that you comply with the law.

- Always state the purpose of the meeting in the notice. Some LLC operating agreements (as well as some state LLC acts) say that only matters listed in the notice can be discussed and voted on at the meeting. To make sure you comply with your operating agreement and your state law, you should always state the purpose of the meeting in the notice. Even if you aren't required to describe the purpose of the meeting, it can be very helpful to the participants to know what will be covered ahead of time. After all, how can a member make an informed decision about whether to attend a meeting if he or she doesn't know what will be discussed and decided there?

If you follow these suggestions, you should be in compliance with any state's statutory notice of meeting rules, and everyone will be fully informed about your upcoming meeting.

> **TIP**
>
> **Use a waiver of notice form if you have to meet right away.** If you don't have time to comply with the meeting call and notice requirements discussed in Steps 3 and 5, you may have other options. If all members of your LLC work easily together, you can simply prepare a waiver of notice form and have each person sign it before, at, or after the meeting. This should meet any notice requirement in your operating agreement or state law. (See "How to Prepare Minutes of Paper LLC Meetings" in Chapter 6, Step 1, for instructions on preparing this waiver form.) However, this less formal approach is definitely not recommended if there is dissension in the ranks of your members and/or managers. The dissidents may simply refuse to sign.

Notice Requirements If Prior Meeting Was Adjourned With Unfinished Business

If a managers' or members' meeting is adjourned to continue business at another time, you usually don't have to send out notices for the second, continued meeting if it's held soon after the adjourned meeting. If you need to carry a meeting over to the next day, for example, you don't have to go to the trouble of giving notice of the second meeting.

Otherwise, give notice of all meetings to be continued. It's not hard to do this, and everyone will be reminded that the business will be carried over at the next meeting. Providing a new notice also gives any managers or members who happened to miss the first meeting a chance to attend the second.

Nonvoting Shares May Be Entitled to Notice

As mentioned above, LLCs occasionally issue nonvoting memberships to investors and other inactive owners. But some states' laws (as well as some LLC operating agreements) require that all members (voting and nonvoting) be given a chance to approve special matters that may affect their investment. Examples of such decisions include:

- amending the articles or operating agreement
- issuing a new membership
- approving a transfer of interest
- continuing the LLC business after a member leaves (state law may require this vote)
- distributing cash or property to members
- requiring additional contributions from members, and
- dissolving the LLC.

State law requirements for these matters are covered in Appendix B. If your state requires unanimous membership approval for special decisions, all members—voting and nonvoting—must approve the decisions. If your LLC has nonvoting memberships, you should take a broad view of who is entitled to receive notice of meetings. Even if a member is not entitled to vote on certain issues, you should go the extra step of inviting all interested parties, voting or nonvoting, to attend important LLC meetings. Doing so can curtail later complaints by members that they were kept in the dark or that major LLC decisions were made behind their back.

Manner and Contents of Notice

All notices should be in writing. The notice should state the time, place, and date of the upcoming meeting. The purpose of the meeting should also be included in the notice. You can hand the notice in person to each participant, or mail (first class, please) the notice to each member, manager, or other meeting participant at his or her address, which should appear in your LLC records. Other forms of providing notice are possible, such as email, fax, voice mail, and the like, as long as you are sure they are reliable (that is, the notice will be received and read by the participant) and the participant will not object to the alternate form of notice.

Fill in Notice of Meeting Form

To give formal notice of a special or annual meeting, you can use the Notice of Meeting form below.

CD-ROM

Below is a sample of the Notice of Meeting form included on the CD-ROM and as a tear-out form in Appendix C. (See Appendix A for information on selecting and using the CD-ROM

Notice of Meeting

Name of LLC: _____[insert name of LLC]_____ ❶

A meeting of ____["members" and/or "managers"]____ of the LLC will be held at

_____[location of meeting]_____,

on ___[date of meeting]___ at ___[time of meeting]___. ❷

The purpose(s) of the meeting is/are as follows:_____

_____[summarize the purpose(s) of the meeting]_____ ❸

❹

_____, LLC Secretary ❺

Signature of Secretary

---

files.) Complete the form following the special instructions provided below.

Special Instructions

❶ Insert the full name of your LLC.

❷ Indicate whether the meeting is of members and/or managers, and insert the place, date, and time of the meeting. LLC meetings are usually held at the principal office of the LLC, although state law and operating agreements usually allow manager and member meetings to be held anywhere.

> **TIP**
>
> **If you are in a hurry, use waiver of notice forms.** If you are sending notice late or need to hold a meeting quickly without giving formal notice, have each member and/or manager sign a written waiver of notice form—see "How to Prepare Minutes of Paper LLC Meetings" in Chapter 6, Step 1. This procedure will help you avoid legal challenges regarding short or informal notice when you are in a hurry to hold a meeting.

❸ Succinctly state the purpose(s) of the meeting. Here are some suggestions:

- "Annual [or regular] meeting of members for electing the managers of the LLC."
- "Annual [or regular] meeting of members and managers to review the prior year's business, discuss LLC operations for the upcoming year, re-elect managers for a one-year term, allow managers to accept election, and transact any other business that may come before the meeting."
- "Special meeting of members for the purpose of [state the specific purpose for which the meeting is being called, for example, 'approval of cash distribution to LLC members']."

> **CROSS REFERENCE**
>
> **Use resolutions for common LLC decisions.** Chapters 8 through 15 contain instructions on approving various types of ongoing LLC business decisions. At the beginning of Appendix

C, you'll find a list of tearout and resolution forms included with this book (as tearout forms and on the CD-ROM), along with cross-references to the chapters and sections of the book that provide instructions for preparing each resolution.

❹ If your operating agreement allows members who cannot attend a meeting to cast their votes by proxy, you should let them know how to do it. If voting by proxy is allowed, members may sign a proxy form that authorizes another person, typically a spouse or another member, to vote their LLC interest at a meeting. Some states specifically allow proxy voting by members, but most state LLC acts don't address this issue. However, operating agreements may establish rules not otherwise prohibited under state law for the regulation of LLC affairs, including proxy voting by members. If your LLC agreement allows proxy voting by members, and the upcoming meeting is a members' meeting, you can insert the following paragraph into the notice form to let members know how to cast a vote by proxy:

> If you are an LLC member and cannot attend the meeting, the LLC operating agreement allows you to designate another person in writing to vote your membership on your behalf. If you wish to do this, please deliver a signed proxy form to the secretary of the LLC before the meeting. Contact the secretary if you need help preparing this proxy form.

If you include this paragraph in your notice, you will probably want to include a blank proxy form with each notice sent out. Refer to Step 8, below, for a sample proxy form and instructions.

As you can see, this paragraph refers only to members, not managers. By and large, managers are not allowed to act by proxy. After

all, if you are specifically selected to act as an LLC manager, it's a bit irresponsible (and legally risky) to let another manager vote in your place on LLC business decisions.

TIP
Include additional information with the notice. You will probably want to send out additional material with your notice to help make your meeting as productive as possible and to help your managers and/or members understand the issues to be discussed at the upcoming meeting. For example, you might prepare and send out an agenda for the meeting, listing all the items and business that will be discussed or proposed for approval. You'll find information on preparing an agenda and other premeeting materials in Step 6, below.

❺ Have the LLC secretary sign the notice form.

Step 6. Prepare a Premeeting Information Packet

You will probably wish to include materials to help participants prepare for an upcoming meeting when you send out notices. You may want to provide this material even if you do not send out a formal written notice of the meeting (if you provide verbal notice of a meeting, for example).

To help people prepare for a meeting, especially those who are not involved in the day-to-day management of the LLC, you may want to send out:

- **An agenda for the meeting.** This should include new items as well as any unfinished business carried over from a prior meeting.

- **Copies of reports, presentations, and background material.** Include all information that may help participants familiarize themselves with the issues to be decided at the upcoming meeting. Doing this not only saves time at the meeting but also helps your LLC make better decisions.

- **Copies of proposed LLC resolutions.** If applicable, use one of the ready-made LLC resolutions contained in this book.

- **Minutes of the last managers' or members' meetings.** One of the first items on your agenda will probably be to approve the minutes from the last meeting. You can send the prior minutes out to members before the meeting, along with an approval form they can sign to approve the prior minutes. Using this form will save time at the next meeting—and provides written proof that all members and/or managers consented to decisions reached at previous meetings. This may be helpful, for example, if some members or managers did not attend the last meeting but you want to create a record showing that they approved of the important decisions reached in their absence. (To prepare a written approval form, see "How to Prepare Minutes of Paper LLC Meetings" in Chapter 6, Step 3.)

- **Proof of receipt.** *(Optional)* If you want participants to acknowledge that they received notice of the meeting, send an Acknowledgment of Receipt of Notice of Meeting form to be signed and returned. (See Step 7, below.)

- **Member proxies.** *(Optional)* You may wish to enclose a blank proxy form with notice of a members' meeting if you anticipate that a member will wish to send another person to the meeting to vote his or her membership interest. (See Step 8, below.)

Step 7. Prepare Acknowledgment of Receipt Forms (Optional)

If you have an important or controversial meeting coming up, or if you generally run

your LLC in a formal manner, you may wish to document that all managers, members, and other upcoming meeting participants actually received notice of the meeting. This may be particularly important if you provide informal (verbal or email) notice or if you have some nonmanaging members. Distributing Acknowledgment of Receipt forms allows you to create a record that notice was properly received by your managers and/or members.

CD-ROM

Below is a sample of the Acknowledgment of Receipt of Notice of Meeting form included on the CD-ROM and as a tearout form in Appendix C. (See Appendix A for information on selecting and using the CD-ROM files.) Prepare the form following the special instructions provided below. You should fill out a separate form for each person acknowledging notice.

Special Instructions

❶ Insert the name of your LLC.

❷ Insert the type of meeting (members' and/or managers'), but leave the date line blank—the person acknowledging receipt of notice will insert the date he or she received notice in this blank.

❸ Check the box to indicate how notice will be (or was) sent to the recipient. Fill in any additional information as requested for a particular type of notice (such as the telephone number used for verbal notice or the address to which mail or email was sent).

❹ Insert the recipient's name on the line just after the signature line in paragraph 3.

❺ If you will send out notice of meeting forms by mail, include an acknowledgment of receipt form with each notice. Also enclose a self-addressed, stamped envelope (SASE) addressed to the LLC officer's at the LLC

Acknowledgment of Receipt of Notice of Meeting

LLC Name: _____ [insert name of LLC] _____ ❶

(Recipient of Notice: In paragraph 1, please fill in the date on which you received notice of the meeting; in paragraph 2, review for accuracy the type of notice checked, making and initialing corrections as appropriate; in paragraph 3, date and sign your name; and mail or deliver a completed copy to the LLC officer listed in paragraph 4.)

1. I received notice of a meeting of the _____ ["members" and/or "managers"] _____ of the LLC on ____ [leave date blank for recipient] ____. The notice of meeting stated the date, time, place, and purpose of the upcoming _____ meeting. ❷

2. The notice of meeting was: ❸

   ☐ received by fax, telephone number _____

   ☐ delivered verbally to me in person at _____

   ☐ delivered verbally to me by phone call, telephone number _____

   ☐ left verbally in a message on an answering machine or on voice mail, telephone number _____

   ☐ delivered by mail to _____

   ☐ delivered via email, email address _____

   ☐ other: _____

3. Date: _____

   Signed: _____

   Printed Name: _____ ❹

4. Please return to: ❺

   Name of LLC Officer: _____

   Name of LLC: _____

   Address: _____

   Phone: _____

   Fax: _____

address. If you gave notice verbally or by email, you may either mail an acknowledgment form to each participant or hand out the forms at the meeting.

When you receive completed, signed receipts from the recipients, place them in the folder for the upcoming meeting or in your LLC records binder.

Step 8. Prepare Proxies for Members' Meetings (Optional)

A proxy lets a member authorize another person to vote his or her shares at an upcoming meeting. Some states specifically authorize member voting by proxy. A few have special restrictions—limiting the proxy's duration, for example. Most states don't address this issue, so your operating agreement can establish its own rules for proxy voting. (See Appendix B for links to your state's LLC act.) Larger LLCs, or those that have members scattered throughout a wide geographic region, may routinely include blank proxy forms with the notice and other premeeting materials sent to members. Many smaller LLCs won't have any reason to send out proxy forms—a member who has to miss a meeting won't need to authorize someone else to vote in his or her stead if all members agree on the issues to be decided. However, in rare instances, a member may ask you to provide a proxy prior to an upcoming meeting.

At a joint managers'/members' meeting, members may be asked to vote on actions proposed by the managers, such as an amendment to the articles or operating agreement of the LLC, so a membership voting proxy is appropriate for this type of meeting, too.

CD-ROM

Below is a sample of the Membership Voting Proxy form included on the CD-ROM and as a tearout in Appendix C. (See Appendix A for information on selecting and using the CD-ROM files.) Complete the form following the special instructions provided below.

Special Instructions

❶ Insert the full name of the LLC in the first blank. Leave the second blank empty—the member inserts the name of the proxyholder here.

❷ Check whether the upcoming meeting is a joint managers'/members' or just a members' meeting (for a joint meeting, check both boxes; for a members' meeting, check the second box only).

❸ Insert the date and time of the upcoming meeting.

❹ Type or print the name of the member after the signature line, but leave the date and signature lines blank—the member making out the proxy will date and sign the form in these two blanks.

❺ Insert the date by which the proxy must be returned (mailed or delivered) to the LLC, and the name and address to which the proxy must be sent (usually, the LLC secretary at the LLC office). You'll probably want to set a date close to—or even on the same day as—the meeting, but if you want (or your operating agreement requires) more notice of the member's vote by proxy, specify an earlier date here.

If a member mails or delivers a completed proxy form to your LLC for use at an upcoming meeting, place it in the meeting folder or your LLC records binder.

Membership Voting Proxy

(Member: Insert name of proxyholder—the person you are authorizing to vote in your place—in first paragraph, then date, sign, and return by the date indicated to LLC officer at address listed below.)

The undersigned member of _____[insert name of LLC]_____, a limited liability company, authorizes __[recipient inserts proxyholder name]__ to act as his or her proxy and to represent and vote his/her LLC membership at a meeting of: ❶

    (Check one or both boxes) ❷

    ☐ managers

    ☐ members

to be held on __[insert date and time of meeting]__. ❸

This proxy is effective for all items of business brought before the meeting.

Date: _____[leave blank]_____

Signature of Member: _____[leave blank]_____

Printed Name of Member: _____[insert printed name of member]_____ ❹

Please return proxy by __[insert latest date for return of signed proxy]__ to: ❺

Name of LLC Officer: _____

Name of LLC: _____

Address: _____

Phone: _____ Fax: _____

! **CAUTION**

Proxies may have a limited life. In the few states whose laws specifically address proxy voting by members, a written proxy may be legally effective only for a limited period, such as 11 months, unless the proxy says otherwise. If you use proxies at all, you should have members sign them no more than a few weeks prior to a meeting, and limit their use to one meeting only. If you wish to have your members sign proxies to be effective for longer durations (so you can use one proxy for more than one meeting), find out whether your state's law requires you to include additional language in the proxies to make them effective for a longer period of time.

Step 9. Distribute Notice Forms and Information Packet

Have the secretary of your LLC deliver (by mail, personally, or electronically) the notice of meeting form to the meeting participants, together with any premeeting information you have prepared, as explained above. If the information is mailed to a member or manager, use the exact address shown in your LLC records. On the meeting summary sheet (see Step 2, above), have the secretary complete the lines at the bottom of the form indicating how and when each manager or member was given the notice form. Place the notated summary sheet in your folder for the meeting or your LLC records binder.

When to Use Certified Mail

Most LLCs provide written notice of meetings by first-class mail. However, if you have a dissident manager or member, or for some other reason you may have to prove that a person actually received a mailed notice, send the notice by certified mail with a return receipt requested. Place the certification number or return receipt in your meeting folder or LLC records binder.

Other Ways to Give Notice

You may occasionally decide to provide notice of LLC meetings verbally: in person or by phone, answering machine, voice mail, or email. This is particularly likely to happen in small, closely held LLCs where a few people who own and run the LLC agree to contact one another by the quickest, most convenient method available. For example, you may decide to fax or email notice of an upcoming meeting instead of mailing it. Although not specifically authorized under most LLC statutes, electronic or other alternative forms of providing notice should work fine if everyone agrees to the method. If you do use a verbal or electronic means of providing notice, it's wise to prepare documentation showing how and when the notice was given and received by the member or manager (or other meeting participant). Step 7, above, explains how to prepare a written acknowledgment of receipt of notice for this purpose.

Certification of Mailing Form (Optional)

If you don't want to take the time to get receipts of notice from each meeting participant (either by sending notice by certified mail, return receipt requested, or by getting each person to sign and submit an acknowledgment of receipt of notice), you can prepare an in-house certification of mailing form. In this form, your LLC secretary certifies that notice for an upcoming meeting was mailed to each participant on time.

CD-ROM

Below is a sample of the Certification of Mailing of Notice form included on the CD-ROM and as a tearout form in Appendix C. (See Appendix A for information on selecting and using the CD-ROM files.) Complete the form following the special instructions provided below.

Certification of Mailing of Notice

I, the undersigned acting secretary of _____ [insert name of LLC] _____ , a limited liability company, certify that I caused notice of the meeting of the ___ ["members" and/ or "managers"] ___ of the LLC to be held on __[insert date and time of meeting]__ to be deposited in the United States mail, postage prepaid, on ___[insert date of mailing]___ , addressed to the following persons at their most recent addresses as shown on the books of this LLC as follows: ❶

_____[names and addresses of persons to whom notice was mailed]___ ❷

_____

_____

A true and correct copy of the notice is attached to this certificate.

Date: _____

Signed: _____ , Secretary

Printed Name: _____ ❸

Special Instructions

❶ Fill in the full name of the LLC, the type of meeting ("members" and/or "managers"), and the date and time of the upcoming meeting. Have your LLC secretary fill in the date of mailing.

❷ Have the secretary fill in the names and addresses of the participants to whom notice was mailed.

❸ Have the secretary date, sign, and print his or her name on the form. Attach a copy of the previously mailed written notice to the certification form, and place the form in your meeting folder or LLC records binder. ●

How to Hold an LLC Meeting

This chapter covers the basic steps necessary to hold a successful LLC meeting. You'll also find a few more premeeting steps. If you've read Chapter 3, you've already learned about premeeting formalities, and I refer you back to these steps to accomplish them quickly. Only a few of the meeting steps are legally required, and you can skip or combine the others as you see fit. Don't worry that you'll miss an important step: The minutes form set out in the next chapter (and in Appendix C) reminds you to take care of all the legally required steps.

SKIP AHEAD

If you know how to hold meetings, skip ahead. If you're experienced in holding LLC meetings and wish to get right to the task of preparing your minutes, skip to Chapter 5. Likewise, if you wish to document a managers' or members' decision without holding a real meeting, skip to Chapter 6 to prepare minutes for a paper meeting or to Chapter 7 to take action by written consent.

SKIP AHEAD

If you have a one-member LLC that you manage yourself, you probably won't hold a real meeting. In practice, member meetings for a one-member LLC and manager meetings for a one-manager LLC are often held on paper only, to formally record decisions that the sole member or manager wishes to document. If you are in this situation, turn to Chapter 6, which covers the steps you need to take to prepare minutes for this type of "paper meeting." You may also record decisions by written consents. (See Chapter 7.) However, a sole LLC member can also hold a real one-person meeting (you can talk to yourself if you wish) or hold a real meeting with others (staff, officers, advisers, or lawyers, for instance), to present reports and discuss proposals.

Step 1. Call and Provide Notice of the Meeting

Before holding your meeting, it's standard procedure to call and provide notice of the meeting, according to the legal requirements contained in your operating agreement. The steps you'll take to accomplish these tasks are fully described in Chapter 3.

SKIP AHEAD

To bypass normal notice requirements If you wish to sidestep all legal requirements for calling and noticing your meeting, your managers or members (or both, if it's a joint meeting) can sign a waiver of notice form. Dispensing with notice of an upcoming meeting is particularly appropriate for small LLCs whose managers or members are all involved in the business and maintain regular contact with each other. (See "How to Prepare Minutes of Paper LLC Meetings" in Chapter 6, Step 1, for instructions on preparing waiver of notice forms.)

Step 2. Prepare an Agenda for the Meeting

Especially for larger meetings, the person in charge of the meeting (referred to as the "chairperson" throughout the remainder of this chapter and this book) will have an easier time if he or she has a written agenda that lists the order of business for the meeting. (See "Steps to Prepare for a Meeting" in Chapter 3, Step 6, for a discussion of preparing a premeeting agenda.) An agenda can help the chairperson keep an eye on the clock, making sure that all proposed items are covered within the time allotted for the meeting.

Step 3. Prepare Meeting Resolutions in Advance

As a practical matter, it is usually best to prepare ahead of time drafts of resolutions to be introduced at a meeting. Drafting suitable resolutions will require you to understand the issues involved, and then put them into language that clearly states the business or matter to be approved at the meeting.

You don't need to use fancy or legal language for your resolution. Just describe, in a short, concise statement, the transaction or matter to be approved. Normally, resolutions start with a preamble of the following sort: "The (members and/or managers) resolved that …", but this is not required.

Following are some examples of resolutions:

EXAMPLE 1 (bank loan):

"The managers resolved that the treasurer be authorized to obtain a loan from _____[insert name of bank]_____ for the amount of $_____ on terms he/she considers commercially reasonable."

EXAMPLE 2 (LLC hiring):

"The members approved the hiring of _[insert name of new employee]_, hired in the position of _[insert job title]_ at an annual salary of $_____ and in accordance with the terms of the LLC's standard employment contract."

EXAMPLE 3 (tax year):

"The members decided that the LLC shall adopt a tax year with an ending date of 3/31."

EXAMPLE 4 (amendment of articles):

"The members resolved that the following new article be added to the LLC's articles of organization: _____[language of new article]_____."

CROSS REFERENCE

Common resolutions are covered in Chapters 8 through 15. All of the above matters (and many others) are covered in a specific resolution included with this book and explained in Chapters 8 through 15.

Step 4. Get Together to Hold the Meeting

Your next step is to have the meeting participants (members and/or managers, as well as any additional people who will present reports or otherwise participate in the meeting) meet at the time and place specified in your notice of the meeting. Most LLC operating agreements select the principal office of the LLC as the place where meetings are held, but they usually also allow meetings to be held at any location inside or outside the state as designated by the members or managers. (For a discussion of several state-of-the-art ways to hold a meeting over phone lines, on a company intranet, or via video conference hookups, see Step 5, just below.)

Step 5. Hold a Meeting in Cyberspace If You Have the Equipment and Know-How

SKIP AHEAD

Skip this material if you plan to meet in person. This section is not really a separate step in the LLC meeting process—rather, it is a discussion of alternative ways of convening LLC meetings. If you plan to meet in person, you can safely skip this "step" and proceed to Step 6. If you're interested in setting up a meeting without the need to get everyone together at the same physical location, this step gives suggestions for using technology to help streamline the LLC meeting process. You'll have to make these arrangements in advance, and make sure everyone can use the technology.

Telecommunications advances now allow a number of people to simultaneously communicate over phone lines using telephone, video, and audio/video computer conferencing software. Most state LLC statutes are worded broadly enough to allow managers and members to meet by using a means of telecommunication that allows each of the participants to hear one another simultaneously. However, if you anticipate that any participant may object to a meeting that's not held in person, or if a matter to be resolved at a meeting is controversial, it's best to meet in person and avoid any challenges to the meeting format.

Step 6. Appoint a Chairperson and Secretary

Before the meeting begins, you'll need to find people to fill two important roles at the meeting:

- **Chairperson.** This person, usually the president, directs the activity at the meeting.

- **Secretary.** The secretary of the meeting—usually the LLC secretary—takes notes of the order and outcome of business discussed and voted on at the meeting. These notes will be used later to fill in the blanks on the minutes form, as explained in the next chapter.

Exactly how a meeting is organized and conducted is up to you. State LLC law generally does not concern itself with parliamentary procedures used at meetings. For a discussion of how to introduce, discuss, and vote on proposals at LLC meetings, see Step 12, below.

Formal Rules for Running a Meeting

Your meeting can be as formal or informal as you wish in terms of raising and making motions and seconding and voting on items of business. This book doesn't cover the many parliamentary rules and procedures (formal rules for conducting meetings) that can be used to run LLC meetings, because they are usually unnecessary. If your LLC has only a few members and/or managers in attendance at a meeting, a conversational format will probably work best. For slightly larger meetings, an agreeable, but no-nonsense, chairperson will be the key to keeping meetings on track.

LLCs with more than about ten participants may need to establish more detailed ground rules for meetings. For example, the chairperson may wish to call on members or managers individually to elicit comments and opinions prior to a vote, setting a time limit of five minutes or so for remarks. Or, the chairperson may wish to have motions formally proposed, seconded, and discussed before the question is called and a vote taken.

If you need guidance in setting ground rules, you can use formal parliamentary procedures. For a remarkably easy-to-use guide to implementing the most commonly used parliamentary procedures at meetings, see *Parliamentary Law at a Glance*, by E.C. Utter (Contemporary Books, Inc.).

Step 7. Chairperson Calls the Meeting to Order

The chairperson normally calls the meeting to order by announcing that it's time to begin. The chairperson then directs the order in which business will be covered at the meeting. Typically, the chairperson will introduce some items and call on other meeting participants to take the lead for certain items of business. For example, the chairperson may ask the meeting secretary to read a proposal and take the votes after an issue is discussed.

Note Taking at Meetings Made Easy

The secretary does not need to provide a longhand narrative of everything that happens at an LLC meeting. It is usually enough to list who is present, the nature of the proposals raised, and the outcome of votes taken. This information can then be used after the meeting to complete the minutes form discussed in the next chapter. The quickest method of all is for the secretary to fill in the minutes form at the meeting (either on copies of the tearout forms in Appendix C, or on the minutes form provided on the CD-ROM included with this book).

Step 8. Secretary Determines Whether a Quorum Is Present

The secretary should note those present and absent from the meeting, making sure that the required number (a quorum) of members or managers (or of each for a joint members'/managers' meeting) is present. If your LLC allows proxy voting by members, and you are tallying up the interests of members at a meeting to compute whether a quorum is present, make sure to include any membership interests represented by proxies. (For more on proxies, see Chapter 3, Step 8.) If a quorum is not present at the start of a meeting, the chairperson should adjourn the meeting to a new time and date, and start over by providing notice of the new meeting date, time, and purpose to all participants, as discussed in Chapter 3, Step 5.

EXAMPLE:

The operating agreement of XYZ LLC states that the LLC must have seven managers and that a majority of the authorized number of managers represents a quorum for managers' meetings. Four managers, therefore, must attend managers' meetings for business to be discussed and approved. This is true even if any manager's slot is currently vacant.

If your operating agreement does not state the minimum quorum requirements for a meeting, see the "Meeting Requirements" heading in Appendix B for your state's default quorum rules. Many states with quorum rules (many do not have them) set a quorum for manager meetings as a majority of the total number of managers authorized in your LLC and a quorum for members' meetings as a majority of the members (or a majority of all of the members' capital and/or profits interests). Again, check your operating agreement or your state's law in Appendix B to be sure.

Your operating agreement or state LLC act may set the minimum quorum requirement for members' meetings as a percentage of capital and/or profits interests held by members. See "Measuring Membership Interests in the LLC" in Chapter 3, Step 3, to understand how to determine whether the required membership percentage is present at your meeting.

EXAMPLE:

Dollars to Donuts, LLC, a bakery, is a manager-managed LLC, operated by three member-managers. Four relatives of the three managers also have invested in the LLC as passive members. Because the LLC is closely held by a few people and their close family members, the LLC operating agreement requires the attendance of the three active member-managers, plus no fewer than two of the three passive members, at membership meetings. Super-majority quorum requirements of this sort are common in the LLC world, particularly when the LLC is owned and operated by a close-knit group.

CAUTION

A quorum must be present to take action. For the managers or members to take action, a quorum must be present at the meeting. For example, if a quorum of members is not present at a members' meeting, or a member leaves and the quorum is broken, the meeting must be adjourned until another time when a quorum of members can be obtained for the meeting.

CAUTION

If your LLC has special membership classes, your quorum requirements may be different. In the great majority of smaller LLCs, all members have voting rights. If the operating agreement does not specifically list the voting rights granted to members, you can assume all members having voting power. But if your operating agreement creates different classes of membership interests (granting voting power to some classes but not to others), a quorum of the membership interests with voting power on a matter must be present before a vote is taken on the matter.

EXAMPLE:

Green Construction LLC has issued six voting and two nonvoting memberships. The operating agreement defines a quorum for members' meetings as a majority of the members who are entitled to vote. The LLC ignores the two nonvoting memberships in its calculation of a quorum. If four out of the six voting members attend a members' meeting, there is a majority quorum in attendance and the meeting can begin.

Very Rare Exception: State LLC law is flexible, and some LLCs with unusual needs may give one member the exclusive vote on a particular matter. For example, the operating agreement may authorize the issuance of a special membership interest to a bank or financial institution, granting it exclusive voting power to approve or veto the distribution of cash to LLC members. Obviously, the holder of this special type of membership interest must be present at a meeting to vote on a proposed distribution of cash to LLC members, whether or not a quorum of the full voting membership is also present at the meeting.

CAUTION

Different quorum rules may apply for special business or important structural changes. In special cases, your operating agreement may require a meeting of all members. (See your operating agreement and check Appendix B for information on finding your state law.) This may be required, for example, when the LLC members are voting to:

- amend articles of organization or the operating agreement
- approve a new member
- sell all LLC assets
- voluntarily dissolve the LLC, or

- continue the LLC after the disassociation of a member (the loss of membership rights due to the death, disability, expulsion, or bankruptcy of a member).

In such cases you cannot vote on these matters unless all members attend. However, members don't have to vote (some may abstain). And the vote need not necessarily be unanimous. Check your state's laws and your operating agreement for details.

Step 9. Secretary Reads Minutes or Summarizes Business of Last Meeting

After determining that a quorum is present at the meeting, it is customary, but not legally required, for the secretary of the meeting to read or summarize the minutes of the last meeting. After that, the minutes are approved by the participants. This is a particularly good idea when the LLC holds regular manager or membership meetings every month or so. It is a polite and efficient way to have everyone agree that the written minutes for the prior meeting properly reflect and summarize the actions taken and decisions reached at that meeting. Often, a member or manager will have a small correction to the minutes. It is up to the president or chairperson to deal with these corrections without having meeting participants completely rehash the proceedings of the prior meeting.

TIP

Save time by sending out minutes in advance. To save the time and trouble of reading and discussing minutes of a prior meeting at the current meeting, you can send them out as part of the premeeting packet discussed in Chapter 3, Step 6. You may also want to send out an "approval of minutes" form in advance instead of waiting for the upcoming meeting to have the participants approve these minutes. Doing this can save time at

the meeting, as well as provide a signed document showing that the managers and/or members specifically approved actions taken at a prior meeting. This is an especially good idea if a manager or member missed a previous meeting. (See Chapter 6, Step 3, for instructions on preparing an approval of LLC minutes form.)

Step 10. Handle Any Unfinished Business

No matter how long meetings last, items of business may have to be carried over to the next meeting. If this happened at your last LLC meeting, make sure to tackle any "old business" first before taking care of the new business items on the agenda. Of course, the notice (or waiver of notice) for the current meeting should have included a summary of any unfinished business to be considered at the current meeting.

Step 11. Officers and Committees Present Reports

The next item on the agenda of many meetings, particularly annual membership or manager meetings, is for the chairperson to call on committees, LLC officers, department managers, and outside consultants or advisers to make presentations or hand out reports. Obviously, if all members or managers work in the business and are fully current on its affairs, presenting formal reports may not be necessary. But when members who are not in day-to-day contact with the business are asked to attend, these summaries can be extremely valuable.

TIP

Do the dollars first. For annual meetings, it makes sense to review the LLC's profit and loss picture first, as these are usually the figures everyone is most interested in, particularly outside investors.

Reports are often made to update those present on past or projected LLC operations (such as upcoming plans for increasing the LLC's market share of sales in a particular area of operation), or on a particular aspect of LLC performance (such as the LLC's net worth reflected on the latest balance sheet). Reports can also provide members or managers with the information necessary to make an informed decision on an issue. For instance, it would be helpful to have a discussion of important options associated with the adoption of a 401(k) profit-sharing plan or a report by the president explaining the reasons for the creation and issuance of a new class of membership.

EXAMPLE 1:

At a management meeting, prior to proposing a vote on a resolution to increase the coverage limits of the LLC's product liability insurance, the chief financial officer summarizes current coverage limits and options for increased coverage, based on data obtained from the LLC's insurance broker. Next, the LLC's outside legal adviser gives a report summarizing current trends and outcomes in product liability law cases involving products similar to the LLC's product line.

EXAMPLE 2:

At the annual managers'/members' meeting for Yolodyne Ltd. Liability Co., the chairperson calls on the treasurer to report on past and projected balance sheet figures, followed by a report by the president outlining new operations planned for the upcoming year. Providing past and prospective information of this sort can help keep outside investors satisfied with the work goals and performance of the LLC. Following the presentation of reports, managers are nominated for election or reelection, and the membership vote is taken.

TIP

Don't surprise members with new reports at the meeting. To save time at meetings, and to avoid surprise, reports and background information should be mailed to managers, members, and other meeting participants prior to the meeting. (See Chapter 3, Step 6.) The presenters can then comment on only the most important issues raised in the reports, rather than go through all of the information in detail.

The Legal and Practical Value of Reports Presented at Meetings

The LLC acts of many states specifically immunize a manager from personal liability if he or she relied on misleading or false reports when reaching a decision. (The typical exception is if the member or manager knew, or should have known, that the information submitted in the report was unreliable.) This gives LLC members (in member-managed LLCs) and managers (in manager-managed LLCs) an additional measure of legal protection, and increases their comfort level when discharging their managerial duties

Reports at LLC meetings can have another, broader purpose: They are an excellent way to keep members informed of LLC operations and performance. Such reports not only provide a good jumping-off point for discussion at the meeting, but they can also head off member objections to a course of business taken by the LLC management team. If reports have been distributed before and read at a meeting, the members can't claim that they haven't been kept informed.

Step 12. Introduce and Discuss Specific Proposals

After any reports or background presentations have been made at the meeting, the chairperson will want to formally introduce proposals for discussion and vote by the managers or members (or both). Proposals are best introduced in the form of resolutions that clearly and legally state the item or business or matter to be approved. This allows you to include the exact language of the resolution in your minutes, with no need to reword it later.

REMINDER

Resolutions. This book provides 80-plus resolution forms, ready for use to tackle common types of ongoing business raised at LLC meetings. If you need, or wish, to prepare your own resolution, short and simple language works best. See the examples given in Step 3, above, and in Chapters 8 through 15.

LLCs can use a variety of procedures to introduce, discuss, and decide resolutions at meetings. Typically, the chairperson or another LLC officer follows a prepared agenda to introduce a proposal, such as whether or not to increase the liability limits of the LLC's general liability insurance policy. The proposal can be introduced by way of a formal motion that is seconded by another participant and then discussed. Or, a proposal can simply be introduced by the chairperson with the assumption that some discussion will occur before a formal motion is made.

Either way, you will probably discuss the merits and possible parameters of the proposal unless all participants are already fully informed and ready to vote. For example, the president,

acting as chairperson, might introduce a resolution to increase LLC insurance coverage. The participants debate whether all that extra insurance coverage is really necessary. Once the general discussion is over, the chairperson can either propose adopting the resolution (if one has been introduced), or propose specific language for the resolution.

After a resolution has been introduced and discussed, the chairperson may move for a voice vote. However, experienced chairpersons, aware of the desirability of achieving a consensus, will be sensitive to divergent views. The chairperson may allow participants to suggest modifications to the resolution prior to calling for a vote, as long as the changes don't completely undercut the purpose of the resolution. For example, a member may propose a resolution for the LLC to purchase $50,000 of additional liability coverage. Another member may propose that the insurance resolution be made more specific by authorizing the purchase of $50,000 of general liability insurance coverage from the lowest bidder, after getting quotes from the LLC's current insurance carrier and outside companies.

After the language of a resolution is decided, the managers or members (or both) vote to approve or veto it. (See Step 13, below.) When a resolution passes, it is inserted into the minutes for the meeting and becomes an official act of the LLC. If it fails, it normally isn't mentioned in the minutes, unless you want a record stating that the resolution didn't pass.

Introducing Resolutions at Joint Managers'/Members' Meetings

At joint managers'/members' meetings (in manager-managed LLCs), managers may propose resolutions for membership approval. For example, management might propose an amendment to the articles to change the LLC name or to authorize an additional class of membership. The chairperson usually asks a manager to introduce and discuss the amendment prior to taking a membership vote on it. (For a discussion of the decision-making roles of LLC managers and members, see Chapter 2.)

When a resolution is introduced by managers for membership approval, the specific language of the resolution is not normally hammered out at the joint meeting. Instead, the managers will have approved the proposed language before the meeting—typically, at a managers' meeting—then mailed the proposed resolution to members as part of the premeeting materials. This gives members a chance to understand the measure ahead of time, and to make an informed decision at the meeting after hearing any additional reports or background on the proposal.

EXAMPLE: At the annual managers'/members' meeting of Rackafrax LLC, a manager-managed LLC, the members are asked to ratify an amendment to the operating agreement that requires additional contributions from members whenever the cash reserves of the LLC fall below a threshold amount. The resolution presented for approval at the members' meeting was approved earlier by the managers at a managers' meeting. This resolution, together with a written summary of the reasons for the amendment, was sent out to the Rackafrax members as part of the premeeting materials. (See Chapter 3, Step 6.)

The chairperson, who is also LLC president and a manager-member of the LLC, introduces the resolution. The managers and members, LLC officers, and staff present at the meeting discuss the resolution. Following the discussion, the chairperson makes a motion for a member vote on the written resolution. After being seconded, the motion carries, and a member vote on the amendment is taken.

Step 13. Take the Votes of Managers or Members

After resolutions have been presented in final form at a meeting, the managers or members must vote on them. Most resolutions require the majority vote of those present at a meeting. A resolution will be submitted to a vote of members, managers, or both, depending on the type of meeting and the type of resolution:

- **Members' meetings.** In a member-managed LLC, all meetings are members' meetings. Members vote either per capita (one vote each) or in proportion to their percentage of capital, profits, or capital and profits interests. (See "Measuring Membership Interests in the LLC," in Chapter 3, Step 3, for information on measuring these interests.) Typically, a majority of the membership interests represented at a meeting is required to approve a resolution. Your operating agreement should tell you how the voting power of your members is computed, and what membership vote is necessary for members to take action at a meeting. If it doesn't, see the "Meeting

Requirements" heading in Appendix B to find out whether your state's LLC act has a default member voting rule that applies in the absence of an operating agreement rule. Remember: If your LLC has issued memberships to nonvoting members, only members with voting rights are typically entitled to vote on a resolution presented at a meeting of members (except when a full membership vote is required for very important decisions—see "Special Membership Voting Rules," below).

- **Manager's meetings and joint members'/managers' meetings.** In a manager-managed LLC, the managers vote on most resolutions presented at meetings, asking for membership approval only for important issues that require a membership vote (see "Special Membership Voting Rules," below). Under standard LLC operating agreements and state default rules for manager voting, managers get one vote each, and the approval of a majority of managers is necessary for the managers to take action at a meeting. Again, check your operating agreement.

If you are confused about who decides what at meetings of manager-managed LLCs, see "How Your Management Structure Affects Decision-Making Requirements" in Chapter 2 for a more in-depth explanation.

EXAMPLE 1:

Wirewrap Electronics, LLC, is member-managed, with four members who have each contributed 25% of the capital to fund the LLC. The operating agreement grants voting rights to members in proportion to the current value of each member's capital account. At the time of the members' meeting, each member's account balance equals $15,000 (25% of the total $60,000

capital contributed to the LLC at its formation). The operating agreement requires the approval of at least a majority of the membership voting power present at a members' meeting to pass a resolution. All four members attend the meeting, so the approval of at least three of the four members (representing 75% of the capital interests of the LLC) is necessary to pass a resolution.

EXAMPLE 2:

Syncopation Sound Recording, LLC, is manager-managed by five active members. The operating agreement requires the majority per capita vote of all managers present at a manager's meeting to pass a resolution. A quorum of three managers attends an LLC managers' meeting. The affirmative votes of two of the three managers present are necessary to pass a resolution.

Here are a few issues that may arise during the voting process:

- **If a member or manager abstains.** When a member or manager abstains, it often means he or she doesn't agree to a particular action, but also doesn't want to annoy others by voting "no." In short, he or she may want to duck the issue by having the minutes reflect a neutral position. Here's how it might play out: If five managers or members are present at a meeting (assuming each gets one vote and a majority vote is necessary to pass a resolution), you need three "yes" votes to pass a resolution. With two "yes" votes, two "no" votes, and an abstention, the resolution fails.
- **Liability of silent managers.** Some states specify that a manager (in a manager-managed LLC) or a member (in a member-

managed LLC) can be held personally accountable for unlawful decisions—such as the approval of a cash distribution that makes the LLC insolvent—if the manager or member voted to approve the decision. Also, courts may hold members or managers personally liable if an LLC decision turns out (perhaps through 20-20 hindsight) to have created a serious risk of injury to others, and others are actually injured because of the decision—for example, a decision by LLC managers to go forward with a product line that causes harm to customers. Will an abstention in either of these situations protect a member or manager from personal liability? In some states, the answer may be "no." It's safer to vote "no" than to abstain if you want to make it clear that you disagree with an LLC management decision or policy. The minutes will record your disapproval of the decision.

- **Method of voting.** Typically, LLC statutes don't say how members or managers should cast their votes. Standard practice is as follows: Unless a specific request for a written vote (ballot) is presented at the meeting, voice votes are normally taken on resolutions raised at meetings. By the time a vote occurs, often everyone is ready to say "yes." But this isn't always the case. If there is any opposition, it's usually best to poll the participants (members, managers, or both) by asking each member to voice his or her vote individually. Written ballots are typically requested only when the issue at hand is controversial or contested, and members of the board don't wish to announce their decision at the meeting.

- **Proxy voting by members.** Members may sign a proxy form that allows another person to vote their membership interest at a meeting.

(See Chapter 3, Step 8, for a discussion of proxies and instructions on preparing proxy forms for membership voting.)

- **Election of managers.** If members of a manager-managed LLC hold a regular (annual or other periodic) meeting to elect managers, this is usually done by taking the voice votes of members. The managers who receive the highest number of votes will be elected to the management team—for example, the top three vote-getters out of five nominees are elected to a three-manager team. Some LLC operating agreements contain specific provisions, based on state statutes, setting out special voting procedures for nominating and electing managers at the members' meeting. For example, some operating agreements provide that any member may request the election of managers to be by written ballot or the use of cumulative voting. The latter is a special type of voting process used primarily to protect minority member interests in larger LLCs. (See "Cumulative Voting by Members," below.)

Unless there is controversy or ill will among LLC principals, the members of small manager-managed LLCs routinely reelect all LLC managers to serve another term at each annual meeting of members. Routine reelection of managers is allowed under state laws, which do not limit the number of consecutive terms a manager may hold. Just as typically, the operating agreement specifies an unlimited term for managers, who serve until they resign or are removed by a vote of members.

Cumulative Voting by Members

Cumulative voting by members to elect managers can help protect minority member interests in larger LLCs. If your operating agreement requires the use of cumulative voting in an election of managers, then each member can cast a total number of votes in the election equal to the number of shares he or she owns, multiplied by the number of persons to be elected to the board. The member can cast all of his or her votes for one candidate or split them up among the candidates as the member sees fit.

EXAMPLE: Members A and B own 2,000 shares each, and Member C owns 1,000 shares. At the annual members' meeting, four candidates are nominated for election to a three-person board. Under normal voting rules whereby one share is equal to one vote, C's candidate can always be outvoted by A's or B's choice. With cumulative voting, however, C is given 3,000 votes (A and B have 6,000 votes each). While still outnumbered, if C casts all 3,000 votes in favor of one candidate and A and B split their votes among two other candidates, C has a chance of electing his or her nominee to the board.

Small LLCs in which members own roughly equal interests don't need to concern themselves with cumulative voting. If each member has the same number of votes, the outcome of a cumulative and a regular election will be the same.

Special Membership Voting Rules

Whether your LLC is manager- or member-managed, your articles or operating agreement may require the vote of all members, or a majority of the total membership interests in your LLC (not just a majority of those present at a meeting), for some decisions. Typically, the following decisions require the approval of all or a majority of all membership interests (check your articles, your operating agreement, and your state's law as summarized in Appendix B):

- amending the articles of organization or operating agreement
- issuing a new membership
- admitting a transferee as a new member
- distributing cash or property to members prior to the sale of a membership or dissolution of the LLC
- continuing the LLC after a member dies, departs, or otherwise loses a membership interest (in some states, this vote must be taken to avoid a dissolution of the LLC)
- selling substantially all LLC assets not in the ordinary course of business, and
- dissolving the LLC.

Very rarely, the articles or operating agreement give one class of memberships the right to a separate vote on certain proposals. So, if you're making decisions fundamental to the organization or operation of your LLC, check your articles and operating agreement for special provisions (and check your state's law in Appendix B). If you find any, make sure you understand what is required, and check your conclusions with your legal adviser if the decision is important.

Step 14. Adjourn the Meeting

After the managers or members have voted on all resolutions, the chairperson should propose adjournment. If no further business is proposed and the motion carries, the meeting is adjourned.

If the secretary didn't prepare minutes at the meeting, your next step is to prepare minutes to place in the LLC records binder. Minutes and related forms are covered in the next chapter. For now, place all papers presented or drafted at the meeting in the folder for the meeting or in your LLC records binder.

TIP

Provide notice if a meeting is adjourned with unfinished business. If an LLC meeting is carried over to another time so unfinished business can be concluded, I recommend providing notice to all participants of the continued meeting (even though your operating agreement and state law may require notice only to persons who didn't attend the original meeting). For instructions on providing notice of the continued meeting, see Chapter 3, Step 5. ●

How to Prepare Written Minutes of LLC Meetings

This chapter explains how to use the LLC minutes form to document actions taken at LLC meetings. You will find a sample minutes form in this chapter, and a ready-to-fill-in form in Appendix C and on the CD-ROM at the back of this book. The minutes form is designed to document the most common procedures and actions taken at LLC meetings. It allows you to insert one or more resolutions to show approval of special business at these meetings. Inserting resolutions in your minutes forms is easy, as explained in "How to Use LLC Resolutions," below.

SKIP AHEAD

If you have a one-member LLC that you manage yourself, skip ahead. In practice, member meetings for a one-member LLC and manager meetings for a one-manager LLC are often held on paper only, to formally record decisions that the sole member or manager wishes to document. If you are in this situation, turn to Chapter 6, which explains the steps you need to take to prepare minutes for this type of "paper meeting." You may also record decisions by written consents. (See Chapter 7.)

However, a sole LLC member or manager can also hold a real one-person meeting (you can talk to yourself if you wish). Or you can hold a real meeting where you invite others (staff, officers, advisers, or lawyers) to present reports and discuss proposals.

How to Use LLC Resolutions

The minutes form includes standard language for the approval of business customarily handled at LLC meetings, such as the review of past LLC business and the election of LLC managers (for a manager-managed LLC with fixed-manager terms). To take other actions at LLC meetings, you will want to add one or more resolutions to show formal approval of LLC legal, tax, and other business decisions. To help you do this, this book provides more than 80 resolutions that cover standard LLC transactions. (See Chapters 8 through 15 for instructions on using the various resolutions forms included with this book.) In most cases, you can simply fill in one of these resolutions and insert it into your minutes, as explained in this chapter.

If you need to prepare your own language for a resolution (one that isn't covered by one of our resolution forms), it's easy to do. You'll find examples in the special instructions for filling out the minutes form, below.

Most LLC resolutions stand on their own and don't require additional documentation. However, some types of resolutions ratify or refer to additional backup agreements or paperwork, and you should attach this supplementary material to your minutes. For example, if members approve a resolution to make a loan to a manager, you can prepare and attach a promissory note to your minutes. This book includes some backup paperwork (for example, promissory note forms) with the appropriate resolutions. But finding and adding your own supplemental forms, if necessary, is also easy to do. For example, standard loan, real estate, and other business forms are available from banks, real estate brokers, legal stationers, business law libraries, and other sources.

When to Prepare Minutes

Minutes should be prepared shortly after the meeting is held (within a few days or so). If you wait longer, you may forget to prepare the minutes, or be unable to follow your notes or recollection as to the proposals made and votes taken. Here are some suggestions:

- **If you hold a real meeting.** If you are preparing minutes for a face-to-face meeting, as described in Chapter 4, the secretary usually waits until after the meeting to fill in the minutes form, based on his or her notes. Or, the secretary may prepare a draft of the minutes form before the meeting and complete it during or shortly after the meeting. Some secretaries prefer to fill out the entire minutes form during the meeting, either by using a fill-in-the-blanks minutes form (see Appendix C) or by filling in the form on the CD-ROM using a computer at the meeting.

Who Attends LLC Meetings?

Here are some common scenarios for attendance at LLC meetings.

Annual meetings (or other regular meetings scheduled periodically in your operating agreement):

- In a member-managed LLC, the entire membership is asked to attend the annual meeting to review the prior year's business and plan upcoming LLC operations. This is a good time to propose any special resolutions that require approval, such as amendments to the articles or operating agreement, or to discuss other important items of LLC business (the possible admission of new members, approval of a cash distribution to members, and the like).

- In a manager-managed LLC in which managers are elected at specific, fixed intervals (such as yearly or every other year), the members attend a regular members' meeting to vote on the election (or reelection) of the managers. Members may also review past business and discuss future operations, and vote on special items of membership business. Managers may be asked to attend the meeting to report to the membership on past and upcoming LLC operations. Following their election or reelection by the members at the annual members' meeting, the managers will attend the annual managers' meeting to accept their management positions for another term.

- In a manager-managed LLC in which managers hold their positions for an indefinite term (until they resign or are removed by the members), the members will probably not hold annual or other regular meetings. The managers may still hold an annual or other regular meeting to discuss past business and future plans. The members may be asked to attend to hear reports given at the meeting, as well as to vote on any special membership resolutions prepared by the managers.

Special meetings (called for a particular purpose by one or more members or managers):

- In a member-managed LLC, the members are sometimes asked by other members to attend a meeting to approve one or more items of LLC business.

- In a manager-managed LLC, if the matter is a standard item of business, only the managers attend special meetings to approve the action. If the matter to be decided requires membership approval (amendment of articles or admission of a new member, for example), the members are also asked to attend. At the meeting, the managers propose the resolution, and the members vote on it.

- **If you hold a paper meeting.** To prepare minutes for a paper meeting (one that doesn't actually occur), follow the instructions in Chapter 6. The secretary normally prepares the minutes form whenever it's convenient; it need not be on the exact paper meeting date. The secretary then distributes a copy to all members for their approval, as explained in "How to Prepare Minutes of Paper LLC Meetings" in Chapter 6, Step 5.

Preparing the Minutes Form

This section shows you how to prepare the minutes for an LLC meeting, using the minutes form included with this book.

The LLC minutes form presented in this section is designed to accommodate a variety of meeting scenarios. It includes check boxes and language to handle each of the options for attendance and the approval of regular and special matters.

CD-ROM

Below is a sample of the minutes form included on the CD-ROM and as a tearout form in Appendix C. (See Appendix A for information on selecting and using the CD-ROM files.) Fill the form out following the special instructions provided below.

Special Instructions

❶ Insert the type of meeting ("members," "managers," or "members/managers") and the date, time, and place of the meeting. Many operating agreements call for meetings to be held at the principal office of the LLC unless the members or managers have decided to hold the meeting elsewhere.

❷ Use one or more check boxes to show the purpose(s) of the LLC meeting. Note that the preamble states that the meeting was held for the transaction of "all business." This means that if the purpose of the meeting was simply to allow the members and/or managers to get together to discuss and decide any matter of importance, you do not need to check any of the boxes—in this case, you are simply holding a general LLC meeting for the discussion of LLC-related business.

Check the third box if a purpose of calling the meeting was to discuss a specific proposal (other than the election of managers or review and planning of LLC business—these matters are covered by the first and second check boxes). In the space provided, briefly summarize the specific items of business for which the meeting was called—such as "a change of LLC tax year," "approval of a cash distribution to members," "admission of a new member," "purchase of the membership interest of a departing member," and the like.

❸ Insert the name and title of the persons who acted as chairperson and secretary of the meeting. Typically, the LLC president will act as chairperson, but you may decide to designate any other officer or a manager or member of the LLC. Usually, the secretary of the LLC acts as secretary of all LLC meetings. In his or her absence, another officer typically assumes this task.

Note: In the instructions for this form, unless otherwise specified, references to the "secretary" are to the secretary of the LLC meeting. Again, this person is usually also secretary of the LLC.

❹ If the meeting is an annual or other regular meeting scheduled in your operating agreement, check the first box, and insert in the blank the period for holding the meeting. For example, if the meeting is an annual meeting, check the first box, then insert "annually" in the blank; if the meeting is a monthly meeting, insert "monthly." Insert another period for

Minutes of LLC Meeting

LLC Name: _____[insert name of LLC]_____

1. A meeting of the ___["members" and/or "managers"]___ of the LLC was held on ___[date of meeting]___ at _[time of meeting]_ at _____[place of meeting]_____, ❶ for the transaction of all business that may properly be brought by participants before the meeting, including any of the special purposes listed below:

   [If applicable, check one or more boxes below, and supply additional information as appropriate.] ❷

   ☐   Election of LLC manager(s) by LLC members

   ☐   Review of past LLC business and discussion of future operations

   ☐   The approval of one or more resolutions as follows:

   　　　　[If this box is checked, insert summaries of resolutions.]

2. _____[name of chairperson]_____ acted as chairperson, and ____[name of meeting secretary]____ acted as secretary of the meeting. ❸

3. The chairperson called the meeting to order.

4. The secretary announced that the meeting was: ❹

   [Check one of the boxes below and supply additional information.]

   ☐   a regular meeting scheduled to be held __[insert period for holding regular LLC meeting]__ under provisions in the LLC operating agreement

   [or]

   ☐   a special meeting called by the following person(s):

_____	☐ Manager	☐ Member	☐ Other: _____
_____	☐ Manager	☐ Member	☐ Other: _____
_____	☐ Manager	☐ Member	☐ Other: _____

5. The secretary announced that the meeting was held pursuant to notice, if required and as required under the operating agreement of this LLC, or that notice had been waived by all participants entitled to receive notice under the operating agreement. Copies of any certificates of mailing of notice prepared by the secretary of the LLC and any written waivers signed by participants entitled to receive notice of this meeting were attached to these minutes by the secretary. ❺

6. ☐ **Members Voting.** [Check if members will vote at the meeting, and supply information below.]

The secretary announced that an alphabetical list of the names and interests held by all members of the LLC was available and open to inspection by any person in attendance at the meeting. The secretary announced that there were present, in person or by proxy, the following voting power of the members of the LLC, representing a quorum of the members. (The secretary attached written proxy statements, executed by the appropriate members, to these minutes for any membership voting power listed below as held by a proxyholder.) ❻

Name of Member   Member's Voting Power

_____   _____

_____   _____

_____   _____

_____   _____

7. ☐ **Managers Voting.** [Check if managers will vote at the meeting, and supply information below.]

The secretary announced that an alphabetical list of the names of the managers of the LLC was available and open to inspection by any person in attendance at the meeting. The secretary announced that the following managers of the LLC were present, representing a quorum of the managers: ❼

Names of Managers

_____

_____

_____

_____

_____

8. The secretary announced that the following persons were also present at the meeting in the following capacities: ❽

    Name   Title

    _____   _____

    _____   _____

    _____   _____

    _____   _____

9. ☐ **Previous Meeting Minutes.** (Check if previous meeting minutes will be approved at this meeting, and supply information, checking one or both additional boxes below.)

    The secretary announced that the minutes of the LLC meeting held on __[date of prior meeting]__ ❾

    ☐ had been distributed prior to the meeting, and the secretary was in receipt of any written approval of minutes forms signed and returned by persons who had read and approved the minutes.

    ☐ were distributed at the meeting, then read by the secretary.

    After counting any written approvals, and, if necessary, taking the voice vote of __["members" and/or "managers"]__ at the meeting, the secretary announced that the minutes as distributed, read, and corrected, as appropriate, were approved. The secretary attached a copy of the approved minutes together with any signed approvals of minutes forms to these minutes.

10. The following reports were presented at the meeting by the following persons: ❿

    _____[describe reports and name of person presenting report(s)]_____

    _____

    _____

11. ☐ **Election of Managers.** (Check if managers will be elected, and supply information below.)

    The chairperson announced that the next item of business was the nomination and election of the managers for another __["one-year" or other period]__ term. The following nominations were made and seconded: ⓫

Names of Manager Nominee(s):

_____

_____

_____

The secretary next took the votes of members entitled to vote for the election of managers at the meeting, and, after counting the votes, announced that the following persons were elected to serve as managers of this LLC:

Names of Elected Manager(s):

_____

_____

_____

_____

☐ **Managers' Acceptance.** [Check if managers accepted positions.]

The above managers, having been elected, accepted their management positions. The secretary announced that the presence of current managers of the LLC at the meeting represented a quorum of managers of the LLC.

12. ☐ **Resolutions.** [Check if resolutions will be passed, and supply information below.]

After discussion, on motion duly made and carried by the affirmative vote of [check one or more boxes and supply any required information]: ⑫

☐ a majority of the membership voting power in attendance

☐ a majority of the managers in attendance

☐ other, as follows:

[insert other member and/or manager approval or list votes of each participant]

_____

_____

The following resolution(s) was(were) approved at the meeting:

_____ [describe the resolution(s) approved by the above voting procedure] _____

_____

_____

☐ **Additional Resolutions.** (Check if additional resolutions will be passed, and supply information below.)

After discussion, on motion duly made and carried by the affirmative vote of [check one or more boxes and supply any required information]: **12**

    ☐ a majority of the membership voting power in attendance

    ☐ a majority of the managers in attendance

    ☐ other, as follows:

    [insert other member and/or manager approval or list votes of each participant]

    _____

    _____

The following resolution(s) was(were) approved at the meeting:

_____ [describe the resolution(s) approved by the above voting procedure] _____

_____

_____

There being no further business to come before the meeting, it was adjourned on motion duly made and carried. **13**

The above minutes were completed in final form on the date shown below by the undersigned secretary of the meeting:

Date: _____

Signature: _____

Title: _____

regular meetings held at other intervals, such as "the first Monday of each calendar quarter."

If the meeting was not scheduled in your operating agreement, check the second box to show the meeting is a special meeting, then list the person(s) who called the meeting. Next to each name, check whether the person is a member and/or manager of the LLC, or has another title. If you check "other," indicate the person's title, such as "president" or "treasurer." Remember: Your operating agreement may specify who may call LLC meetings—typically a manager, a specified number of members, or an LLC officer. (See Chapter 3, Step 3.)

If your operating agreement doesn't address this issue, state law may specify who may call LLC member or manager meetings. (See the "Meeting Requirements" section for your state in Appendix B for any state default rules.)

❺ This paragraph states that *if required by your operating agreement* each meeting partici-pant either (1) was given notice if and as required by your operating agreement or (2) waived notice by signing a written waiver of notice form. Although your operating agree-ment (or state law if your agreement is silent on providing notice of meetings) may not require notice for some or all LLC meetings—particularly regular LLC meetings scheduled in your operating agreement—it's a good idea to give written notice prior to each meeting. This is the best way to make sure each member or manager knows about the meeting well in advance and understands the nature of the proposals to be discussed there. (See Chapter 3, Step 5, for notice of meeting requirements and recommendations.) If you own and run a closely held LLC, you may be able to use waiver of notice forms.

If notice was mailed to members, attach to the minutes any Certificate of Mailing of Notice or Acknowledgment of Receipts. (See

Chapter 3, Steps 7 and 9.) Attach any written waivers of notice for the meeting that were signed by members. (See Chapter 6, Step 1, for instructions on preparing waiver of notice forms.)

TIP

Closely held LLCs: Hand out waiver of notice forms at the meeting to save time. Small LLCs with only a few members or managers—who are almost guaranteed to attend meetings—sometimes decide to dispense with official premeeting notice formalities entirely. Instead, the LLC secretary informally notifies all members of the meeting. The secretary of the meeting then hands out written waiver of notice forms for each participant to sign at the start of the meeting. This is perfectly legal and won't create any problems if you are sure each member knows about the meeting and its purpose well in advance, and all members and managers are getting along fairly well.

❻ Check this box if members attended and voted at your LLC meeting. This paragraph applies to a meeting of members or a joint meeting of managers and members where members were asked to vote. If only managers attended the meeting, or if members were in attendance to hear or participate in discussions, but not to vote, don't check this box—skip to item 7, below.

The first sentence of the paragraph restates a common practice that an alphabetical list of members was made available for inspection during the meeting (to allow the secretary and members to assess the voting interests of other members). You can prepare a meeting participant list as explained in Chapter 3, Step 4, or you can simply make your LLC records binder available for inspection at the meeting, if it includes a membership register with a current list of your members and their membership interests. The paragraph also states that a quorum of the membership was in attendance at the meeting. If a quorum is not present, members can attend the meeting but can't vote on LLC business.

If you check the box at the start of the paragraph (because members attended and voted at the meeting), list the names of the members present at the meeting. To the right of each name, show the voting power of each member. How to measure voting power should be set out in your operating agreement or, if your agreement doesn't address it, by state law. (See Appendix B.) Generally, members vote either (1) per capita (one vote each), (2) according to their capital account balances in the LLC, (3) according to their profits interests (rights to receive profits of the LLC), or (4) according to both their capital and profits interests in the LLC. Unless members vote per capita, a member's voting power will be specified as a percentage of the total voting power in the LLC. (For example, a member whose capital account reflects 10% of the LLC's capital will have 10% of the LLC voting power.) For more on calculating a member's voting power, see "Measuring Membership Interests in the LLC," in Chapter 3, Step 3.

The total voting power listed here should add up to at least a quorum of your membership as defined in your operating agreement or under state law. Typically, a quorum is defined as (1) a majority of the total number of members or (2) a majority of the total capital and/or profits interests in your LLC. (For more information on quorum requirements, see Chapter 4, Step 8.)

EXAMPLE:

The annual meeting of Raster Graphics, LLC, a manager-managed LLC, was held as scheduled in the LLC operating agreement. Both managers and members were in attendance, with the members voting to approve a resolution proposed by management to seek an additional $2,000 capital contribution from each of the members. (Notice of the proposal was mailed to each member before the meeting.) The LLC managers are the CEO and VP, neither of whom is a LLC member. The LLC has four members, with each member voting according to his or her profits interests in the LLC. A majority of the profits interests constitutes a quorum of members under the operating agreement.

Stan, the LLC and meeting secretary, notes at the meeting that profits interests in the LLC are proportionate to capital contributions. In other words, a member who contributed 10% of the capital to the LLC also gets a 10% profits interest in the LLC and 10% of the LLC voting power. (This is the way most LLC operating agreements set up capital and profits interests.) He also notes that the following members, who made the following capital contributions, are present at the meeting: Max Nyquist, $10,000; Carol Starling, $25,000; Rudy Caruthers, $6,000.

Stan also notes that one member, Sarah Schelling, who made a $9,000 capital contribution, is not present. (She called a few days prior to the meeting to say that she would not attend, but was comfortable letting the other members vote to decide on the membership proposal without sending a proxy to represent her membership interest.) Stan computes that members who contributed $41,000 of the LLC's total capital of $50,000 were in attendance, which represented a majority of the capital and profits interests of the LLC. A majority of the LLC's voting power was, therefore, in attendance, and the members could vote on the additional capital contribution proposal presented by the managers. After the meeting, Stan fills out this portion of the minutes to read as follows:

Name of Member	Member's Voting Power
Max Nyquist	20%
Carol Starling	50%
Rudy Caruthers	12%

How to record proxyholders. If a member was represented by written proxy at a meeting, list the proxyholder's name on the left, followed by the words "proxyholder for" and the name of the member. Show the member's voting power (that has been delegated to the proxyholder) in the column at the right. Attach to the minutes a written proxy statement dated and signed by each member whose voting power is represented by proxy. See Chapter 3, Step 8, for a discussion of when to use and how to prepare a written proxy for use at members' meetings.

❼ Check this box if managers attended your LLC meeting (which will be the case whenever you hold a manager meeting or joint meeting of LLC managers and members). If you check it, list the managers in attendance at the meeting below the paragraph. Of course, a quorum of managers—a majority of the number of managers under most operating agreements and state default rules—must be present for the managers to take action at the meeting.

❽ Specify any LLC officers and others in attendance at the meeting. If a manager or member was also present as an LLC officer, a committee chairperson, a consultant, or in another capacity—for example, as CEO to present a report—list that person here again in their nonmember or nonmanager capacity.

❾ For some LLC meetings—particularly those scheduled within a month or so of the past meeting—participants may be asked by the secretary to approve the minutes of the previous LLC meeting. This applies only if the last meeting was of the same type as the current meeting—for example, if both meetings were a meeting of members or a joint meeting of managers and members. Mostly, approving prior minutes is meant to remind everyone of any special business approved at the last meeting, and to allow any objections to the minutes before they are placed in the LLC records book. If you review prior minutes at the current meeting, check this box, and insert the date of the prior meeting in the first paragraph. Then check one or both of the next two boxes as follows:

Box 1. If you sent copies of the minutes of the last meeting to each participant prior to the meeting (as part of the premeeting materials prepared as explained in Chapter 3, Step 6), check this box. To save time and get everyone's approval to the prior minutes, the secretary also may have sent out a written approval of minutes forms to be signed and returned by people receiving the premeeting materials. (This form is covered in Chapter 6, Step 3). The text following this box acknowledges that these approval forms may have been sent, signed by participants, and returned to the secretary.

Box 2. If you distributed copies of the minutes at the current meeting, check this box.

Boxes 1 and 2. You can check both boxes 1 and 2 if you combine these procedures to approve the minutes of the last meeting. For example, the secretary may have distributed the minutes prior to the meeting, but not received written approvals back from all of the participants. In this case, the secretary should redistribute copies of the prior meeting's minutes at the current meeting and read them, then take a voice vote to make sure everyone approves the minutes.

Usually, the prior meeting's minutes are routinely approved. But if any member or manager brings up any objections or mistakes, the secretary will need to work these out. This can be done either by making appropriate corrections to the prior minutes and taking a new approval vote, or by obtaining a majority vote to approve the final version of the minutes over the objection of one or more participants.

In the last paragraph of this section, indicate whether members and/or managers approved the minutes of the last meeting. Again, this assumes the prior and the current meeting are of the same type. Insert "members" if both meetings were members' meetings, "managers" if both were manager meetings, or "members and managers" if both were joint managers'/members' meetings. The secretary should attach the approved minutes of the prior meeting to the minutes of the current meeting, and also attach any written approval of minutes forms signed and returned to the secretary.

❿ Managers, members, or LLC officers may have presented annual or special reports at the meeting. For example, the president may have presented an annual operating report and the treasurer may have summarized the past year's financial profits or losses. List a description of the reports given, such as "treasurer's report of year-end profits and loss," along with the name and title of the presenter. The secretary should attach any written copies of reports to the minutes.

⓫ This box does not apply to member-managed LLCs. For manager-managed LLCs, check this box if the meeting was held for members to elect managers of the LLC. In LLCs where managers are elected to fixed terms, this is a typical item of business for the annual members' (or joint managers'/members') meeting, but also can be an agenda item for a specially called members' meeting held at the end of managers' terms. It also can apply to manager-managed LLCs in which managers serve for indefinite terms. For instance, the members may be asked to attend a meeting

to fill a vacancy in management after a manager resigns or is removed. However, LLC operating agreements and default state law rules often allow the remaining managers to fill a temporary manager vacancy themselves.

If you check this box, supply the additional information in this section. In the first sentence, insert the terms of office of managers in the blank. If managers have a fixed term, a one-year term is the most common, but your operating agreement may set a longer term. If managers are elected to serve for indefinite terms, insert "indefinite" in this blank.

Under "Name of Manager Nominee(s)," fill in the names of all nominees for whom the members may vote. Many small LLCs simply nominate (and reelect) the current manager team for another term of office, but members or managers may place other names in nomination. Just as in a small corporation where the directors who are majority shareholders are routinely nominated and reelected, everyone in an LLC typically nominates and reelects the current managing members unless they decide it's time for a change.

In the spaces under the heading "Names of Elected Manager(s)," indicate the persons who were elected by the members to serve as managers for another term (or for an indefinite term). Of course, if your manager-managed LLC has just one manager, only one name will be inserted here.

There are different ways to hold membership votes. Most LLCs elect managers by voice vote or written ballot, and the nominees who receive the most votes win. Although sometimes each member gets one vote (a per capita voting scheme), under a different operating agreement the voting power of each member may be expressed as a percentage of total membership voting power, because it may be tied to the member's proportionate share of capital and/or profits interests in the LLC. (See item 6, above.)

EXAMPLE:

Ten members of a manager-managed LLC, each with 10% of the LLC voting power, are voting to elect three of five nominees to a three-person management team. Each member may cast his or her 10% vote in favor of each of three candidates (each may cast a 10% vote three times). The results are as follows:

Candidate	Percent of Vote Received	Result
Nominee 1	100%	Elected (Ten members voted for this candidate)
Nominee 2	100%	Elected (Ten members voted for this candidate)
Nominee 3	50%	Elected (Five members voted for this candidate)
Nominee 4	30%	Not Elected (Three members voted for this candidate)
Nominee 5	20%	Not Elected (Two members voted for this candidate)

Note that a total of 300% of the voting power of the LLC was exercised. This makes sense since the ten members, who hold 100% of the LLC voting power, each get to vote for three candidates. The total voting power percentage cast for each candidate is totaled, and then these candidate totals are compared to find the three candidates who received the three highest percentages of LLC voting power. In the above example, Nominees 1 and 2 received votes from all ten members, while Nominees 3, 4, and 5 received the votes of five, three, and two members, respectively. The three candidates receiving the largest number of votes, Nominees 1, 2, and 3, are elected to the board.

Cumulative voting procedures. Some LLCs elect by cumulative voting procedures. Your articles or operating agreement should state whether your members may ask to cumulate their votes to elect managers of the LLC. (Most LLCs do not allow cumulative voting.) Cumulative voting differs from standard voting (called "plurality" voting) in that a member gets to cumulate his or her entire election voting power in favor of any one candidate, or to split it up as he or she sees fit. In the above example, this means that each member gets to vote 30% of the LLC voting power (the 10% voting power possessed by the member multiplied by the number of managers to be elected) for one or a combination of candidates.

EXAMPLE:

Using the same ten members and five nominees in the previous example, cumulative voting rules give each member a total of 30% to cast for one or more manager nominees. This means that any one member has a better chance of tipping the scales in favor of one candidate, because he or she can cast more than 10% voting power for a particular candidate. Of course, a member will lose a chance to vote for any other candidates by casting all 30% for one nominee. This is the purpose of cumulative voting, and a reason it is used in larger LLCs: It gives minority members a better shot at electing at least one candidate to the management team, despite the voting power of the majority members. (For a further discussion of cumulative voting rules, see Chapter 4, Step 13.)

At the end of item 11 is a check box. If the managers were elected at a membership-only meeting, leave this box blank. Check this box only if all of the following are true:

- you held a joint managers'/members' meeting

- the members elected managers at the meeting

- a quorum of the newly elected managers were present at the meeting after their election, and

- the managers accepted their management positions.

12 This section of the minutes allows you to record the passage of one or more resolutions that were discussed and voted on at the LLC meeting. If your meeting was held simply to present reports, hold discussions, and, if appropriate, elect managers of a manager-managed LLC to another term, you can skip this section. (The previous sections of the minutes form cover these areas.) For most LLC meetings, however, this section should be used to show the actual business of the meeting—that is, the discussion and approval of one or more special items of business—by the passage of resolutions by LLC managers and/or members.

If your meeting was held to approve one or more specific resolutions, check the box at the start of this section, then check one or more of the subsequent three boxes to show the type of vote used to approve the resolution. Check the first box if a majority of the membership voting power present at the meeting passed the

resolution. This is the usual membership voting rule for most member-managed LLCs or for membership approval of matters brought before the members in a manager-managed LLC.

Check the second box if a majority of managers present at the meeting passed the resolution. This is the usual manager voting rule for manager-managed LLCs. Check both boxes if both members and managers approved the proposal by a majority vote. If your members and/or managers approved the proposal by a different vote—for example, by the unanimous vote of all members or managers—check the "other" box, then insert the vote of members and/or managers used to pass the resolution. Checking the "other" box is also appropriate if you wish to list the "yes" or "no" votes of each member and/or manager, regardless of the type of vote required to pass the resolution.

> **CAUTION**
>
> **Special requirements apply to certain votes.** Your LLC operating agreement or state law may require a special vote for certain matters. For example, commonly all, or a majority of all, members (not just a majority of members present at a meeting) must approve amendments to LLC articles or operating agreements. See "How Your Management Structure Affects Decision-Making Requirements" in Chapter 2 for more information.

After checking the appropriate boxes, insert the resolution approved by members and/or managers at the meeting. In many instances, you can insert one of the ready-to-use resolutions included in Chapters 8 through 15. See the beginning of Appendix C for a list of tearout and CD-ROM resolution forms included with this book, with cross-references to the chapters and sections of the book that contain instructions for preparing each resolution.

If you wish to approve business not covered by one of our resolutions, supply your own language for the resolution in this space in your minutes. You don't need to use fancy or legal language for your resolution. Just describe as specifically as you can the transaction or matter approved by your members and/or managers at the meeting in a short statement. Resolutions often start with a preamble of the following sort: "The members resolved that …", but this is not required. Here are a couple of examples of resolution language.

EXAMPLE 1 (amendment of articles):

"The members ratified a managers' resolution adding the following new articles to the LLC's articles of organization: [language of new articles] ."

EXAMPLE 2 (amendment of operating agreement):

"The members approved an amendment to the operating agreement of the LLC. The text of the changed operating agreement provision is as follows: [language of amended operating agreement provision] ."

⑬ This concluding adjournment paragraph and signature line are included on a separate page. It should be attached at the very end of your minutes, after your resolution page or pages (see item 12, above). The secretary of the meeting should date and sign the form, then type his or her title (usually LLC secretary or another LLC officer). The date inserted should be the date the minutes are completed, not the date of the meeting.

> **TIP**
>
> **Save your minutes.** Remember to file the completed minutes in your LLC records binder together with all attachments. If you prepared a separate meeting folder for the meeting (see Chapter 3, Step 1), now is the time to transfer all forms and attachments related to the meeting from the folder to your LLC records binder.

What If More Than One Resolution Is Approved at an LLC Meeting?

If you use the same voting procedure to pass more than one resolution, you can list the other resolutions below the first one in the space provided in Section 12 of the minutes form. But if you use different voting procedures for different resolutions, you need to group them together according to the voting procedure used to pass them.

EXAMPLE: Cake Walk Custom Bakery, L.L.C., is member-managed. At the LLC's annual meeting, three proposals were presented by the secretary for approval by the members. Two were passed by normal voting procedures—that is, by a majority of membership voting power present at the meeting. The third proposal—an amendment to the LLC operating agreement—required the vote of all members. It also passed. After the meeting, the LLC secretary filled in Section 12 in the minutes form as follows:

What If More Than One Resolution Is Approved at an LLC Meeting? (continued)

12. ☒ Resolutions. [Check if resolutions will be passed, and supply information below.]

　　After discussion, on motion duly made and carried by the affirmative vote of (check one or more boxes and supply any required information);

　　　☒ a majority of the membership voting power in attendance

　　　☐ a majority of the managers in attendance

　　　☐ other, as follows: _____ _____ .

　　The following resolution(s) was(were) approved at the meeting:

　　　The members resolved that the accounting and tax period of this LLC shall end on May 31 of each year.

　　　The members approved the hiring of Laurence Kernan for the position of Chief Financial Officer.

And on the next page:

☒ **Additional Resolutions.** (Check, if additional resolutions will be passed, and supply information below.)

　　After discussion, on motion duly made and carried by the affirmative vote of (check one or more boxes and supply any required information);

　☐ a majority of the membership voting power in attendance

　☐ a majority of the managers in attendance

　☒ other, as follows: __unanimous vote of all of the members of the LLC.__

The following resolution(s) was(were) approved at the meeting:

The members approved an amendment to the operating agreement of the LLC. The text of the changed operating agreement provision is as follows: __[language of amended operating agreement provision]__ .

　As you can see, the secretary used the first page of Section 12 of the minutes form to show approval of the first two resolutions by normal membership voting. The secretary then filled in the "Additional Resolutions" section to show the approval of the operating agreement amendment by all members.

　The tearout minutes form in this book includes an additional page that duplicates the first page of Section 12 to allow you to do this. If you need to show the separate passage of additional resolutions, just copy this page as many times as you need, then fill them in. If you use the forms on CD-ROM, just copy and paste the page that follows the first page of Section 12 as many times as you need.

How to Hold a Paper LLC Meeting

This chapter presents the few simple steps necessary to document a "paper" meeting of your LLC members and/or managers. With a paper meeting, members or managers don't actually get together but instead arrive at decisions informally. To make a clear record of these decisions, minutes are prepared (usually by the LLC president or secretary), and the managers or members approve them by signing them.

Decide Whether to Hold a Paper Meeting

The paper meeting procedure works best for family LLCs or for LLCs with only a few managers or members who work together or know each other well and agree on most LLC decisions. Of course, paper meetings also work well for a one-person LLC, where the sole member really doesn't need to sit down and talk to himself (or if he does, then perhaps it's time for a two-week vacation).

In such small LLCs, the paper meeting procedure allows LLC principals to conduct and document routine LLC business without going through the motions of holding a face-to-face meeting. Legally, preparing and ratifying paperwork for a fictional LLC meeting will not create problems for your LLC as long as every member or manager agrees to the procedure and, of course, approves the decisions reflected in the minutes of the paper meeting.

CAUTION

Avoid paper meetings if there is conflict or disagreement. Paper meetings can work well for small, closely held LLCs with no more than a few members and managers. However, even for small LLCs, you should use this procedure only when everyone is really in agreement. If there is even a whiff of dissent in the wind, or if the decision requires additional discussion, it is far better to hold a real meeting.

Documenting Past Decisions With Paper Meetings

If you failed to properly document past LLC meetings of your managers and/or members, you are not alone. Many, if not most, smaller LLCs that do their own paperwork forget to document important legal and tax decisions as they occur, putting off the task of preparing the paperwork until later. Often, the impetus for preparing this overlooked paperwork is an IRS audit or a request for minutes of a meeting from members or managers, or a bank or other financial institution.

As long as all managers and members agreed to the past actions when they were taken, using the paper meeting approach to re-create LLC records after the fact should work well for your LLC.

EXAMPLE:

Small Systems, LLC, is a small, closely held member-managed LLC with six members who work in the business. The LLC has been in operation for five years when the treasurer is notified of an IRS audit of the LLC's informational income tax returns from the last two years. (A multimember LLC files informational partnership returns unless it has elected corporate tax treatment—see Chapter 9.) For the audit, the treasurer is asked to produce minutes of any LLC meetings for the years in question.

As often happens in small LLCs, the daily grind of business has consumed the energies of the co-owners. Procedural niceties, such as annual membership meetings (required to be held under provisions in the LLC operating agreement), have been skipped.

The only special items of formal legal or tax paperwork executed during the LLC's first five years were the signing of a lease by the LLC president and treasurer, as well as the approval by members of a change of accounting period recommended by the LLC tax adviser. These decisions were approved by all members informally.

The members decide it is best to formalize these past decisions by preparing paper minutes for annual membership meetings for the last five years. They also decide to prepare minutes of two special membership meetings to formally document the approval of the LLC lease and the change of accounting period. These minutes are placed in the LLC records binder, and copies of the minutes of meetings for the two years in question are given to the IRS.

Comparing Paper Meetings and Written Consents

For those who don't want to hold a formal LLC meeting (or for those who missed holding one), there are two alternative procedures:

- preparing minutes of a paper meeting, or
- acting by written consent.

If you prepare minutes for a paper meeting, you are, in essence, approving LLC business by the written consent of your managers and/or members (assuming all members and/or managers will be listed in your minutes of the paper meeting). So the two procedures are quite similar. Which one you use depends on your preferences and your reasons for preparing the documentation. If you think minutes look better than a written consent to document the approval of an LLC decision, use the minutes of a paper meeting approach; if it seems simpler to obtain the written consent of members and/or managers to a decision, use written consents instead.

Here are a few points to consider when you're deciding whether paper meetings or written consents would best meet your immediate needs:

- **For standard annual business, use minutes of paper meetings.** Minutes of paper meetings summarize the discussion and approval of items of business taken up annually by the members and/or managers. Such business includes the annual review of past and present LLC business by LLC members or managers, as well as the annual election of managers (in a manager-managed LLC). The reason to use minutes of paper meetings for standard decisions is simple: The IRS, courts, financial institutions, and others generally expect LLC records to contain standard minutes of meeting forms. Written consent forms with no supporting documentation may not be enough to convince others that you paid attention to the ongoing formalities of LLC life, particularly if your LLC operating agreement requires you to hold regular LLC meetings.

- **Written consents can be used to show approval of special items of business.** Written consent forms are generally used to document special decisions that would normally be approved at special meetings of members and/or managers. In smaller LLCs, these isolated decisions, approved as needed, are commonly approved and documented with written consent forms rather than the more formal minutes of a paper meeting.

- **LLC records may contain both minutes and consent forms.** It's fine to prepare minutes of paper meetings for some decisions and written consents for others.

EXAMPLE:

Bert and Jennifer are a married couple and the only two managers of a small manager-managed LLC. Their children have an investment interest in the business as nonmanaging minority members. Bert and Jennifer routinely reelect themselves as managers at the end of each year. (The LLC operating agreement gives managers a one-year term.)

After a few years of operation, they realize that they haven't kept up their LLC records. Bert prepares minutes of the annual membership meetings for the past two years, showing the nomination and reelection of each manager for another one-year term. He accompanies these with minutes of annual manager meetings showing the managers' (Bert's and Jennifer's) acceptance of their reelection for another year. Of course, these minutes forms also restate the discussion and approval of standard agenda items and business taken up at these meetings, such as reading and approval of past minutes and the review of LLC business operations.

To save time, Bert prepares a written consent form showing membership approval of a special decision approved by Bert and Jennifer during the second year of the LLC: the admission of their children as new members of the LLC. Approval of the admission of the children as LLC members could also be documented by preparing minutes of a paper membership meeting attended by Bert and Jennifer (at the time, the only two members of the LLC). But consent forms seem adequate, especially given the fact that the annual meetings are now fully documented.

How to Prepare Minutes of Paper LLC Meetings

If you've decided to hold a paper meeting, follow the steps below to prepare the necessary paperwork.

Step 1. Prepare a Waiver of Notice of Meeting Form

If you're going to prepare minutes for an LLC meeting that will never actually occur, you'll obviously want to sidestep (legally) any formal call and notice requirements for holding the meeting. (See Chapter 3, Steps 3 and 5, for an overview of call and notice requirements.) The best way to do this is to have each meeting participant entitled to notice—each member and/or manager who will be shown as in attendance at the meeting—sign a written Waiver of Notice of Meeting form. The waivers may be dated before, on, or after the meeting date that will be shown in the minutes.

You should always summarize the purpose(s) of the upcoming meeting in your waiver form. In some cases, this is legally required. Even if it isn't, however, listing the purpose will help you make sure that all managers and/or members appreciate the nature of the business to be reflected in your minutes. Plus, state laws sometimes prohibit the transaction of any business not specified in the notice, or the waiver of notice, for a special LLC meeting.

 TIP

Other reasons to use a waiver of notice form. You may use a waiver of notice form even if you are planning to hold a real meeting. As discussed in Chapters 3 through 5, you should use a waiver of notice form whenever you wish to hold a meeting of your members and/or managers and do not have the time, or choose not to spend the time, to provide everyone with advance notice.

CD-ROM

Below is a sample of the Waiver of Notice of Meeting form included on the CD-ROM and as a tearout form in Appendix C. (See Appendix A for information on selecting and using the CD-ROM files.) Fill the form out following the special instructions provided below.

By signing this form, the manager or member waives any meeting notice requirements imposed by state law, as well as any additional or alternative notice rules set out in your operating agreement. You can prepare one waiver form for multiple managers and/or members to sign, or you can prepare one form for each person.

TIP

Handle all of the paperwork at once. Steps 2 through 5, below, provide instructions on filling out paper minutes and approval forms that you'll send to your managers and/or members. So, to avoid multiple mailings or meetings, prepare the waiver forms and include them for signing when you distribute the rest of the paperwork.

Waiver of Notice of Meeting

Name of LLC: _____

The undersigned waive(s) notice of and consent to the holding of the meeting of the LLC held at_____[location of meeting]_____ on _____[date of meeting]_____ at __[time of meeting]__. The purposes of the meeting are as follows:
[insert summary of purpose(s) of meeting] ❶

_____

_____

_____

_____

_____

_____

Dated: _____ ❷

Signature   Printed Name

_____   _____

_____   _____

_____   _____

_____   _____

_____   _____

Special Instructions

❶ When preparing a waiver of notice form, whether for a real or paper meeting, it's always important to state the purpose(s) of the meeting. Be as specific as you can regarding the proposals to be presented at the meeting.

EXAMPLE:

A paper meeting of members is held to approve an amendment to the operating agreement that requires additional capital contributions from members whenever a majority of managers decides additional capital is needed by the LLC. The purpose of the meeting stated in the waiver of notice form reads as follows: "to add a new provision to the LLC operating agreement to allow managers to require additional capital contributions from members."

❷ If more than one person will sign the form, the date inserted here should be the date the first person signs the waiver form. If the waiver is for notice of a members' meeting, have all members sign it. If the meeting is a managers' meeting, have all managers sign it. If it is a joint managers'/members' meeting, all members and managers should sign it.

Step 2. Prepare Minutes of the Paper Meeting

Your next step is to prepare the actual minutes for your paper LLC meeting. Usually, the secretary of the LLC prepares and distributes this paperwork, but the task can be assigned to anyone. Have the designated person follow these steps:

- To prepare minutes, use the sample LLC minutes form with instructions provided in Chapter 5. Fill out all blanks as if you were holding a real meeting, with all members

or managers present. For example, for the date and time, fill in the date and time the minutes were prepared. For location of the meeting, fill in the principal office of the LLC.

- Make copies of the minutes for each manager and/or member (who will review them prior to signing the Approval of LLC Minutes form discussed in the next step).

- Place a copy of the minutes of the paper meeting in your LLC records binder.

Step 3. Prepare an Approval of LLC Minutes Form

After preparing minutes for your paper meeting, you should have each manager and/or member specifically sign off on the decisions approved in the minutes by signing an approval of minutes form. *This step is essential when you use the paper meeting procedure to document past LLC decision making.* Because a real meeting was not held, you need to be sure everyone agrees to your summary of the decisions reflected in your minutes. (Again, if the meeting is a members' meeting, get the signature of *all* members; if a managers' meeting, obtain the approval of *all* managers. For a joint managers'/members' meeting, have all members and all managers sign the approval.)

TIP

When to use an approval form for minutes of a real LLC meeting. The approval form can come in handy to obtain approval of minutes of a real LLC meeting, after the meeting has been held and the minutes have been prepared. For example, prior to holding a regularly scheduled LLC meeting, you may wish to send the minutes of the previous regular meeting to the participants so they can read them before the new meeting. Instead of waiting for the upcoming meeting to have the participants approve these minutes, you may wish to ask them to sign and mail an approval form beforehand. Doing this can save time at the upcoming meeting, as well as create a signed document showing that the managers and/or members specifically approved actions taken at a prior meeting. If a manager or member missed a previous meeting, it's an especially good idea to get a written record of their signed approval to important decisions that were reached at that earlier meeting.

CD-ROM

Below is a sample of the Approval of LLC Minutes form included on the CD-ROM and as a tearout form in Appendix C. (See Appendix A for information on selecting and using the CD-ROM files.) Fill the form out following the special instructions provided below.

You can prepare one approval form for all managers and/or members to sign, or you can prepare one form for each person to sign individually.

Approval of LLC Minutes

Name of LLC: _____

The undersigned consent(s) to the minutes of the LLC meeting held at _____ [location of meeting]_____ on ____[date of meeting]____ at ___[time of meeting]___, and attached to this form, and accept(s) the resolutions passed and the decisions made at such meeting as valid and binding.

Dated: _____ **❶**

Signature	Printed Name
_____	_____
_____	_____
_____	_____
_____	_____
_____	_____
_____	_____
_____	_____
_____	_____

Special Instruction

❶ If multiple signatures will be obtained for the approval form, list the date the first person signs.

Step 4. Prepare a Cover Letter to Meeting Participants

You may wish to send along a cover letter to members and/or managers when you send the paper minutes and approval form. This letter explains the reasons for asking them to approve paper minutes. If the people asked to sign the approval form are not LLC insiders or are unfamiliar with LLC formalities, you will need to explain the procedure.

CD-ROM

Below is a sample of the cover letter included on the CD-ROM and as a tearout form in Appendix C. (See Appendix A for information on selecting and using the CD-ROM files.) Fill the form out following the special instructions provided below.

Special Instruction

❶ The secretary usually signs the letter, inserting the title of "secretary" under the signature line. The secretary's name, and the address and telephone number of the LLC, are inserted on the remaining lines.

Step 5. Get Managers' and Members' Approval

After you've completed the forms (Steps 1–4, above), make copies of all of them. Then distribute the copies to each manager and/or member. If it's easier, you may send around one copy of the forms to be signed—this is particularly efficient when the members and/or the managers all work at the business.

Remember to include these documents:

- waiver of notice form
- minutes, including resolutions for the approval of special items of business along with any reports or other attachments (see Chapter 5 for instructions on including resolutions in your minutes), and
- approval of minutes form.

Remember to place signed copies of these forms in your LLC records binder.

TIP

You may want to include other background materials. You can send out additional material with your written minutes and approval forms to help your members and/or managers understand the issues involved in the decision at hand. Such material might include copies of reports and background material that may help your members and/or managers familiarize themselves with the issues.

Cover Letter for Approval of Minutes of LLC Meeting

Date: _____

Name: _____

Mailing Address: _____

City, State, Zip: _____

Re: Approval of LLC Minutes

Dear _____:

I am enclosing minutes of a meeting of _____ [name of LLC] _____ that show approval of one or more specific resolutions.

Since these items were agreeable to the members and/or managers entitled to vote on them, we did not hold a formal meeting to approve these decisions. We are now finalizing our LLC records and preparing formal minutes that reflect these prior LLC decisions.

To confirm that these minutes accurately reflect past decisions of the LLC and to formally signify your agreement to them, please date and sign the enclosed Approval of LLC Minutes form and mail it to me at the address below. If you have corrections or additions to suggest, please contact me so we can hold a meeting or make other arrangements to finalize and document these changes.

Sincerely,

_____, ❶

Title: _____

enclosures: Minutes & Approval of LLC Minutes form

Please return to:

Name: _____

LLC: _____

Mailing Address: _____

City, State, Zip: _____

Phone: _____ Fax: _____

How to Take Action by Written Consent Without an LLC Meeting

State statutes (either explicitly or implicitly) allow the managers and members of an LLC to take action without holding a meeting (real or paper), simply by signing written consent forms. Under the usual procedure allowed by state law, you simply insert the language of the decision or action to be approved into a written consent form. (You may use one of the resolutions covered in Chapters 8 through 15 of this book or you may write your own.) Then, all members and/or all managers sign the consent form, legally approving the resolution.

Taking the written consent approach to LLC decision making is often appropriate for small LLCs with only a few members and/or managers. Written consents are sometimes even suitable for slightly larger companies that have a deadline for making a decision and don't have time to assemble the full membership or management at a special meeting.

Action by written consent is most appropriate if the issue at hand is a routine tax or financial formality—for instance, the approval of standard loan terms offered by a bank or the approval of a tax election recommended by the LLC's accountant. It is not appropriate where a decision may cause debate or disagreement among managers or members.

TIP

Absent managers and/or members can use written consents to approve decisions. Written consent forms also come in handy when one or more managers and/or members are not able to attend an important LLC meeting. Even if you obtain a quorum that can approve decisions, it's wise to also get the written consent of any nonattending members or managers, especially if important resolutions were adopted at the meeting. Doing this ensures that all managers and/or members are informed of actions taken at a particular meeting, and it provides clear evidence that they approved the action taken.

TIP

Some states allow less-than-unanimous votes to pass resolutions with written consents. Some states laws specifically allow a majority or other less-than-unanimous percentage of votes to take action by written consent (or allow the LLC's operating agreement to establish its own voting rule for written consents, regardless of what the state statute says). But to be legally safe and avoid controversy within the LLC, we recommend getting the signatures of all members and/or managers on written consent forms.

When to Use Minutes of Paper Meetings Instead of Written Consents

You can safely use written consents to show the approval of most special decisions that would otherwise be documented by preparing minutes of a special LLC meeting (one held specifically to approve that decision). But for decisions usually made at annual meetings, larger LLCs will want to use minutes. Even small LLCs usually prepare minutes of a real or paper meeting to document the decisions made at annual or other regularly scheduled meetings. Written minutes take a little more time to prepare than written consents, but minutes look more convincing and official in the LLC records binder. As a result, written minutes are better for more important LLC decisions that may someday become the subject of controversy. (For instructions on preparing minutes for real and paper meetings, see Chapters 5 and 6.) For more information on when to use face-to-face meetings, paper meetings, and written consents, see Chapter 2.

Step 1. Check Your Operating Agreement for Any Written Consent Rules

Start by checking your operating agreement to determine your LLC's rules for taking action by written consent. A common requirement found in operating agreements is that members (and managers in a manager-managed LLC) can take action without a meeting only by unanimous written consent. But some state LLC acts, and some operating agreements, allow fewer than all members or all managers to approve decisions by written consent.

> **CAUTION**
>
> **Get unanimous written consent to avoid problems.** Don't get too caught up in your operating agreement's language on this issue. If you have all written consents signed by every member or manager, you should meet the statutory requirements for written consents in your state. You'll also have proof that everyone approved of the decision at issue.

Step 2. Prepare Written Consent Form

You'll see that it only takes a minute or two to fill out written consent forms, which must then be distributed to your managers and/or members for signing.

The people entitled to vote on the decision at hand should sign the consent form. In a member-managed LLC, this means the members. In a manager-managed LLC, this generally means the managers. But the members must also sign for certain important decisions, such as amendments to the articles or operating agreement, the admission of new members, the approval of additions of capital, distributions of cash or property to members, or a vote to dissolve the LLC. (For more information on who makes LLC decisions, see Chapter 2.)

> **CD-ROM**
>
> Below is a sample of the Written Consent to Action Without Meeting form included on the CD-ROM and as a tearout form in Appendix C. (See Appendix A for information on selecting and using the CD-ROM files.) Fill the form out following the special instructions provided below.

Special Instructions

❶ Insert a description of the actions or decisions (in the form of resolutions) agreed to by the members and/or managers. Chapters 8 through 15 contain instructions for preparing the ready-to-use resolutions included with this book. (See the beginning of Appendix C for a list of these resolutions with cross-references to the chapters and sections of the book that cover each one.) If you wish to approve a matter not covered by one of our resolutions, insert your own resolution language in the consent form. You don't need to use fancy or legal language for your resolution. Just describe as specifically as you can the transaction or matter approved by your members and/or managers, in a short, concise statement. Resolutions often start with a preamble of the following sort: "The [members and/or managers] resolved that…", but this is not required.

The following are examples of the language typically found in resolutions:

EXAMPLE 1 (bank loan):

"It is resolved that the LLC treasurer be authorized to obtain a loan from _____[name of bank]_____ for the

Written Consent to Action Without Meeting

Name of LLC: _____

The undersigned hereby consent(s) as follows:

[insert one or more resolutions] ❶

_____

_____

_____

_____

_____

_____

_____

Dated: _____ ❷

Signature   Printed Name

_____   _____

_____   _____

_____   _____

_____   _____

_____   _____

amount of $_____ on terms he/she considers commercially reasonable."

EXAMPLE 2 (LLC hiring):

"Managers resolved that ___[name of new employee]___ be hired in the position of ___[job title]___ at an annual salary of $_____ and in accordance with the terms of the LLC's standard employment contract."

EXAMPLE 3 (tax year):

"It is resolved that the LLC adopt a tax year with an ending date of _____ _____."

EXAMPLE 4 (amendment of articles):

"Resolved that the following new article be added to the LLC's articles of organization: _____[language of new article]_____."

If you need to draft your own resolution language and you have trouble doing so, or if the matter has important legal or tax consequences, you may wish to turn to a lawyer or accountant for help. (See Chapter 16.)

❷ Date the consent form and have your members and/or managers sign their names.

As mentioned above, if you have only a few members or managers, it may be easiest to prepare one master consent form to be relayed to each of your members or managers to sign. In this case, date the form as of the date of the first signature by a member or manager. Another method, more appropriate when you have a larger number of members or managers, is to prepare separate consent forms for dating and signing by each person. Either method (or a combination of both methods) will work.

> **TIP**
>
> **You may want to include background materials.** You may send out additional material with your written consent forms to help your members and/or managers understand the issues involved in the decision at hand. Such material could include copies of reports and background material that may help your members and/or managers familiarize themselves with the issues.

Step 3. Place Signed Consent Forms in Your LLC Records Binder

After distributing your consent forms and obtaining the signatures of your members and/or managers, make sure to place each completed form in your LLC records binder. It's common to place these papers in the minutes section of the LLC records binder, arranged according to the date of the action by written consent. ●

Standard LLC Business Resolutions

This chapter presents resolutions that allow LLC members and/or managers to authorize standard items of ongoing LLC business, including:

- opening a bank account for the LLC
- adopting a fictitious LLC name
- approving LLC contracts and purchasing, or
- leasing real property.

This chapter also provides forms that can be used to delegate, approve, rescind, or certify LLC decision-making authority. Where appropriate, it provides relevant legal and tax information to help you select and use the resolutions.

If you don't find a resolution you need for a standard item of LLC business in this chapter, scan this book's index or table of contents for Chapters 8 through 15. It's quite possible you'll find it in a later chapter.

When to Use Resolutions Included in This Chapter

Much of the paperwork covered in this chapter may not be legally or sometimes even practically required to consummate a standard LLC business deal (depending on the importance of an LLC decision or action). In fact, many smaller LLCs forgo passing formal resolutions for all but the most important items of ongoing LLC business, such as the purchase or sale of LLC real estate or the approval of long-term business or financial commitments. But even small LLCs sometimes decide to prepare formal paperwork for less critical business matters when an outsider wants to be sure of full member or manager approval before entering into a business deal with the LLC. For example, perhaps a vendor wants proof that the full membership approved a long-term purchase order before agreeing to grant a hefty discount for goods or services.

Who Approves Resolutions?

The LLC resolutions contained in this chapter must be approved by the person or persons responsible for managing the LLC. In a member-managed LLC, this means the voting members; in a manager-managed LLC, this means the person or persons appointed as managers. For convenience, I refer to the "members" as the persons who approve standard LLC business resolutions (because most smaller LLCs are member-managed). Just keep in mind that if your LLC is manager-managed, you will want to have these business resolutions approved by your LLC manager(s).

Of course, you may choose to have all members (not just voting members) or both members and managers (in a manager-managed LLC) approve or ratify a really important decision. This would be a good idea if you want to cover all bases before committing the LLC to a substantial financial commitment, or if the decision at hand may provoke controversy (such as a contract with an outside company owned by a current LLC member or manager). You probably won't want to take this extra precaution unless it is legally required or the decision is important enough to warrant the extra time and effort.

How to Use LLC Resolutions

- Scan the table of contents at the beginning of the chapter to find the right resolutions for the business at hand.

- When you find one you need, read the background material that precedes the resolution.

- Follow the instructions included with the sample resolution to complete a draft of the resolution on your computer. If you need guidance on selecting and using the computer disk files, see Appendix A. (You'll have to fill in the tearout resolution included in Appendix C if you aren't using a computer.)

- Complete any needed attachment forms, such as an account authorization form or a lease agreement.

- If the resolution involves complex issues that will benefit from expert analysis, have your legal or tax adviser review your paperwork and conclusions.

- Prepare meeting minutes or written consent forms as explained in Chapters 5–7, inserting the completed resolution into the minutes or consent form.

- Have the LLC secretary sign the printed minutes or have members and/or managers sign the written consent forms. Then place the signed forms, together with any attachments, in your LLC records binder.

Bank Account Resolutions

One of the first items of business any LLC will undertake is to open an LLC account from which checks can be written. Checks may be drawn against a standard bank checking account, a stock brokerage money-market account, or another type of interest-bearing account set up to provide a reasonable return on the LLC's funds.

Opening and maintaining financial accounts in the name of the LLC is not just a practical nicety; it's also a legal safeguard. If you, as a member or manager of an LLC, intermingle LLC funds with your own personal money, a court may hold you personally liable for LLC debts or taxes. One of the reasons you organized an LLC was to gain personal protection from legal liability for your business. You don't want to let sloppy financial habits destroy this important LLC benefit.

In small, closely held LLCs, the first deposit to the LLC account is often money advanced by the LLC organizers to help pay initial organizational and operational costs. The LLC can reimburse the founders after the company is fully organized, or the money can be applied toward members' initial capital contributions. The second deposit into an LLC bank account often consists of personal checks from members who paid cash for their capital interests (memberships).

Start-Up Money: Funding Your LLC Bank Account

When you should deposit operating funds into your LLC checking account, and how much you should deposit, is often a matter of common sense. Generally, under state LLC statutes, you can fund ("capitalize" in legal jargon) your LLC with as little or as much money as you wish.

However, if you fail to pay into your LLC at least enough money to cover its foreseeable short-term debts and liabilities, and the LLC is later sued, a court may decide to "pierce the LLC veil" and hold the owners personally liable for LLC debts. This is more likely to occur if a court finds that the owners have used the LLC form to defraud creditors or other outsiders.

EXAMPLE: The principals of Think Thin, LLC, begin doing business with no money or assets, hoping to obtain initial capital by franchising a national chain of hypnotherapy weight-reduction clinics. A few outsiders buy initial franchises in the mistaken belief (reinforced by the Think Thin sales force) that the LLC has sufficient operating capital to advertise and otherwise actively promote the franchise chain. In a later lawsuit brought by the franchisees, a court holds the LLC business owners personally liable for monetary damages to the franchise purchasers, stating that it would be unfair to let the LLC business structure protect LLC principals from personal liability under these circumstances.

General Resolution to Open LLC Bank Account

This resolution will work well for most small LLCs that have a treasurer who handles the LLC's day-to-day finances, such as writing checks and making deposits. The resolution authorizes the treasurer to open one or more unspecified accounts in the name of the LLC. The treasurer alone is permitted to withdraw funds from these accounts, although anyone authorized by the treasurer may make deposits.

If you wish to designate someone other than the treasurer to deal with LLC funds, you can change the title of the officer in this resolution (and also in the resolutions that follow). For example, you may substitute the title "vice president of LLC finance" for the word "treasurer."

CD-ROM

Below is a sample of the resolution you can use to authorize the treasurer to open and use accounts on behalf of the LLC. You'll find this resolution on the CD-ROM and as a tearout form in Appendix C. (See Appendix A for information on selecting and using the CD-ROM files.)

CAUTION

Your bank may require additional paperwork. Many banks require you to fill out an account authorization form signed by the person authorized to sign LLC checks, as provided in one of the bank account resolutions in this chapter. Your bank may also ask you to submit a certified copy of your LLC bank account resolution. (For instructions on preparing a certification form, see "Certification of LLC Resolution," below.)

Authorization of Treasurer to Open and Use LLC Accounts

The treasurer of this LLC is authorized to select one or more banks, trust companies, brokerage companies, or other depositories, and to establish financial accounts in the name of this LLC. The treasurer and other persons designated by the treasurer are authorized to deposit LLC funds in these accounts. However, only the treasurer is authorized to sign checks and withdraw funds from these accounts on behalf of the LLC.

The treasurer is further authorized to sign appropriate account authorization forms as may be required by financial institutions to establish and maintain LLC accounts. The treasurer shall submit a copy of any completed account authorization forms to the secretary of the LLC, who shall attach the forms to this resolution and place them in the LLC records binder.

Specific LLC Bank Account Resolution

The next resolution authorizes the LLC treasurer to open an account with specific banks or other institutions. Again, the resolution allows only the treasurer to write checks drawn against the funds in this account, although anyone authorized by the treasurer may make deposits. Once again, you may delegate this authority to someone other than the treasurer by changing the resolution.

CD-ROM

Below is a sample of the resolution you can use to authorize the treasurer to open and use specific accounts. You'll find this resolution on the CD-ROM and as a tearout form in Appendix C. (See Appendix A for information on selecting and using the CD-ROM files.) Fill the form out, following the special instruction provided below.

Special Instruction

❶ If you wish to authorize only one account, delete the additional account information lines. For three or more accounts, add additional account information lines.

Authorization of Treasurer to Open and Use Specific LLC Account(s)

The treasurer of this LLC is authorized to open the following account(s), in the name of the LLC, with the following depositories:

Type of account: __["checking," "petty cash," or other]__

Name, branch, and address of financial institution:

_____

_____

_____

Type of account: __["checking," "petty cash," or other]__ ❶

Name, branch, and address of financial institution:

_____

_____

_____

    The treasurer and other persons authorized by the treasurer must deposit the funds of the LLC in this account. Funds may be withdrawn from this account only on the signature of the treasurer.

    The treasurer is authorized to complete and sign standard authorization forms for the purpose of establishing the account(s) according to the terms of this resolution. A copy of any completed account authorization form(s) must be submitted by the treasurer to the secretary of the LLC, who will attach the form(s) to this resolution and place them in the LLC records binder.

Bank Account Resolution With Multiple Signers

This resolution allows you to authorize one or more persons, such as officers and staff personnel, to sign LLC checks in order to withdraw LLC funds from the LLC accounts. You also can specify how many persons from this list are required to sign each LLC check.

CD-ROM

Below is a sample of the resolution you can use to authorize the treasurer to open a bank account and designate one or more persons who may sign checks for the LLC. You'll find this resolution on the CD-ROM and as a tearout form in Appendix C. (See Appendix A for information on selecting and using the CD-ROM files.) Complete the form using the special instruction provided below.

Authorization of LLC Account and Designation of Authorized Signers

The treasurer of this LLC is authorized to open a ___[type of account, such as "checking" or "petty cash"]___ account in the name of the LLC with ___[name and branch address of bank or other institution]___.

Any officer, employee, or agent of this LLC is authorized to endorse checks, drafts, or other evidences of indebtedness made payable to this LLC, but only for the purpose of deposit.

All checks, drafts, and other instruments obligating this LLC to pay money must be signed on behalf of this LLC by ___[number]___ of the following:___[names and titles of persons authorized to sign checks]___.

The above institution is authorized to honor and pay any and all checks and drafts of this LLC signed as provided in this authorization.

The persons designated above are authorized to complete and sign standard account authorization forms for the purpose of establishing the account(s), provided that the forms do not vary materially from the terms of this resolution. The treasurer must submit a copy of any completed account authorization forms to the secretary of the LLC, who will attach the forms to this resolution and place them in the LLC records binder.

Special Instruction

❶ You may designate two or more persons allowed to write checks payable out of LLC accounts. One or more—or all of them—may be required to sign each check.

EXAMPLE 1:

"All checks, drafts, and other instruments obligating this LLC to pay money must be signed on behalf of this LLC by any one of the following: Janice Spencer, President; James Williams, Treasurer; William Yarborough, Assistant Treasurer."

EXAMPLE 2:

"All checks, drafts, and other instruments obligating this LLC to pay money must be signed on behalf of this LLC by any two of the following: Janice Spencer, President; James Williams, Treasurer; William Yarborough, Assistant Treasurer."

TIP

Add terms or conditions if you wish. You may customize this resolution to add other conditions or requirements for check-writing. For example, you could add an additional sentence to the above paragraph in Example 2 to require the approval of the president for all checks written for more than $1,000, $5,000, $10,000, or any other amount you choose.

EXAMPLE OF ADDITIONAL TERMS:

"All checks, drafts, and other instruments obligating this LLC to pay money must be signed on behalf of this LLC by any one of the following: Janice Spencer, President; James Williams, Treasurer; William Yarborough, Assistant Treasurer. However, the verbal or written approval of the LLC president is required prior to the signing by the treasurer or assistant treasurer for checks with a face amount of one thousand dollars ($1,000) or more."

Authorization of LLC Safe Deposit Account

Some LLCs decide to open a safe deposit box at a local bank or other financial institution to store important LLC documents, such as promissory notes, investment securities owned by the LLC, or trade secrets. LLC owners who run their shop formally may want to use the resolution shown below to authorize this item of business.

CD-ROM

Below is a sample of the resolution you can use to authorize the rental of a safe deposit box. You'll find this resolution on the CD-ROM and as a tearout form in Appendix C. (See Appendix A for information on selecting and using the CD-ROM files.)

Authorization of Rental of Safe Deposit Box

The treasurer of the LLC is authorized to rent a safe deposit box in the name of the LLC with an appropriate bank, trust company, or other suitable financial institution, and to deposit in this box any securities, books, records, reports, or other material or property of the LLC that he or she decides is appropriate for storage and safekeeping in this box.

Assumed or "Fictitious" LLC Name Resolution

Sometimes an LLC wishes to do business under a name different from the one stated in its articles of organization (or similar organizing document, such as the certificate of formation), without giving up its formal LLC name.

EXAMPLE:

An LLC files articles of organization under the name "Accelerated Business Computer, LLC." Later, the managers decide to use stationery, advertise, and otherwise do LLC business under the abbreviated name ABC, LLC. However, the managers still wish to keep the formal LLC name stated in its articles.

The easiest solution is to register the new name you want to use as an assumed LLC name. Assumed names (also called fictitious or "dba" names—for "doing business as") must be filed with a state and/or local office. In most states, the filing is made in the county clerk's office for each county in which the assumed LLC name will be used. For example, an LLC that sells goods and services locally would file assumed LLC name documents in the office of the county where the principal office of the LLC is located.

To find out how to register your assumed LLC name, call or email the state LLC filing office first. (A list of each state's LLC filing offices, including email addresses, is provided in Appendix B.) This office should provide fictitious or "dba" forms if you must register the name at the state level, and/or refer you to a local state office (county clerk) if the assumed name must be registered locally. To register locally, you may be required to publish a notice of assumed name and file a proof of publication with the local county clerk's office. Your local county clerk's office can provide instructions.

If you must file an assumed LLC name with the state office, it cannot be identical to a name already registered by another LLC. The state will refuse to accept the name for filing if it finds that the name is already taken, on a master list that includes registered LLCs. For local filings, the new name probably won't be checked against other names. However,

it's worth doing a little research, both in your county and in the state, to avoid using a name that's too similar to an existing business's name. See "Perform a Trade Name and Trademark Search Before Adopting or Charging Your LLC Name," below.

TIP

Amend your articles to change the LLC's formal name. If an LLC wishes to change its name and conduct business exclusively using this new name, the best way to do this is to change its formal name in the articles of organization (or similar organizing document). You will have to amend the articles and file the amendment with the LLC filing office. (See "Amending Articles of Organization" in Chapter 10 for a resolution to approve an amendment to the LLC articles.)

CD-ROM

Below is a sample of the resolution you can use to adopt an assumed or fictitious LLC name. You'll find this resolution on the CD-ROM and as a tearout form in Appendix C. (See Appendix A for information on selecting and using the CD-ROM files.)

Adoption of Assumed LLC Name

It was decided that this LLC will do business under a name that is different from the formal name of the LLC stated in its articles of organization (or similar organizational document that was filed with the state to commence the legal existence of the LLC). The assumed name selected for the LLC is _____ [assumed name] _____.

The secretary of the LLC was instructed to register the assumed LLC name as required by law.

Perform a Trade Name and Trademark Search Before Adopting or Changing Your LLC Name

Registering an assumed LLC name, just like registering a formal LLC name by filing LLC articles of organization, does not guarantee you the absolute legal right to use the name. If another business has been using this name or a similar name in connection with its business, products, or services, a court can award the other business the right to the name. The court may also hold your LLC liable for damages, including any profits the other business lost because you used the name.

That's why you should make sure, before adopting a new name, that another business is not using a name similar to it. You'll have to check business names in your county and state and, if your business involves interstate commerce, business names used in other states where you operate. You can perform a search in your own state by checking telephone books, business directories, and names registered with the state trademark office. (Typically, this office is a division within the state secretary or department of state's office.) In addition, you can check nationwide using the Federal Register maintained by the U.S. Patent and Trademark office in Washington, DC, which contains a list of nationally registered names. You can do a free federal trademark search over the Internet—point your Internet browser to www.uspto.gov and go to the trademarks area. You can also just put parts of the name you want to use into a search engine like Google, Yahoo, or MSN and see what comes up. For more information on performing your own name search, see *Trademarks: Legal Care for Your Business & Product Name,* by Stephen Elias (Nolo).

Resolution to Approve an LLC Contract

Before one of your LLC members or officers signs an important contract, you may want to obtain formal approval from your LLC members and/or managers. It's a good idea to obtain formal approval of a contract ahead of time if the contract concerns an important undertaking by the LLC or obligates it to expend substantial funds. Other types of contracts that are appropriate for formal approval include:

- business deals that extend over a period of time, such as a five-year purchase-option contract on a building

- complicated business arrangements that would benefit from formal review and approval, and

- contracts where the other party wants the LLC to back up its commitment with a formal approval process—for example, a potential long-term supplier or service provider requests formal LLC management approval in writing before fulfilling a large order.

The resolution below allows you to record management approval of a proposed contract between your LLC and an outside person or business and to delegate an LLC officer to enter into the contract on the LLC's behalf.

CROSS REFERENCE

Resolutions for granting specific authority to LLC members, managers, officers, or employees. For a discussion of resolutions specifically geared to authorizing LLC officers to transact business for the LLC, or to ratify a contract made by an LLC member or manager after it has been signed, see "Delegation of Authority and Approval of Individual Contracts," below.

Approval of Contract

The   ["members" and/or "managers"]   were presented a proposed contract to be entered into between this LLC and   [name of outside business or party]   for the purpose of   [subject matter of contract, such as "the renovation of LLC offices"] , together with the following attachments: [specify additional material submitted with contract for approval, such as "building plans, schedule for performance of services under the contract, etc."]   .

Next, a report on the proposed contract was given by   [name of LLC officers or other employees] , who made the following major points and concluded with the following recommendation: [if applicable, cite major points provided in verbal or written reports given at the meeting and the conclusions of the reports]   .

After discussion,   [If you wish, you may add: "including discussion of the following points:" and cite specific statements or conclusions given by individual members or managers.] , it was decided that the transaction of the business covered by the contract was in the best interests of the LLC, and the proposed contract and attachments were approved.

The _____ [title of LLC officer] _____ was instructed to execute the contract submitted to the meeting in the name of and on behalf of the LLC, and to see to it that a copy of the contract executed by all parties, together with all attachments, be placed in the records of the LLC.

CD-ROM

Above is a sample of the resolution you can use to approve a proposed contract. You'll find this resolution on the CD-ROM and as a tear-out form in Appendix C. (See Appendix A for information on selecting and using the CD-ROM files.)

Real Property Resolutions

These resolutions address the lease, purchase, or sale of real property (real estate) by the LLC. Because real estate transactions usually involve a lot of money and/or long-term commitments, all LLCs will want to formally approve these transactions with the resolutions provided below.

Resolution Approving Lease by LLC

Your LLC should pass a formal resolution to approve a lease of business premises by the LLC, particularly if the lease is long term or requires a substantial deposit or payments by the LLC, or if the members and/or managers need to discuss the lease terms.

Use the following resolution to show LLC approval of lease terms negotiated with a property owner or manager. Attach a copy of the lease to the resolution and file both documents in your LLC records binder.

CD-ROM

Below is a sample of the resolution you can use to approve a commercial lease. You'll find this resolution on the CD-ROM and as a tearout form in Appendix C. (See Appendix A for information on selecting and using the CD-ROM files.)

Consider a Lease of Personally Owned Real Estate to Your LLC

A member of a small LLC may wish to lease property to the LLC to get cash out of the LLC and obtain favorable tax benefits. Of course, the IRS will expect the LLC to pay a reasonable rent (because the LLC can deduct the rent as a business expense in computing net LLC income, which is then allocated to the owners). The LLC member-landlord reports the rent payments as ordinary income on his or her tax return. A portion of the rental income, in turn, can be offset by depreciation deductions taken by the landlord member. Ask your tax adviser before deciding to rent, rather than sell, real property to your LLC; the tax implications can be complex. If an LLC manager or member does rent property to the LLC, you should read Chapter 15, which covers business deals between the LLC and its members or managers.

Approval of Lease of Premises by LLC

A proposed lease agreement between _____[name of LLC]_____ and _____[name of owner]_____ for the premises known as _____[address of property]_____ was presented for approval. The lease covered a period of _[term of lease]_, with _[interval of lease payments, such as "monthly" or "quarterly"]_ rent payments payable by the LLC of _[dollar amount or formula used to compute rent payments]_.

After discussion, it was decided that the lease terms were commercially reasonable and fair to the LLC and that it was in the best interests of the LLC to enter into the lease.

The lease and all the terms contained in it were approved, and the secretary of the LLC was authorized to instruct the appropriate LLC officers to execute the lease on behalf of the LLC, and that a copy of the executed lease agreement be attached to this resolution and filed in the LLC records binder.

Who Can Buy or Sell Property on Behalf of the LLC?

Some states allow any LLC member (in a member-managed LLC) or manager (in a manager-managed LLC) to transfer real property on the LLC's behalf. If you want to restrict this right to only certain members or managers, you can do so in your articles of organization or operating agreement.

If you authorize only some members or managers to deal with property transactions, however, you should make this limitation known. For example, you should give a copy of this limitation to anyone who is considering buying or selling property from or to the LLC. If you don't make this restriction known, the LLC might have to go through with a property transaction set up by an unauthorized member or manager—most state laws require an LLC to honor a deal made with an outside party if the outside party reasonably believed that the person he or she was dealing with was authorized to make the deal.

In addition to giving outsiders who want to transfer property to or from the LLC a copy of the limiting language from your operating agreement or articles, you can take further steps to protect your LLC from unauthorized property deals. For example, your state may allow your LLC to file a statement with the secretary of state's office, listing the people who are authorized to make real estate deals on the LLC's behalf. You can also record a resolution, your articles, or a state form listing those authorized to make property transactions with the county recorder. These filings will put outsiders on notice that only certain members or managers are authorized to transfer real property on the LLC's behalf.

If you want to authorize particular members, managers, or officers to enter into a particular real estate deal, use one of the resolutions below. If you want to authorize just one member, manager, or officer to enter into all real estate transactions, use the Delegation of LLC Authority resolution, below.

Resolution Authorizing LLC to Purchase Real Property

The members or managers may want to formally authorize a purchase of real property by the LLC. This is a significant business transaction that warrants a little extra formality. What's more, title and trust companies may require a members' or managers' (for a manager-managed LLC) resolution before escrow papers are finalized.

Buying real property gives rise to significant mortgage interest and depreciation deductions for the LLC and, if the property is purchased from an LLC member, a source of cash to the selling member. Of course, to ward off possible challenges from other members, the LLC should pay no more than fair market value for property purchased from a member. (See Chapter 15 for more on business deals between the LLC and its members or managers.) The tax ramifications of a purchase of real property by

---

Purchase of Real Property by LLC

The purchase by this LLC of real property commonly known as _____[street address
of property]_____ was discussed. The president announced that the property had
been offered to the LLC for sale by the owner at a price of __$ [seller's asking price]__. After
discussing the value of the property to the LLC and comparable prices for similar properties, it
was agreed that the LLC should __["accept the offer" or "make a counteroffer for the property
at a price of $(counteroffer price)"]__.

It was also agreed that the LLC will seek financing for the purchase of the property on
the following terms: _____[insert, if applicable, the terms and interest rate of financing
the LLC will seek for financing the purchase of the property, for example, "this offer or counteroffer is contingent on the LLC's ability to obtain financing for the purchase under a 30-
year note carrying an interest rate not to exceed 10%"]____.

The president was authorized to instruct the appropriate LLC officers to prepare all
financial and legal documents necessary to submit the offer or counteroffer to the seller
and to seek financing for the purchase of the property according to the terms discussed and
agreed to in this resolution.

---

the LLC are complex, both for the LLC and its
members (particularly if one or more members
own the property being sold to the LLC).
Always check with your tax adviser before
deciding to go ahead with an LLC real estate
purchase.

CD-ROM

Above is a sample of the resolution you
can use to approve the purchase of real property
by the LLC. You'll find this resolution on the CD-
ROM and as a tearout form in Appendix C. (See
Appendix A for information on selecting and using
the CD-ROM files.)

Resolution Authorizing LLC to Sell Real Property

Another important LLC transaction that should
be formally approved is the sale of real property
owned by the LLC. As with a purchase of
real estate, a sale of real estate is a significant
business transaction that warrants a little extra
formality. Title and trust companies may also
require a formal LLC resolution that approves
the sale before final escrow papers can be
prepared. The resolution shown below can be
used for this purpose.

CD-ROM

Below is a sample of the resolution you can
use to approve the sale of real property by the LLC.
You'll find this resolution on the CD-ROM and as a
tearout form in Appendix C. (See Appendix A for
information on selecting and using the CD-ROM files.)

Authorization of Sale of Real Property by LLC

After discussion, it was agreed that the president of this LLC is authorized to contract to sell real property of the LLC commonly known as: _____ [street address of the property to be sold] _____ on the following conditions and terms: ____ [provide price and other terms that the president should seek to obtain; for example: "at a sales price of at least $100,000, with at least 10% down and the balance carried through a 10-year or shorter note at current commercial interest rates"] .

The president of the LLC and any other officers of the LLC authorized by the president can execute all instruments on behalf of the LLC necessary to make and record a sale of the above property according to the above terms.

Delegation of Authority and Approval of Individual Contracts

State law typically says that any member in a member-managed LLC and any manager in a manager-managed LLC can act as an "agent" of the LLC. An agent can legally act on the LLC's behalf to accomplish any business reasonably within its general business purposes. This also goes for officers and key employees. This means that an LLC is bound by the acts of its members (in a member-managed LLC), its managers (in a manager-managed LLC), and other agents (including officers and other key employees), as long as the transaction is within the apparent authority of the person—that is, the transaction is the type of action or decision an outsider would reasonably expect the person to be able to perform or make for the LLC—and as long as the outsider has no knowledge of a limitation on the authority of the LLC member, manager, officer, or employee.

For major actions or decisions, however, you may wish to give only one or two people the authority to enter into a particular transaction. If the matter is important enough, and your

LLC will benefit by having it handled only by a particular LLC person with the necessary expertise, then using a "delegation of authority" resolution makes sense. For example, if the LLC wishes to allow a talented employee to commit significant funds for certain projects or to handle a critical area of LLC operations—such as purchasing real property or signing long-term service contracts—it makes sense to have the LLC officially delegate authority to the employee for these actions. Doing this can be useful to emphasize to the employee the limits of his or her authority. And it can provide a paper trail of the decision if it is later questioned by others. Finally, if you are worried that an outsider may inadvertently deal with the wrong LLC member, manager, officer, or employee, you can give the outsider a copy of the resolution, to put the outsider on notice that the person specified in your resolution is the person the outsider should deal with.

The following sections provide resolutions your LLC can use to approve the authority of an LLC member, manager, officer, or employee to undertake LLC business or enter into LLC contracts. They also provide ratification resolutions that can be used to approve business transactions already undertaken by individuals on behalf of the LLC. Such after-the-fact approval can be helpful, as explained below.

Resolution Delegating LLC Authority

Use the following resolution to delegate specific authority for one or more contracts, decisions, or business matters to an LLC member, manager, officer, or employee. This resolution can help make the authorized individual aware of his or her primary role in upcoming business transactions, and let the person (and others) know how far the person can go in acting for the LLC.

EXAMPLE:

Tired Treads, LLC, a used-car leasing company, wants one of its LLC officers to negotiate and sign a long-term, wholesale, car rental agreement with a used-car dealer. Before the dealer will close the deal, however, he wants to see a formally approved resolution from Tired Treads, LLC, that sets out the LLC officer's authority to close the deal. The LLC approves a resolution that delegates authority to the LLC officer to handle this particular transaction.

CD-ROM

Below is a sample of the resolution you can use to delegate LLC authority. You'll find this resolution on the CD-ROM and as a tearout form in Appendix C. (See Appendix A for information on selecting and using the CD-ROM files.)

Delegation of LLC Authority

After discussion, it was agreed that the following individual, whose LLC title is indicated below, is granted authority to perform the following tasks or transact the following business by and on behalf of the LLC, or to see to it that such tasks are performed for the LLC under his or her supervision as follows:

_____ [state the name and title of LLC member, manager, officer, or employee and the specific authority granted to the person, including any limitations to his or her authority]_____ .❶

This person is also granted the power to perform any and all incidental tasks and transact incidental business necessary to accomplish the primary tasks and business described above.

Special Instruction

❶ You can limit the individual's authority to specific business transactions, certain monetary or time limits, or in any other way you wish.

EXAMPLE:

GyroCopter Tours Ltd. Liability Co. uses this resolution to help define the authority of an LLC vice president to negotiate the renewal of its flight insurance policies with its insurer. Specific minimum terms are set out in the resolution—the VP can only make a deal that covers the entire gyro fleet, for a minimum term of one year, with a minimum insured amount per gyro of $1 million. The resolution further states that if the policy is not obtained within the following 90 days, the delegation of authority automatically terminates, and the vice president must request additional approval from LLC management to continue the insurance negotiations on behalf of the LLC.

Resolution Ratifying a Contract or Other Business Approved by an Individual

When a business decision needs to be made in a hurry, an LLC member, manager, officer, or employee sometimes does not have time to obtain management's prior approval of the transaction. If the transaction is important or potentially controversial—that is, some members or managers may object without hearing more about the business deal or transaction—it is wise to seek formal approval of the transaction after the fact. This gives the person who made the deal a chance to explain his or her reasons and obtain formal approval from the LLC members or managers. Legally, this sort of after-the-fact approval—called a ratification—takes the individual off the hook personally for any monetary loss from the transaction and, as a practical matter, helps ease personal tensions by bringing management in on the deal.

EXAMPLE:

The treasurer of Master Mind Enterprises, LLC, gets a large cash payment from a client. It's Friday, just before closing—too late to talk to management—and the treasurer decides to maximize the yield from the funds by depositing the check in a short-term certificate of deposit rather than in the LLC's interest-bearing checking account, which currently pays a lower interest rate. On Monday, the treasurer asks the managers to approve the transaction.

CD-ROM

Below is a sample of the resolution you can use to ratify a transaction entered into by an LLC member, manager, officer, or employee. You'll find this resolution on the CD-ROM and as a tear-out form in Appendix C. (See Appendix A for information on selecting and using the CD-ROM.)

TIP

Use this resolution for joint decisions. This resolution also can be used to approve joint decisions, not just those undertaken by a particular individual. For example, by changing the language of the resolution slightly, you can use this resolution to have all members approve a contract or transaction that was made by the LLC managers (in a manager-managed LLC) or by some, but not all, members.

EXAMPLE:

The managers of Ovoid Egg Supply L.L.C. recently approved and paid for the renovation of its packaging plant, even though the final cost exceeded the contracted price by 25%. The managers decide it would be wise to tell the members why they agreed to pay the excess amount, then ask the members to vote on a resolution to ratify the final payment.

Ratification of Contract or Transaction

After discussion, it was agreed that the following contract or other business transaction undertaken on behalf of the LLC by the following individual whose title appears below is hereby adopted, ratified, and approved as the act of the LLC and is accepted as having been done by, on behalf of, and in the best interests of the LLC:

[insert the name and title of the LLC member, manager, officer, or employee and the date and nature of the contract or other business transaction]   .

The Right Way for Officers and Other Employees to Sign LLC Contracts

Whenever an LLC member, manager, officer, or employee signs a contract for the LLC—whether before or after obtaining LLC authority for the contract—the document should always be signed as follows:

[name of LLC]   ,

by [signature]

[name and title of individual]

For example:

Ovoid Egg Supply L.L.C.   ,

by   *Bud Breedy*

Bud Breedy, Secretary

If someone signs a contract in his or her own name instead of signing for the LLC, a third party may be able to hold the individual personally responsible for doing what was promised in the contract.

Resolution Rescinding Employee's Authority

An LLC may wish to cancel the previously approved authority of an individual to transact business or negotiate the terms of a contract. This may happen, for instance, if the original LLC resolution was open-ended—that is, it did not specify a time limit for the individual's authority. Business conditions may have since rendered the delegation of authority to the person unnecessary or inappropriate. For example, the LLC might rescind the treasurer's authority to seek loan funds once the treasurer has borrowed sufficient funds under the prior open-ended authority.

CD-ROM

Below is a sample of the resolution you can use to revoke previously approved authority of an LLC member, manager, officer, or employee. You'll find this resolution on the CD-ROM and as a tearout form in Appendix C. (See Appendix A for information on selecting and using the CD-ROM files.)

Rescission of Authority

After discussion, it was agreed that prior authority granted to [name and title of LLC member, manager, officer, or employee] on [date of approval of authority] for the purpose of [describe the authority granted to the individual] is no longer necessary to the interests of the LLC and that any and all authority granted under the prior approval of authority is hereby rescinded and no longer in effect.

Certification, Affidavit, or Acknowledgment of LLC Decision or Document

Your LLC members, managers, officers, or employees may need to certify to others that a given LLC decision, act, or document was properly approved by your LLC. For example, prior to granting a loan, a bank may require the LLC secretary to certify that the LLC members (or managers in a manager-managed LLC) approved the loan.

This section provides three forms your LLC secretary (or other officer) can use for this purpose. Note that the forms do not require approval by members or managers—the secretary's signature certifies that the members or managers previously approved an act or decision. In other words, none of these forms is a resolution. The first two forms are ways to validate or certify a resolution that is attached to or quoted in the form; the third is a legal statement that can be added to the end of another legal document, such as a contract.

Certification of LLC Resolution

The following form can be used by the LLC secretary to certify to outsiders that an LLC resolution is authentic and was properly adopted. This is the least formal of the three forms in this section, and the most common means of certification.

CD-ROM

You'll find this resolution on the CD-ROM and as a tearout form in Appendix C. (See Appendix A for information on selecting and using the CD-ROM files.) Complete the certification following the instructions below.

Certification of LLC Resolution

The undersigned, duly elected and acting _____["secretary" or title of other officer]_____ ❶ of

_____[name of LLC]_____, ❷ certifies that the attached resolution ❸ was

adopted by the _["members" and/or "managers"]_

    ☐ at a duly held meeting at which a quorum was present, held on __[date of meeting]__

    or,

    ☐ by written consent(s) dated on or after __[date of first written consent]__ ,

and that it is a true and accurate copy of the resolution and that the resolution has not been rescinded or modified as of the date of this certification. ❹

Dated: _____

_____
    [signature]

_____, Secretary [or other title]
    [typed or printed name]

Special Instructions

❶ Although it is most common for the secretary to sign this form, any officer, member, or manager can do so. Insert the title of the officer, member, or manager who is certifying the LLC decision in the first and last blank of the certification.

❷ Fill in the name of the LLC.

❸ Attach a copy of the LLC resolution or written consent approved by the members and/or managers before submitting this resolution form. Remember to place copies in your LLC records binder.

❹ Fill in the rest of the blanks as indicated.

Affidavit of LLC Resolution

A more formal way for the LLC secretary to certify that a particular LLC decision was formally approved by the LLC is through the use of an affidavit. This is a sworn statement, signed by the secretary in the presence of a notary, that attests to the truth of the statements it contains. The legal language for affidavits varies from state to state, but a typical affidavit follows the format of the sample below.

CD-ROM

You'll find this resolution on the CD-ROM and as a tearout form in Appendix C. (See Appendix A for information on selecting and using the CD-ROM files.)

CAUTION

Check your state's notarization form. Before using this form, ask a notary in your state for a copy of your state's standard affidavit. Make any necessary modifications so that the language of your affidavit conforms to your state's standard language. (Of course, you can also use the state's standard form instead.)

Affidavit of LLC Resolution

STATE OF _____

COUNTY OF _____

Before me, a Notary Public in and for the above state and county, personally appeared
_____ [name of LLC secretary] _____ who, being duly sworn, says:

    1. That he/she is the duly elected and acting _____ [title] _____
of _____ [name of LLC] _____ , a _____ [name of state] _____ LLC.

    2. That the following is a true and correct copy of a resolution duly approved by
the _["members" and/or "managers"]_ of the LLC _["at a duly held meeting at which
a quorum was present, held on [date of meeting]" or "by a sufficient number of written
consents dated on or after [date of first written consent obtained for approval of
resolution]"]_ :

        _____ [insert language of resolution here] _____

    3. That the above resolution has not been rescinded or modified as of the date of this
affidavit.

    [signature of secretary taken in the presence of Notary]

    [typed or printed name] , Secretary

Sworn to and subscribed before me this _____ [date] _____ day of _____.

    _____ [signature of Notary Public] _____

Notary Public

My commission expires: _____

Notary Seal

Acknowledgment of LLC Document

An LLC officer, member, or manager may be asked to acknowledge a legal document, such as a lease or deed. An acknowledgment states that the person is who he or she claims to be and that he or she actually signed the document in question. Acknowledgments, like affidavits, often must be signed in the presence of a notary. An acknowledgment form is appended or attached to the end of a legal document signed by an LLC officer, member, or manager.

CAUTION

Check your state's acknowledgment form. Before using this form, ask a notary in your state for a copy of your state's standard acknowledgment language, then make any necessary changes to have your acknowledgment language conform to state requirements.

CD-ROM

You'll find this resolution on the CD-ROM and as a tearout form in Appendix C. (See Appendix A for information on selecting and using the CD-ROM files.)

Acknowledgment

STATE OF _____

COUNTY OF _____

I hereby certify that on _____[date]_____, before me, a Notary Public in and for the above state and county, personally appeared __[name of officer, member, or manager]__, who acknowledged himself/herself to be the _____[title]_____ of _____[name of LLC]_____ and that he/she, having been authorized to do so, executed the above document for the purposes contained therein by signing his/her name as _____[title]_____ of _____[name of LLC]_____.

__[signature of Notary Public]__
     Notary Public

My commission expires: _____

Notary Seal

LLC Tax Resolutions

This chapter contains a few common LLC tax resolutions to be approved by members or managers. Of course, this is not an extensive treatment of the various tax issues that can come up in an LLC. Often, the LLC's tax adviser will provide the impetus to consider and approve tax matters. These few resolutions are examples of ways to formally approve tax elections or decisions. More commonly, tax decisions are made informally, at both the LLC and the individual member levels. Later chapters discuss other common tax issues that arise during the course of LLC operations, such as contributions of capital and loans made by members to the LLC, the admission of new members, the withdrawal of existing members, and the transfer of a membership interest by a current member to an outsider.

Who Approves Resolutions?

Unless otherwise noted below, the LLC resolutions contained in this chapter should be approved by the person or persons responsible for managing the LLC. In a member-managed LLC, this means the voting members; in a manager-managed LLC, this means the person or persons appointed as managers. Of course, in a member-managed LLC you may choose to have all members (including nonvoting members if you have them), or in a manager-managed LLC both members and managers, approve or ratify a really important tax decision. Usually, you will not wish to take this extra step unless this additional approval is legally required or the decision is important enough to warrant the extra time and effort.

How to Select and Use LLC Resolutions

- Scan the table of contents at the beginning of the chapter to find the right resolutions for the business at hand.

- When you find one you need, read the background material that precedes the resolution.

- Follow the instructions included with the sample resolution and complete a draft on your computer. If you need guidance on selecting and using the computer disk files, see Appendix A. (You'll have to fill in the tear-out resolution included in Appendix C if you aren't using a computer.)

- Complete any needed attachment forms, such as tax forms.

- If a resolution involves complex issues that will benefit from expert analysis, have your legal or tax adviser review your paperwork and conclusions.

- Prepare meeting minutes or written consent forms as explained in Chapters 5–7, and insert the completed resolution into the appropriate form.

- Have the LLC secretary sign the printed minutes or have members and/or managers sign the written consent forms. Then place the signed forms, together with any attachments, in your LLC records binder.

LLC Corporate Tax Treatment Election

By default, a multimember LLC is taxed by the IRS as a partnership, and a single-owner LLC is taxed as a sole proprietorship. But that's only by default: An LLC can also elect to be treated by the IRS as a corporation. Most LLCs will not wish to do this—after all, one of the advantages of forming an LLC is the benefit of being treated as a "pass-through" tax entity. (LLC profits and losses and credits and deductions "pass through" the business and are allocated to members at the end of each LLC tax year.) But your tax adviser may decide that it would be a good idea for your LLC to elect corporate tax treatment. Generally, this happens if LLC profits are substantial, and the owners wish to shelter business income in the LLC. If you do elect corporate tax treatment, the retained income in the LLC is taxed at lower corporate tax rates (15% and 25% for taxable net corporate incomes up to $75,000), instead of the sometimes higher individual tax rates members may have to pay on income allocated to them.

If you want to elect corporate tax treatment for your LLC, you must file IRS Form 8832, *Entity Classification Election*, and check the corporation box on the form (the actual language of this box is "a domestic eligible entity electing to be classified as an association taxable as a corporation"). The form must be signed by all LLC members unless the members have authorized a particular officer, member, or manager to sign it on their behalf.

CD-ROM

Below is a sample of the resolution you can use to approve a corporate tax election by the LLC. You'll find this resolution on the CD-ROM and as a tearout form in Appendix C. (See Appendix A for information on selecting and using the CD-ROM files.) Complete the resolution according to the special instruction below.

Note that this resolution must be approved by all members, even in a manager-managed LLC.

LLC Election of Corporate Tax Treatment

After consultation with the LLC's tax adviser, the LLC treasurer recommended that the LLC elect to be taxed as a corporation, starting ___[insert date when election is to start]___ . ❶ After discussion, all members agreed that this election should be made, and the treasurer was authorized by the members to complete IRS Form 8832, "Entity Classification Election," to accomplish this election, and to sign the form on behalf of each of the members of this LLC, and to file it with the IRS.

It was also agreed that, if applicable, the treasurer file any additional forms necessary to elect corporate tax treatment of the LLC for state income tax purposes. ❷

Special Instructions

❶ Your tax adviser can tell you when your election should start, and this date should be inserted here. The start date of the corporate tax treatment election must also be specified on IRS Form 8832.

❷ Most states that impose a corporate income tax follow the federal tax rules, treating an LLC that has elected corporate tax treatment as a corporate tax entity for state income tax purposes (if the state imposes a corporate income tax). But some states impose their own requirements, or have their own forms that must be completed to achieve corporate tax treatment at the state level. Ask your tax adviser for information on your state's requirements.

Resolution for Approval of Independent Audit

As part of the LLC's annual tax accounting procedures, a tax audit of the LLC's books may be necessary. Or, a special audit may be requested by the IRS or required by a bank prior to approval of a loan or credit application. Audits of this sort are called "independent audits," and they are usually done by an outside accounting firm that does not handle ongoing tax or bookkeeping chores for the LLC.

TIP

There are less expensive alternatives to independent audits. To avoid the expense and hassles of a full-blown outside audit, financial institutions sometimes allow LLCs to submit financial statements that have been "reviewed" by the LLC's accountant, using standard auditing rules (Generally Accepted Accounting Practices, or GAAP). If this alternative is available when you are preparing financial statements that will be examined by others, you will probably want to choose it.

CD-ROM

Below is a sample of the resolution you can use to authorize an independent audit of the LLC's financial records and transactions. You'll find this resolution on the CD-ROM and as a tearout form in Appendix C. (See Appendix A for information on selecting and using the CD-ROM files.)

Approval of Independent Audit of LLC Financial Records

After discussion, it was agreed that the accounting firm of   [name of accountant or firm]   was selected to perform an independent audit of the financial records of the LLC for the   [year]   fiscal year and to prepare all necessary financial statements for the LLC as part of its independent audit.

The LLC treasurer was instructed to work with the auditors to provide all records of LLC finances and transactions that may be requested by them, and to report to the LLC on the results of the audit on its completion.

Approval of LLC Tax Year

Choosing appropriate dates for your LLC's tax year is important—and best done with the guidance of the LLC's accountant. The deadlines for preparing and filing LLC informational tax returns, and the tax consequences of specific transactions made during the year, will turn on this decision. Further, the LLC's accounting period (the period for which the LLC keeps its books) must correspond to its tax year.

Generally, an LLC's tax year must be the same as the tax year of LLC members who hold a majority share of the LLC's profits and capital interests (individual members will have calendar tax years; corporate or other business entity members may not). If the members who own the majority of the LLC's interests do not share a common tax year (for example, one corporate member's tax year ends July 31 and another's tax year ends December 31), the LLC must choose the tax year of all of its "principal members." These are defined as members owning a 5% or greater share of LLC profits and capital. If the principal members don't share a common tax year, the LLC must choose a tax year that results in the least deferral of income. (A mathematical test is applied under Income Tax Regulation 1.706-1.)

LLC members typically are individuals, so most LLCs have a calendar tax year (from January 1 to December 31). But special IRS rules allow LLCs to elect a noncalendar tax year—called a "fiscal year"—in a couple of instances:

- **Natural business year.** Revenue Procedure 74-33 allows an LLC to choose a noncalendar tax year if the LLC's natural business year concludes in a month other than December. (Generally, at least 25% of business revenue must occur within the last two months of the natural business year.) For example, a summer resort might choose a tax year that ends on September 30 if this is the end of the lodge's peak income season.

- **Three-month deferral of income.** LLCs can adopt a noncalendar tax year if it will result in a deferral of income of three months or less. For example, if a fiscal year ending September 30 is requested, this will generally be allowed, since it results in a three-month deferral of income when compared to the normal calendar tax year. Use of this three-month deferral exception comes at a price: Your LLC will have to make an extra tax payment to the IRS each year in an amount equal to the estimated deferral of tax that results from the noncalendar year. You'll have to pay tax on deferred LLC income at the members' highest individual tax rate plus one percentage point. (See Sections 444 and 7519 of the Internal Revenue Code.) You must also file an IRS Form 8752, *Required Payment or Refund under Section 7519,* available at the IRS website, www.irs.gov.

For further information on these technical tax year rules, check with your accountant.

> **CAUTION**
>
> **The IRS must approve your change of tax year.** If your LLC has already adopted a tax year, and now wants to change it, you'll need IRS approval to make the change. Normally, the IRS will not approve a change of tax year unless you can show a substantial business purpose. (For example, you are converting from a calendar tax year to a tax year that meets the natural business year of your LLC.) However, there's an exception to this rule: An LLC can change its tax year without IRS approval if it adopts the tax year used by the members who hold a majority interest or by all the principal members (holders of 5% or more of the LLC's interests). To seek IRS approval for a change of tax year, the LLC must file IRS Form 1128, *Application to Adopt, Change, or Retain a Tax Year,* available at the IRS website, www.irs.gov.

CD-ROM

Below is a sample of the resolution you can use to approve the selection of a tax year for the LLC. You'll find this resolution on the CD-ROM and as a tearout form in Appendix C. (See Appendix A for information on selecting and using the CD-ROM files.) Complete the resolution using special instruction below.

Note that the language of this resolution assumes that the LLC has consulted the LLC's accountant prior to making this decision.

Special Instruction

❶ If the LLC qualifies for a noncalendar tax year, it need not choose the last day of whatever month it picks to end its tax year—it may choose to have its tax year end on the same day each year, such as the last Friday of June. A tax year of this sort is called a 52-53 week tax year.

Approval of LLC Tax Year

After discussion and a report from the treasurer, which included advice obtained from the LLC's accountant, it was resolved that the tax year of the LLC will end on _[ending date, such as "December 31" or the last day of another month if the LLC qualifies for a noncalendar tax year]_ ❶ of each year. The treasurer was appointed to file the necessary tax forms on behalf of the LLC to adopt or change the tax year of the LLC with the IRS [add, if applicable, "and the appropriate state tax agency"].

Resolutions to Amend the LLC Articles and Operating Agreement

Many, if not most, LLCs eventually amend their articles of organization (referred to as a "certificate of formation" or a "certificate of organization" in some states) and their operating agreement. To do so, the LLC must follow rules contained in its state's LLC laws.

Get Everyone's Approval for Amendments

Under most state laws, members must approve amendments to the LLC articles or to the LLC operating agreement by either unanimous or majority approval. This can be arrived at by a vote or by written consent. Even if your state law allows less-than-unanimous consent, amendments to the articles or the operating agreement are important enough to warrant discussion and approval by all LLC members. Check your operating agreement to find out the requirements for amending the articles or agreement; if your operating agreement doesn't address the issue, you can find your state's rules in Appendix B, under the heading "Amendments."

In a manager-managed LLC, the managers normally need not approve the amendments (except in a few states). As a practical matter, however, it is usually the managers who decide on an amendment to the articles or operating agreement, then propose it to the members for approval.

How to Select and Use LLC Resolutions

- Scan the table of contents at the beginning of the chapter to find the right resolutions.
- When you find one you need, read the background material that precedes the resolution.
- Follow the instructions included with the sample resolution and complete a draft of the resolution on your computer. If you need guidance on selecting and using the computer disk files, see Appendix A. (You'll have to fill in the tearout resolution included in Appendix C if you don't use a computer.)
- Complete any needed attachment forms.
- If a resolution involves complex issues that will benefit from expert analysis, have your legal or tax adviser review your paperwork and conclusions.
- Prepare meeting minutes or written consent forms as explained in Chapters 5–7, and insert the completed resolution in the appropriate form.
- Have the LLC secretary sign the printed minutes or have members and/or managers sign the written consent forms. Then place the signed forms, together with any attachments, in your LLC records binder.

Decide Whether You Need to Amend Your Articles or Your Operating Agreement

If you want to add provisions to your founding documents, state law may actually allow you to choose between placing them in your articles or your operating agreement. When you have this choice, it is best to add new provisions to your operating agreement rather than to your articles. That's because the operating agreement can be amended more easily and inexpensively than articles. Amendments to articles must be filed with your state's LLC filing office for a fee.

EXAMPLE:

The current members of Della Frattoria Wood-Fired Bread, LLC, wish to impose a requirement that all members be at least 18 years of age. In their state, member qualifications don't have to be placed in the articles. The members decide to amend the operating agreement to add this requirement.

To find out what provisions must be included in your articles of organization, take a look at your state's business or LLC law (you can find a citation to the law and instructions for searching it online in Appendix B). Typically, one section of the law lists the provisions that *must* be included in articles. Usually the next section lists provisions that *may* be placed in articles. These optional article provisions may be placed in either your articles or your operating agreement.

Amending Articles of Organization

From time to time, LLCs may need to amend their original articles of organization to add, change, or delete provisions. Like the original articles, amendments to the articles must be filed with the state LLC filing office, accompanied by a filing fee. (Appendix B lists each state's LLC filing office address and telephone number.)

LLCs often amend their articles because they wish to:

- change the structure of the LLC from member-management to manager-management or vice versa
- authorize special classes of membership, such as nonvoting memberships
- change the formal name of the LLC
- add additional provisions to the articles, such as limitations on the personal liability of members and managers officers, or
- delete provisions that the LLC wishes to repeal or that list outdated information. For example, an LLC may want to delete a provision that specifies the LLC will dissolve on a specified future date (no longer required under most LLC statutes).

An Easier Way to Change an LLC's Name

If you're planning to change your LLC's name—either to better identify your business or to benefit from a name that has become associated with your LLC's products or services—there's an easier way to change the name than amending your articles.

In most states, an LLC wishing to do business under a name different from that specified in the articles may file a fictitious or assumed business name statement with the state LLC filing office or local county clerk's office. This simple procedure allows the LLC to use the new name locally without having to file a formal amendment to its articles. (Read more about adopting an assumed or fictitious LLC name in Chapter 8.)

You Can't Change Certain Article Provisions

In most states, you can delete—but cannot change—article provisions that specify the initial agent, initial registered office, or initial members or managers of the LLC. The reason is simple: These people always remain the initial agent, members, or managers, and this address remains the initial registered office. You may delete any reference to them—for example, to take out the reference to your first registered agent, who has been replaced. You can't, however, specify other people or other office locations as the initial agent, members, managers, or registered office.

To notify the state of any change in your registered agent or registered office, file a statement of change of agent or registered address with the state LLC filing office. If you request it, most state LLC offices provide a form for this purpose.

In a member-managed LLC, typically one or more members suggest a change to the articles, then ask the LLC secretary to call a membership meeting or circulate written consent forms to obtain membership approval of the amendment. In a manager-managed LLC, typically the managers first agree on the language of proposed amendments, then ask the members to approve the amendments. Amendments to articles almost always have to be approved by all or a majority of the members. (See the "Amendments" section for your state in Appendix B.)

TIP

Always give notice of a meeting to amend the articles. You will want to give all members ample notice of a meeting to amend the LLC articles, even if this isn't required under state law or your operating agreement. Disclose in the notice that the upcoming meeting is being held to amend the articles of the LLC, and include a copy of the proposed amendment along with the notice.

It's easy to prepare a resolution to amend your articles for membership approval, which you'll then insert in your minutes or written consent forms. The resolution can show approval of:

- only the specific language that you wish to change, or
- a restatement of your entire articles—which, of course, includes any changes you are making.

Specific Amendment to Articles Resolution

CD-ROM

Below is a sample of the resolution you can use to approve a specific change to your articles (rather than to approve completely restated articles as explained later). You'll find this resolution on the CD-ROM and as a tearout form in Appendix C. (See Appendix A for information on selecting and using the CD-ROM files.) Complete the resolution according to the special instructions below.

Because you are not changing the entire text of your articles, you should attach a copy of the approved resolution with the new articles language to the current articles in your LLC records binder.

Approval of Amendment to Articles of Organization ❶

RESOLVED, that Article __[number or letter of article that is being amended, added, or deleted]__ of the articles of organization of this LLC be __["amended to read," "added," or "deleted"]__ as follows: __[insert the language of the changed or new article, or show a struck-through version of the wording to be deleted]__ . ❷

Special Instructions

❶ If your organizing document goes under another name, such as "certificate of organization" or "certificate of formation," change the references in the resolution to correspond to the name of your organizational document.

❷ Here are a few examples of ways to use this resolution:

EXAMPLE 1 (changing the LLC name):

"RESOLVED, that Article ONE of the articles of organization be amended to read as follows: The name of this LLC is Big Wheels, LLC."

EXAMPLE 2 (changing from member-management to manager-management):

"RESOLVED, that Article TWO of the articles of organization be amended to read as follows: Management of the LLC shall vest exclusively in one or more managers. The initial manager shall be: __[name and address of first manager]__ ."

EXAMPLE 3 (adding a new article):

"RESOLVED, that Article TEN of the articles of organization be added as follows: One of the LLC managers shall be elected annually by the Hingham Investment Group, Ltd., with the initial election date to be determined by majority vote of the current LLC managers."

EXAMPLE 4 (deleting a limitation on the duration of the LLC that's no longer required to be included in articles under state law):

"RESOLVED, that Article B of the articles of organization be deleted as follows: ~~The duration of this LLC shall be thirty years from the date of filing of these articles of organization.~~"

Amendment by Restatement of Articles Resolution

Members sometimes decide to approve a restatement of the entire articles, which contains all old and new provisions (minus any deletions).

CD-ROM

Below is a sample of the resolution you can use to approve a restatement of your articles. You'll find this resolution on the CD-ROM and as a tearout form in Appendix C. (See Appendix A for information on selecting and using the CD-ROM files.) Complete the resolution according to the special instruction below.

Special Instruction

❶ If your organizing document goes under another name, such as "certificate of organization" or "certificate of formation," change the references in the resolution to correspond to the name of your organizational document.

Approval of Restatement of Articles of Organization ❶

RESOLVED, that the articles of organization be amended and restated to read in full as follows:

   [insert the entire text of your articles, including any new or changed provisions and
minus any provisions that are being deleted]   .

File Amendment of Articles With State LLC Filing Office

After obtaining the approval of your members to an amendment resolution, you'll need to file an Amendment of Articles form with your state's LLC filing office. A sample form should be available from the LLC filing office in your state. (A list of LLC filing office addresses and phone numbers, along with website addresses, can be found in Appendix B.) Typically, the amendment form is referred to as an Amendment of Articles or Amendment of Certificate form. You will probably have to pay a small fee to file the form.

The sample form below contains the basic information normally required in an amendment of articles. It provides space for the text of the amended or restated articles and information on how, when, and by whom the amendment was approved.

After filing your amendment form with your state's LLC filing office, remember to place a copy in your LLC records binder. Also include a copy of the minutes of a membership meeting or the written consent of members used to obtain approval of your amendment resolution.

CD-ROM

The following sample amendment form is included as a guide, but you should use the form provided by your state's LLC filing office instead, if one is available. You'll find this form on the CD-ROM and as a tearout form in Appendix C. (See Appendix A for information on selecting and using the CD-ROM files.)

Amendment of Articles Form

To: [name and address of state LLC filing office]

Articles of Amendment

of

_____ [name of LLC]_____

One: The name of the LLC is _____ [name of LLC] _____ .

Two: The following amendment to the articles of organization was approved by the members on

[date of LLC meeting or written consent] :

____ [insert language of amendment or full restatement of articles here] _____

_____

_____

_____

_____ .

Three: The number of members required to approve the amendment was _[insert the membership vote required for approval, usually "all members"]_ , and the number of members that voted to approve the amendment was _[number of members (or percentage of membership interests) voting in favor of the amendment, again, usually "all members"]_ .

Date: _____

By:

_____ [signature of president] _____

_____ [typed name] _____ , President

_____ [signature of secretary] _____

_____ [typed name] _____ , Secretary

Amending the LLC Operating Agreement

LLCs sometimes wish to add, delete, or change provisions in their operating agreement. Typically, all or a majority of members must approve such an amendment. (See the "Amendments" heading for your state in Appendix B). Unlike articles amendments, amendments to the LLC operating agreement do not need to be filed with the state's LLC filing office.

You may wish to amend your existing operating agreement to accomplish one or more of the following:

- After the admission of a new member, to show the capital, profits, and voting interests of the new member, as well as the changes in the existing members' interests brought about by the new member's admission.

- After the departure of a member, to show the recomputed capital, profits, and voting interests of the remaining members.

- To add comprehensive buy-sell provisions that specify how, when, and for how much a member may transfer a membership interest, and to control transfers of a membership interest by a member to family, heirs, or creditors.

- To change the date, time, or place of the annual or other regular members' or managers' meetings.

- To specify special notice, call, or voting rules for meetings of members or managers. For example, the members may wish to require written notice well in advance of all membership meetings, even if not required under state law.

- To change the authorized number of managers of the LLC (in a manager-managed LLC).

- To change the duties and responsibilities of one or more LLC officers.

In a member-managed LLC, one or more members typically ask the LLC secretary to arrange a members' meeting to discuss a proposed amendment to the operating agreement. If the wording of the amendment has already been worked out, and if the matter is one all members will readily agree to, the member may, instead, ask the secretary to circulate written consents to obtain members' approval to the proposed amendment. In a manager-managed LLC, one or more managers propose the amendment to the operating agreement. After the wording is worked out by the managers, the amendment is proposed at a meeting of members for full membership approval or is circulated to all members as part of a written consent.

TIP

Always provide notice of a meeting to amend the operating agreement. If you hold a membership meeting to approve an amendment to your LLC operating agreement, you should provide written notice of the meetings well in advance to all members. The notice should state that the meeting is being held to amend the operating agreement of the LLC. Also, include a copy of the proposed amendment with the notice. State law and your operating agreement may not require this much preliminary planning, but an operating agreement change warrants this extra measure of premeeting formality.

Resolution to Amend LLC Operating Agreement

CD-ROM

Below is a sample of the resolution you can use to approve an amendment to your LLC operating agreement. You'll find this resolution on the CD-ROM and as a tearout form in Appendix C. (See Appendix A for information on selecting and using the CD-ROM files.) Complete the resolution according to the special instruction below.

Amendment of LLC Operating Agreement

RESOLVED, that ___[number and/or letter designation of amended operating agreement provision]___ of the operating agreement of the LLC is ___["added," "amended" or "deleted"]___ as follows:

___[insert language of new or changed operating agreement provision or show a struck-through version of wording to be deleted]___.❶

Special Instruction

❶ Here are examples of a completed resolution:

EXAMPLE 1:

RESOLVED, that Article TWELVE of the operating agreement of the LLC is added as follows: "Article TWELVE: Nontransferability of Shares. All shares of this LLC are nontransferable, except with the written approval of all members."

EXAMPLE 2:

RESOLVED, that Article II, Section A (3), of the operating agreement of the LLC is amended as follows:

"Article II: Meetings of LLC Managers, Section A (3): The managers of this LLC must meet annually on the first Wednesday of June of each year, and also on the same day as, and immediately following, the annual members' meeting required under other provisions of this operating agreement."

💡 **TIP**

Make sure to update your operating agreement on file with the LLC. An operating agreement is a contract among your LLC members. Therefore, you will want to make sure that the agreement on file with the LLC reflects the changes approved by resolution or written consent of the members.

There are two ways to do this: First, you can retype the entire operating agreement (including the approved changes), then have it signed by all current members (and their spouses, if spouses signed your original agreement). A second way is to attach the resolution or written consent that contains the new language to the appropriate section of your current operating agreement, and to have all members initial or sign the resolution to show their approval (spouses should also sign or initial the attached resolution or written consent if they signed the original agreement).

LLC Membership Resolutions

This chapter covers LLC resolutions that approve changes in the rights and interests of members, plus other items of business that directly affect LLC members. For example, during the life of an LLC, a new member might be admitted. Or, one or more members might withdraw or sell their membership interests (whether to insiders or outsiders). In other membership matters, the LLC might approve distributions of profits to members or ask for additional capital contributions to fund ongoing LLC operations. These membership matters are discussed here, along with their legal and tax consequences.

All Members Should Approve Membership Resolutions

The LLC resolutions contained in this chapter should be approved by LLC members (as well as by managers in a manager-managed LLC). I recommend that all members approve these resolutions, not just a majority of members or another percentage specified in your LLC operating agreement. Although unanimous approval is not always legally necessary, it is the most practical choice for these important membership decisions. The surest way to avoid future disputes within the membership ranks, particularly when approving resolutions that affect one or more members' shares of LLC capital or profits, is to come up with a decision that all members can support.

How to Select and Use LLC Resolutions

- Scan the table of contents at the beginning of the chapter to find the right resolution for the matter at hand.

- When you find one you need, read the background material that precedes the resolution.

- Follow the instructions included with the sample resolution to complete a draft of the resolution on your computer. If you need guidance on selecting and using the computer disk files, see Appendix A. (You'll have to fill in the tearout resolution included in Appendix C if you don't use a computer.)

- Complete any needed attachment forms.

- If a resolution involves complex issues that will benefit from expert analysis, have your legal or tax adviser review your paperwork and conclusions.

- Prepare meeting minutes or written consent forms as explained in Chapters 5–7, and insert the completed resolution into the appropriate form.

- Have the LLC secretary sign the printed minutes, or have members and/or managers sign the written consent forms and waivers. Then place the signed forms, together with any attachments, in your LLC records binder.

SEE AN EXPERT

Check tax issues with a professional. This chapter doesn't deal with the more complex tax issues that inevitably arise in connection with the membership transactions discussed below, such as the "inside basis" of assets contributed to an LLC (the LLC's basis in its assets, as opposed to a member's individual basis in the member's LLC interest), as well as tax elections that can be made to change how this basis is computed. Extra tax complexities also surround the purchase and sale of a member's interest in the LLC if the member contributed property for that interest. And there can be tax consequences when you want to reward an active member or manager with an increase in his or her LLC ownership share. In short, you should check the full tax consequences of any of the transactions covered in this chapter before approving and implementing them.

Distributions of LLC Profits to Members

People invest and work in LLCs to receive a share of their profits. Sure, when LLC cash is short, profits are often kept and used in the business. But most LLC owners don't wait too long before paying themselves a fair share of the revenue earned by the LLC. The members and/or managers of an LLC should consider several factors before deciding whether to pay out distributions of profits—including the legal rules for when an LLC can pay distributions and the tax ramifications of such distributions.

Tax Effects of LLC Distributions

At the end of the LLC's tax year, profits (or losses) are automatically allocated to LLC members in proportion to each member's "distributive share," or "profits (and losses) interest," in the LLC. The distributive share for each member should be defined in your operating agreement—it simply means the percentage of profits and losses to be allocated to each member. Normally, a member's distributive share of profits and distributive share of losses is the same—that is, a member

with a 10% distributive share is allocated 10% of the LLC's profits and 10% of its losses. But this is not always so. For example, your operating agreement may say that a particular member's distributive share is set at 15% of the profits and 20% of the losses.

 CROSS REFERENCE

How to measure membership interests.
There are several ways an LLC can calculate a member's ownership. A member's capital interest is the capital he or she has contributed as a percentage of the total contributions by all members, less any distributions from the LLC to the member. A profits interest is the right to receive a certain percentage of LLC earnings—it often tracks the member's capital interest. A capital and profits interest is the average of the member's capital interest and profits interest. For more on these methods, see "Measuring Membership Interests in the LLC," in Chapter 3, Step 3.

At the end of the tax year, the IRS treats profits as income to the LLC members (not to the LLC itself), whether the distributions are actually paid or not. As profits are allocated, they are taxed to the individual members.

EXAMPLE:

Ted's LLC has net profits of $20,000 at the end of its tax year on November 30, 2007. Ted has a 50% capital interest in the LLC, and his distributive share is 50% of LLC profits and losses. Half the profits— $10,000—are allocated to him at the end of the LLC tax year, although these funds are not distributed. (He doesn't get a $10,000 check from the LLC.) On his 2007 individual tax return, Ted reports and pays taxes on the $10,000 of allocated profits at his individual tax rate.

Allocating Losses to LLC Members

Planning to divide profits is a pleasant prospect, but you also have to consider how you will share the losses. In the startup phase of an LLC, the business may generate losses—that is, business expenses may exceed profits.

This is not always a bad thing, however. Unlike a corporation, the LLC can pass businesses losses through the business onto the individual tax returns of the owners, where these losses can be used to offset their other income, whether from a salaried day job or an investment portfolio. (Your tax adviser can tell you about special loss rules that limit how business losses can be used to reduce active or passive income.)

In contrast, business losses are "locked into" a corporation. Even though they may be carried back and forward (within limits) to offset corporate income in earlier or later corporate tax years, the shareholders can't use corporate losses to offset income on their individual income tax returns. (S corporations are an exception to this rule: An S corporation is a pass-through tax entity, so shareholders can use losses to offset other personal income. However, special rules restrict how much income a shareholder can reduce in this way.)

In an LLC, an owner can also use entity-level debt (for example, a loan taken out on property that the LLC owns) to increase the owner's basis in his or her LLC interest.

EXAMPLE: Big Plans, LLC is a property development LLC owned by Sam and Zena, who each contributed $50,000 to start it. Big Plans buys a $500,000 property for $100,000 down (the total amount of cash paid in by the two members) and a $400,000 mortgage. After the sale, each owner has a $250,000 basis in his or her LLC interest ($50,000 initial basis plus $200,000, which is each owner's ½ share of the $400,000 entity-level debt).

Because of property development costs (including mortgage payments), the LLC reports a loss of $140,000 in its first year. Each member shares 50/50 in profits and losses, so each is allocated a $70,000 loss. Because each member has $250,000 of basis, each can use the entire amount of the loss on his or her individual tax return to offset other income (assuming other technical tax rules are met). The allocation of this loss to each owner reduces each owner's basis to $180,000 ($250,000 minus $70,000).

Capital Accounts vs. Tax Basis

A member's capital account in the LLC and a member's tax basis in his or her share of the LLC are two ways of measuring the value of ownership. However, they are calculated differently and used for different purposes. It's important to understand the distinction as you decide whether to take any action that might affect a member's ownership share, such as distributing profits or admitting a new member.

- A member's **capital account** shows, in bookkeeping terms, the book value of the member's ownership interest in the LLC—the amount the member would expect to be paid if the company were liquidated and its assets divided between the members at their book value.

- A member's **tax basis** is the tax value or "basis" of what he or she has paid into the LLC, for purposes of computing any capital gains tax owed when the member sells his or her share of the company. The higher a member's basis, the lower the taxes the member will owe; a lower basis means higher taxes. Basis also limits how much of the LLC's allocated losses a member can use to offset other income on his or her tax return; a member can deduct losses only up to the amount of his or her tax basis in the LLC.

When a member contributes cash or property to the LLC, his or her capital account is credited with the dollar amount or fair market value of the contribution. When profits are allocated to the member at the end of the LLC's tax year, his or her capital account balance goes up (because the business owes the member money). As profits are distributed, the member's capital account balance goes back down (to show that the business no longer owes this money). These adjustments are similar to the adjustments made to the member's tax basis, which also goes up when profits are allocated and goes back down when profits are distributed.

Your tax adviser can help you calculate the value of each member's capital account and tax basis in the LLC—and explain how distributing profits, asking for additional contributions, or admitting new members will affect these numbers.

When profits are allocated to a member, they also increase the member's basis in his or her membership interest. (See "Capital Accounts vs. Tax Basis," above). Conversely, an allocation of LLC losses to a member decreases the member's basis in the membership interest, until the basis is reduced to zero. If allocated profits did not increase a member's tax basis, the member would pay a double tax on these profits—once when they were allocated, and again (as capital gains tax) when the member sold his or her interest in the LLC.

When previously allocated LLC profits are actually distributed to a member, they are not taxed again to the member—they were already taxed when they were allocated to the member. But the distribution does affect a member's basis, as follows: When LLC profits are actually distributed, a member decreases his or her basis by the amount of cash distributed. Only if the amount distributed exceeds a member's basis is a tax due (on the amount by which the distributed profits exceed the member's basis). This downward adjustment when profits are distributed offsets the upward adjustment that was made when profits were allocated to the member, and puts the member's basis back where it started before the distributed profits were earned by the LLC.

Legal Rules for LLC Distributions of Profits

You also have to consider your state's laws when deciding whether to distribute profits. State law may regulate when and how profits can be paid.

When Distributions Can Legally Be Made

Many states regulate when an LLC can legally distribute profits to members. Generally, a distribution of profits will be valid if, after the distribution, both of the following are true:

1. The LLC remains solvent—that is, the LLC will be able to pay its bills as they become due in the normal course of business, and

2. LLC assets equal or exceed its liabilities (or conform to a higher asset-to-liability ratio set out in a state statute).

Members or managers can rely on the LLC's financial statements, such as a balance sheet, in deciding whether a distribution meets these standards. (Some states allow an LLC to revalue its assets and liabilities prior to a distribution, as long as it discloses this fact to members.) Members or managers should also be allowed to base their decision to distribute profits on financial information from reliable sources, such as the LLC's treasurer or tax adviser.

CAUTION

You could be on the hook for invalid distributions. Members or managers who approve a distribution in violation of the statutory standard can be held personally liable for the amount of the invalid distribution.

Some states have no statutory standards for paying out profits. In these states, a state court, if faced with a legal challenge to a distribution brought by a disgruntled member or creditor, will probably apply standards similar to those listed above.

TIP

Check your articles and your operating agreement for rules on distributions. Check your articles and operating agreement to see if any rules are set out for when and how distributions may be made. If you need more information, check your state LLC act. (See Chapter 1.)

How Distributions Must Be Made

Most states allow LLCs to decide how profits should be distributed by setting out the rules in their operating agreement. Generally, unless the LLC operating agreement provides for special allocations of profits and losses, each member is given a share of profits and losses (a distributive share) according to the member's capital interest with the LLC (but check your operating agreement to be sure). In the absence of a provision in the operating agreement, some states require distributions to be allocated in proportion to members' profit-sharing interests in the LLC. Here's an example.

Oregon LLC Act, Section 63.195
[...]
If neither the articles of organization nor any operating agreement provides for [... allocations of LLC distributions of cash or assets prior to LLC dissolution], such distributions shall be allocated among the members in proportion to their right to share in the profits of the limited liability company.

Other states require LLCs to allocate distributions of profits in proportion to the members' capital account balances.

Ohio LLC Act, Section 1705.11

[...]

Unless otherwise provided in the operating agreement, distributions that are made shall be made to the members in proportion to the value as stated in the records of the company [...] of the contributions made by each member to the extent the contributions have been received by the company and have not been returned.

State law typically requires distributions of profits to be made proportionately to all LLC members (according to their distributive shares). In other words, the LLC can't give one member his share of the profits in one distribution, and a second member her share in another. Members also cannot be forced to accept distributions from the LLC that are disproportionate to their distributive shares, in most states.

LLCs typically distribute profits in cash, not LLC property. In fact, many states prohibit members from demanding distributions in property. Likewise, members usually do not have to accept property distributions from the LLC. This is because members don't have to accept LLC distributions that are disproportionate to their distributive shares. The nature of property distributions would usually require distributions that are disproportionate to members' shares because the value of property parceled out to members rarely matches their exact distributive percentage. Here's a typical statute that embodies these requirements.

Ohio LLC Act, Section 1705.13

Except as provided in writing in the operating agreement and regardless of the nature of his contribution, a member has no right to demand and receive any distribution from a limited liability company in any form other than cash. Except as provided in writing in the operating agreement, a member may not be compelled to accept a distribution of any asset in kind from a limited liability company if the percentage of the asset distributed to him is greater or less than the percentage in which he shares in distributions from the company.

Resolution to Approve LLC Distribution of Profits

State laws don't generally require LLC members or managers to formally approve a resolution to distribute profits. A simple verbal consensus to do so is usually sufficient. It's up to you to decide when it makes sense to prepare and approve a formal LLC resolution. For smaller LLCs with plenty of cash, it may not be necessary to prepare this paperwork. But if the LLC is short of funds and a distribution may affect LLC performance, or if all members are not in agreement on the amount or other terms of distribution, preparing and approving a formal resolution can help show that the distribution was lawfully made (according to the standards discussed above). For larger LLCs, it usually makes sense to formally approve distributions by resolution to avoid controversies later.

Of course, if the LLC is making a cash distribution that all members readily agree to, there is little likelihood of a legal challenge to the distribution, unless the LLC is in debt and an unpaid creditor makes a fuss. (In that case, you will want to be sure your LLC can continue to pay off the debt after the distribution.) A formal resolution, in this case, can document that the LLC is able to afford the payout of cash and that a sufficient number of members voted to approve it.

The following resolution can be used to approve a management decision to make a distribution of LLC profits to members.

CD-ROM

Complete the resolution according to the special instructions below. You'll find this resolution on the CD-ROM and as a tearout form in Appendix C. (See Appendix A for information on selecting and using the CD-ROM files.)

Approval of LLC Distribution

The LLC resolves that the LLC will make the following distribution of profits of the LLC to the following members: ❶

Name of Member	Amount ❷
_____	$_____
_____	$_____
_____	$_____
_____	$_____
_____	$_____

It was announced that the above distribution of LLC profits was in accordance with the requirements for the allocation of distributions to members as set out in the LLC operating agreement, or as required under state law. The treasurer presented a current balance sheet of the LLC at the meeting for review by the attendees, and announced that the LLC's tax adviser had been consulted. It was agreed that, after giving effect to the distribution, the LLC would continue to be able to pay its obligations as they become due in the normal course of its operations, and that the LLC would meet any applicable financial and legal tests under state law for making distributions to members. The treasurer was instructed to attach a copy of the balance sheet to this resolution for inclusion in the LLC's records binder. ❸

The treasurer of the LLC is instructed to prepare and deliver or mail a check drawn on the LLC's account in the appropriate amount to each member entitled to the distribution no later than   [date of distribution payment] . ❹

Special Instructions

❶ Check your operating agreement to see how many managers or members are required to approve distributions to members. I suggest that you always obtain full membership approval for distributions. For example, some members with sufficient personal cash reserves may object to the distribution, preferring that money be kept in the business to help the LLC grow. It's best to deal with these objections before, not after, making a distribution.

❷ Insert the name of each member and the amount of cash distribution to be made to each. You can adapt this resolution to show the distribution of LLC assets to members, but such property distributions are less common and may invoke special state law requirements, as discussed above.

❸ This resolution states that the LLC members have consulted a current balance sheet presented by the treasurer prior to approving a distribution, and that a copy of the balance sheet was attached to the resolution. This precaution is recommended to show that members had good reason to conclude that the LLC would be solvent after the distribution. It also states that the treasurer consulted a tax adviser to make sure the distribution makes sense. You can delete or change these assertions as you see fit. Again, if you are making a cash distribution that all members readily agree to, there is little likelihood of a legal challenge to the distribution unless your LLC is in debt.

❹ The distribution date should be shortly after the date of the LLC decision, usually within one or two weeks. If you wait too long—say, more than one month—the financial condition of your LLC may change and you will need to analyze whether your LLC still meets the applicable financial tests for making the payout.

Additional Capital Contributions by Members

During the life of an LLC, there may be times when cash runs low and the LLC needs to seek additional operating funds from its existing members. One way to do this is by asking members to make loans to the LLC (covered in Chapter 13). Another way is to ask members to make additional capital contributions. If the LLC is on track to be successful over the long term, and added funds would benefit the LLC, some or all members may agree to pay additional cash into the LLC as capital.

Tax Considerations

Making a capital investment in an LLC is usually a tax-free transaction—the members do not owe any taxes on the membership interests they receive, nor does the LLC pay any taxes on the cash or property it accepts in exchange. Additional capital contributions simply increase each contributing member's capital account and tax basis in his or her membership interests. (See "Distributions of LLC Profits to Members," above, for a discussion of basis.) In effect, the tax effects of paying capital into an LLC are deferred until a later time, when the member's basis in his or her LLC interest is used to determine the amount of taxes the member owes when the interest is sold or the LLC is liquidated.

EXAMPLE 1:

Dianne capitalizes her one-person advertising consulting LLC with $50,000 in cash. Her initial $50,000 basis is adjusted up and down over the years as she contributes money to, and receives distributions from, the LLC. When she decides to sell her LLC seven years later, her basis is $40,000. She sells the LLC for $150,000. Her taxable profit on the sale is $110,000: $150,000 minus her $40,000 tax basis.

EXAMPLE 2:

Barbara is a member and vice president of Biz Wiz, a small member-managed LLC. As part of its formation, Barbara's LLC issues her a 30% capital (membership) interest in exchange for her cash payment of $70,000, plus the patent she owns for "Biz Wiz" software. Barbara's $30,000 basis in her patent plus her cash payment of $70,000 are added to make up her starting basis of $100,000 in her LLC membership.

When Barbara leaves the company several years later, her LLC basis is $150,000, reflecting her share of LLC liabilities as well as allocations of profits made to her during the LLC's prior tax years. The LLC has done well, and expects to do better, so the remaining LLC members value Barbara's interest at $200,000 and pay her this amount. Barbara recognizes a taxable gain of $50,000 on her sale of her LLC interest—the $200,000 sales price minus her basis of $150,000.

You can expect to pay a tax on any gain you make when you sell your ownership interest. In most cases, your profit should be eligible for capital gains tax rates, which are often lower than ordinary individual income rates paid by the owners. Therefore, it's almost always an advantage to have the profit from a sale of an ownership interest taxed at capital gains rates.

EXAMPLE:

Let's revisit Barbara, and assume her sale of her membership interest is eligible for long-term capital gains treatment (at a 15% capital gains tax rate), rather than ordinary income tax treatment. Had Barbara's sale not qualified for capital gains tax rates, she would have been taxed on the sale proceeds at a 33% rate—her personal income tax bracket.

The tax effects of selling or liquidating an interest are discussed more in "Admitting LLC Members" and "Withdrawal of LLC Members," below.

REMINDER

Taxes also result from distributions of members' distributive shares. Members may owe taxes when they receive profits from their LLC in the form of distributions. The tax effects of distributions of profits and losses are covered in "Distributions of LLC Profits to Members," above.

Legal Considerations

On the legal side, LLCs are generally free to ask for additional capital as needed, unless the LLC articles or operating agreement impose special requirements. For example, before a request for additional capital can be made, an LLC's operating agreement might require the unanimous or majority vote of members, or the specific approval of any members who won't make additional contributions (because contributions by the other members will lower noncontributing members' percentages of capital interest in the LLC, as discussed below). Before asking members to contribute additional capital, check your operating agreement to make sure it allows the LLC to make the request, and to see if any special voting or other requirements apply.

Commonly, members are asked to make capital contributions in proportion to their current capital interests (as shown by their capital account balances). Doing this maintains the status quo of the LLC, because each member's ownership percentage remains the same. But if your LLC needs cash, and only some members can afford to give it, you may want to go ahead and accept the capital contributions of the members who can afford to make them. This will diminish the relative capital percentage of the noncontributing members, but that may be acceptable to them. After all, the added funds will benefit the LLC, and they want the business to succeed as long as they hold an interest in it.

Of course, if a noncontributing member sees the request for additional capital as a scheme for the cash-rich members to increase their relative capital interests, he or she may object. The best way to handle scenarios of this sort is to discuss the reasons for the capital request with the entire membership, and to allow additional contributions only if all members agree. If you can convince all members—including those who cannot afford to make additional cash contributions—that there is a valid and pressing need for additional LLC capital, they probably will approve the pay-in by the other members, despite the fact that their relative capital and profit-sharing interests in the LLC will be diminished afterwards.

TIP

Update your operating agreement, if necessary. The relative capital contributions (or capital account balances) of your members may change if members contribute additional capital disproportionately, or some contribute and some don't. This may also change the voting and profit-and-loss-sharing ratios in your operating agreement. If out-of-date profit-and-loss-sharing ratios are hardwired into your agreement, you will want to change it. Also, if your agreement includes a schedule of capital contributions, you will want to update it to show the additional capital contributions. For these reasons, you should always review your agreement and make any necessary changes after you get extra capital from your members. (See Chapter 10 for a resolution to use to approve amendments to your operating agreement.)

Should You Pay Interest on Additional Capital Obtained From Members?

One way to reward members who make additional capital contributions to the LLC is to have the LLC pay interest on the contributed capital. This is particularly true if members are already receiving interest payments for their initial capital contributions to the LLC. If the LLC decides to pay interest on additional capital contributions made by members, make sure your operating agreement allows this; many agreements say that interest cannot be paid on contributed capital. If your agreement prohibits interest payments, you will need to amend it to allow the LLC to pay interest on capital. (See "Resolution to Amend LLC Operating Agreement" in Chapter 10.)

From a tax standpoint, if interest payments to members are not dependent on profits (usually they are not), they are treated as a "guaranteed payment" by the LLC. (For a discussion of guaranteed payments vs. distributive share payments, see "Tax Treatment of Salaries Paid to Members" in Chapter 12.) This means that the LLC can deduct or capitalize the payments, and each member reports the interest as income on his or her tax return. (A "capitalized" payment is put on the balance sheet as an asset cost. This reduces taxes later when LLC assets or interests are sold.) If the interest is payable to members only if profits of the LLC are sufficient that year, interest payments are treated as allocations and distributions of a member's distributive share of profits.

Resolution to Approve Additional Capital Contributions by Members

The following resolution can be used to approve additional contributions of capital by members.

CD-ROM

Complete the resolution following the special instructions below. You'll find this resolution on the CD-ROM and as a tearout form in Appendix C. (See Appendix A for information on selecting and using the CD-ROM files.)

Special Instructions

❶ Be sure to follow any voting requirements in your operating agreement for approval of additional capital contributions. I recommend that all members approve additional capital contributions, even if a smaller number is allowed under your operating agreement.

❷ List the names of members and their additional capital contributions. Usually cash contributions will be made, but, if appropriate, the fair market value of property contributions can be shown instead.

❸ If you wish to pay interest to members on their additional capital contributions, check this box and complete this paragraph. Specify the annual interest rate and show the terms for payment of the interest. For example, if the interest will be dependent on sufficient LLC profits, you can provide: "Interest is payable within one month following the close of each tax year of the LLC only if LLC profits are sufficient to pay the interest. If LLC profits are not sufficient in a given year, the interest will not be payable for that year." Or, if interest is guaranteed, regardless of LLC profits: "Interest payments will be paid yearly, within one month of the close of the LLC tax year."

Approval of Additional Contributions of Capital by Members

It was agreed that the following members will make the following contributions of capital to the LLC, on or by ___[date for payment]___ : ❶

Name of Member	Amount ❷
_____	$_____
_____	$_____
_____	$_____
_____	$_____
_____	$_____

☐ It was agreed that the operating agreement of the LLC will be amended, if necessary, to reflect the capital, profits, voting, and other interests of all members of the LLC as a result of the making of the above capital contributions.

☐ It was agreed that the LLC will pay interest at the rate of ___% per year on the above capital contributions, subject to the following terms: ___[specify time for payments and whether interest payments are dependent on sufficient LLC profits]___ . ❸

Admitting LLC Members

The admission of a new member is a big change in the life of an LLC. An LLC may need a new member's additional capital investment to fund future growth, or perhaps a relative or friend of a current member has asked to be let in. You may also have a new member if a current member decides to sell his or her interest to another person, and the remaining members are asked to approve the new member. If all current members agree that the new person would get along well with LLC management and add to LLC productivity, the admission of the new member makes sense. This section examines these situations and includes a resolution LLC members can use to formally admit a new member.

Admitting a New Member

This section outlines the general tax and legal rules for admitting a new member to an LLC. This section deals with brand-new, additional members. (Admitting a new member to replace an existing member is covered in "Admitting a Transferee to the LLC," below.)

Tax Consequences of Admitting New Members

For tax purposes, admitting a new member is handled just like the original admission of the founding LLC members. The new member makes a capital contribution in return for an interest in the capital, profits, and losses of the LLC. The transaction is usually nontaxable to the member, but the member is given a basis in his or her interest that affects the amount of taxes the member will pay when the membership interest or LLC is later sold or liquidated. The new member's basis is the amount of cash paid, plus the member's tax basis in any property transferred to the LLC.

(Read more in "Distributions of LLC Profits to Members," above.)

CAUTION

A new member who will work for the LLC may owe taxes. If you admit a new member in return for the performance of services, that member may owe taxes on his or her membership interest. If the member receives a "capital interest" in an LLC (a right to share in the assets of the LLC on its liquidation in return for services), the interest is treated like income and is taxable. The same is true if the person receives a predictable payment of LLC profits. Either way, the member immediately owes taxes on the fair market value of the membership interest. If this tax result is likely to occur, the member may be better off borrowing the money necessary to buy into the LLC, and paying off the debt as he or she receives an LLC salary or a distributive share of LLC profits. This is covered in more detail in "Tax Treatment of Salaries Paid to Members" in Chapter 12.

When you admit a new member, the member's capital contribution is carried in the member's capital account on the LLC books. (For an explanation of capital accounts, see "Capital Accounts vs. Tax Basis," above.) But a new member's capital contribution can change the relative capital account balances of the members. Because a member's share of LLC assets and profits and losses is tied to the member's proportionate capital interest in the LLC, bringing in a new member can reduce existing members' interests. As a result, your LLC may need to adjust its balance sheet, perhaps adding a value for goodwill, before the new member is brought in. Here's an example.

EXAMPLE:

Janet is being admitted as a new member to Icarus Films, LLC, a company with three existing members (Sally, Justin, and Barbara), each of whom has a current capital account balance of $40,000. Janet is to become an equal member of the company, so, after her contribution, her capital account should represent 25% of the total capital account balances of all members. The existing members agree that the current value of the film company is $200,000, and that Janet should pay $50,000 for her one-quarter stake in the business. If Janet's $50,000 contribution is simply reflected on the LLC books, her capital account balance will equal approximately 29% of all LLC capital accounts ($50,000/$170,000), meaning that Janet would own more of the company than any of the others.

One way to handle this is to "capitalize" the goodwill (or reputation) of the company prior to Janet's admission. This means adding goodwill to the balance sheet as a new asset. The amount of the goodwill should be equal to the excess of the value of the company after Janet's admission over the member's total capital account balances. In other words, the goodwill amount is the difference between the value of the company ($200,000) and the sum of the current account balances ($120,000) plus Janet's contribution ($50,000). In this case, goodwill equals $30,000 ($200,000 value of LLC minus $170,000). This $30,000 worth of goodwill should be divided equally among the three members on the balance sheet so that, just prior to Janet's admission, Sally, Justin, and Barbara each have capital account balances of $50,000 ($40,000 plus a $10,000 share of the newly capitalized goodwill).

There is no basis change, no allocation or distribution, and no tax arising from this recalculation—it is an event that takes place only on the balance sheet. Total capital account balances before Janet's admission should equal $150,000. When Janet is

admitted, her capital account balance is $50,000, exactly one-quarter of the total capital account balances of all members after her admission ($200,000).

You don't need to get involved with these calculations when admitting a member to your LLC—your tax person can handle the details for you. All you need to know is that capital account balances are affected by the admission of a new member, so adjustments may need to be made to capital accounts to make sure the members end up with their fair share of total LLC capital interests after the admission.

Legal Requirements for Admitting New Members

As usual, your LLC operating agreement is your first and best source for the requirements for admitting new members to your LLC. Most agreements restate the default state LLC rule, which suggests that all existing members must approve the admission of a new member into an LLC unless the articles or operating agreement provide otherwise. It's a sensible rule. All members should be included in the discussion to admit a new member and agree to it. This avoids forcing the existing LLC members to share ownership and management responsibilities with an incompatible person.

CROSS REFERENCE

Look up your state's default admission rule in Appendix B. You'll find the default rules for admitting new members into an LLC for each state in Appendix B, under the heading "Admission of Members." This section includes the state rules for admitting both new members and members who have been transferred an interest from a prior member (see "Admitting a Transferee to the LLC," below). However, because state laws may change, it's important to look at your state's LLC act as well—you'll find instructions for accessing it online in Appendix B.

There is another important legal implication to admitting a new member. As you know, the basic rights, responsibilities, and interests (capital, profits, and voting interests) of members and managers are spelled out in your LLC operating agreement. You'll want a new member to consent to the terms of the operating agreement—it is, after all, a contract between the members of the LLC. Also, the admission of a new member changes the relative capital, profits, and voting interests of all members, so your operating agreement may need to be updated to reflect these new numbers (if actual capital, profits, and voting interests are specified for each member in the operating agreement). To get a new member's consent to the operating agreement, have the new member sign a statement agreeing to be bound by its terms. Or, if you are updating your operating agreement, have all members, including the new member, sign the updated agreement. Getting the signatures of all members' spouses is also a good idea, because a member's spouse may have a property right in a membership interest. (To formally approve changes to your operating agreement, use the Resolution to Amend LLC Operating Agreement in Chapter 10.)

EXAMPLE:

Ninja Programming Consultants Group, LLC, is bringing in Jeff, a new master C++ programmer with a Black Belt in the Java language. He will be given a one-third capital interest in exchange for his contribution of a Java code kernel, which will form the basis for an advanced Internet search engine the LLC plans to market to clients. He will also receive a one-third profits interest in the business for maintaining this kernel and creating other cutting-edge code critical to the continued success of the company. Obviously, Jeff's newly created capital and profits interests change the relative capital and profit-sharing interests of the existing members. They agree to admit Jeff as a new member, so a new LLC operating agreement is prepared that reflects the new capital and profits interests of all members. The existing members and Jeff, together with their spouses, sign the new operating agreement.

CAUTION

Watch out for securities laws. An investment in a business, including a capital interest in an LLC, may be defined under state and federal law as a "security." If it is, the sale of the interest must be registered with the federal Securities and Exchange Commission and the state securities agency, unless an exemption from federal and state registration applies. Fortunately, states are starting to say that an investment in an LLC where all members are active in the business is not a "security," because securities are traditionally defined as investments to reap profits from the work or energies of others. Also, federal and state securities laws contain exemptions for small, private sales of securities. However, you should still proceed with caution in offering and selling LLC memberships to outsiders. To be sure you can safely issue a membership interest under the securities law, consult with a knowledgeable small business lawyer.

If you are considering selling an interest to a passive (inactive) member, be particularly careful, because the securities laws were set up to protect just this type of outside investor. If the investor became dissatisfied with the performance of her investment in your LLC, she could sue you to recover her losses, claiming that her membership interest was issued in violation of the securities laws.

Resolution to Admit a New LLC Member

The following resolution can be used by the LLC to formally approve the admission of a new, additional member. (To admit a member who has bought a membership from a existing member, see "Admitting a Transferee to the LLC," below.)

CD-ROM

Complete the resolution following the special instructions below. You'll find this resolution on the CD-ROM and as a tearout form in Appendix C. (See Appendix A for information on selecting and using the CD-ROM files.)

Special Instructions

❶ Insert the name of the new member and a description of the cash or property to be paid or transferred to the LLC by the new member. If the member is contributing property, state the fair market value of the property in your description. (The property will be carried on the LLC's books at this value.) In describing any property transferred, be as specific as you can. For example, give the year, make, and vehicle ID number for a truck or the make, model, and serial number of a computer. As an alternative to writing this information in the resolution, you can attach a receipt or other description of the property to the resolution, and refer to this paperwork in the resolution, such as "computer equipment listed in attached Schedule 1."

If the member will sign a promissory note to pay for the membership interest in installments, refer to the promissory note in the description. The note should carry commercially reasonable terms, such as the rate of interest and repayment schedule. (See Chapter 14 for several forms of promissory notes you can adapt for this purpose.)

Admission of New Member

After discussion, it was agreed that the LLC will issue the following membership interest to the following person for the following payment or transfer of property to the LLC:

Name   Payment

___[insert name of new member]___ ❶   ___[insert amount paid for membership interest]___

It was agreed that the operating agreement of the LLC will be amended, if necessary, to reflect the capital, profits, voting, and other interests of all members of the LLC as a result of the admission of the person named above. It was also agreed that, as a condition to being formally accepted as a member of this LLC, the new member agrees to the rights and responsibilities associated with membership by signing the most current LLC operating agreement or by signing a statement, attached to the most current LLC operating agreement, in which the new member agrees to be bound by the terms of the agreement. ❷

> **TIP**
>
> **How to transfer assets to the LLC.** Additional legal paperwork may be necessary to transfer some types of property to the LLC. For example, to transfer a car to an LLC, the new member must sign over a title slip and send a copy to the department of motor vehicles in your state. For transfers of real estate, new deeds transferring the property to the LLC should be prepared and recorded at your county recorder or deeds office. Check with a real estate broker or office supply store for copies of standard deed or transfer forms. An excellent source of deed forms and legal information on transferring real property interests in California is *Deeds for California Real Estate*, by Mary Randolph (Nolo).

Sometimes the LLC will issue a new member an interest in return for canceling a debt that the LLC owed to the new member. For example, the new member loaned the LLC startup funds under a note, but decides to exchange the note for an interest in the LLC rather than seek repayment under the note. If this is the case, describe the specifics of the debt cancellation in this resolution—for example, "cancellation of loan to LLC issued on October 1, 2000, principal and accrued unpaid interest owing in the amount of $35,500." Or, if the loan was documented with a promissory note, you can refer to the note instead—for example, "see attached promissory note dated October 1, 2000." Make sure the new member (the former lender) marks the note "paid in full," signs and dates the note, and attaches a copy of it to the resolution. Alternatively, the new member can sign a release. (For instructions on preparing promissory notes to document loans made by members, see Chapter 13. A release form is included in Chapter 14.)

❷ Make sure to obtain the new member's signature on an updated operating agreement, or a statement agreeing to be bound by your current operating agreement, after the new member reads a copy of the agreement. Place copies of the paperwork in your LLC records binder.

Admitting a Transferee to the LLC

During the life of your LLC, a member may want to leave and cash out his or her membership interest by selling it to an outsider. Of course, this scenario presupposes that the member can find someone who is willing to buy the member's stake in the LLC, manage or work for it, and perform any other duties required under the LLC's operating agreement.

Tax Consequences of Admitting a Transferee

The basic tax consequences for a new member who receives a former member's interest are similar to those for a new member who buys an interest from the LLC. The transaction is nontaxable to the new member, but the new member is given a basis in the interest that affects the amount of taxes the new member will pay when the membership interest or LLC is later sold or liquidated. The transferee (the buying member) takes a tax basis in the interest equal to the amount of cash paid to the transferor (the selling member) plus the buyer's tax basis in any property that he transferred to the selling member. (See "Distributions of LLC Profits to Members," above, for a discussion of tax basis.)

However, a transfer of a membership interest is handled differently than the admission of a new member by the LLC, because the selling member rather than the LLC itself receives the payment for the interest. One common way to treat the transfer of a former member's interest to a new member is to keep the transfer "off the books" of the LLC. In other words, the old member's capital account balance is simply transferred to the new member's capital account. The actual amount paid for the interest by the transferee is not reflected on the LLC capital accounts.

Selling Economic Rights Is Different From Selling All Membership Rights

The sale of a membership interest as discussed in this chapter means the sale of all of a departing member's membership rights—economic (profits and capital), managerial, voting—the whole ball of wax, with all associated membership rights and responsibilities. However, a member can also transfer all or part of his or her economic rights to an outsider but remain a managing, voting member of the LLC. This sort of transfer of economic rights is under state LLC law without consent by the other LLC members, unless the LLC operating agreement says otherwise.

EXAMPLE: Billy is one of two members of Taxi-Cology Cab Company LLC, which owns two taxicab licenses and oversees a fleet of electric-powered cabs, contracted for use under an experimental clean-the-air program funded by a nonprofit ecology consortium. Billy, short of funds for his son's college tuition, pledges his membership interest as collateral for a personal loan. LLC profits are adequate for Billy to make loan repayments, but Billy has difficulty budgeting his finances and falls behind on the loan. The bank does not wish to foreclose, and its loan department suggests that Billy transfer his right to collect his share of LLC profits to the bank until the loan principal is reduced to a specified amount. Any excess of LLC profits over the loan payments will be applied to loan principal unless Billy requests a return of the excess. Billy agrees to the temporary transfer of economic rights in his membership, committing himself to keeping a closer track of his finances, at least until his LLC's profits substantially increase.

EXAMPLE:

Dominic buys Alicia's LLC membership interest for its fair market value, $60,000. When she sells her interest, Alicia's capital account balance was $45,000. This $45,000 balance is zeroed out of Alicia's account when she withdraws and is posted to Dominic's new capital account. The payment of $60,000 for the interest is not reflected on the LLC books; it is a private transaction between the former and new member.

There are other ways to handle a transfer of membership interest. For example, the LLC can take the opportunity to record the amount by which the LLC's fair market value has increased over its book value at the time of the transfer. In the above example, Alicia's stake in the net assets of the LLC as reflected in her capital account was only $45,000, but she was able to sell it for $60,000. One of the ways to update the LLC balance sheet at the time of the transfer is to account for the goodwill of the LLC—the excess of its fair market value over its net asset value—on its balance sheet. This is done in a manner similar to the Icarus Films example discussed in "Admitting a New Member," above, where adjustments for goodwill were made to the existing member's capital accounts when a new member bought an interest in the LLC. The same sort of adjustments can be made when a former member sells an interest to a new member.

EXAMPLE:

Let's still assume that Alicia wants to sell her LLC interest to Dominic for $60,000. Let's also assume that Alicia is a 25% owner and Rachel is a 75% owner of the LLC. Their capital account balances, respectively, are $45,000 and $135,000, making total LLC capital—the "net asset" or "book value" of the LLC—$180,000. Because Alicia can sell her 25% interest for $60,000, however, the LLC is really worth $240,000 ($60,000 x 4)—$60,000 more than its book value. This additional amount represents the LLC's "goodwill," an additional LLC asset.

Prior to the transfer of Alicia's membership, this goodwill asset is posted on the LLC books at $60,000, and the capital account of each member increases proportionately according to their relative interest in the LLC—Alicia's capital account increases by $15,000 ($60,000 x 25%), Rachel's by $45,000 ($60,000 x 75%). The result is that Alicia has a capital account balance of $60,000 ($45,000 + $15,000) and Rachel $180,000 ($135,000 + $45,000). The capital accounts are now properly established to reflect the terms of the sale of Alicia's membership to Dominic. He pays Alicia $60,000 for her interest, and Alicia's $60,000 capital account balance is transferred to his new LLC capital account. This amount is equal to 25% of the total capital of the LLC, which now equals $240,000.

Again, you don't need to worry about bookkeeping adjustments when a member sells an interest. Just make sure the LLC's tax adviser goes over the options and adjustments to the LLC books prior to a transfer of a member's interest to a new member.

When a Member Transfers a 50% or Greater Membership Interest

When a member who owns a 50% or greater interest in an LLC sells or transfers the member's interest, special IRS rules kick in. These can have significant tax effects on the LLC and its members. Specifically, Section 708 of the Internal Revenue Code says that an LLC is "terminated for tax purposes" if, within a 12-month period, there is a sale or exchange of 50% or more of the total capital and profits interests in the LLC. Transfers of interests by gift, will, inheritance, or buyouts by the LLC itself (where the LLC buys back the interest of a departing member) do not count, but sales of interests to outsiders (who become new members) or to the continuing LLC members do.

Here's the problem: If this type of transfer of a 50% or greater interest does occur, the IRS says that the LLC is terminated for tax purposes. This means the books of the company are closed and all assets are considered to have been distributed to the LLC members, who then are assumed to have recontributed the distributed assets to a new LLC owned by the same LLC members (not counting the member whose 50% or greater transfer triggered the tax termination). Because a deemed distribution to members can result in a taxable gain and the payment of taxes, the tax effect of this type of forced tax termination can be enormous and costly. Make sure you plan ahead.

Whenever a member is planning to transfer an interest, even if the member's stake in capital and profits of your LLC is less than 50%, check with your tax adviser well in advance to handle or minimize any tax results that may occur, including a possible tax termination of the LLC.

Under current Internal Revenue Code § 708 regulations, a tax termination also occurs when an LLC is left with one member only (or when the LLC stops doing business). But, when one member of a two-member LLC dies, the LLC does not terminate as long as the deceased member's estate, or an inheritor of the interest, continues to share in the profits or losses of the LLC. Ask your tax adviser for further information.

Legal Issues on the Transfer of a Membership

State statutes vary, but most require that members approve a sale by a member to a new member, unless the articles or operating agreement say otherwise. Typically, the law requires the consent of all or a majority of the nontransferring members (either per capita or according to capital and/or profits interests in the LLC).

If the transfer of a membership interest to a new member is not covered in your articles or your operating agreement, and your members do not agree to admit a transferee (the person who buys an LLC interest), state law usually says the buyer gets only an economic interest in the LLC membership. In other words, the buyer receives a right to profits and capital distributions, but not full LLC membership voting or management rights. Obviously, a buyer usually wants the whole kit and caboodle, so you will want to poll your members to get their consent for the buyer to join the membership ranks.

CROSS REFERENCE

How to find your state's rule for admitting new members. Each state's membership voting requirement for approving the admission of a transferee is in Appendix B under the heading "Admission of Members." (This heading also shows the approval requirement for issuing a new membership to someone who contributes capital directly to the LLC.) Make sure to also check your operating agreement, and, if you want to be sure of the most current state rules, your state LLC act.

Admitting a new member is an important decision. Because the nontransferring members may not have had any dealings with the proposed admittee in the past, I recommend that you have all members approve the admission of the new member, no matter what your operating agreement or state law has to say on the subject. This is particularly true when the LLC is member-managed. If the new member is not compatible personally and managerially with the other members, LLC business can suffer severely. As part of this approval process, the existing members can let the new member know what they expect, and the members can try to work out any differences at the outset. If it is clear that the new member is not compatible, it's probably best to handle the problem head-on, letting the selling or transferring member know that his or her choice of buyer is not satisfactory to the other members. In this case, the transferring member can decide to transfer only economic rights in the membership to the buyer or continue the search for a new buyer (if the member is determined to transfer all membership rights in order to be completely free of the LLC).

There is another important legal implication to admitting a new member. As you know, the basic rights, responsibilities, and interests (capital, profits, and voting interests) of members and managers are spelled out in your LLC operating agreement. You'll want a new member to consent to the terms of the operating agreement, because it is, after all, a contract between the members of the LLC. Also, the admission of a new member may change the relative capital, profits, and voting interests of all members, so your operating agreement may need to be changed to reflect these new numbers (if actual capital, profits, and voting interests are specified for each member in the operating agreement). For both reasons, it's important to take a close look at your operating agreement when you admit a new member. It may need to be updated.

Make sure the new member agrees to be bound by the LLC operating agreement. To accomplish this, either have the new member sign a statement consenting to be bound by all terms of the current operating agreement or, if you are updating your operating agreement, have all members, including the new member, sign the updated agreement. All members' spouses should also sign, because they may have a property right in a membership interest. (To formally approve changes to your operating agreement, use the Resolution to Amend LLC Operating Agreement in Chapter 10.)

> **CAUTION**
>
> **State law may dissolve your LLC when a member sells his or her interest.** Some states' LLC statutes say that an LLC automatically dissolves, or "legally terminates," when a member sells or otherwise disposes of a membership interest, unless the remaining (nontransferring) members agree in writing to continue the LLC. This may seem like a strange and unnecessary requirement, but your state may have enacted this sort of provision to comply with old tax rules. It's easy to comply with this requirement if it's imposed in your state. (But you can check to see whether your state has this type of provision in Appendix B, under the heading "Continuation of the LLC"). The resolution shown below, for approving the transfer of a member's interest, includes the nontransferring members' consent to continue the LLC after the transfer.

Resolution to Approve Transfer of Membership to a New Member

The following resolution can be used to formally approve the transfer of an LLC membership interest by a departing member to a new member. Under typical state statutes, unless the remaining members approve the transfer, the buyer only gets economic rights (rights to profits and losses and, when the LLC dissolves, liquidated distributions), but not full membership voting and management rights.

> **CD-ROM**
>
> Complete the resolution following the special instructions below. You'll find this resolution on the CD-ROM and as a tearout form in Appendix C. (See Appendix A for information on selecting and using the CD-ROM files.)

Special Instructions

❶ Insert the names of the former member and the new member.

❷ Make sure to obtain the new member's signature to an updated operating agreement, or have the new member sign a statement agreeing to be bound by your current operating agreement after the new member reads a copy of the agreement. Place copies of the paperwork in your LLC records binder.

❸ As mentioned above, state statutes and/or the LLC operating agreement may require the written consent of the nontransferring members to continue the LLC after a member sells an interest. If so, the written consent of the nontransferring members must be obtained within 90 days after the former member withdraws. I assume you will approve and sign this resolution before a member's sale to a new member, and therefore meet any deadline imposed in your operating agreement or under state law for obtaining this consent.

To make it clear that you wish to continue your LLC after a member sells an interest, have all nontransferring members sign in the space provided, and indicate the date of their signatures. (If they sign at different times, insert the date of the first signature.) If you have any questions about your state's current default rule for voting to continue your LLC after a member sells an interest, check your state LLC act or ask a lawyer for guidance.

Approval of Transfer of Membership

After discussion, it was agreed that the LLC approves the transfer of the membership interest of ___[name of transferring member]___, "former member," to ___[name of new member]___, "new member." ❶ The new member is admitted as a full member of this LLC, with all economic, management, voting, and any other rights associated with the membership interest of the former member.

It was agreed that the books of this LLC will be adjusted to show the termination of membership rights of the former member and the establishment of membership rights of the new member.

The operating agreement of the LLC will be amended, if necessary, to reflect the capital, profits, voting, and other interests of all members of the LLC as a result of the admission of the new member named above. It was also agreed that, as a condition to being formally accepted as a member of this LLC, the new member must agree to the rights and responsibilities associated with membership by signing the most current LLC operating agreement or by signing a statement, which will be attached to the most current LLC operating agreement, agreeing to be bound by the terms of the agreement. ❷

It was further resolved that the nontransferring members of the LLC, whose signatures appear below, consent to the continuance of the business and legal existence of the LLC following the withdrawal of the former member and the admission of the new member. ❸

Date: _____

Signature: _____

Signature: _____

Signature: _____

Signature: _____

Withdrawal of LLC Members

The flip side of the admission of a member is the withdrawal of a member. A member may withdraw from an LLC in any one of the following scenarios:

- The LLC is not sufficiently profitable, and the member wishes to withdraw capital and invest it elsewhere.

- The member needs funds to meet other business or personal needs, and wants to cash out the membership interest now rather than waiting for the LLC to be sold or liquidated.

- The member is having a personal or business conflict with the other members, isn't enjoying working in the LLC any longer, or wants to depart for other personal reasons.

- The member is disabled and is no longer able to manage and/or work for the LLC as a result.

- The member is a thorn in the side of the other members and is being expelled. Expulsions are not common; they can only occur in LLCs with more than two members. (In a two-member LLC, if one member wants to force the other out, this dissolves the LLC as a practical matter.)

When a member wishes to leave, the first thing you should do is look at your LLC articles and operating agreement. In many LLCs, the members have agreed in their operating agreement that a member is not allowed to cash out prior to the liquidation or sale of the LLC or may cash out only if the member accepts a discounted value for his or her membership interest. Some operating agreements contain comprehensive "buy-sell provisions" that specify exactly when a member's interest may be bought, how a member's interest will be valued, and how the LLC will pay for it. These provisions may give both the LLC and/or the remaining members a chance to buy the withdrawing member's interest.

RESOURCE

For more information on buy-sell provisions. If you want to learn more about the options typically included in LLC (as well as partnership and corporate) buy-sell provisions—perhaps to include in your own LLC operating agreement—see *Business Buyout Agreements: A Step-by-Step Guide for Co-Owners,* by Anthony Mancuso and Bethany K. Laurence (Nolo).

Often, however, the LLC documents don't include buy-sell provisions or other ways to handle a member's withdrawal. In this situation, you will need to check your state's LLC act to find out the legal options and consequences of the departure of an LLC member. Some of these legal issues are covered in the "Legal Issues" section below, but first I'll explain the basic tax consequences of the departure of a member.

Tax Effects of a Member's Withdrawal

The buyout of a member's interest, by the LLC or the remaining members, is, of course, a taxable event. The withdrawing member calculates any gain he or she realizes on the sale—the amount by which the sales price for the interest exceeds the member's basis—and pays taxes on the gain. (For a general discussion of tax basis, see "Tax Effects of LLC Distributions," above.) The member's gain is usually taxed at capital gains rates, which are generally lower than the normal individual income tax rates. If the amount paid to the withdrawing member is less than his or her basis in the interest, the member realizes a loss on the sale, which the member may be allowed to deduct on his or her individual tax return. (The IRS "at-risk" and "passive income" rules affect the deductibility of losses by a member. Your tax adviser can tell you more about these loss limitation rules.)

TIP

Don't forget to include LLC liabilities when calculating the value of a sale. An LLC member's basis in an LLC interest includes the member's share of LLC liabilities. When the member's interest is sold, the member is relieved of these liabilities. Therefore, the tax rules say that a member's share of LLC liabilities is added to the amount received in a sale of the LLC interest. In effect, the member is treated as having received an additional cash payment equal to the member's share of LLC debts at the time of departure.

EXAMPLE:

José withdraws from his LLC, and the remaining members buy out his interest for $40,000. José's basis in his interest was $25,000, and his share of LLC liabilities at the time of his withdrawal was $5,000. His gain on the transfer of his interest is $20,000 ($40,000 payment plus $5,000 in liabilities he no longer has to worry about, minus $25,000 basis).

These standard tax rules regarding basis and gain apply when a withdrawing member sells a membership interest back to one or more of the remaining LLC members or to an outsider who is then admitted into the LLC (as discussed in "Admitting a Transferee to the LLC," above). But special tax rules kick in if a withdrawing member sells an interest back to the LLC itself. The payment the LLC makes to buy back the interest of a withdrawing member is known as a "liquidating distribution." Essentially, the rules regarding liquidating distributions allow more wiggle room than the standard rules and let the LLC and its members structure the tax consequences of the sale in more than one way.

Here's how the liquidating distribution rules generally work (but you should always ask your tax adviser for the latest information): When the LLC itself buys back a withdrawing member's interest, the member pays capital gains tax rates only if the LLC pays the book value of actual LLC assets.

EXAMPLE:

Chuck withdraws from his LLC, which pays him the book value of his interest. This value is computed as the balance sheet value of LLC assets minus LLC liabilities, multiplied by Chuck's percentage of LLC ownership (the percentage of his capital interest compared to total LLC capital interests).

If LLC assets equal $150,000, and liabilities equal $75,000, the balance sheet (net asset) value of the LLC is $75,000. If Chuck holds a 25% capital interest in the company, the LLC pays him $18,750 ($75,000 x 25%) for his interest. In this situation, Chuck is paid for his proportionate interest in the net assets of the LLC, and the sale is eligible for capital gains tax treatment—that is, Chuck pays capital gains taxes on the amount of gain he realizes on the sale of his interest back to the LLC.

Of course, withdrawing members usually want to get more for their membership interest than its book value. That's because the book value of LLC assets does not normally include appreciation on the assets that has occurred since the transfer of the assets to the LLC (unless the assets have recently been revalued to update the balance sheet), but does reflect depreciation deductions taken by the LLC on its assets. Also, book value does not normally include the "goodwill" of the business—the added value of a business due to its recognition by its customers and its continuing ability to earn profits because of this recognition. Because of this, the buy-sell provisions of LLC operating agreements often provide for additional payments to a withdrawing member. For example, the agreement may provide that a withdrawing member is entitled to the book value of the member's interest plus an additional amount, which may be a set amount or a percentage of book value or LLC profits. This bonus amount is intended to compensate the withdrawing member for his or her share of the fair market value of the LLC over and above its book value.

Here's what the IRS rules say (under IRC Section 736) regarding liquidating payments over and above book value: The extra amount will be treated as ordinary income to the withdrawing member, taxable at the member's individual income tax rates instead of the lower capital gains rates (unless the LLC operating agreement specifically provides for and allocates an extra payment as "goodwill," discussed below). The LLC can treat the additional payment for goodwill either as a payout of profits, which reduces the distributive share of income payable to the other members, or as an expense, which reduces the net income of the LLC. In either case the LLC (and, therefore, the continuing members) get the tax benefit of the additional payout, which reduces the net taxable income passed along to the other members.

EXAMPLE:

Using Chuck again as an example, if the buy-sell provisions of Chuck's LLC operating agreement stated that Chuck should be paid his 25% share of the net asset value of the LLC on his withdrawal, plus a bonus of 15% of this balance sheet figure, this extra 15% bonus amount is taxable to him as ordinary income, and reduces the net income reported by the LLC on its tax return. (Chuck pays ordinary income tax rates on the 15% amount, but still gets to treat the 25% share as capital gains, taxable at the lower capital gains tax rates.)

The big exception to this rule is that an LLC payment that exceeds the book value will be treated under the capital gains rules if the LLC's operating agreement specifically says that the extra payment is for the "goodwill" of the business. An example best illustrates this important tax exception.

EXAMPLE:

Using the previous LLC example, if the LLC's operating agreement says that the extra 15% payment to a withdrawing member is payment for a member's share of the LLC's "goodwill," the extra amount will be taxed at capital gains rates to Chuck, and the LLC can't use the extra payment to reduce its taxable income.

The purpose of this exception is to give LLC members some say in structuring the tax consequences of a payout to a withdrawing member. If they want the withdrawing member to bear the tax cost of an additional payment by paying ordinary income tax on it, then there's no need to say anything in the operating agreement. But if the members agree that the LLC should bear the tax burden of these additional payments (payments over and above the book value of LLC assets) to withdrawing members, they can allocate the extra payments to goodwill in their operating agreement. By doing so, a withdrawing member gets favorable capital gains tax treatment on the additional payment, but the LLC can't use it to reduce its income.

! CAUTION

Always check your operating agreement before a buyout! Because the tax consequences of a buyout of a withdrawing member can generate very different tax outcomes depending on the exact wording of your operating agreement, always review your operating agreement before a withdrawing member leaves your LLC. Your lawyer or tax adviser may decide to amend your agreement to include (or exclude) magic language relating to payments for goodwill, which can be critical to achieve a tax result in favor of your LLC or a withdrawing member.

Legal Issues on the Withdrawal of an LLC Member

State law varies concerning a member's right to withdraw from an LLC, particularly when the LLC operating agreement doesn't address the issue. State statutes also differ with respect to the amount of compensation a member is legally entitled to when he or she withdraws from an LLC (again, assuming the operating agreement is silent on this). If your operating agreement doesn't deal with member withdrawal, it's probably time to give your agreement a tune-up. As discussed above, this once-over is also important from a tax perspective. You'll want to make sure the language of your agreement leads to the desired tax result when a departing member's interest is bought back by your LLC.

RESOURCE

How to prepare basic buy-sell provisions. One self-help resource that shows you how to prepare basic buy-sell provisions to include in your operating agreement is Nolo's *Business Buyout Agreements: A Step-by-Step Guide for Co-Owners*, by Anthony Mancuso and Bethany K. Laurence. This book shows you how to prepare provisions that specify how, when, and how much to pay a business owner who withdraws, dies, or proposes to sell an interest to an outsider. It applies to LLCs as well as small corporations and partnerships.

Of course, the best way to find out how your state handles membership withdrawal is to check your state's LLC act. Each state's default rule for the withdrawal of members is summarized in Appendix B, under the heading "Withdrawal of Members." That section indicates your state's rules, if any, for the procedures when a member wishes to withdraw from the LLC, as well as the rules for payments to a withdrawing member. Check your state LLC act for the latest information. Generally, these default rules apply only if the LLC articles and operating agreement don't address these issues.

A state may allow members to withdraw without notice. Some states require six months' notice while others have shorter notice requirements. For example, Indiana requires only 30 days' prior notice by a withdrawing member; Missouri, 90 days.

As compensation for a withdrawing member's interest, the following statute is fairly typical:

District of Columbia LLC Act, Section 29-1027

(a) Except as otherwise provided in [this LLC Act], upon resignation, any resigning member is entitled to receive any distribution to which such member is entitled under the articles of organization or an operating agreement, and, if not otherwise provided in the articles of organization or an operating agreement, such member is entitled to receive, within a reasonable time after resignation, the fair value of such member's membership interest as of the date of resignation.

(b) If the resignation of the member is a breach of an operating agreement, or the resignation occurs as a result of otherwise wrongful conduct of the member, the limited liability company may recover from the resigning member damages for breach of the operating agreement or as a result of the wrongful conduct, including the reasonable costs of obtaining replacement of the services that the resigning member was obligated to perform, and may offset the damages against the amount otherwise distributable to the resigning member, in addition to pursuing any remedies provided for in an operating agreement or otherwise available under applicable law.

Under this common scheme, a member is entitled to current distributions—that is, a member's distributive share of profits earned but unpaid prior to the withdrawal of the member. Unless the articles or operating agreement say otherwise, a member must get also the *fair value* of his or her interest. What does this mean? The LLC act does not define this important standard, but court cases involving partnerships—which, it is safe to assume, apply to LLCs as well—generally say that the fair value of a business interest is its fair market value, not just its book value.

In other words, if an LLC's operating agreement doesn't address the rights of withdrawing members and a member resigns from an LLC, the withdrawing member is probably entitled to more than the balance of the member's capital account or the book value of his or her interest. In fact, the member may decide to sue for more if it appears likely that the fair market value of the member's interest is more than he or she received. And, the member may have a fair chance of winning, particularly if the operating agreement is not clear on how much a departing member is entitled to be paid and state law does not specifically limit the amount a departing member is entitled to receive.

The second portion of the D.C. statute is also typical of how states handle member withdrawal. Obviously, state law cannot prohibit a member from leaving an LLC, no matter what the statutes or the LLC operating agreement say. This section addresses this problem. It says that a member who resigns in violation of a provision of the LLC operating agreement (or leaves due to wrongful conduct—for example, a member is expelled for violating standards specified in the operating agreement) can be required to pay for the cost of replacing him- or herself or for other monetary damages caused to the LLC because of the withdrawal. These costs can be deducted from the amount the LLC is otherwise required to pay the withdrawing member.

EXAMPLE:

Hilda is a one-third member of Goody-Goody Two Shoes Supply, LLC. (She has a one-third capital and profits interest.) In addition to her initial capital contribution of $10,000, her deal with her LLC is that she work full-time, including weekends if needed, running the business in return for her share of the profits.

Hilda becomes tired of working long days for her one-third share of LLC profits. She hands in her walking papers to her fellow members, giving them six months' advance notice of her departure. Because the LLC operating agreement forbids Hilda from leaving without finding a replacement member who will work in the business and is suitable to the other members, Hilda tries to find a replacement. She has no luck finding anyone willing to work the number of hours required for her current level of profit-sharing, but she leaves anyway.

The remaining members understand Hilda's need to leave, but want to be fair to the LLC as well as to Hilda. They value the business at a fair market value of $240,000, which makes Hilda's capital interest worth $80,000. The LLC has to hire and train a replacement for Hilda, at least until another member willing to invest and work in the business comes along. They estimate these training costs at $10,000 and deduct this amount from the check they issue to Hilda on her departure. (They don't deduct the ongoing salary of the replacement worker—after all, the LLC receives value for these services.) Hilda is happy getting $70,000 back on her investment of money and time in the LLC and moves on to greener—that is, more profitable—pursuits.

TAX NOTE:

Because Goody-Goody's LLC operating agreement does not allocate to goodwill any part of an LLC's payments made to a withdrawing member (discussed above), the LLC will be able to deduct the amount of the payment that exceeds Hilda's share of the book value of the business. They remind Hilda in their cover letter sent with the check that the portion of the LLC payment that exceeds her share of the book value of the business is likely taxable to her as ordinary income, and that her tax adviser can help her meet the requirements for reporting the payment on her tax return.

It is common for states to allow the LLC to offset the amount paid to a departing member if the LLC has to find a replacement worker to perform the withdrawing member's services or if the member is withdrawing in violation of the operating agreement or for other wrongful conduct. Some states allow the LLC in such cases to reduce the payment otherwise required under the operating agreement by the amount of profits lost by the LLC or, in the alternative, by the portion of the goodwill, or "going concern" value, of the LLC otherwise allocated to the member's interest.

Other states take a less generous approach to a withdrawing member, even one who

gives the LLC adequate notice, and say that a withdrawing member is entitled to the fair market value of the member's interest (determined on a going-concern basis or a liquidation basis, whichever is less). Liquidation value means the amount the LLC assets would bring when sold separately upon liquidation of the LLC (when a buyer is simply paying for assets, not paying to step into a going business)—and is likely to be the lowest measure of a business's worth. Other states may limit the amount a withdrawing member receives to the balance of the member's capital account. This is normally substantially less than the fair market value of the member's interest in a profitable company.

A number of states take an even less generous approach—that is, they don't even allow withdrawing members to be paid for their membership interest unless and until the LLC dissolves (as always, unless otherwise provided in the LLC operating agreement). Instead, the withdrawing member is given the status of a transferee or assignee of a membership interest. This means that the withdrawing member can no longer vote or manage the LLC, but retains a right to receive ongoing allocations and distributions of the LLC profits, losses, credits, and deductions passed along to all LLC members. In other words, the withdrawing member is not paid the value of the member's membership interest until the LLC is later sold or liquidated in its entirety. Here's an example, which provides that a withdrawing member is treated as a transferee.

Nebraska LLC Act, Section 21-2619. Withdrawal or Reduction of Member's Contribution to Capital

[…]

(3) A member of the limited liability company who has withdrawn from membership, but whose capital account has not been liquidated pursuant to the articles

of organization or the operating agreement, shall have the status of a transferee as provided in section 21-2621 [which lists the rights to profits and other economic rights of transferees] unless otherwise provided in the operating agreement.

Lastly, a number of states simply say that a member may not withdraw from the LLC unless allowed to do so under the operating agreement or by consent of the remaining members. But, remember: Even in a state with this type of law, a member is always free to leave in violation of the operating agreement, as long as that member is willing to live with (or challenge in court) not receiving payment for the membership interest or receiving a reduced amount.

CAUTION

Sometimes, an LLC can't legally pay for a withdrawing member's interest. State LLC laws usually restrict management's ability to make distributions to members. If a distribution will lower the book value of LLC assets below the current liabilities of the LLC, or if a distribution is likely to make it difficult for an LLC to be able to pay its bills as they become due, an LLC should not make the distribution. These distribution restrictions apply not just to the payout of LLC profits; they apply to all LLC distributions, including a payout to a withdrawing member to purchase a membership interest.

If the LLC is unable to pay cash to a departing member because of these legal requirements and cannot borrow the money from a bank, it may be forced to pay for the departing member's interest in installments. It would do so either by signing a promissory note to pay the member monthly or quarterly or, if the future liquidity of the LLC is difficult to predict, by forestalling payments until the LLC has more cash on hand. If the LLC cannot buy back the departing member's interest,

even under an installment payment plan, the withdrawing member will continue to own an economic interest in the LLC and will continue to share in LLC profits and losses until his or her membership is bought out by the LLC.

CROSS REFERENCE

Check your state's LLC act to find out the rules for handling member withdrawals. You'll find instructions for searching your state's laws online in Appendix B.

Resolution to Approve LLC Purchase of a Withdrawing Member's Interest

The following resolution can be used to approve the LLC's purchase of a withdrawing member's interest (and to agree to continue the LLC after a member withdraws).

CD-ROM

Complete the resolution following the special instructions below. You'll find this resolution on the CD-ROM and as a tearout form in Appendix C. (See Appendix A for information on selecting and using the CD-ROM files.)

Special Instructions

❶ In the first blank, specify the name of the withdrawing member. In the second blank, put the date when the LLC will purchase the departing member's interest. In the third, spell out the terms of purchase of the interest, including the form of payment (cash or property—usually cash) and whether the payment will be in installments. (If payment is to be in installments, specify repayment terms, and attach a promissory note embodying the terms of repayments. See Chapter 13 for promissory note forms.)

Approval of LLC Purchase of Interest of Withdrawing Member

The LLC resolves that the LLC will purchase the entire membership interest of ____[name of withdrawing member]____, a member of this LLC, on the terms specified below. It was agreed that the purchase of the membership interest will terminate all capital, profits, loss, and voting, and all other management, ownership, and economic interests of the member in this LLC.

The date of purchase is: ___[insert proposed purchase date]___

The terms of the purchase are as follows: ___[specify amount, type, and timing of payment, plus any other terms]___. ❶

After a report of the treasurer, which included an analysis of the most recently prepared balance sheet of the LLC and LLC operations since its preparation, it was agreed that the LLC was able financially and in accordance with any applicable state legal requirements to purchase the withdrawing member's interest according to the terms set out above. ❷

The treasurer was instructed to prepare a balance sheet of the LLC as of the date set for purchase of the withdrawing member's interest, and to see to it that a copy of the balance sheet, plus any additional supporting documentation, be given to the member prior to the date of purchase for the member's review and, if requested, signature. A copy of the balance sheet and any supporting documentation, signed by the withdrawing member if appropriate, will be attached to this resolution and placed in the LLC records binder.

On completion of the necessary paperwork, the treasurer will pay, or make appropriate arrangements for payment, on behalf of the LLC to purchase the withdrawing member's interest on the terms specified above.

It was further resolved that the remaining members of the LLC, whose signatures appear below, consent to the continuance of the business and legal existence of the LLC following the withdrawal of the member named above. ❸

Date: _____

Signature: _____

Signature: _____

Signature: _____

Signature: _____

❷ Attach a balance sheet to the resolution. It should show that the LLC is financially able to buy back the departing member's interest according to the terms set out in the resolution. If you have questions about your LLC's ability to afford the buyback or about your state's legal distribution requirements, check out your state LLC act or see a lawyer or tax person for help.

❸ Some state statutes and/or LLC operating agreements may require the written consent of the remaining members to continue the LLC after a member withdraws. If this is true of your LLC, then have the remaining LLC members sign in the space provided, and indicate the date of their signatures. (If they sign at different times, insert the date of the first signature.) Remember, state requirements vary, but typically the written consent of the remaining members must be obtained, if at all, within 90 days of the member's withdrawal. You will probably approve and sign this resolution before a member's departure, and therefore meet any deadline imposed in your operating agreement or under state law for obtaining this consent. ●

LLC Hiring and Compensation Resolutions

An important part of any LLC's business is to hire personnel and set salaries. This is true for small, closely held LLCs as well as big companies with large payrolls.

Another increasingly important issue is when and how to contract for services offered by outside individuals and companies (independent contractors). Hiring independent contractors can be a cost- and tax-effective strategy for obtaining help with an LLC project without having to place the worker on the payroll.

Also, LLCs may decide to pass special compensation resolutions for members, managers, and officers, such as approving year-end salary increases and bonuses, payment for attending meetings, and indemnification for members, managers, and employees. This chapter covers all of the above issues and provides instructions for selecting and using resolutions to approve these and related matters.

LLC Management Generally Approves Resolutions

The LLC resolutions contained in this chapter can be approved by LLC management—that is, by the members of a member-managed LLC or by the managers of a manager-managed LLC.

How to Select and Use LLC Resolutions

- Scan the table of contents at the beginning of the chapter to find the right resolutions for the business at hand.

- When you find one you need, read the background material that precedes the resolution.

- Follow the instructions included with the sample resolution to complete a draft of the resolution on your computer. If you need guidance on selecting and using the computer disk files, see Appendix A. (You'll have to fill in the tearout resolution included in Appendix C if you aren't using a computer.)

- Complete any needed attachment forms.

- If a resolution involves complex issues that will benefit from expert analysis, have your legal or tax adviser review your paperwork and conclusions.

- Prepare meeting minutes or written consent forms as explained in Chapters 5–7, and insert the completed resolution in the appropriate form.

- Have the LLC secretary sign the printed minutes or have members and/or managers sign the written consent forms and waivers. Then place the signed forms, together with any attachments, in your LLC records binder.

Approving Salaries for Members and Employees

This section provides resolutions to approve the hiring and compensation of LLC members and nonmember employees. These resolutions provide a useful way to explain the payment of substantial salaries and to list the responsibilities of member and nonmember workers.

Before getting into the language of the resolutions, I'll explain the tax ramifications of paying salaries to LLC members. (As always, please check with your tax adviser for the latest rules and strategies.)

Tax Treatment of Salaries Paid to Members

Even though a member of an LLC, like a partner in a partnership, may be paid a salary, the member is not generally considered an employee for legal and tax purposes. So while it is customary for some LLCs to give members a guaranteed salary in return for the performance of services, these payments are classified as "guaranteed payments" under the tax rules (unless they are tied to the LLC's net income—see below). This means that the payments are taxed as ordinary income to the member at the close of the LLC's tax year in which the payments accrue (become payable), even if they are distributed to the member at a later time. Of course, the LLC gets to deduct (or capitalize in some cases) the payments as a business expense.

On the other hand, if a member's salary is tied to the net income of the LLC, it is treated as a member's "distributive share" of LLC profits. That means the salary payments are taxed to the member when allocated to him or her by the LLC (again, usually at the end of the LLC's tax year).

Although both guaranteed payments and distributive share payments are taxed as ordinary income to the member, the net tax results to the members as a whole are a bit different. For example, allocations and distributions of members' distributive shares of profits can affect the members' basis in their membership interests; guaranteed payments do not. And, guaranteed payments come off the top. In other words, they are deducted before the net LLC income available for distribution to all members is computed—that is, before the members' distributive shares are allocated. This means that guaranteed payments affect all LLC members, because they lower the net income that will be allocated to the members at the end of the LLC tax year.

So (you may be asking), should an LLC member who works for the company be compensated with guaranteed payments or distributive shares? The answer will vary. It is common to allocate profits to a working member in recognition of the fact that the member is entitled to compensation (like wages or salary) in return for working for the business, separate from what he or she might receive for merely being an owner.

EXAMPLE:

Jeff and Roberta form the Magic Carpet Cleaning LLC. Each pays equal cash to start the LLC in return for a 50% capital interest. Because Jeff will work for the business and Roberta won't, they agree that the first $30,000 of annual net profits, if any, go to Jeff, and any remaining profits are divided equally between Jeff and Roberta. In other words, Jeff receives a greater distributive share of profits in recognition of his work as a member of the LLC.

It is also common to give a mix of guaranteed payments and a percentage of profits to a member who works for the LLC.

EXAMPLE:

Magic Carpet decides to guarantee Jeff a yearly payment of $30,000. It does this by providing in its LLC operating agreement that Jeff will receive 50% of the annual profits, but no less than $30,000 each year. First-year profits are $50,000, so Jeff is allocated half of the profits at the end of the year—$25,000—as his distributive share of profits for the year, plus $5,000 to reach his minimum of $30,000 for the year. Only the $5,000 is treated as a guaranteed payment to Jeff (because actual profits were not sufficient to pay the $5,000). In its second tax year, the LLC's net income is $60,000. Jeff receives $30,000 at the end of the year—half of the profits. This allocation is treated entirely as Jeff's distributive share of profits (because profits were sufficient to pay Jeff's guarantee of $30,000).

If an LLC member is paid for services in a nonmember capacity—for example, a member is paid for providing occasional legal or accounting services as a consultant—the payment usually can be handled like any payment for outside services. That is, the LLC deducts the payment from its income (or capitalizes it if required to do so), and the member reports and pays income tax on the payment only when the member actually receives it. (Read more in "Using Independent Contractors," below.)

Paying for Services With a Future Interest

Some LLCs pay members who provide services by giving them an interest in the future profits or value of the business. The tax consequences of the type of deal depend on what the member receives.

If a member receives a "capital interest" in an LLC—this generally means a right to share in the assets of the LLC on its liquidation—in return for the performance of services, the capital interest is treated like income and is taxable. The member immediately owes taxes on the fair market value of the membership interest. If a member receives an interest only in the profits of the LLC in return for services—called a "profits" interest—the profits interest is normally not taxed, unless the amount of profits the member will receive is clearly discernible or predictable. (See Revenue Procedure 93-27.)

But note the following additional points:

Even if a profits-only interest is issued to a member, the member may owe taxes if his or her interest is sold or transferred within two years of its issuance grant.

Under proposed Treasury Regulation 105346-03, dated May 24, 2005, LLCs and their members must follow special rules, adopt special agreements, and make sure that special tax elections are filed by persons receiving LLC interests in return for the performance of services within 30 days of the issuance of the interest to obtain favorable tax treatment of that interest.

Ask your tax adviser how to comply with these and the other special rules and requirements before you decide to issue profits or other LLC interests in return for the performance of services. For more information, see Notice 2005-43, "Proposed Revenue Procedure Regarding Partnership Interests Transferred in Connection With the Performance of Services." At the time of this edition, this notice was published at the following IRS website address: http://www.irs.gov/irb/2005-24_IRB/ar10.html (although the notice speaks in terms of partnership interests, it also applies to LLC interests).

SEE AN EXPERT

Check with your tax adviser before compensating members. The tax issue relating to paying members for their services can get pretty complicated. For example, all members who are actively involved in the LLC generally have to report all money they receive from it—whether in the form of allocated profits, guaranteed payments, or profits paid in return for services—as self-employment income. This means the member has to pay not only ordinary income tax but also self-employment taxes (which go to Social Security and Medicare) on this money. Your tax adviser can let you know the rules and help you figure out the best way to compensate members for their work.

Resolution Approving LLC Hiring

The following resolution can be an excellent means of formalizing the hiring of an LLC worker (who can be an LLC member, manager, officer, or employee). But you should think twice before putting the terms of any employment relationship, particularly with a nonmember, in writing—whether in this resolution, an employment contract, or other LLC paperwork. Here is the reason: State law will most likely impose limits on terminating the employment relationship of a nonmember worker who is hired for a set employment term (as opposed to an "at-will" nonmember employee, who is hired for an unspecified period).

RESOURCE

Want more information on employment laws? For an excellent resource on employment law requirements, see *The Employer's Legal Handbook*, by Fred Steingold (Nolo). It contains a wealth of information, including rules on hiring and firing employees of a business.

CD-ROM

Below is a sample of the resolution you can use to approve the hiring of an LLC worker. You'll find this resolution on the CD-ROM and as a tearout form in Appendix C. (See Appendix A for information on selecting and using CD-ROM files.) Complete it following the special instruction below.

Approval of LLC Hiring

After discussion, the hiring of _____ [name of member or employee] _____ to the position of _____ [job title] _____ was approved.

It was agreed that the duties of this position and compensation for performing these services will be as follows: ___ [specify job duties and compensation] ___ . ❶

Special Instruction

❶ This is an optional paragraph. If you include this paragraph, a court may decide that your language gives a nonmember employee extra rights to work for your LLC. But you may decide to use this clause to specify the duties of an executive you know will be around for a while—for example, an organizing member and key employee of your LLC.

Resolution for Salary Increases or Bonuses

It is customary for LLCs to increase the pay of top executives from time to time and to award annual bonuses to working members, managers, and employees as well. If the increase or bonus is substantial, you may wish to pass a resolution showing LLC approval of the additional payment. Doing so helps show that the additional expenses were carefully considered before

---

Approval of Bonuses and Salary Increases

The LLC considered the question of salary increases and bonuses to persons who performed compensated services for the LLC. After discussion, the LLC approved the following salary increases and bonuses, to be paid to the following persons:

Name and Title	Amount	Type	
_____	$ _____	☐ Salary Increase	☐ Bonus
_____	$ _____	☐ Salary Increase	☐ Bonus
_____	$ _____	☐ Salary Increase	☐ Bonus
_____	$ _____	☐ Salary Increase	☐ Bonus
_____	$ _____	☐ Salary Increase	☐ Bonus
_____	$ _____	☐ Salary Increase	☐ Bonus
_____	$ _____	☐ Salary Increase	☐ Bonus

The above salary amounts or bonuses will be paid as follows: __[specify when bonuses will be paid, such as "on December 15, 2010," or the LLC tax year when salary increases are effective, such as "for the year 2010"]__ .

---

approval, a formality that may help in case any nonworking members wonder whether the pay increases were warranted.

CD-ROM

Above is a sample of the resolution you can use to approve bonuses and salary increases. You'll find this resolution on the CD-ROM and as a tearout form in Appendix C. (See Appendix A for information on selecting and using the CD-ROM files.)

Using Independent Contractors

As a way to keep costs down, LLCs often hire outside individuals (called independent contractors, or ICs) to perform work for their LLC, thus saving on payroll taxes, workers' compensation insurance, health insurance, disability insurance, and other employment costs.

IRS Filing Requirements

Even though you do not need to withhold or pay employment taxes for independent contractors, you must prepare and file IRS Form 1099-MISC, *Miscellaneous Income,* for each independent contractor to whom you pay more than a small threshold amount during the tax year. Keep tabs on this 1099 requirement if you hire independent contractors; the threshold amount for this filing is subject to change and is posted each year on the IRS website at www.irs .gov. (You can download the form there as well.)

! **CAUTION**

The IRS may assess substantial penalties for misclassification of independent contractors. The IRS and state tax agencies are becoming increasingly concerned about companies that treat too many workers as "independent contractors." These agencies routinely perform employment audits that result in independent contractors being reclassified as employees, with back taxes and penalties assessed against the employer (even if the worker filed tax returns and paid income taxes and self-employment taxes on the earnings).

If you misclassify an employee as an independent contractor, the unpaid payroll taxes and withholding amounts can easily equal 20% to 40% of the compensation paid to the worker. Worse, after additional penalties and interest are added, the total employer liability resulting from an employment tax audit can exceed what you paid the worker.

IRS Independent Contractor Classification Criteria

The IRS uses a number of tests when deciding whether a worker is an independent contractor or an employee. (This is for outside workers only; members who work for their LLC are not treated as employees. See "Approving Salaries for Members and Employees," above.) Here are some of the more important independent contractor (IC) tests:

- **If it looks like the worker runs a separate business.** One of the most heavily weighted factors the IRS uses to determine IC status is whether the person who provides the services for the LLC has a substantial investment in his or her own business and facilities (in a business other than the LLC) and is pursuing personal profit motives in performing the work. If so, the person will likely be treated as an IC.

- **If the worker does outside work.** Does the worker work for other companies while working for your LLC? If so, this helps establish IC status.

- **If the worker is supervised like an employee.** If the worker must account for his or her actions on an ongoing basis or is directed not just as to the results of the work but also as to when and how it must be done, the worker looks more like an employee.

- **If the work is very important to the LLC.** If the success or failure of the LLC's business hinges in a major way on the outcome of the work being performed, or if it is the primary business of the company, this will weigh heavily toward a finding of employee status.

- **If the worker is hired by the LLC continually.** If you constantly employ the same person to perform the same task over an extended period of time, this factors against IC status.

- **If the worker needs help from the LLC to perform the services.** If you must give the worker extra help or training to perform the task, this figures in favor of employee status.

- **If the worker's business is incorporated.** If the outside worker has incorporated his or her business (or, perhaps, has formed an LLC), this is often persuasive evidence that the person should be treated as in independent contractor. In fact, more and more companies that use outside help—for example, firms that contract for programming services—are requiring individuals to be incorporated (or to have established another type of business entity, such as an LLC) to avoid any employment tax issues that might otherwise arise.

Resolution Approving Independent Contractor Services

In many situations, you can use your regular procedure for hiring outside contractors without worrying about formalities. But if you want to obtain formal approval of the arrangement—for example, if an outside IC requests formal approval by your LLC—this resolution can come in handy.

CD-ROM

Below is a sample of the resolution you can use to approve the hiring of ICs. You'll find this resolution on the CD-ROM and as a tearout form in Appendix C. (See Appendix A for information on selecting and using the CD-ROM files.) Complete it following the special instruction below.

Approval of Independent Contractor Services

After discussion, the following independent contractor services were approved to be performed by ___[name of independent contractor firm or individual]___:

___[specify services and payment schedule for services to be performed]___. ❶

Special Instruction

❶ If the outside firm or individual has submitted a schedule of services or an agreement for approval, you can refer to it here and attach it to your resolution after the resolution is approved. In that case, insert the following language in this portion of the resolution: "See attached schedule/agreement, which was approved and is attached to this resolution."

TIP

Use written independent contractor agreements. An independent contractor agreement not only sets the terms of the work to be performed and the schedule for payments for the work by the LLC, but can also help the arrangement qualify for independent contractor status with the IRS. Standard independent contractor agreements reference many of the tax factors used by the IRS for classifying the worker as an outside contractor. For example, agreements often make the service provider liable for all employment taxes, withholding, and the like. To prepare an independent contractor agreement and learn more about the various tax criteria used by the IRS in classifying workers as employees and independent contractors, you'll need outside help. Two excellent resources are *Hiring Independent Contractors: The Employer's Legal Guide,* and *Consultant and Independent Contractor Agreements,* both by Stephen Fishman (Nolo).

Appointing and Paying Officers

State LLC laws usually allow an LLC to appoint whatever officers it decides are necessary or convenient to carry out its business. Typically, an LLC has a president, a treasurer, and a secretary, plus any additional officer positions it decides to fill. In a small one- or two-owner LLC, one person might hold more than one officer position. State law typically allows this. In many instances, officer titles such as president and secretary are formal, administrative titles only. They are used by the officer only when signing or approving LLC legal or tax papers. In other words, even though a person may be granted the title of LLC president or treasurer, he or she is typically paid a salary in connection with other full-time work for the LLC.

EXAMPLE 1:

Beth is the president of the Dynamite Deli LLC, and Bob is its treasurer/secretary. Beth is paid a salary as the manager of the deli and Bob as the counter chief. (Their formal LLC officer positions are unpaid.)

EXAMPLE 2:

Nate, Nancy, and Nick are the three members of a member-managed financial planning services LLC. Nate is the CEO (chief executive officer, which can be an alternate title for president), Nancy is the CFO (chief financial officer, an alternate title for treasurer), and Nick is the CIO (chief information officer—in charge of the financial software systems of the company). He also doubles formally as the LLC secretary. Each is paid a salary for filling these traditional officer positions (president, vice president, and secretary). Nick is paid for performing both jobs.

Use the resolution shown below to appoint LLC officers and to set compensation (hourly or salary) if an officer is to be paid for officer duties.

CD-ROM

Below is a sample of the resolution you can use to approve the appointment of LLC officers. You'll find this resolution on the CD-ROM and as a tearout form in Appendix C. (See Appendix A for information on selecting and using the CD-ROM files.) Complete it following the special instruction below.

Appointment of LLC Officers

After discussion, the following individuals were appointed to serve in the following LLC officer positions. Any annual salary to be paid to any officer and approved is shown below next to the name of the officer:

Title of Officer	Name	Compensation, if any
_____ :	_____	$_____ ❶
_____ :	_____	$_____
_____ :	_____	$_____
_____ :	_____	$_____

Each officer has the duties that are specified in the operating agreement of the LLC and as may be designated from time to time by the LLC management. An officer serves until his or her successor is elected and is qualified to replace the officer.

Special Instruction

❶ If a person will be paid for serving as an officer, fill in the annual salary. If salaries will be set later, insert "to be determined" in the appropriate salary blanks. If officers will not receive salaries in their capacities as officers, fill in "N/A" or "none" in the salary blanks.

Compensation for Attending LLC Meetings

Your LLC may want to pay members or managers for attending LLC meetings, as well as for incurring travel and other expenses. This compensation will be taxable income to the individual. They are also deductible by the LLC in determining its net income that is distributable to members on its annual information return.

Resolution Authorizing Payment for Attending LLC Meetings

Members and managers may be paid a per diem (per day) amount for attending LLC manager or member meetings. In addition, members or managers who must travel to attend these meetings may be reimbursed additional reasonable travel expenses. This occurs most often where closely held LLCs have outside members—perhaps an out-of-state relative who holds a membership interest in the LLC and attends annual membership meetings.

CD-ROM

Below is a sample of the resolution you can use to authorize special compensation. You'll find this resolution on the CD-ROM and as a tear-out form in Appendix C. (See Appendix A for information on selecting and using the CD-ROM files.) Complete it following the special instruction below.

Authorization of Payment for Attending LLC Meetings

After discussion, it was agreed that all of the following persons will be paid the following amounts for each day, or fraction of a day, during which they attend a meeting of the LLC.

Name and Title	Per Diem Amount
_____	$_____
_____	$_____
_____	$_____
_____	$_____

It was also discussed and agreed that the following persons will be   ["advanced" or "reimbursed"]   the following reasonable and necessary travel expenses incurred to attend meetings of the managers and/or members of the LLC:

Name and Title	Per Meeting Travel Allotment ❶
_____	$_____
_____	$_____
_____	$_____
_____	$_____

Special Instruction

❶ You can specify a set travel expense allotment, or you can simply set a maximum amount to be advanced or reimbursed (for example, "actual travel expenses up to a maximum amount of $500").

Resolution Authorizing Stipend for Attending LLC Meetings

Another way to compensate members or managers for attending LLC meetings is by authorizing the payment of an annual amount, regardless of the number of meeting days per year or the actual travel expenses incurred.

CD-ROM

Below is a sample of the resolution you can use to authorize annual stipends. You'll find this resolution on the CD-ROM and as a tearout form in Appendix C. (See Appendix A for information on selecting and using the CD-ROM files.) Complete it following the special instruction below.

Special Instruction

❶ Insert a month and date, such as "March 31." Do not include a year.

Indemnification for Members, Managers, Officers, and Employees

Indemnification means that the LLC will pay any fines, settlements, court awards or judgments, attorneys fees, penalties, or other amounts that are personally assessed against:

- a member
- a manager
- an officer
- an employee, or
- another person acting as an agent of the LLC.

These amounts might be assessed because of unwise decisions or omissions made while performing services for the LLC. They are usually imposed as the result of lawsuits or investigations.

Indemnification is an LLC's way of guaranteeing LLC members, managers, employees, and other agents that the LLC will pay certain costs and amounts that may be assessed against them as a result of working for the LLC. Some LLCs indemnify only certain categories of LLC representatives, such as managers or officers, or

---

Annual Stipend for Attendance at LLC Meetings

After discussion, it was agreed that, on or by ___[date of payment]___ ❶ of each year, the following persons will be paid the following annual amounts, which comprise a yearly travel allotment for traveling to and attending regular and special meetings of the LLC:

Name and Title	Annual Stipend and Travel Allotment
_____	$_____
_____	$_____
_____	$_____
_____	$_____

set certain conditions that must be met before indemnification occurs.

EXAMPLE:

Tosh Imato, the sole manager of Lox Box LLC, approved the LLC's use of certain suppliers, who turned out to be lax in their refrigeration procedures. A customer sues Tosh personally for medical bills resulting from a food-poisoning incident. Tosh wins the suit, after a finding by the court that he could not have reasonably known of or foreseen the inferior food-processing procedures used by the supplier. The victory is not complete, however, because Tosh is liable for hefty lawyers' fees incurred in his own defense. Because the LLC has authorized indemnification for all legal costs associated with lawsuits that are resolved in favor of managers, the LLC—not Tosh—pays these fees.

The extent and amount of indemnification that can or must be paid by LLCs to managers, members, and officers may be set by state LLC statutes. Some states don't require or address indemnification; others have lengthy statutes covering this issue. Typically, if a state LLC act has a provision for indemnification, it requires the LLC to indemnify an LLC member, manager, officer, employee, or agent of the LLC for legal expenses, including attorney's fees, if that LLC representative is sued and wins the lawsuit. Other types of indemnification, such as payment of a court judgment or settlement if an LLC representative doesn't win a lawsuit, may or must be paid if certain conditions are met. For example, indemnification might be authorized if the LLC determines that the person acted in good faith and in the best interests of the LLC

and, in criminal cases where fines are levied, that the person did not believe the conduct was unlawful.

Here is a typical statute.

Minnesota Limited Liability Company Act, Section 322B.699

2. […] a limited liability company shall indemnify a person made or threatened to be made a party to a proceeding by reason of the former or present official capacity of the person against judgments, penalties, and fines, including, without limitation, excise taxes assessed against the person with respect to an employee benefit plan, settlements, and reasonable expenses, including attorney's fees and disbursements, incurred by the person in connection with the proceeding, if, with respect to the acts or omissions of the person complained of in the proceeding, the person:

1. has not been indemnified by another organization or employee benefit plan for the same judgments, penalties, fines, [etc.];

2. acted in good faith;

3. received no improper personal benefit …

4. in the case of a criminal proceeding, had no reasonable cause to believe the conduct was unlawful; and

5. in the case of acts or omissions occurring [when the person was acting as a governor/manager, member, or employee of the LLC], reasonably believed that the conduct was in the best interests of the limited liability company ….

The provision goes on to say that this otherwise mandatory indemnification can be denied by an express provision in the articles or operating agreement of the LLC as long as the denial of indemnification applies to all persons within a given class (such as all managers or members).

Managers' and Members' Liability Insurance May Be Important

Even if your LLC indemnifies you to the maximum extent possible under state LLC statutes, this may not be enough. If a manager, member, or officer loses a lawsuit, state law may not allow indemnification unless an independent committee of the LLC or a judge finds that the person acted in good faith. Moreover, even if indemnification can be authorized in a particular case, the LLC may not have the funds to pay these bills.

Consequently, some LLCs decide that the best way to protect members and managers from personal liability for their LLC acts or omissions is to purchase a special managers', members' and officers' liability policy. (In the corporate world, this type of insurance is called a D & O liability policy, which stands for "directors and officers" liability policy.) These policies can be used instead of, or in conjunction with, indemnification by the LLC. For example, they can pick up the cost of legal expenses not paid directly by the LLC, or they can pay in addition to any indemnification made. Policies of this sort may be costly, and some contain a lot of exclusions. So if obtaining this type of coverage is important to you, do some insurance shopping. Check with different insurance brokers to find a suitable and affordable policy.

The articles or your operating agreement might already contain a summary or restatement of the mandatory or permissible indemnification rules in your state. Or it might authorize indemnification payments for your LLC's principals and agents according to its own preference. In either case, you will not need to use the resolution below. But if your articles and your operating agreement don't deal with indemnification, I suggest you use the following resolution as a starting point only. Because state indemnification rules vary, you should check the resolution against the rules in your state's LLC act and, if you need more information, ask a small business lawyer for guidance.

SEE AN EXPERT

There's more to indemnification than meets the eye. This general resolution is not tailored to meet the details of each state's indemnification scheme. If indemnification is of crucial concern to you—perhaps because your particular line of business or the legal climate in your field means that you can expect lawsuits directed against your managers, members, or officers—check with a small business lawyer to explore just how helpful your state's indemnification statutes really are. Also check into buying a managers' and members' liability policy to cover any nonindemnified legal costs.

CD-ROM

Below is a sample of the resolution you can use to provide for indemnification and insurance. You'll find this resolution on the CD-ROM and as a tearout form in Appendix C. (See Appendix A for information on selecting and using the CD-ROM files.)

The general indemnification resolution provided below can be used by the LLC to authorize the maximum indemnification for LLC members, managers, officers, and other LLC agents permitted by state law. It also authorizes the LLC to purchase managers' and members' liability insurance to cover legal expenses, settlements, fines, and other costs not covered by indemnification.

LLC Indemnification and Insurance

The LLC will indemnify its current and former [insert "members," "managers," "employees" and/or "other agents"] to the fullest extent permitted under the laws of this state. Such indemnification is not deemed to be exclusive of any other rights to which the indemnified person is entitled, consistent with law, under any provision of the LLC articles of organization (or similar organizing document of this LLC) or the LLC operating agreement; as a result of any general or specific action of the members or managers of this LLC; under the terms of any contract; or as may be permitted or required by law.

The LLC may purchase and maintain insurance or provide another arrangement on behalf of any person who is or was a [insert "member," "manager," "employee," and/or "other agent"] of this LLC against any liability asserted against him or her and incurred in such a capacity or arising out of his or her official capacity with this LLC, whether or not the LLC would have the power to indemnify him or her against that liability under the laws of this state.

Loans to the LLC

When an LLC needs money, it typically applies to a bank for a loan or asks its members for funds, in the form of additional capital contributions or as loans. Some smaller LLCs may prefer to borrow funds from members, because they are usually active in the business and willing to help out when cash flow is tight. (If your LLC wishes to lend money to—rather than borrow from—an LLC member, manager, officer, or employee, see Chapter 14.)

This chapter discusses the tax and legal ins and outs of borrowing money. It includes resolutions that allow the LLC to formally approve finalized loans taken out from financial institutions, existing members, or family and friends. Setting out this type of specific approval in a formal resolution helps an LLC control the borrowing behavior of its principals. It also helps everyone in the LLC agree on how much to borrow when cash is short.

This chapter also includes resolutions that can be used to authorize LLC members, managers, or officers to go out and borrow funds on behalf of the LLC. These resolutions are preliminary in nature—that is, they grant LLC officers permission to seek a loan, sometimes with a limit placed on the maximum amount that may be borrowed or other restrictions on the terms of the financing.

To help you keep your loans in order, this chapter also explains how to select and use different types of promissory notes to help you document the payback terms of your LLC's loans.

SEE AN EXPERT

Tax and legal considerations. Borrowing money is a serious business, even if the lender is a member, manager, or other LLC insider. You should use the information in this chapter to discuss the tax, legal, and practical considerations of taking out loans with your tax adviser or business lawyer before approving any sizable LLC loan.

Who Should Approve Loans to the LLC?

Typically, only LLC managers (the managing members of a member-manager LLC or the managers of a manager-managed LLC) need to approve loan transactions. If the loan transactions are substantial in amount or frequency, or if your LLC has outside investors (nonmanaging members) who might raise eyebrows at a particular loan transaction, however, you should have all members (in addition to any managers) approve the loan.

CAUTION

Members and managers can enter into loans on the LLC's behalf without express approval. Under the laws of most states, any member of a member-managed LLC, any manager of a manager-managed LLC, and any LLC officer can enter into legally binding contracts—including loan agreements—on the LLC's behalf. (This general rule doesn't apply if the outside lender knows that the proposed loan is outside the authority actually granted to the member, manager, or officer.) You probably don't plan to give copies of your borrowing resolution(s) to every potential lender in town, but adopting a resolution specifying who has the authority to enter into loans can serve as a powerful check on those inside the LLC. Once you approve a borrowing resolution, everyone will know what is expected of them—and chances are good that members, managers, and officers will abide by the terms of the resolution and avoid committing the LLC to loans that go beyond its terms.

Bank Loans to the LLC

Many LLCs borrow funds from time to time from banks and other commercial institutions, such as savings and loans and credit unions. This chapter refers to all of these institutions as "banks."

There are two common ways LLCs borrow from banks:

- **Lump-sum loan.** The LLC receives the entire amount of borrowed funds all at once and repays it over time, usually over two to five years. Banks often charge the prime interest rate currently in effect plus two or three percentage points, or an adjustable rate that changes in step with a particular financial index. Especially at the start of its relationship with a bank, your LLC should also expect to be asked to pay a point or two as a loan fee and to pledge the personal assets of LLC principals, the LLC's accounts receivable, or the LLC's inventory as collateral for the loan. As your LLC's credit history develops with the bank, you should be able to negotiate lower points on future loans and might get away without a pledge of personal collateral. (This is a good thing, of course, because when an LLC member pledges personal assets for a loan, he or she gives up the limited liability protection that otherwise applies to LLC debts and is personally liable for the loan if the LLC fails to repay it.)

- **Revolving line of credit.** Funds may be borrowed by the LLC, paid back, and reborrowed over a period of time (usually one year) on an as-needed basis, up to the LLC credit limit. Interest rates and fees are similar to those for a loan, but for the credit limit to be renewed for another year, the bank may require the line of credit to be paid off for at least part of the year. "Out of debt for thirty days once in each 12 months" is a typical requirement for renewal.

  As with lump-sum loans, your LLC may be required to pledge either the personal assets of LLC principals, the LLC's accounts receivable, or the LLC's inventory as collateral for the line of credit.

EXAMPLE:

The Hinterland Campwear LLC needs additional funds to take up the slack in cash flow during slow periods of its yearly business cycle. It applies for and obtains a $75,000 line of credit at a local bank. Throughout the year, authorized officers may call the bank and ask to have funds transferred to the LLC account. Requests for additional funds may be made as often as needed, as long as cumulative borrowing under the line of credit does not exceed the credit limit of $75,000 in a fiscal year. Hinterland may pay back as little or as much of the amount borrowed as it chooses, which allows the LLC to save on interest payments when it has extra cash.

Understanding Important Loan Terms

Make sure you fully understand the terms of any LLC loan before you sign on the dotted line. Here are some loan terms to read carefully:

- **Security pledge.** Depending on the LLC's and its members' net worth and credit history, as well as the amount of the LLC loan, the bank may ask members to pledge personal assets as collateral for the note—such as equity in a house. If the LLC defaults on repayment of the note, the bank can foreclose on the house and sell the property to satisfy the delinquent debt.

- **Right of setoff.** In case of default, the bank will have the right to reach all of the money, securities, and other property that the LLC and the guarantors have deposited as security for the debt with the bank.

- **Subordination agreement.** If the LLC signs a subordination agreement and then defaults on its bank loan, the bank has a legal right to be paid before other lenders (including LLC members) listed in this agreement. In other words, if you previously loaned money to your LLC, either during the LLC's formation or at a later date, the bank has a right to be paid before you.

Tax Effects of a Bank Loan to an LLC

The money an LLC borrows from the bank (also called the principal of the loan) is not considered income. Therefore, it is not allocated to members and taxed to them. After all, the principal amount of a loan must be repaid—the LLC and its members don't get to keep this money. The interest that the LLC pays on a bank loan can be deducted from the LLC's income as an LLC business expense. This reduces the LLC's net profits, which are allocated and taxed to members at the end of the LLC's tax year.

A bank loan to an LLC can also affect the members' tax basis in their membership interests. This is a complicated area; here are a few basics, but you'll probably want to talk to a tax adviser for help.

First, as discussed in Chapter 11, the term "income tax basis," or simply "basis," refers to the value assigned to your LLC ownership interest for the purposes of determining the taxable gain or loss from it after it is sold. Generally, your income tax basis in an ownership interest is the cash amount you pay, along with your current basis in any property you transfer, to buy the interest. If you transfer property that's subject to a debt that the business assumes—for example, you transfer real estate subject to a mortgage—your basis in your interest is decreased by the amount of the assumed debt.

An increase in basis generally results in lower capital gains taxes when an LLC member sells his or her interest; likewise, a decrease in basis generally results in higher taxes. In addition, members sometimes want to increase their basis in a membership interest so they can deduct LLC losses on their individual income tax returns. Members generally get to deduct LLC losses allocated to them, but only up to the amount of their basis in their interest. If the loss exceeds the basis amount, the loss cannot be deducted that year but must be held for deduction in future years.

A member's basis can be affected when a member personally guarantees repayment of a bank loan—that is, when the member agrees to pay off the loan balance if the LLC defaults and the LLC assets pledged as collateral don't cover it. The tax rules classify this type of loan as a "recourse debt," because the lender has recourse to seek repayment from the member who made a personal guarantee. When a member takes on a "recourse debt," the tax rules allow that member to increase his or her basis in a membership interest by the full amount of the loan. (This tax treatment is similar to the increase of basis that occurs when a member makes a capital contribution to an LLC—read more in "Legal Issues on Insider Loans," below). Of course, any time a member's basis increases because of an LLC loan, the member's basis decreases as the loan is paid off.

There are other ways that a member's basis in a membership interest can be increased when the LLC takes out a loan. Bank loans can sometimes be classified as recourse debt of the members, even if they don't personally guarantee the loans. For example, if the bank that has loaned money to the LLC can force the members to pay cash into the LLC to bring their capital account balances back up to zero any time they are negative, the bank loan can be classified as recourse debt. In this situation, a member's basis is increased by multiplying the total loan amount by the member's percentage of profits interest in the LLC.

If a loan to an LLC does not qualify as recourse debt, the tax rules call it "nonrecourse debt." Although nonrecourse debt may allow LLC members to increase their basis in their membership interests, the benefit of this basis increase may be limited by other tax rules. (See

"An Increase in a Member's Tax Basis Doesn't Always Allow Members to Deduct More LLC Losses," directly below.)

An Increase in a Member's Tax Basis Doesn't Always Allow Members to Deduct More LLC Losses

As mentioned above, members can deduct LLC losses allocated to them up to the amount of their basis in their interest. If the loss exceeds the basis amount, the member cannot deduct the loss that year but must hold the deduction for future years.

Here's the rub: Another set of IRS loss-deduction rules—called the "at-risk" loss rules—say that even if a member has sufficient basis to absorb a loss, no deduction can be taken unless the member's "at-risk" basis is at least as large as the amount of the loss the member seeks to claim. At-risk basis is generally the amount of money an LLC member stands to lose as a result of an investment in the LLC, including his or her liability for any LLC debt. However, most nonrecourse LLC loans—loans taken out by an LLC for which no member is personally responsible—do not increase a member's at-risk basis (with the exception of some secured real estate loans).

Other loss limitations rules can kick in when a member seeks to use losses and deductions generated by LLC loans to offset income on a member's individual tax return. Ask your tax adviser for more information.

SEE AN EXPERT

See your tax adviser for further informa-tion. This is only the briefest introduction to the complexities surrounding this area of LLC operations. I strongly recommend that you talk to your tax adviser if you wish to learn more about the various ways loans affect a member's basis in an LLC interest and tax obligations.

Resolutions to Approve Loans to the LLC by Lending Institutions

If you plan to borrow money from a bank or other financial institution, the bank will probably require a formal resolution. But check with its loan department before preparing any of the resolutions provided in this chapter. You may find that the bank will do much or all of the paperwork for you. All banks will at least provide you with a promissory note to sign. Some use their own loan resolution forms for signature by LLC members or managers.

If a bank does not provide its own resolution form, it may ask you to submit a copy of an LLC resolution that shows member and/or manager approval of the loan or line of credit. Below, you'll find samples of various resolutions that you can use to record LLC approval of loans from banks and other outside lending institutions. Pick the one that applies best to your situation.

TIP

Certification may be necessary. A bank may require that a loan approval resolution be certified by your LLC secretary. This means the secretary attaches a statement to the resolution stating that it was properly approved by the LLC and is still in effect. See "Certification of LLC Resolution" in Chapter 8 for a form the LLC secretary can use to certify the LLC's approval of a resolution.

Resolution Authorizing Bank Loan to LLC at Specific Terms

Use this resolution if you are seeking approval of a loan already negotiated with a local bank or other lender. This resolution shows approval of the specific terms of the loan.

CD-ROM

Complete this resolution following the special instructions below. You'll find this resolution on the CD-ROM and as a tearout form in Appendix C. (See Appendix A for information on selecting and using the CD-ROM files.)

Special Instructions

❶ As a shortcut, on the line "Terms of the Loan," you can use the words "terms according to the attached promissory note" and attach a copy of the promissory note to your resolution.

❷ Ordinarily, the LLC authorizes a member, manager, or officer (such as the president or treasurer) to borrow loan funds on its behalf. However, you may specify another officer or employee if you wish.

Authorization of Loan to LLC at Specific Terms

It was announced that the officers of the LLC have received a loan commitment from the following bank, trust company, or other financial institution on the following terms:

Name of Lender: [name of bank or other financial institution]

Loan Amount: [principal amount of the loan—amount you plan to borrow, not including interest]

Terms of the Loan: [state the terms of the loan, including rate of interest, the full repayment period, number and amount of installment payments, and date and amount of final payment if different from other payments]   ❶

It was resolved that the proposed terms of the loan are fair and reasonable to the LLC and that it is in the best interests of the LLC to borrow the funds on the terms stated above.

It was further resolved that the following member, manager, or officer is authorized to execute the notes and documents necessary to make the above loan on behalf of the LLC:

Name   Title ❷

_____   _____

_____   _____

Resolution Authorizing Maximum Loan to LLC on General Terms

The next resolution allows the LLC to authorize an LLC member, manager, or officer to go out and secure a bank loan (one that has not yet been arranged with a bank). This resolution allows the designated LLC representative to seek financing from a bank or other financial institution for a maximum loan amount on currently available terms, without limiting the transaction to a specific interest rate or other repayment provisions.

CD-ROM

Complete this resolution form following the special instruction below. You'll find this resolution on the CD-ROM and as a tearout form in Appendix C. (See Appendix A for information on selecting and using the CD-ROM files.)

Special Instruction

❶ Again, the LLC typically authorizes a member, manager, or officer, such as the president or treasurer, to borrow loan funds on its behalf.

Authorization of Maximum Loan Amount to LLC

It was resolved that it is in the best interests of the LLC to borrow up to the following amount from the following bank, trust company, or other financial institution:

Name of Lender: _____ [name of bank] _____

Loan Amount: ____ [principal amount of the loan not including interest] ____

On behalf of the LLC, the following member, manager, or officer is authorized to sign the appropriate notes and documents necessary to borrow an amount that does not exceed the amount noted above, on terms commercially reasonable to the LLC:

Name   Title ❶

_____   _____

_____   _____

Resolution Authorizing LLC Representative to Borrow Funds on Behalf of LLC as Needed

You may use this resolution to give an LLC member, manager, or officer unlimited authority to borrow money on behalf of the LLC from one or more banks whenever necessary for LLC business. An LLC should delegate this much financial leeway to an LLC principal only if all members have a significant amount of personal trust in an LLC principal. Such trust is most typically found in small LLCs where the person in question is actively involved with day-to-day operations.

CD-ROM

Complete this resolution form following the special instruction below. You'll find this resolution on the CD-ROM and as a tearout form in Appendix C. (See Appendix A for information on selecting and using the CD-ROM files.)

Special Instruction

❶ Again, the LLC typically authorizes a member, manager, or officer, such as the president or treasurer, to borrow loan funds on its behalf.

Authorization of LLC Representative to Borrow Funds on Behalf of LLC as Needed

It was resolved that the following member, manager, or officer of the LLC is authorized to borrow funds on behalf of the LLC from one or more banks or other financial institutions in the amounts he or she decides are reasonably necessary to meet the business needs of the LLC:

Name   Title ❶

_____   _____

_____   _____

Resolution Authorizing Specific Loan Terms Secured by LLC Property

You may use the following resolution to approve and document an LLC loan that is secured by personal or real property owned by the LLC. While the earlier loan resolutions can be modified to allow you to do this, here you can specifically list the LLC assets pledged as security. This extra bit of detail makes sense if the LLC is pledging significant LLC assets, such as LLC real estate, accounts receivables, or inventory, as collateral for the loan.

TIP

Get permission from all members before pledging substantial LLC assets. To avoid member discontent if the LLC can't repay the debt and the lender liquidates the LLC assets that secured the loan, you should have all members approve this resolution, whether your LLC is managed by some (or all) members or by managers.

CD-ROM

Complete this resolution form following the special instructions below. You'll find this resolution on the CD-ROM and as a tearout form in Appendix C. (See Appendix A for information on selecting and using the CD-ROM files.)

Authorization of Loan Terms Secured by LLC Property

It was resolved that the following LLC member, manager, or officer is authorized to borrow the sum of _$ [principal amount of loan]_ on behalf of the LLC from _____ [name of bank]_____ :

Name	Title ❶
_____	_____
_____	_____

The person named above is authorized to execute a promissory note for the principal amount shown above, together with a mortgage, deed of trust, or security agreement and any other documents necessary to secure payment of the note with the pledge of the following LLC property:

Property Used as Security for Note:____ [insert a description of the property]____ ❷

The terms for repayment of the note will be as follows:

Terms of Note: _____ [specify loan terms or refer to promissory note]_____ ❸

Special Instructions

❶ Again, the LLC typically authorizes a member, manager, or officer, such as the president or treasurer, to borrow loan funds on its behalf.

❷ Describe the LLC property pledged for the loan. For personal property, provide serial or ID numbers and a description of the property. An example might be "1994 Jeep Grand Cherokee, ID # XXX0099." For real estate, a street address (rather than a legal description) will do fine.

❸ Spell out the terms of the loan, such as the rate of interest and the number and amount of monthly payments. If terms have not been arranged, insert the following statement: "on best terms available from lender." If you prepare a promissory note for the loan, you may refer to it here as follows: "See the terms of the promissory note between the LLC and _____ [name of lender] _____, attached to this resolution" and attach a signed copy to the resolution.

Resolution Authorizing Line of Credit

The next resolution authorizes an LLC member, manager, or officer to arrange for and use an ongoing line of credit at a bank. Before you go forward, however, consider that once the authority is granted, an authorized person may tap the line at any time, up to the credit line limit that the bank authorized. (If you want a resolution that places a cap on the amount of money an LLC principal may borrow from a line of credit in any one transaction, see the resolution that follows this one.)

Note that the authority granted under this resolution is more limited than the authority given under the previous resolution. Here, the designated person may enter into repeated borrowing transactions only after the LLC obtains a line of credit. The result is that the person can't borrow more than the maximum amount authorized by the credit line. By contrast, in the previous resolution, an LLC member, manager, or officer is given the power to apply repeatedly for different bank loans, with no maximum overall limit established.

CD-ROM

Complete this resolution form following the special instructions below. You'll find this resolution on the CD-ROM and as a tearout form in Appendix C. (See Appendix A for information on selecting and using the CD-ROM files.)

Authorization of Line of Credit

It was resolved that it is in the best interests of the LLC to obtain a line of credit for borrowing funds from _____ [name of bank] _____.

The following LLC member, manager, or officer is authorized to complete all necessary forms, documents, and notes and to pledge as security for the loan any LLC assets necessary to obtain and use the line of credit:

Name   Title ❶

_____   _____

_____   _____

It was further decided that the authority granted by this resolution be limited and that the person named above not be allowed to establish a line of credit that exceeds _____ [credit line limit] _____. ❷

Special Instructions

❶ Again, the LLC typically authorizes a member, manager, or officer, such as the president or treasurer, to borrow loan funds on its behalf.

❷ You can use this paragraph to restrict the amount the LLC representative can borrow from the credit line during a certain period.

EXAMPLE:

Execuflex Time Management Systems, LLC, authorizes its treasurer to establish and borrow against an LLC line of credit as she sees fit, subject to an annual borrowing limit of $100,000 or up to $50,000 in a given quarter. Here's how to complete this provision:

"It was further decided that the authority granted by this resolution is limited and that the person named above is not allowed to borrow funds against the line of credit that exceed $100,000 per year or $50,000 in any calendar quarter."

If you don't wish to limit the amount of borrowing, simply delete the last paragraph. If you wish to limit the per-transaction amount of borrowing under a line of credit, see the next resolution.

Resolution Authorizing Line of Credit With Cap on Each Transaction

The sample resolution below authorizes a line of credit but restricts the amount that may be borrowed in any given transaction under this line of credit.

CD-ROM

Complete this resolution form following the special instructions below. You'll find this resolution on the CD-ROM and as a tearout form in Appendix C. (See Appendix A for information on selecting and using the CD-ROM files.)

Authorization of Line of Credit with Cap on Each Transaction

It was resolved that it is in the best interests of the LLC to obtain a line of credit from _____ [name of bank] _____ .

The following LLC member, manager, or officer was authorized to complete all necessary forms, documents, and notes necessary to obtain and use the line of credit to allow borrowing by the LLC in an aggregate amount that does not exceed __$[credit line limit and period if you wish—for example, $50,000 per fiscal year]__ : ❶

Name	Title ❷
_____	_____
_____	_____

It was further resolved that the amount borrowed under the line of credit in one transaction will not exceed __$[maximum amount that can be borrowed against the line of credit in one transaction, such as $10,000]__ unless any excess amount is specifically approved by further resolution of the LLC. ❸

Special Instructions

❶ You can use this paragraph to restrict the amount the LLC representative can borrow from the credit line in one transaction.

EXAMPLE:

Execuflex Time Management Systems, LLC, authorizes its treasurer to establish and borrow against an LLC line of credit as she sees fit, subject to an annual borrowing limit of $100,000 or up to $25,000 per transaction. Here's how to complete this provision:

"The following LLC member, manager, or officer was authorized to complete all forms, documents, and notes necessary to obtain and use the line of credit to allow borrowing by the LLC in an aggregate amount that does not exceed <u>$100,000 per year or $25,000 in any one transaction</u>."

❷ Again, the LLC typically authorizes a member, manager, or officer, such as the president or treasurer, to borrow loan funds on its behalf.

❸ You can use this paragraph to restrict the amount the LLC representative can borrow from the credit line in any one transaction. If you don't wish to limit the authority of the person named in this resolution in this way, simply delete the last paragraph.

Resolution Authorizing a Line of Credit Secured by LLC Property

You may use the following resolution to approve and document an LLC line of credit that is secured by personal or real property owned by the LLC. While the earlier line of credit resolutions can be modified to allow you to do this, here you can specifically list the LLC assets pledged as security. This extra bit of detail makes sense if the LLC is pledging significant LLC assets, such as LLC real estate, accounts receivables, or inventory, as collateral for the line of credit.

TIP

Get permission from all members before pledging substantial LLC assets. To avoid member discontent if the LLC can't repay the debt and the lender liquidates the LLC assets that secured the line of credit, you should have all members approve this resolution, whether your LLC is managed by some (or all) members or by managers.

CD-ROM

Complete this resolution form following the special instructions below. You'll find this resolution on the CD-ROM and as a tearout form in Appendix C. (See Appendix A for information on selecting and using the CD-ROM files.)

Authorization of Line of Credit Secured by LLC Property

It was resolved that it is in the best interests of the LLC to obtain a line of credit for borrowing funds from _____ [name of bank] _____.

The following LLC member, manager, or officer is authorized to complete all necessary forms, documents, and notes and to pledge as security for the loan any LLC assets necessary to obtain and use the line of credit:

Name   Title ❶

_____   _____

_____   _____

The person named above is authorized to execute a promissory note for the line of credit amount shown above, together with a mortgage, deed of trust, or security agreement and any other documents necessary to secure payment of the note with the pledge of the following LLC property:

Property Used as Security for Note: _____ [insert a description of the property] _____ ❷

The terms for repayment of the note will be as follows:

Terms of Note: _ [specify line of credit terms or refer to promissory note] _____ ❸

Special Instructions

❶ Again, the LLC typically authorizes a member, manager, or officer, such as the president or treasurer, to open a line a credit on its behalf.

❷ Describe the LLC property pledged for the line of credit. For personal property, provide serial or ID numbers and a description of the property. An example might be "1994 Jeep Grand Cherokee, ID # XXX0099." For real estate, a street address (rather than a legal description) will do fine.

❸ Spell out the terms of the line of credit, such as the rate of interest and how monthly payments are calculated. If terms have not been arranged, insert the following statement: "on best terms available from lender." If you prepare a promissory note for the credit line, you may refer to it here as follows: "See the terms of the promissory note between the LLC and _____ [name of lender] _____, attached

to this resolution" and attach a signed copy to the resolution.

Loans to the LLC by Members and Other Insiders

In small LLCs, the members often have a choice as to how to fund their business endeavors. They may pay money into the business as "capital" or they may lend funds to the LLC as "debt." This choice applies whether the funds are obtained at the startup of the LLC enterprise or after the LLC has been in business for a while.

CAUTION

Always get formal approval of insider loans to the LLC. Insider loans are loans between an LLC member, officer, or manager and the LLC. This is one of the areas of LLC decision making in which formal approval with a resolution is absolutely necessary. All LLCs should use resolutions and promissory notes (provided in Appendix C and on disk) to formally approve and record insider loan transactions. This precaution will maintain the limited liability of the members, avoid internal controversy, and help combat problems with the IRS.

Legal Issues on Insider Loans

Some LLCs borrow funds from time to time from members or managers (or sometimes from a member's family or friends). These loans may supplement bank loans or replace them. The purpose is usually to increase the LLC's cash reserves or to cover operational expenses. These insider loans can benefit both the LLC and a lending member or other insider.

As opposed to an additional capital contribution, a loan payable with interest results in an immediate investment return to the lending member. (In comparison, a capital contribution is a "risk" investment that depends on the success of the LLC—when you make a capital payment to your LLC, you are paying for the right to receive a share of any profits of the LLC as well as a portion of LLC assets when the LLC is sold or liquidated, if any remain after paying off creditors.) Obviously, unlike an interest-bearing loan made to an LLC, a capital contribution does not guarantee you a return on your money.

Even a loan agreement signed by the LLC, however, doesn't always assure the lender an investment return on the loaned funds. It's always possible that the LLC could fail to turn a profit and not be able to make repayments on the loan. And unlike a bank, an LLC insider probably won't have asked the other members to sign personal guarantees for the loan. For this reason, in larger LLCs, it may be difficult to find members or other individuals willing to offer funds unless the LLC is doing well and the lender feels assured of receiving timely

interest and principal payments under the loan. That's why loans of this sort mostly occur in the context of smaller, closely held LLCs. In such cases, there is considerable overlap between the fortunes of the LLC and the personal finances of its main members.

EXAMPLE:

Larry's Reality, LLC, is a one-person computer arcade and virtual reality parlor in the Westmont Mall complex. To keep his adolescent clientele interested in making return visits to the arcade, Larry must purchase the latest in expensive computer and virtual reality game gear, regardless of the current condition of his business's bottom line. As a result, he finds that he must occasionally make short-term (one- to three-month) personal loans to his LLC.

It is particularly important to document this type of insider loan transaction with LLC resolutions. If you don't do any extra paperwork when you routinely lend your one-person or small LLC operational funds by writing checks out of your personal checking account, a court could well decide that your LLC is simply your alter ego. The court could then hold you personally liable for LLC debts.

EXAMPLE:

For each of the personal loans made by Larry to his LLC, he prepares an LLC loan resolution and a basic promissory note to place in his LLC records binder. These should stand him in good stead should he ever land in court. Even if a disgruntled creditor claims that Larry's Reality operation is nothing more than his own personal limited liability checking account, Larry will probably win in court and hold on to his limited liability.

Another reason to prepare resolutions for insider loan transactions is to avoid internal controversy among your members. While LLC members or managers usually lend funds to help the LLC, not themselves, it is natural that repeated loan transactions between an LLC and a principal member or manager may arouse the curiosity of other LLC insiders. They may wonder if the lending member or manager is taking advantage of his or her LLC leverage to get too good a deal on repayment terms, essentially making money at the expense of the LLC. Getting formal approval for these loan transactions can answer nonborrowing members' questions and avoid this type of problem.

EXAMPLE:

Larry's brother-in-law, Fred, invests in Larry's Reality for a 20% nonvoting (nonmanaging) membership share. Larry calls an annual LLC membership meeting. At the meeting, he assures Fred that all personal loans made by Larry to the LLC carry commercially competitive interest rates and other repayment terms. Larry gives Fred copies of the loan resolutions and promissory notes. After examining the loan terms, Fred is satisfied that Larry has made the loans simply to help the business succeed, not to receive a special individual benefit.

TIP

Use a fixed interest rate. A member may wish to lend money to the LLC at no or low interest rates (though this may raise the hackles of IRS auditors—read more in "Tax Effects of Insider Loans," below). More sensibly, a member might wish to charge a commercially reasonable rate of interest for going to the trouble of lending personal funds to the LLC. But while commercial banks commonly charge variable interest rates that float two or three points above prime, members usually do not like to set up loans with fluctuating rates, because it's too complicated to do all the calculations. Instead, member loans usually contain a fixed interest rate. This is often fixed at a point or two above the prime rate that's in effect when the loan documents are signed. Or, members can choose a commercial rate, such as the "applicable federal rate."

Federal Loan Rates

The federal rates are the rates paid by the federal government on borrowed funds. They are set monthly. There are three federal rates: short term for loans with a three-year term or less (or for demand notes that can be called due at any time); mid term for loans from three years to nine years; and long term for loans with a term more than nine years.

The applicable federal rates are changed each month. You can find them online at www.irs.gov as the current month's "imputed interest rates" or "AFR rates" (technically called the "applicable federal rates under Section 1274(d) of the Internal Revenue Code"). Major business newspapers also list the current applicable fed rates, typically in their stock quotations section.

CAUTION

Beware of state usury laws. Whatever rate you come up with for an individual loan to your LLC, it must comply with your state's usury law. This law limits the maximum interest rate individuals can charge on loans, usually to 10%–12% per year (but sometimes much less). Check with your accountant or your local bank or other financial institution if you're not sure of the usury regulations in your state. You can also check the Caine-Weiner resource center at www.caine-weiner.com for a 50-state chart of permitted interest rates.

Other Ways Members Can Help Their LLC Financially

Investing capital or making loans to an LLC is not the only way members can fund their LLC or make assets available for its use. Here are a few other methods:

- The LLC may not need to go to the trouble of raising money to buy property that is currently owned by a member. Instead, the member can lease property to the LLC and receive rental income in return. Rent payments, like interest payments for a loan, are deductible by the LLC as business expenses (and, like interest income, rental income is taxed to the member who leases out the property).

- If the LLC needs funds to buy property (real estate or personal property, such as equipment or automobiles), it may be more advantageous for a member to purchase the property and lease it to the LLC (similar to the previous scenario).

- If the LLC needs cash, it can borrow from a bank rather than from its members, using the members' personal collateral to qualify for the loan. In other words, the members help out by pledging personal assets to guarantee repayment of the loan in case the LLC defaults on its payments. (Read more in "Bank Loans to the LLC," above.)

Tax Effects of Insider Loans

The basic tax effects of a member loan to the LLC are straightforward (and are the same as the tax effects of loans made to an LLC by a bank, as discussed above), as long as the loan is legitimate.

The money the LLC borrows (the principal of the loan) is not considered business income, and so is not taxed to the LLC. The LLC gets to deduct the interest it pays on the loan as a business expense. This, in turn, reduces the net profit of the LLC allocated and taxed to members at the end of its tax year. The member who lends the money to the LLC reports the interest payments received from the LLC on his or her individual income tax return, and is taxed at his or her individual income tax rate. When the LLC repays the principal, these proceeds are not taxable to the member.

Potential problems arise only when an LLC or an LLC member is selected for a tax audit. In that case, the IRS may carefully scrutinize a loan made to the LLC by a member, particularly if the LLC is closely held by just a few members.

If the IRS thinks a loan is just a disguised capital investment in the LLC, it will treat it as such. This means that interest payments the LLC makes to the member will be considered "guaranteed payments" (much like fixed salary payments), which have certain technical differences in their tax treatment that can be important to some LLCs. (Guaranteed payments and fixed salary payments are discussed briefly in "Tax Treatment of Salaries Paid to Members" in Chapter 12.)

More important, if the IRS treats a loan like a capital contribution to the LLC, the loan principal repayments the LLC makes to the member will be treated as distributions of LLC profits from the member's capital account. Generally, distributions of profits lower the member's basis in his or her interest. If the distributions exceed the member's basis, the member will have to pay taxes on the excess amount. A lower basis also results in higher capital gains taxes, if and when the member sells the membership interest or the LLC is liquidated. A lower basis can also limit the amount of LLC losses the member can claim on an individual tax return to offset other income.

One reason the IRS is leery of insider loans is that some LLC members use unpaid LLC debts to generate immediate deductions and losses, instead of waiting to claim them when the business folds. This is an unlikely scenario for readers of this book, who actively engage in a business to make a profit, not to generate deductible losses on their individual tax return. Nevertheless, here's an example of what the IRS is worried about:

EXAMPLE:

Tradewinds Travel Agency, LLC, is in the financial doldrums. It's short on profits due to a downturn in the economy, which resulted in less discretionary travel spending by the agency's regular clientele. To shore up the agency over the short-term, Sarah and Lewis, the two equal member-managers of the LLC, each lend the company $20,000. This will keep the office open and pay the salary of their sole booking agent. (Sarah and Lewis have income from other, more lucrative businesses.) They do not prepare formal promissory notes for the loans, deciding to treat them informally as non-interest-bearing demand notes—meaning that they will wait until the LLC is profitable before paying themselves back.

After two years, the LLC still hasn't turned around, and Sarah and Lewis realize that the LLC is unlikely to ever pay them back on the loans. They claim the loans as bad-debt deductions on their individual tax returns, using them to offset other income and save on taxes. Unfortunately for them, the IRS audits the LLC's and Sarah and Lewis's tax returns, disallowing the bad-debt losses. Why? Because the loans look to the IRS like investment of additional capital by the owners, which should be paid back only when the profits of the business warrant

it—or when the owners sell their interests. After all:

- The loans did not carry a set rate of interest.
- There was no repayment schedule.
- They were made in proportion to the member's capital interests in the business.
- They were commercially unreasonable loans (a bank would have required collateral for the loans and interest payments).

Because the IRS treats the loans as capital contributions, Sarah and Lewis will have to wait until they liquidate or sell their LLC membership interests to take their losses on the loan.

To avoid this kind of trouble with the IRS, you should follow a few basic rules. Following these rules will help ensure that the IRS treats loans from your members as legitimate lending transactions rather than capital contributions.

The idea behind these rules is simple: If all the facts and circumstances of a loan transaction show that a member advanced money to an LLC with a reasonable expectation of repayment regardless of the success of the LLC, the transaction will be treated as a loan. If the facts show otherwise, the loan will be treated as a capital contribution.

The key to surviving IRS audit scrutiny is to make sure your loan is *commercially reasonable*. The loan should be backed up by a written promissory note that includes at least the following terms:

- An unconditional promise by the LLC to repay the loan amount. If the LLC can delay payment to a member until the member liquidates his or her interest, the IRS is more likely to see the loan as a capital contribution.

- A fixed maturity date. The IRS prefers short-term notes over long-term notes, although repayment terms as long as ten years are usually considered acceptable. If a promissory note lacks a maturity date (a demand note, for instance) or if payments are contingent on earnings of the LLC, the IRS is more likely to disregard the loan.

- Interest payments at or close to the prevailing commercial rates. For small businesses, this hovers around, or perhaps a little above, the prime rate.

- A pledge of collateral as security for repayment, if a commercial lender probably would have required collateral.

Also, if loans are made by more than one member in proportions that correspond roughly to their capital interests, the "loans" will start looking more like capital contributions than valid loan transactions.

To avoid such conflicts with the IRS (and to maintain your limited liability and avoid controversy among the members), it's important to record LLC management's approval of an insider loan in a resolution and to use a promissory note, discussed below.

Resolution to Approve Loan to the LLC by Insider

If your LLC is borrowing funds from an LLC member, manager, or other individual, rather than a bank or other outside business, you should always get LLC approval in a formal resolution, backed up with a promissory note that spells out the terms for repayment. Doing this creates a paper trail that the LLC and the individual lender can refer to later to handle any disputes. It's surprising how often undocumented loans to and from individual owners can lead to trouble. Lenders and borrowers might remember the terms of

the deal differently or walk away from the transaction with different expectations. If you put all loan transactions in writing, you can resolve later controversies with a quick look at your LLC records. Preparing proper LLC loan documentation can also, of course, help avoid problems with the courts and the IRS.

The resolution below records the LLC's acceptance of a loan of funds from one or more members, managers, or other individuals (friends or relatives of a member, for instance). This resolution uses language designed to verify that the loan is properly documented by a written promissory note, is being made on commercially acceptable terms, and can be paid back without jeopardizing the financial viability of the LLC. These recitals help establish the loan as a valid debt transaction.

TIP

Use a special resolution to approve a member or manager loan to the LLC. If the LLC borrows from a member or manager at payback terms that are generous to the lender (for example, the lending member will receive a high rate of interest from the LLC), you may want to have the loan approved by the nonlending members. They will first want to verify that the loan terms do not unduly benefit the lending members (that is, the terms are similar to the terms that any outsider would insist on when making a loan to the LLC). An easy way to do this is to approve the loan using the resolution in "Resolution for Approval of Member or Manager Self-Interested Business Deals" in Chapter 15. The resolution in Chapter 15 includes extra space to show disclosure of the member's or manager's interest in the loan transaction and allows the LLC to state the reason the loan transaction is fair to the LLC.

CD-ROM

Complete this resolution following the special instructions below. You'll find this resolution on the CD-ROM and as a tearout form in Appendix C. (See Appendix A for information on selection and using the CD-ROM files.)

Special Instructions

❶ Specify the amount to be lent along with the name of each member, manager, or other individual making the loan to the LLC. If a loan is made jointly by spouses, list both spouses on one line.

❷ Before presenting the resolution to the LLC, prepare a proposed promissory note that contains the loan terms and present it for approval by the LLC. After approval, it should be signed by the LLC treasurer and the lender, and a copy should be attached to the resolution.

Approval of Loan to the LLC

It was resolved that it is in the best interests of the LLC to borrow the following amount(s) from the following individuals:

Name of Lender	Amount ❶
_____	$_____
_____	$_____

The terms of each loan were included in a proposed promissory note presented for approval at the meeting. ❷ The LLC determined that these terms were commercially reasonable. The LLC also determined that LLC earnings should be sufficient to pay back the loan(s) to the lender(s) according to the terms in the note(s), and that such repayment would not jeopardize the financial status of the LLC.

Therefore, the LLC approved the terms of each note and directed the treasurer to sign each note on behalf of the LLC. The secretary was directed to attach a copy of each note, signed by the treasurer, to this resolution and to place the resolution and the attachment(s) in the LLC records binder.

Promissory Notes Overview

A promissory note is the contract behind a particular loan—a written promise by the borrower to pay back the lender the principal amount borrowed, with interest, in a specific time frame.

Before looking at the various promissory note forms included with this book, this section explains the different ways notes are commonly structured. This discussion will help you select the most appropriate form for your loan transaction.

SKIP AHEAD

Skip ahead if you're borrowing from a bank. All banks will provide you with a promissory note to sign when your LLC borrows money from them. Use the promissory notes below only for loans to the LLC by members, managers, and other individual lenders.

Our Promissory Notes Use Simple Interest

The notes discussed in this chapter call for simple, rather than compound, interest. With simple interest, interest is charged on the remaining unpaid principal due under the note, but not on any unpaid interest that accumulates during the term of the loan.

As a practical matter, compound interest is usually not necessary for LLC loans from insiders. If the loan is paid off in installments, the LLC will usually pay off all accrued interest with each installment. For long-term loans that don't call for any payments for quite a while (perhaps a year or more), it's possible to compound the interest due, although most smaller LLCs won't choose to do so. If you want to figure out compound interest, you can use a future value table; check with your tax adviser, your bank, or a real estate broker.

Lump-Sum Repayment With Interest

If your note provides for a lump-sum repayment, both principal and interest are repaid at the end of the agreed repayment period. To compute the interest due with the repayment, multiply the full amount of principal owed under the note times the annual interest rate times the number of years (and any fraction of a year) the loan will be outstanding.

EXAMPLE:

Kyle will lend $10,000 to his LLC at an annual interest rate of 6%. Under the terms of the promissory note, repayment of principal plus interest is due in one lump sum at the end of a five-year period. To compute the interest due with the lump-sum payment, Kyle multiplies $10,000 x .06 x 5 to arrive at an interest payment of $3,000. The total lump-sum payment due at the end of the loan period will be $13,000.

It may be necessary to calculate the interest on a monthly basis, such as when a note calls for a 15- or 30-month repayment period. In that case, figure out the monthly interest and multiply it by the appropriate number of months. Then add that amount to the principal.

EXAMPLE:

Kyle will lend $10,000 to his LLC at an annual interest rate of 6%. Repayment of principal plus interest is due in one lump sum at the end of an eight-month period. To compute the interest due, Kyle multiplies $10,000 x .06 to arrive at an annual interest payment of $600. He then divides that by 12, to get monthly interest of $50, which he multiplies by 8, for a total of $400. Finally, he adds the total interest to the principal to calculate the total lump-sum payment due at the end of the loan period: $10,400.

Periodic Payment of Interest Only

If your note provides for periodic payments of interest with a lump-sum payment of principal at the end of an agreed period, you have to figure out the amount of interest that should be paid periodically. The easiest way to do this is to figure out the total amount of interest the LLC will end up paying. As you'll see, the LLC will pay the same total amount of interest this way as it would if it repaid the entire amount (principal and interest) at the end of the repayment period.

To compute the total interest charged under this type of note, multiply the principal amount times the annual interest rate times the number of years (and any fraction of a year) of the loan term. Then divide this total interest amount by the number of periodic interest payments required under the note. The result is the amount of each interest-only payment the LLC must pay.

EXAMPLE:

Maria, an LLC manager, lends $15,000 to her LLC. The note provides for quarterly interest-only payments at the rate of 6% over the three-year life of the note. That's 12 quarterly interest payments the LLC will make. Total interest due on the $15,000 over the three-year period is $2,700 ($15,000 x .06 x 3). The amount of each quarterly interest payment is $225—the total $2,700 interest amount divided by 12.

Periodic Payments of Interest Plus Principal (Amortized Loans)

This type of repayment plan, which allows for monthly or quarterly payments of principal and interest, is probably the one small LLCs use most often.

When both principal and interest are paid in periodic installments under a note, the interest owed under the note declines with each payment, as the outstanding principal balance declines. It's possible, however, to charge equal installment payments if the percentage that goes to paying off the principal increases with each payment.

Fortunately, it's not difficult to figure out the amount required for each payment, using the basic amortization schedule below. If you can't find the interest rate and time period you want, real estate brokers, banks, credit unions, financial publications, and business books have amortization schedules that show amortization multipliers for other interest rates and periods. In addition, standard computer spreadsheets such as Microsoft *Excel* and others can compute interest due on amortized loans, as can online calculators, which you can find on numerous websites, including www.timevalue.com.

To use the amortization schedule below, you need to know the annual interest rate and term of the note in years. Find your interest rate percentage in the left-hand column of the schedule and the number of years for the terms of your note in the top row. Then, extend the column and row until they intersect. Multiply this number by the total principal amount of your loan. The result is the monthly principal and interest payment under the note that will pay off the principal in the specified number of years.

EXAMPLE:

Martina, an LLC member, plans to lend her LLC $20,000 at 8% over a period of ten years, to be paid back in equal monthly principal and interest payments. She finds the 8% row on the left side of the schedule and follows it to the right to meet the ten-year column extending down from the

Amortization Schedule for Monthly Payments

Interest Rate	Number of Years																	
	1	1.5	2	2.5	3	4	5	6	7	8	9	10	11	12	13	14	15	20
3.0%	.0847	.0569	.0430	.0346	.0291	.0221	.0180	.0152	.0132	.0117	.0106	.0097	.0089	.0083	.0077	.0073	.0069	.0055
3.5%	.0849	.0571	.0432	.0349	.0293	.0224	.0182	.0154	.0134	.0120	.0108	.0099	.0091	.0085	.0080	.0075	.0071	.0058
4.0%	.0851	.0573	.0434	.0351	.0295	.0226	.0184	.0156	.0137	.0122	.0110	.0101	.0094	.0088	.0082	.0078	.0074	.0061
4.5%	.0854	.0576	.0436	.0353	.0297	.0228	.0186	.0159	.0139	.0124	.0113	.0104	.0096	.0090	.0085	.0080	.0076	.0063
5.0%	.0856	.0578	.0439	.0355	.0300	.0230	.0189	.0161	.0141	.0127	.0115	.0106	.0099	.0092	.0087	.0083	.0079	.0066
5.5%	.0858	.0580	.0441	.0358	.0302	.0233	.0191	.0163	.0144	.0129	.0118	.0109	.0101	.0095	.0090	.0085	.0082	.0069
6.0%	.0861	.0582	.0443	.0360	.0304	.0235	.0193	.0166	.0146	.0131	.0120	.0111	.0104	.0098	.0092	.0088	.0084	.0072
6.5%	.0863	.0585	.0445	.0362	.0306	.0237	.0196	.0168	.0148	.0134	.0123	.0114	.0106	.0100	.0095	.0091	.0087	.0075
7.0%	.0865	.0587	.0448	.0364	.0309	.0239	.0198	.0170	.0151	.0136	.0125	.0116	.0109	.0103	.0098	.0094	.0090	.0078
7.5%	.0868	.0589	.0450	.0367	.0311	.0242	.0200	.0173	.0153	.0139	.0128	.0119	.0111	.0106	.0101	.0096	.0093	.0081
8.0%	.0870	.0591	.0452	.0369	.0313	.0244	.0203	.0175	.0156	.0141	.0130	.0121	.0114	.0108	.0103	.0099	.0096	.0084
8.5%	.0872	.0594	.0455	.0371	.0316	.0246	.0205	.0178	.0158	.0144	.0133	.0124	.0117	.0111	.0106	.0102	.0098	.0087
9.0%	.0875	.0596	.0457	.0373	.0318	.0249	.0208	.0180	.0161	.0147	.0135	.0127	.0120	.0114	.0109	.0105	.0101	.0090
9.5%	.0877	.0598	.0459	.0376	.0320	.0251	.0210	.0183	.0163	.0149	.0138	.0129	.0122	.0117	.0112	.0108	.0104	.0093
10.0%	.0879	.0601	.0461	.0378	.0323	.0254	.0212	.0185	.0166	.0152	.0141	.0132	.0125	.0120	.0115	.0111	.0107	.0097
10.5%	.0881	.0603	.0464	.0380	.0325	.0256	.0215	.0188	.0169	.0154	.0144	.0135	.0128	.0122	.0118	.0114	.0111	.0100
11.0%	.0884	.0605	.0466	.0383	.0327	.0258	.0217	.0190	.0171	.0157	.0146	.0138	.0131	.0125	.0121	.0117	.0114	.0103
11.5%	.0886	.0608	.0468	.0385	.0330	.0261	.0220	.0193	.0174	.0160	.0149	.0141	.0134	.0128	.0124	.0120	.0117	.0107
12.0%	.0888	.0610	.0471	.0387	.0332	.0263	.0222	.0196	.0177	.0163	.0152	.0143	.0137	.0131	.0127	.0123	.0120	.0110

top row of the schedule. She multiplies the resulting number, .0121, by $20,000 to arrive at the monthly principal plus interest payment amount of $242.

Securing Loans With Interests in LLC Property

Sometimes, although not often, individual lenders (members, managers, their friends or family) may ask for the loan to be secured with collateral. After all, this is exactly what outside commercial lenders often require. Securing a loan with collateral means that property owned by the LLC is pledged as security for the loan. If the LLC defaults, the lender may take the collateral and keep it or sell it as repayment for the debt.

Collateral for loans typically consists of the LLC's equity and share in real or personal property such as land or a building, a boat, a car, or computers. The accounts receivable of the LLC—amounts owed to the LLC and carried on the LLC books as an asset—also may be pledged for a loan. Product inventory is another likely source of collateral for loans. In all cases, lenders must make sure that the property has not already been pledged for the repayment of another LLC loan, such as a bank loan or line of credit.

After assuring that the property is "unencumbered" (that is, has not been used to secure another note), the lender should request that paperwork be prepared to put third parties on notice that the property is being used to secure a note, thus making it more difficult for the LLC (the debtor) to dispose of the secured property without the lender's (creditor's) permission. This is always done when real estate is used as security: A mortgage or deed of trust is prepared and recorded at the office of the county recorder. A legal stationer who carries legal forms, a local real estate broker, a bank officer, or your legal or tax adviser may have copies of these forms available. You'll find a basic secured, amortized promissory note below, to which you can attach copies of any security agreements (deeds of trust or mortgages) necessary in your state.

Demand Notes

A demand note allows the lender to "call the loan due" (request repayment of the entire loan) at any time. Rather than specifying a particular date in the future for repayment, the lender is given the power to call the loan due by making a written demand for payment. The borrower is usually given a short period of time, 30 to 60 days, for instance, after the written demand in which to pay off the loan balance.

Some demand notes limit when the lender can demand repayment. For example, a note might prohibit a lender from demanding repayment until at least three years have elapsed from the date of signing of the loan.

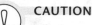 **CAUTION**

Proceed cautiously with a demand note. Although relations within the LLC may be cozy now, it's possible that there could be a falling out between your LLC and the lender. It's not unheard of for a lender to decide to get even by making an unexpected demand on a demand note. If you think there's any chance that this could happen when the LLC may not have the cash necessary to fulfill the loan repayment demand, choose another type of promissory note.

CAUTION

The IRS may look askance on demand notes. As mentioned above, if a promissory note lacks a maturity date and a repayment schedule, the IRS is more likely to regard a loan from an LLC member as a capital contribution to the LLC rather than a valid loan transaction.

Promissory Notes for Loans to LLC

This section explains how to use the promissory note forms included with this book. As discussed earlier, you should prepare a promissory note for each loan transaction made by an individual to your LLC. Attach it to your LLC resolution approving the loan.

SEE AN EXPERT

When to get outside help. It's always a good idea to have your tax adviser or lawyer give an LLC note the once over before using it, to ensure favorable legal and tax treatment. This is particularly important if you decide to add additional provisions to your note or wish to make any of the changes discussed in "Changing the Terms of the Basic Note Forms," directly below.

Changing the Terms of the Basic Note Forms

There are a great many terms and variations of terms that may be included in promissory notes, including interest rates, maturity dates, collateral, default provisions, and periodic payments of interest, principal, or both. The promissory notes included with this book contain the most common terms used by smaller LLCs. However, you may wish to add, delete, or change provisions on these forms to suit your own loan transaction. Here are some examples:

- **Acceleration clause.** All notes in this book contain an acceleration clause that allows the lender to declare the entire unpaid amount of the loan due if the LLC misses a payment for a specified number of days after its due date. While it's unlikely that an individual lender closely associated with the LLC will actually enforce this provision if one payment is missed,

the fact that he or she has the right to do so helps establish that the lender and the LLC intend to create a valid creditor/debtor relationship. If, however, you don't want your LLC to be obligated by this type of instant repayment provision, you can delete this clause.

- **Collection costs.** Another provision included in the notes allows the lender to charge collections costs in the event of a default by the LLC. This also helps establish the commercial reasonableness of the loan transaction. These collection costs include "reasonable attorneys' fees." Some readers may wish to define or place a limit on these fees, perhaps limiting the attorneys' fees that the LLC will pay in the event of a default to 10%–15% of the principal amount of the loan.

Promissory Note: Installment Payments of Principal and Interest (Amortized Loan)

Most smaller LLCs will prefer to use a promissory note that provides for periodic payments of principal plus interest until the principal amount of the loan is paid off.

CD-ROM

Complete this note following the special instructions below. You'll find this resolution on the CD-ROM and as a tearout form in Appendix C. (See Appendix A for information on selecting and using the CD-ROM files.)

LLC Promissory Note:
Installment Payments of Principal and Interest (Amortized Loan)

For value received, _____[name of LLC]_____, the borrower, promises to pay to the order of _____[name of member, manager, or other individual lender]_____, the noteholder, the principal amount of $ _[principal amount of loan]_, together with simple interest on the unpaid principal balance from the date of this note until the date this note is paid in full, at the annual rate of _[annual rate of interest]_ %. Payments will be made at _____[address of lender]_____.

Principal and interest will be paid in equal installments of $_[amount of each payment]_, ❶ beginning on _[date of first payment]_, and continuing on _[day for ongoing payments, for example, "the fifteenth day of each month"]_ until the principal and interest are paid in full. Each payment made by the borrower shall be applied first to accrued but unpaid interest, and the remainder will be applied to unpaid principal.

This note may be prepaid by the borrower in whole or in part at any time without penalty. This note is not assumable without the written consent of the noteholder. Consent will not be unreasonably withheld. This note is nontransferable by the noteholder. ❷

If any installment payment due under this note is not received by the noteholder within _[number of days]_ of its due date, the entire amount of unpaid principal and accrued but unpaid interest due under this note will, at the option of the noteholder, become immediately due and payable without prior notice by the noteholder to the borrower. In the event of a default, the borrower is responsible for the costs of collection, including, in the event of a lawsuit to collect on this note, the noteholder's reasonable attorneys' fees as determined by a court hearing the lawsuit.

Date of Signing: _____

Name of Borrower:_____[name of LLC]_____

Address of Borrower: _____[address of principal office of LLC]_____

City, or County, and State Where Signed: _____

Signature of Borrower:_____[signature of treasurer]_____, Treasurer

on behalf of _____[name of LLC]_____

Special Instructions

❶ Use an amortization schedule to calculate the monthly payment. (See Amortization Schedule, above.) Payments are usually made on a monthly basis, but you can establish a different interval if you choose. If you do, you'll need to use an amortization table based on your loan's repayment interval, such as quarterly or every other month. Check with a library, bookstore, or bank for other amortization tables.

❷ This paragraph specifies that the loan may be repaid by the LLC at any time without triggering a prepayment penalty. This allows your LLC to pay back the loan whenever it makes economic sense to do so. The loan is also made assumable (meaning another company or person can take over the payment obligation for the LLC) with the permission of the noteholder. However, it is unlikely that another company or person will wish to assume payments under the loan. The note is nontransferable—the individual lender may not transfer the note to another person to collect the payments from the LLC. This provision is common for insider loans in a small LLC. You can easily change this sentence to allow transfers if you wish, though it's highly unlikely that a noteholder will wish to transfer an LLC loan.

Promissory Note: Installment Payments of Principal and Interest (Amortized Loan) Secured by LLC Property

This promissory note is the same as the previous note but adds a clause that pledges LLC property as security for repayment of the loan. Again, loans that individuals make to your LLC are not usually secured, but this may be necessary in some cases to help make the individual lender feel more comfortable.

TIP

You can use the security clause in other note forms. To allow the LLC to pledge property as security for the repayment of a different type of note, you may copy the security clause in this note—the last paragraph in the text of the note shown below—to any of the other note forms covered below.

CD-ROM

Complete this note following the special instructions below. You'll find this resolution on the CD-ROM and as a tearout form in Appendix C. (See Appendix A for information on selecting and using the CD-ROM files.)

Special Instructions

❶ Use an amortization schedule to calculate the monthly payment. (See Amortization Schedule, above.) Payments are usually made on a monthly basis, but you can establish a different interval if you choose. If you do, you'll need to use an amortization table based on your loan's repayment interval, such as quarterly or every other month. Check with a library, bookstore, or bank for other amortization tables.

❷ This paragraph specifies that the loan may be repaid by the LLC at any time without triggering a prepayment penalty. This allows your LLC to pay back the loan whenever it makes economic sense to do so. The loan is also made assumable (meaning another company or person can take over the payment obligation for the LLC) with the permission of the noteholder. However, it is unlikely that another company or person will wish to assume payments under the loan. The note is nontransferable—the individual lender may not transfer the note to another person to collect the payments from the LLC. This provision

LLC Promissory Note:
Installment Payments of Principal and Interest
(Amortized Loan) Secured by LLC Property

For value received, _____ [name of LLC] _____ , the borrower, promises to pay to the order of _____ [name of member, manager, or other individual lender] _____ , the noteholder, the principal amount of __$[principal amount of loan]__ , together with simple interest on the unpaid principal balance from the date of this note until the date this note is paid in full, at the annual rate of __[annual rate of interest]%__ . Payments will be made at _____ [address of lender] _____ .

Principal and interest will be paid in equal installments of __$[amount of each payment]__ , ❶ beginning on ____[date of first payment]____ , and continuing on __[day for ongoing payments, for example, "the fifteenth day of each month"]__ until the principal and interest are paid in full. Each payment made by the borrower will be applied first to accrued but unpaid interest, and the remainder will be applied to unpaid principal.

This note may be prepaid by the borrower in whole or in part at any time without penalty. This note is not assumable without the written consent of the noteholder. Consent will not be unreasonably withheld. This note is nontransferable by the noteholder. ❷

If any installment payment due under this note is not received by the noteholder within __[number of days]__ of its due date, the entire amount of unpaid principal and accrued but unpaid interest due under this note will, at the option of the noteholder, become immediately due and payable without prior notice from the noteholder to the borrower. In the event of a default, the borrower is responsible for the costs of collection, including, in the event of a lawsuit to collect on this note, the noteholder's reasonable attorney fees as determined by a court hearing the lawsuit.

Borrower agrees that until the principal and interest owed under this note are paid in full, the note is secured by the following described mortgage, deed of trust, or security agreement: ____[describe security agreement, deed of trust, or mortgage used to pledge security of the property, including a description of the property]____ . ❸

Date of Signing: _____

Name of Borrower: _____ [name of LLC] _____

Address of Borrower: _____ [address of principal office of LLC] _____

City, or County, and State Where Signed: _____

Signature of Borrower: _____ [signature of treasurer] _____ , Treasurer

on behalf of _____ [name of LLC] _____

is common for insider loans in a small LLC. You can easily change this sentence to allow transfers if you wish, but it's highly unlikely that a noteholder will wish to transfer an LLC loan.

❸ This is the security clause. Specify the security agreement used to pledge the property as repayment for the loan in case of default, together with a description of the property. For real estate, you will want to complete and record a mortgage deed or deed of trust with the county recorder. For personal property, state law may require you to complete and file a security agreement to enforce the security clause in your note. A legal forms stationer may have security agreements on hand, or you can contact a real estate broker, tax adviser, or lawyer to obtain these forms or have them prepared for you. Attach a completed copy of the security document to the resolution.

EXAMPLE (real estate used as security):

"Deed of Trust to real property commonly known as _____ [address] _____, owned by _____ [name of LLC] _____, executed on _ [date of signing of deed of trust] , at _ [city and state where signed] _, and recorded at _ [place recorded] _, in the records of _ [name of recording office] _, _____ [name of county and state] _____ ."

EXAMPLE (LLC-owned automobile used as security):

"Security Agreement signed by _____ [name of officer] _____, on behalf of _ [name of LLC] _, on _ [date of signing] _, pledging title to _ [make and model and year of automobile with Vehicle ID #] ."

Promissory Note: Installment Payments of Principal and Interest (Amortized Loan) With Balloon Payment

The next promissory note differs from the standard amortized note discussed above by requiring a "balloon payment" at the end of the repayment term. A balloon payment is a complete payoff of all remaining principal on a specified installment date, one that's prior to the date the loan would normally be paid off by regular installment payments. Use this note if the lender wishes to receive regular payments of principal and interest for a period of time, but then wants full repayment of principal on a particular future date. You will need to use an amortization guide that includes a remaining loan balance table, which will allow you to calculate the amount of the balloon payment (see the special instructions to the note form, below).

CD-ROM

Complete this note following the special instructions below. You'll find this resolution on the CD-ROM and as a tearout form in Appendix C. (See Appendix A for information on selecting and using the CD-ROM files.)

Special Instructions

❶ Start by calculating the periodic payments using an amortization schedule, as discussed above. But with this note, you will amortize the loan for a longer period than the loan will be outstanding; the balloon payment date will occur before the end of the full amortization term. For example, if the LLC plans to provide for a balloon payment in seven years, it may wish to amortize monthly payments over ten or fifteen years, which will allow the lender to make relatively low payments. Choose the

LLC Promissory Note:
Installment Payments of Principal and Interest
(Amortized Loan) With Balloon Payment

For value received, _____[name of LLC]_____, the borrower, promises to pay to the order of _[name of member, manager, or other individual lender]_, the noteholder, the principal amount of _$[principal amount of loan]_, together with simple interest on the unpaid principal balance from the date of this note until the date this note is paid in full, at the annual rate of _[annual rate of interest]%_. Payments will be made at _____[address of lender]_____.

Principal and interest will be paid in equal installments of _$[amount of each payment]_, beginning on _[date of first payment]_, and continuing on _[day for ongoing payments, for example, "the fifteenth day of each month"]_. On the installment payment date on _[date of final (balloon) payment]_, a balloon payment of $____[amount of remaining principal owed on the loan on final installment date]_____ ❶ will be added to the installment amount paid by the borrower in order to pay off this note in its entirety on this final installment payment date. Each payment made by the borrower will be applied first to accrued but unpaid interest, and the remainder will be applied to unpaid principal.

This note may be prepaid by the borrower in whole or in part at any time without penalty. This note is not assumable without the written consent of the noteholder. Consent will not be unreasonably withheld. This note is nontransferable by the noteholder. ❷

If any installment payment due under this note is not received by the noteholder within _[number of days]_ of its due date, the entire amount of unpaid principal and accrued but unpaid interest due under this note will, at the option of the noteholder, become immediately due and payable without prior notice from the noteholder to the borrower. In the event of a default, the borrower is responsible for the costs of collection, including, in the event of a lawsuit to collect on this note, the noteholder's reasonable attorney fees as determined by a court hearing the lawsuit.

Date of Signing: _____

Name of Borrower:_____[name of LLC]_____

Address of Borrower: _____[address of principal office of LLC]_____

City, or County, and State Where Signed:_____

Signature of Borrower:_____[signature of treasurer]_____, Treasurer

on behalf of _____[name of LLC]_____

amortization term for the loan, then find the monthly payment amount under the interest rate on the Amortization Schedule, above. Payments are usually made on a monthly basis, but you can establish a different interval if you choose. If you do, you'll need to use an amortization table based on your loan's repayment interval, such as quarterly or every other month. Check with a library, bookstore, or bank for other amortization tables.

Next, figure the amount of the balloon payment to be added to the last installment payment—this will be the principal balance owed on the note on this date.

 RESOURCE

Find a remaining loan balance table. The easy way to find the remaining principal balance is to use a table called a "remaining loan balance table" that is included in standard loan amortization pamphlets and books. This table will show the percentage of the principal remaining in a given year of a loan. These percentages vary according to the interest rate and the full amortization term of the loan, as well as the date when the balloon payment is made. *McGraw-Hill's Interest Amortization Tables*, by Jack Estes and Dennis Kelley, gives remaining loan balance tables for five- to 30-year loans. You can find a balloon payment calculator at www. timevalue.com.

Insert into the last blank in this section of the note the additional principal payment amount—the balloon payment—due on the last installment payment date.

EXAMPLE 1:

Sheryl Shore, the sole member of For Shore Electronics, LLC, proposes to lend $10,000 to her LLC at a 5% interest rate. The loan will be amortized over 15 years, with the LLC making regular monthly payments of principal and interest for the first seven

years, until a balloon payment becomes due—exactly seven years from the original loan date. Using the Amortization Schedule, above, Sheryl multiplies the principal amount of the loan by .0079 to arrive at a monthly payment amount of $79. Next, Sheryl looks at a remaining loan balance table. She finds that the percentage of the original principal amount owed after seven years on a loan amortized over 15 years at a 5% interest rate is 62.464% (the same as .62464). Sheryl multiplies .62464 by $10,000, and comes up with $6,246.40. This is the principal amount that will be owed on the date the last installment is due (on the date the LLC makes the last payment of $79, at the end of seven years). Sheryl adds the remaining principal payment of $6,246.40 to $79 to come up with a total final (balloon) payment of $6,325.40. The LLC will end up paying a total of $12,882.40— that's ($79 x 12 x 7) plus $6,246.40.

EXAMPLE 2:

Sheryl's LLC wants to amortize the monthly interest and principal amounts over ten years instead of 15. Looking at the Amortization Schedule, above, the loan payments will be $106 per month ($10,000 x .0106). A remaining loan balance table shows that the remaining loan balance after seven years is 35.390% of the original principal amount. In this case, $3,539 ($10,000 x .35390) will be owed on the seven-year anniversary balloon payment date, plus the regular amortized payment of $106. This balloon payment is less than the balloon payment in the previous example because here the loan is paid off more quickly ($106 per month instead of $79 per month), so less principal remains on the note when the final payment is due.

❷ This paragraph specifies that the loan may be repaid by the LLC at any time without triggering a prepayment penalty. This allows your LLC to pay back the loan whenever it makes economic sense to do so. The loan is also made assumable (meaning another company or person can take over the payment obligation for the LLC) with the permission of the noteholder. However, it is unlikely that another company or person will wish to assume payments under the loan. The note is nontransferable—the individual lender may not transfer the note to another person to collect the payments from the LLC. This provision is common for insider loans in a small LLC. You can easily change this sentence to allow transfers if you wish, though it's highly unlikely that a noteholder will wish to transfer an LLC loan.

Promissory Note: Periodic Payments of Interest Only With Lump-Sum Principal Payment

This promissory note provides a designated period of monthly payments of interest only, to be followed by a lump-sum payment of the entire principal amount of the loan. This form of loan makes sense if the loan amount is not excessive and the LLC will be able to come up with the entire principal amount at the end of the loan period.

EXAMPLE:

Gerard, as sole member, lends his LLC $10,000 at a 7.5% rate for five years. Gerard uses the Amortization Schedule, above, to calculate that the total interest owed by the LLC for these funds will be $3,750 ($10,000 x .075 x 5). The amount of each monthly interest installment under the note is thus $62.50 (total interest for the five-year loan period—$3,750—divided by the 60 installments made in this period). At the end of the five-year period during which the LLC pays monthly interest only, the LLC must pay Gerard the entire $10,000.

CD-ROM

Complete this note following the special instructions below. You'll find this resolution on the CD-ROM and as a tearout form in Appendix C. (See Appendix A for information on selecting and using the CD-ROM files.)

Special Instructions

❶ Multiply the principal amount by the interest rate. That is the amount of interest payable per year. Divide that number by 12 to come up with a monthly interest payment. Payments are usually made on a monthly basis, but you can establish a different interval if you choose. If you do, divide the annual interest payable by the amount of payments to be made in one year.

❷ See "Promissory Note: Installment Payments of Principal and Interest (Amoprtized Loan) With Balloon Payment," above, item 2.

LLC Promissory Note:
Periodic Payments of Interest
with Lump-Sum Principal Payment

For value received, _____ [name of LLC] _____, the borrower, promises to pay to the order of _[name of member, manager, or other individual lender]_ , the noteholder, the principal amount of _$[principal amount of loan]_ , together with simple interest on the unpaid principal balance from the date of this note until the date this note is paid in full, at the annual rate of _[annual rate of interest]%_ . Payments will be made at ____[address of lender]____ .

Interest will be paid in equal installments of _$[amount of each interest payment]_ , ❶ beginning on _[date of first payment]_ , and continuing on the _[day for ongoing payments, for example, "the fifteenth day of each month"]_ until _[ending date of loan period]_ , on which date the entire principal amount, together with total accrued but unpaid interest, will be paid by the borrower.

This note may be prepaid by the borrower in whole or in part at any time without penalty. This note is not assumable without the written consent of the noteholder. Consent will not be unreasonably withheld. This note is nontransferable by the noteholder. ❷

If any installment payment due under this note is not received by the noteholder within _[number of days]_ of its due date, the entire amount of unpaid principal and accrued but unpaid interest due under this note will, at the option of the noteholder, become immediately due and payable without prior notice from the noteholder to the borrower. In the event of a default, the borrower is responsible for the costs of collection, including, in the event of a lawsuit to collect on this note, the noteholder's reasonable attorney fees as determined by a court hearing the lawsuit.

Date of Signing: _____

Name of Borrower:_____ [name of LLC] _____

Address of Borrower: _____ [address of principal office of LLC] _____

City, or County, and State Where Signed: _____

Signature of Borrower:_____ [signature of treasurer] _____, Treasurer

on behalf of _____ [name of LLC] _____

Promissory Note: Lump-Sum Payment of Principal and Interest on Specified Date

This promissory note is similar to the previous note in that the entire amount of principal is paid in one lump sum at the end of the loan period. However, unlike the previous note, where interest payments are made in installments during the loan period, here the entire interest amount is paid along with the entire principal amount at the end of the loan term.

EXAMPLE:

Ubiquity Movers, LLC, borrows $10,000 for three years at 9% interest. Using the Amortization Schedule, above, to calculate the total interest owed by the LLC for these funds, a one-time payment of $12,700 ($10,000 principal plus the entire $2,700 interest amount) is due at the end of the three-year loan term.

CD-ROM

Complete this note following the special instruction below. You'll find this resolution on the CD-ROM and as a tearout form in Appendix C. (See Appendix A for information on selecting and using the CD-ROM files.)

Special Instruction

❶ This paragraph specifies that the loan may be repaid by the LLC at any time without triggering a prepayment penalty. This allows your LLC to pay back the loan whenever it makes economic sense to do so. The loan is also made assumable (meaning another company or person can take over the payment obligation for the LLC) with the permission of the noteholder. However, it is unlikely that another company or person will wish to assume payments under the loan. The note is nontransferable—the individual lender may not transfer the note to another person to collect the payments from the LLC. This provision is common for insider loans in a small LLC. You can easily change this sentence to allow transfers if you wish, though it's highly unlikely that a noteholder will wish to transfer an LLC loan.

LLC Promissory Note:
Lump-Sum Payment of Principal
and Interest On Specified Date

For value received, _____[name of LLC]_____, the borrower, promises to pay to the order of __[name of member, manager, or other individual lender]__, the noteholder, the principal amount of ____$[principal amount of loan]____, together with simple interest on the unpaid principal balance from the date of this note until the date this note is paid in full, at the annual rate of ___[annual rate of interest]%___. Payments will be made at _____[address of lender]_____.

The entire principal amount of the loan, together with total accrued but unpaid interest, will be paid by the borrower on __[due date for payment of all principal and interest]__. Any payment made by the borrower prior to the due date specified above will be applied first to accrued but unpaid interest, and the remainder will be applied to unpaid principal.

This note may be prepaid by the borrower in whole or in part at any time without penalty. This note is not assumable without the written consent of the noteholder. Consent will not be unreasonably withheld. This note is nontransferable by the noteholder. ❶

In the event of a default, the borrower is responsible for the costs of collection, including, in the event of a lawsuit to collect on this note, the noteholder's reasonable attorney fees as determined by a court hearing the lawsuit.

Date of Signing: _____

Name of Borrower: _____[name of LLC]_____

Address of Borrower: _____[address of principal office of LLC]_____

City, or County, and State Where Signed: _____

Signature of Borrower: _____[signature of treasurer]_____, Treasurer

on behalf of _____[name of LLC]_____

Promissory Note: Lump-Sum Payment of Principal and Interest on Demand by Noteholder

Here is a classic "demand note" that allows the noteholder (lender) to call the note due at any time. A demand note may make sense when an LLC has only one or two members who borrow money for personal uses from time to time when the LLC has positive cash flow.

CD-ROM

Complete this note following the special instructions below. You'll find this resolution on the CD-ROM and as a tearout form in Appendix C. (See Appendix A for information on selecting and using the CD-ROM files.)

LLC Promissory Note:
Lump-Sum Payment of Principal
and Interest on Demand by Noteholder

For value received, _____[name of LLC]_____, the borrower, promises to pay to the order of _____[name of member, manager, or other individual lender]_____, the noteholder, the principal amount of ____$[principal amount of loan]____, together with simple interest on the unpaid principal balance from the date of this note until the date this note is paid in full, at the annual rate of _____[annual rate of interest]%_____. Payments will be made at _____[address of lender]_____.

The entire principal amount of the loan, together with total accrued but unpaid interest, will be paid within __[period, for example, "30 days or other period agreeable to the LLC and borrower"]__ of receipt by the LLC of a demand for repayment by the noteholder. A demand for repayment by the noteholder shall be made in writing and will be delivered or mailed to the borrower at the following address: _____[address of principal office of LLC]_____. If demand for repayment is mailed, it will be considered received by the borrower on the third business day after the date when it was deposited in the U.S. mail as registered or certified mail. ❶

Any payment made by the borrower prior to the due date specified above will be applied first to accrued but unpaid interest, and the remainder will be applied to unpaid principal.

This note may be prepaid by the borrower in whole or in part at any time without penalty. This note is not assumable without the written consent of the noteholder. Consent will not be unreasonably withheld. This note is nontransferable by the noteholder. ❷

In the event of a default, the borrower is responsible for the costs of collection, including, in the event of a lawsuit to collect on this note, the noteholder's reasonable attorney fees as determined by a court hearing the lawsuit.

Date of Signing: _____

Name of Borrower:_____[name of LLC]_____

Address of Borrower: _____[address of principal office of LLC]_____

City, or County, and State Where Signed: _____

Signature of Borrower:_____[signature of treasurer]_____, Treasurer

on behalf of _____[name of LLC]_____

Special Instructions

❶ Specify how much time the LLC has to pay the loan off after the demand by the noteholder. This period will vary depending on the cash flow requirements of the LLC and the lender. Thirty days is often specified as the period, but up to three months or more may be allowed if the loan amount is substantial. A longer period is appropriate if the LLC might need to seek a bank loan to satisfy the call on the note by the noteholder.

You can, if you wish, add language to the note limiting when the lender can demand repayment. For example, you can prohibit the lender from demanding repayment on the loan until at least three years have elapsed from the date of signing of the loan. You might make an exception to this prohibition by allowing a member-lender to make a demand for repayment at any time during the life of the note if he or she no longer owns an interest in the LLC.

❷ This paragraph specifies that the LLC may repay the loan at any time without triggering a prepayment penalty. This allows your LLC to pay back the loan whenever it makes economic sense to do so. The loan is also made assumable (meaning another company or person can take over the payment obligation for the LLC) with the permission of the noteholder. However, it is unlikely that another company or person will wish to assume payments under the loan. The note is nontransferable—the individual lender may not transfer the note to another person to collect the payments from the LLC. This provision is common for insider loans in a small LLC. You can easily change this sentence to allow transfers if you wish, though it's highly unlikely that a noteholder will wish to transfer an LLC loan.

Promissory Note: Special Schedule of Payments of Principal and Interest

This promissory note allows you to specify a special (nonuniform) schedule for repayment of principal and interest under the loan. For example, your schedule may show changes in principal and/or interest payments over the life of the note, often ending with a final balloon payment of the remaining principal plus all accrued unpaid interest due on a certain date. The options here are unlimited, but here's one example to give you the general idea.

EXAMPLE:

On July 1, Laura lends her LLC $10,000 for five years at 8% interest. She and the LLC agree that Laura will receive no payments until the end of the second year. Using the Amortization Schedule, above, they agree she'll then receive $1,600 in interest-only payments for the first two years of the loan ($10,000 x .08 x 2). The LLC will then make an interest-only payment of $800 at the end of the third year. At the end of the fourth year, it will make an $800 interest payment along with a payment of $4,000 in principal, leaving a principal balance of $6,000. Finally, at the end of the fifth year, the LLC will make its last payment, consisting of the balance of $6,000 principal along with $480 interest ($6,000 x .08 x 1). Here is the repayment schedule:

June 31, 2nd year:	$1,600	(interest)
June 31, 3rd year:	$800	(interest)
June 31, 4th year:	$4,800	($4,000 principal; $800 interest)
June 31, 5th year:	$6,480	($6,000 principal; $480 interest)
Total Payments:	$13,680	($10,000 principal; $3,680 interest)

TIP

An LLC may pay less with an amortized loan. If the same loan had been amortized over five years, Laura's LLC would have paid $203 per month in principal and interest—or $2,436 per year—for a total of $12,180 over five years. In that case, the LLC would have paid only $2,180 in interest.

CD-ROM

Complete this note following the special instruction below. You'll find this resolution on the CD-ROM and as a tearout form in Appendix C. (See Appendix A for information on selecting and using the CD-ROM files.)

Special Instruction

❶ This paragraph specifies that the loan may be repaid by the LLC at any time without triggering a prepayment penalty. This allows your LLC to pay back the loan whenever it makes economic sense to do so. The loan is also made assumable (meaning another company or person can take over the payment obligation for the LLC) with the permission of the noteholder. However, it is unlikely that another company or person will wish to assume payments under the loan. The note is nontransferable—the individual lender may not transfer the note to another person to collect the payments from the LLC. This provision is common for insider loans in a small LLC. You can easily change this sentence to allow transfers if you wish, though it's highly unlikely that a noteholder will wish to transfer an LLC loan.

LLC Promissory Note:
Special Schedule of Payments of Principal and Interest

For value received, _____ [name of LLC] _____, the borrower, promises to pay to the order of _____ [name of member, manager, or other individual lender] _____, the noteholder, the principal amount of __$[principal amount of loan]__, together with simple interest on the unpaid principal balance from the date of this note until the date this note is paid in full, at the annual rate of __[annual rate of interest]%__. Payments will be made at _____[address of lender]_____.

Principal and interest will be paid as follows:

__[Include schedule of payments here. For the last payment, you can insert the following:__ "The borrower will make a final payment in the amount of all remaining principal and all accrued but unpaid interest on (date)."]____

This note may be prepaid by the borrower in whole or in part at any time without penalty. This note is not assumable without the written consent of the noteholder. Consent will not be unreasonably withheld. This note is nontransferable by the noteholder. ❶

If any installment payment due under this note is not received by the noteholder within __[number of days]__ of its due date, the entire amount of unpaid principal and accrued but unpaid interest of the loan will, at the option of the noteholder, become immediately due and payable without prior notice by the noteholder to the borrower. In the event of a default, the borrower is responsible for the costs of collection, including, in the event of a lawsuit to collect on this note, the noteholder's reasonable attorney fees as determined by a court hearing the lawsuit.

Date of Signing: _____

Name of Borrower:_____ [name of LLC] _____

Address of Borrower: _____ [address of principal office of LLC] _____

City, or County, and State Where Signed: _____

Signature of Borrower:_____ [signature of treasurer] _____, Treasurer

on behalf of _____ [name of LLC] _____

Loans by the LLC

This chapter covers loans made by an LLC to LLC insiders such as members, managers, officers, and other employees. This is the flip side of the loan transactions covered in the previous chapter, which covers loans made to the LLC. This chapter also includes a promissory note for LLC insiders to fill out and sign, along with explanations and an example, and a release form for the LLC to sign when the loan is paid off.

Overview of Loans to Insiders

Unless your LLC is in the business of making loans to outsiders (and in most states, it needs special permission from the state to do so), it will probably lend money only to an individual associated with the LLC, such as a member, manager, or key employee, if at all. This type of insider loan transaction is not common. If a member needs cash, the LLC can pay the member's "distributive share" of profits to him or her. And if a member wants a cash distribution of profits before these profits have been earned by the LLC and allocated to the member (which happens at the end of the LLC's tax year), the member can seek an advance payment (draw) of these profits instead of seeking a personal loan from the LLC.

Loans by an LLC to nonmember managers, officers, or employees are also unusual. LLC profits are more productively reinvested in the business of the company than loaned out to LLC individuals. In addition, nonborrowing members in a co-owned LLC are likely to cast a leery eye on special loans made to a particular LLC person. They may feel that such a loan deal smacks of unacceptable favoritism and constitutes an inappropriate diversion of LLC operating funds.

Despite all of this, there may be times when your LLC decides it really does make sense to grant an LLC loan to a member, manager, officer, or employee. For example, if an LLC member is experiencing a personal cash crunch, management may decide that making a personal loan will help keep the person focused on LLC business, especially if the LLC is flush with profits. In that situation, making the loan can serve the best interests of both the LLC and the borrowing member. Here's another example, one that relates more to the LLC business.

EXAMPLE:

A small semiconductor chip fabricator, MegaChips, LLC, decides to entice LLC officers to relocate close to its main headquarters by lending funds to newly hired officers to purchase nearby residential housing. Doing this benefits the LLC by making it easier to attract key employees. The loans should be considered fair to the LLC as long as they:

- carry a reasonable rate of interest (which may be slightly lower than the rates charged by commercial lenders)

- are secured by the property purchased by the officers (a second deed of trust or mortgage on the purchased property)

- are approved by the members, and

- will not impair the LLC's ability to pay its ongoing bills.

Legal Considerations for Loans to Insiders

State law, either explicitly or implicitly, usually permits LLCs to make loans to members and other individuals. But check your state's LLC act to be sure, and to see whether any special approval requirements apply.

Any loan the LLC makes should meet these basic requirements:

- The terms of the loan are commercially competitive—or at least reasonable.
- The disbursal of loan funds will not impair the financial condition of the LLC.

- All members approve loans to nonmembers. Also, keep the following tips in mind when approving a loan by your LLC:

  - Over and above your state's LLC laws, your LLC articles and operating agreement may impose conditions on LLC loans made to insiders. Before approving an insider loan, make sure loans to members, managers, officers, or employees are not prohibited or limited by your articles or operating agreement.

  - In LLCs owned and operated by one or just a few managing members, if all members agree to lend money to themselves, they can be more relaxed about formalities. After all, if there are no nonmanaging members, who's to complain that the interest rates are noncompetitive? But you still need to think about the IRS—more on this in "Tax Consequences of Insider Loans," below—and whether the LLC could invest its money more productively elsewhere.

  - Avoid making loans during hard times. If your LLC is on shaky financial footing when it considers making a loan, or you suspect it soon may be, I suggest you wait until the LLC is more solvent. Making an insider loan when your LLC is cash-poor risks financial, as well as legal, trouble.

  - Get outside help if you need it. As just noted, any time your LLC makes a loan, you will want to make sure that it can afford to do so. You should discuss with your tax adviser or business lawyer any special tax or legal or practical considerations that may make a loan problematical. The information in this chapter should help you when seeking this advice.

Tax Consequences of Insider Loans

A legitimate LLC loan to an insider usually has minimal tax consequences. On the lender's (LLC's) side of the transaction, the LLC does not deduct the disbursement of loan funds from its income, nor does it report the repayment of principal from the borrower as income. The LLC does, however, report interest it collects from the borrower as income on its LLC tax return. This increases revenue and thereby affects the amount of net income allocated to members at the end of the LLC tax year.

Similarly, the borrower (member, manager, or officer) does not report the loan funds as income, because they must be paid back. And the borrower cannot ordinarily deduct interest payments made on the loan for federal income tax purposes. However, there is an exception if the borrower legitimately uses the income for business or investment purposes (in which case, it's an ordinary business expense) or secures it with an interest in the borrower's residence (ask your tax adviser for more information). A legitimate loan usually does not affect the borrower's tax basis in his or her membership interest, but an illegitimate loan may do so (see below).

CAUTION

Check tax issues with an expert. No matter how straightforward and sound your LLC loan to an insider may appear to be, you still risk IRS problems. The IRS often scrutinizes insider loans as a part of business audits. The following sections summarize some tax issues that can arise. But please treat this discussion as an introduction, not a thorough treatment. As always, for authoritative tax advice, see your tax adviser. (Chapter 16 discusses finding a tax adviser to work with.)

Illegitimate Member Loans Treated as Distributions of Profit

One risk with insider loans is that the IRS might decide that a loan to an LLC member was not a bona fide loan transaction but was instead a distribution of a member's distributive share of LLC profits—in other words, an advance against future LLC profits. If this happens, the member's basis in his or her membership interest will be reduced by the amount of the loan disbursement.

A reduced basis can lead to several results (as discussed more thoroughly in Chapter 13):

- More taxes are owed when the membership interest is sold.

- If the loan amount exceeds the member's basis, the member will have to pay income taxes on the excess.

- In addition, a low basis can limit the amount of LLC losses a member can claim on his or her individual tax return to offset other income.

To make sure the IRS doesn't recharacterize a loan as a distribution of profits, the transaction should include as many of the following features as possible.

- A promissory note to document the loan. It should state a commercially reasonable rate of interest and a maturity date—either payable on demand by the LLC, or, better yet, at a specific date or in specified installments.

- Formal approval of the loan transaction by the LLC and by all members (even in a manager-managed LLC or in a member-managed LLC managed by fewer than all members). The transaction should also be documented in LLC minutes or written consents, to be placed in the LLC records binder.

- The debt should be carried on the LLC books and reported on its tax returns as a loan transaction.

- The insider-borrower should make interest and principal payments according to the terms of the note.

- If the note is a demand note (as opposed to one with a due date or payment schedule), demand for payment should be made by the LLC within a reasonable time (two to three years, for instance). In other words, the loan should not be carried on the books indefinitely.

- Repeated loans to members should not be made (and paid off) on a regular schedule. To the IRS, repeated loans to members on a regular basis look more like payments of LLC profits.

- Avoid issuing loans to members in proportion to capital or profits interests in the LLC, which makes the loan transactions look like taxable payments of members' distributive shares of profits.

Below-Market Member Loans

Another possible problem the IRS can have with an insider loan is a too-low interest rate. The IRS doesn't like to see LLC loans to insiders that call for inadequate interest, or none at all, for this reason: The IRS loses taxes on interest income that the LLC would normally receive in connection with the loan transaction. As a result, if the IRS determines that the LLC has made this type of loan, called a "below-market loan" under IRC Section 7872, it will tax the borrower on the interest saved. That is, the borrower will have to pay taxes on the interest he or she would have had to pay on a commercially reasonable loan. Generally, a "below-market" loan is one that carries a rate of interest lower than the "applicable federal rate" in effect at the time the loan is made.

Below-market loans arise mostly in the corporate context, where a closely held corporation makes low-interest loans to shareholders instead of reinvesting the money and paying corporate taxes on returns from the investments. But it can also apply to LLCs that devise a clever scheme to lend money at low or no interest to LLC members so that the LLC members can save on taxes.

Federal Loan Rates

The federal rates are the rates paid by the federal government on borrowed funds. They are set monthly. There are three federal rates: short term for loans with a three-year term or less (or for demand notes that can be called due at any time); mid term for loans from three years to nine years; and long term for loans with a term over nine years.

The applicable federal rates are changed each month, and can be found online at www.irs.gov as the current month's "imputed interest rates" or "AFR rates" (technically called the "applicable federal rates under Section 1274(d) of the Internal Revenue Code"). Major business newspapers also list the current applicable fed rates, typically in their stock quotations section.

TIP

You may want to charge competitive interest on insider loans anyway. For business reasons, your LLC may want to charge competitive interest rates on all LLC loans to insiders. For example, your LLC may decide to make an LLC loan to members at the current prime interest rate plus two percentage points to provide your LLC with interest income on the loan amounts and to encourage a timely payback by borrowing members (the longer they take to repay the loan, the more interest they end up paying to the LLC). Competitive

loans made to members are also more likely to be acceptable to nonborrowing members and other LLC principals.

Resolution for LLC and Member Approval of LLC Loans to Insiders

As mentioned above, preparing resolutions for insider loan transactions can avoid internal controversy among your members. It is natural that repeated loan transactions between an LLC and a principal member or manager may arouse the curiosity of other LLC insiders, who may wonder if the borrowing member or manager is taking advantage of his or her LLC leverage to get too good a deal on interest and repayment terms. Getting formal approval for these loan transactions can answer nonborrowing members' questions and avoid this type of insider controversy.

Use the following resolution to show approval of a loan made by the LLC to a member, manager, officer, employee, or other LLC insider. To summarize: If you can, get the approval of all managers (in a manager-managed LLC) and all members (in both manager- and member-managed LLCs) who are not borrowing money from the LLC. In all cases, make sure that the LLC can afford to make the loan and that the loan terms are fair to the LLC. Use a commercially reasonable rate of interest and a repayment schedule.

CD-ROM

Complete the resolution following the special instructions below. You'll find this resolution on the CD-ROM and as a tearout form in Appendix C. (See Appendix A for information on selecting and using the CD-ROM files.)

Approval of LLC Loan to Insider

It was resolved it is in the best interests of the LLC to make the following loan to the following persons under the following terms:

Name and Title of Borrower: [name and title of member, manager, officer, employee, or other individual who is borrowing the funds]

Principal Amount of Loan: $ [principal amount of the loan—or refer to promissory note: "see attached note for terms of loan" and leave all loan terms below blank] ❶

Rate of Interest: [interest rate] %

Term of Loan: [number of months or years if the loan has a set term, or "payable on demand by LLC" if it's a demand loan]

Payment Schedule: [number and amount of payments (whether they consist of interest only or principal and interest) and date and amount of final payment]   ❷

It was further resolved that the above loan could reasonably be expected to benefit the LLC and that the LLC would be able to make the loan without jeopardizing its financial position, including its ability to pay its bills as they become due.

Therefore, the LLC approved the terms of the note and directed the borrower to sign the note. The secretary was directed to attach a copy of the note, signed by the borrower, to this resolution and to place the resolution and the attachment(s) in the LLC records binder.

Special Instructions

❶ You may insert the specific terms of the loan in the blanks, or you can simply refer to the terms of the promissory note that you complete and attach to your resolution. If you refer to the promissory note, either leave all loan terms blank or delete them from the resolution.

❷ Here's an example of a repayment schedule for a five-year $10,000 member loan carried at a 7% annual interest rate: "Four interest-only payments of $700 shall be made on June 15 of each year, starting on June 15, 2011. The fifth annual payment shall be made on June 15, 2015, consisting of $700 in remaining accrued but unpaid interest, plus the full amount of the unpaid principal of $10,000, for a total final payment of $10,700." For further examples of repayment options and terms, as well as an amortization table, see Chapter 13.

Promissory Notes for Loans by LLC

I recommend that you prepare a promissory note for each loan transaction and attach it to your LLC resolution approving the loan. Doing this records the terms of the loan and can help convince the IRS and others that the loan was a bona fide business transaction between the LLC and its member, manager, officer, or employee.

The sections below discuss promissory notes you can use to document the terms of LLC loans to insiders. These forms are similar to the promissory notes covered in Chapter 13 for loans to the LLC by insiders. However, key wording, instructions, and commentary are a bit different to reflect that the underlying loan transaction is reversed. For example, instead of being titled "LLC Promissory Notes," the notes below are entitled "Individual Promissory Notes"—that is, they are signed by individual persons, not the LLC.

All promissory note forms in this section allow two borrowers to sign for the loan. Normally, two borrowers will take out the same loan only when they are spouses, who are jointly liable for repayment of the note. This means that, if there is a default, the LLC may seek to collect against either spouse for the full amount owed under the note. By doing this, each borrower agrees to the repayment obligation—something that can avoid later legal complications should there be a default, a dissolution of marriage, or another change in the spouses' legal status. A borrower is who unmarried should sign the note alone.

To select a note appropriate for your situation, scan the promissory notes that follow and choose one that suits the lending arrangement at hand. Most of the notes are self-explanatory, but additional information is provided as needed in instructions below each note. (For additional background information on the various loan repayment terms reflected in the notes below, see Chapter 13.)

Our Promissory Notes Use Simple Interest

The loans provided in this chapter call for simple, rather than compound, interest. With simple interest, interest is charged on the remaining unpaid principal due under the note, but not on any unpaid interest that accumulates during the term of the loan.

As a practical matter, compound interest is usually not necessary for LLC loans to insiders. If the loan is paid off in installments, the borrower will usually pay off all accrued interest. For long-term loans that don't call for any payments for quite a while (perhaps a year or more), it's possible to compound the interest due, although most smaller LLCs won't choose to do so. If you want to figure out compound interest, you may use a future value table; check with your tax adviser, bank, or real estate broker.

Individual Promissory Note: Installment Payments of Principal and Interest (Amortized Loan)

This note form provides for the regular payments of principal plus interest over the term of the loan. Typically, payments are scheduled to be made monthly, but you can decide on any payment plan you wish.

CD-ROM

Complete the note following the special instructions below. You'll find this resolution on the CD-ROM and as a tearout form in Appendix C. (See Appendix A for information on selecting and using the CD-ROM files.)

Individual Promissory Note:
Installment Payments of Principal
and Interest (Amortized Loan)

For value received, _____ [name of member, manager, officer, employee, or other individual (plus name of spouse if the LLC borrower is married)] _____, the borrower(s), promise(s) to pay to the order of _____ [name of LLC] _____, the noteholder, the principal amount of $ [principal amount of loan] , together with simple interest on the unpaid principal balance from the date of this note until the date this note is paid in full, at the annual rate of [annual rate of interest] %. Payments will be made at _____ [address of LLC] _____.

Principal and interest will be paid in equal installments of $ [amount of each payment] , beginning on [date of first payment] , and continuing on [day for ongoing payments, for example, "the fifteenth day of each month"] until the principal and interest are paid in full. Each payment made by the borrower(s) will be applied first to accrued but unpaid interest, and the remainder will be applied to unpaid principal. ❶

This note may be prepaid by the borrower(s) in whole or in part at any time without penalty. This note is not assumable without the written consent of the noteholder. Consent will not be unreasonably withheld. This note is nontransferable by the noteholder. ❷

If any installment payment due under this note is not received by the noteholder within [number of days] of its due date, the entire amount of unpaid principal and accrued but unpaid interest due under this note will, at the option of the noteholder, become immediately due and payable without prior notice by the noteholder to the borrower(s). In the event of a default, the borrower(s) is/are responsible for the costs of collection, including, in the event of a lawsuit to collect on this note, the noteholder's reasonable attorney fees as determined by a court hearing the lawsuit.

If two persons sign below, each is jointly and severally liable for repayment of this note. ❸

Name of Borrower #1: _____

Signature: _____

Address: _____

City, or County, and State Where Signed: _____

Date of Signing: _____

Name of Borrower #2: _____

Signature: _____

Address: _____

City, or County, and State Where Signed: _____

Date of Signing: _____

Special Instructions

❶ For instructions on computing the amount of installment payments due under your note, see "Periodic Payments of Interest Plus Principal (Amortized Loans)" in Chapter 13.

❷ This paragraph specifies that the loan may be repaid by the borrower at any time without triggering a prepayment penalty. This allows the borrower to pay off the loan at any time. The loan is assumable (meaning another company or person can take over the payment obligation for the borrower) with the permission of the noteholder (the LLC), but it is unlikely that another person will wish to assume payments under the loan. The note is also nontransferable—the LLC may not transfer the note to another company or person to collect payments from the borrower. This provision is customary for loans from a small LLC. You can easily change this sentence to allow transfers if you wish, though it's highly unlikely that anyone would wish to buy this type of note, even at a discount.

❸ The borrower should complete and sign the first set of signature lines. If the borrower is married, the spouse should complete and sign the second set; otherwise, it should be deleted.

Individual Promissory Note: Installment Payments of Principal and Interest (Amortized Loan) Secured by Property

This promissory note is the same as the previous note but adds a clause that secures the loan with the borrower's real estate or personal property.

TIP

You can use the security clause in other note forms. To allow the borrower to pledge property as security for the repayment of a different type of note, you may copy the security clause in

this note—the last paragraph in the text of the note shown below—to any of the other note forms covered below.

CD-ROM

Complete the note following the special instructions below. You'll find this resolution on the CD-ROM and as a tearout form in Appendix C. (See Appendix A for information on selecting and using the CD-ROM files.)

Special Instructions

❶ For instructions on computing the amount of installment payments due under your note, see "Periodic Payments of Interest Plus Principal (Amortized Loans)" in Chapter 13.

❷ This paragraph specifies that the loan may be repaid by the borrower at any time without triggering a prepayment penalty. This allows the borrower to pay off the loan at any time. The loan is assumable (meaning another company or person can take over the payment obligation for the borrower) with the permission of the noteholder (the LLC), but it is unlikely that another person will wish to assume payments under the loan. The note is also nontransferable—the LLC may not transfer the note to another company or person to collect payments from the borrower. This provision is customary for loans from a small LLC. You can easily change this sentence to allow transfers if you wish, though it's highly unlikely that anyone would wish to buy this type of note, even at a discount.

❸ This is the security clause. (For general information, see "Securing Loans With Interests in LLC Property" in Chapter 13.) Specify the security agreement used to pledge the property as repayment for the loan in case of default, together with a description of the property.

**Individual Promissory Note:
Installment Payments of Principal and Interest
(Amortized Loan) Secured by Property**

For value received, _____ [name of member, manager, officer, employee, or other individual (plus name of spouse if LLC person is married)]_____ , the borrower(s), promise(s) to pay to the order of _____ [name of LLC]_____ , the noteholder, the principal amount of $_[principal amount of loan]_ , together with simple interest on the unpaid principal balance from the date of this note until the date this note is paid in full, at the annual rate of __[annual rate of interest]__ %. Payments will be made at __[address of LLC]__ .

　Principal and interest will be paid in equal installments of $ _[amount of each payment]_ , ❶ beginning on __[date of first payment]__ , and continuing on _[day for ongoing payments, for example, "the fifteenth day of each month"]_ until the principal and interest are paid in full. Each payment made by the borrower(s) will be applied first to accrued but unpaid interest, and the remainder will be applied to unpaid principal.

　This note may be prepaid by the borrower(s) in whole or in part at any time without penalty. This note is not assumable without the written consent of the noteholder. Consent will not be unreasonably withheld. This note is nontransferable by the noteholder. ❷

　If any installment payment due under this note is not received by the noteholder within _[number of days]_ of its due date, the entire amount of unpaid principal and accrued but unpaid interest of the loan will, at the option of the noteholder, become immediately due and payable without prior notice by the noteholder to the borrower(s). In the event of a default, the borrower(s) is/are responsible for the costs of collection, including, in the event of a lawsuit to collect on this note, the noteholder's reasonable attorney fees as determined by a court hearing the lawsuit.

　Borrower(s) agree(s) that until such time as the principal and interest owed under this note are paid in full, the note will be secured by the following described mortgage, deed of trust, or security agreement: _[describe security agreement, deed of trust, or mortgage used to pledge security of the property, including a description of the property]_ . ❸

　If two persons sign below, each is jointly and severally liable for repayment of this note. ❹

Name of Borrower #1: _____

Signature: _____

Address: _____

City, or County, and State Where Signed: _____

Date of Signing: _____

Name of Borrower #2: _____

Signature: _____

Address: _____

City, or County, and State Where Signed: _____

Date of Signing: _____

For real estate, you will want to complete and record a mortgage deed or deed of trust with the county recorder. For personal property, state law may require you to complete and file a security agreement to enforce the security clause in your note. A legal forms stationer may have security agreements on hand, or you can contact a real estate broker, tax adviser, or lawyer to obtain these forms and/or have them prepared for you. Attach a completed copy of the security document to the resolution.

EXAMPLE (real estate used as security):

"Deed of Trust to real property commonly known as _____ [address] _____, owned by _____ [name of borrower(s)] _____, executed on _[date of signing of deed of trust]_, at ___[city and state where signed]___, and recorded at _____[place recorded]_____, in the records of _____[name of recording office]_____, _____[name of county and state]___."

EXAMPLE (automobile used as security):

"Security Agreement signed by _____[name of borrower(s)]_____, on _____[date of signing]_____, pledging title to _____[make and model and year of automobile with Vehicle ID #]_____."

❹ The borrower should complete and sign the first set of signature lines. If the borrower is married, the spouse should complete and sign the second set; otherwise, it can be deleted.

Individual Promissory Note: Installment Payments of Principal and Interest (Amortized Loan) With Balloon Payment

The next promissory note differs from the standard amortized note discussed above by requiring a "balloon payment" to be made at the end of the repayment term. A balloon payment is a complete payoff of all remaining principal on a specified installment date, one that's prior to the date when the loan would normally be paid off by regular installment payments. Use this note if the lender wishes to receive regular payments of principal and interest for a period of time, but then wants full repayment of principal on a particular future date. You will need to use an amortization guide that includes a remaining loan balance table, which will allow you to calculate the amount of the balloon payment. (See the special instructions to the note form, below.) For more information on computing the balloon payment amount, see "Promissory Note: Installment Payments of Principal and Interest (Amortized Loan) With Balloon Payment" in Chapter 13.

CD-ROM

Complete the note following the special instructions below. You'll find this resolution on the CD-ROM and as a tearout form in Appendix C. (See Appendix A for information on selecting and using the CD-ROM files.)

Individual Promissory Note:
Installment Payments of Principal and Interest
(Amortized Loan) with Balloon Payment

For value received,_____[name of member, manager, officer, employee, or other individual (plus name of spouse if LLC person is married)]_____ , the borrower(s), promise(s) to pay to the order of _____[name of LLC]_____ , the noteholder, the principal amount of $__[principal amount of loan]__ , together with simple interest on the unpaid principal balance from the date of this note until the date this note is paid in full, at the annual rate of __[annual rate of interest]__ %. Payments will be made at _____[address of LLC]_____ .

   Principal and interest will be paid in equal installments of $ __[amount of each payment]__ , beginning on __[date of first payment]__ , and continuing on __[day for ongoing payments, for example, "the fifteenth day of each month"]__ . On the installment payment date on __[date of final (balloon) payment]__ , a balloon payment of $__[amount of remaining principal owed on the loan on final installment date]__ ❶ will be added to the installment amount paid by the borrower in order to pay off this note in its entirety on this final installment payment date. Each payment made by the borrower(s) will be applied first to accrued but unpaid interest, and the remainder will be applied to unpaid principal.

   This note may be prepaid by the borrower(s) in whole or in part at any time without penalty. This note is not assumable without the written consent of the noteholder. Consent will not be unreasonably withheld. This note is nontransferable by the noteholder. ❷

   If any installment payment due under this note is not received by the noteholder within __[number of days]__ of its due date, the entire amount of unpaid principal and accrued but unpaid interest of the loan will, at the option of the noteholder, become immediately due and payable without prior notice by the noteholder to the borrower(s). In the event of a default, the borrower(s) is/are responsible for the costs of collection, including, in the event of a lawsuit to collect on this note, the noteholder's reasonable attorney fees as determined by a court hearing the lawsuit.

   If two persons sign below, each is jointly and severally liable for repayment of this note. ❸

Name of Borrower #1: _____

Signature: _____

Address: _____

City, or County, and State Where Signed: _____

Date of Signing: _____

Name of Borrower #2: _____

Signature: _____

Address: _____

City, or County, and State Where Signed: _____

Date of Signing: _____

Special Instructions

❶ For instructions on computing the balloon payment, see the special instructions in "Periodic Payments of Interest Plus Principal (Amortized Loans)" in Chapter 13.

❷ This paragraph specifies that the loan may be repaid by the borrower at any time without triggering a prepayment penalty. This allows the borrower to pay off the loan at any time. The loan is assumable (meaning another company or person can take over the payment obligation for the borrower) with the permission of the noteholder (the LLC), but it is unlikely that another person will wish to assume payments under the loan. The note is also nontransferable—the LLC may not transfer the note to another company or person to collect payments from the borrower. This provision is customary for loans from a small LLC. You can easily change this sentence to allow transfers if you wish, though it's highly unlikely that anyone would wish to buy this type of note, even at a discount.

❸ The borrower should complete and sign the first set of signature lines. If the borrower is married, the spouse should complete and sign the second set; otherwise, it should be deleted.

Individual Promissory Note: Periodic Payments of Interest Only With Lump-Sum Principal Payment

This promissory note provides for regular payments of interest only for a designated period, to be followed by a lump-sum payment of the entire principal amount of the loan. This form of loan makes sense if the loan amount is not excessive and the borrower can come up with the entire principal at the end of the loan period. For more information on this type of payment plan, see "Periodic Payment of Interest Only" in Chapter 13.

EXAMPLE:
Frank's LLC lends him $10,000 at a 7.5% rate for five years. The LLC uses the amortization table in Chapter 13 to calculate that the total interest owed by Frank for these funds will be $3,750 ($10,000 x .075 x 5). The amount of each monthly interest installment under the note is thus $62.50 (total interest for the five-year loan period—$3,750—divided by the 60 installments made in this period). At the end of the five-year period during which Frank pays monthly interest only, Frank must pay the LLC the entire $10,000 amount.

CD-ROM

Complete the note following the special instructions below. You'll find this resolution on the CD-ROM and as a tearout form in Appendix C. (See Appendix A for information on selecting and using the CD-ROM files.)

Special Instructions

❶ For instructions on computing the interest-only payments, see the special instructions in "Promissory Note: Periodic Payments of Interest Only With Lump-Sum Principal Payment" in Chapter 13.

❷ This paragraph specifies that the loan may be repaid by the borrower at any time without triggering a prepayment penalty. This allows the borrower to pay off the loan at any time. The loan is assumable (meaning another company or person can take over the payment obligation for the borrower) with the permission of the noteholder (the LLC), but it is unlikely that another person will wish to assume payments under the loan. The note is also nontransferable—the LLC may not transfer the note to another company or person to collect

---

Individual Promissory Note:
Periodic Payments of Interest
with Lump-Sum Principal Payment

For value received,_____ [name of member, manager, officer, employee, or other individual (plus name of spouse if LLC person is married)]_____ , the borrower(s), promise(s) to pay to the order of _____ [name of LLC] _____ , the noteholder, the principal amount of $ [principal amount of loan] , together with simple interest on the unpaid principal balance from the date of this note until the date this note is paid in full, at the annual rate of [annual rate of interest] %. Payments will be made at _____ [address of LLC]_____.

Interest will be paid in equal installments of $ [amount of each payment] , beginning on [date of first payment] , and continuing on [day for ongoing payments, for example, "the fifteenth day of each month"] until [ending date of loan period] , on which date the entire principal amount, together with total accrued but unpaid interest, will be paid by the borrower(s). ❶

This note may be prepaid by the borrower(s) in whole or in part at any time without penalty. This note is not assumable without the written consent of the noteholder. Consent will not be unreasonably withheld. This note is nontransferable by the noteholder. ❷

If any installment payment due under this note is not received by the noteholder within [number of days] of its due date, the entire amount of unpaid principal and accrued but unpaid interest of the loan will, at the option of the noteholder, become immediately due and payable without prior notice by the noteholder to the borrower(s). In the event of a default, the borrower(s) is/are responsible for the costs of collection, including, in the event of a lawsuit to collect on this note, the noteholder's reasonable attorney fees as determined by a court hearing the lawsuit.

If two persons sign below, each is jointly and severally liable for repayment of this note. ❸

Name of Borrower #1: _____

Signature: _____

Address: _____

City, or County, and State Where Signed: _____

Date of Signing: _____

Name of Borrower #2: _____

Signature: _____

Address: _____

City, or County, and State Where Signed: _____

Date of Signing: _____

payments from the borrower. This provision is customary for loans from a small LLC. You can easily change this sentence to allow transfers if you wish, though it's highly unlikely that anyone would wish to buy this type of note, even at a discount.

❸ The borrower should complete and sign the first set of signature lines. If the borrower is married, the spouse should complete and sign the second set; otherwise, it should be deleted.

Individual Promissory Note: Lump-Sum Payment of Principal and Interest on Specified Date

This promissory note is similar to the previous note in that the entire amount of principal is paid in one lump sum at the end of the loan period. However, unlike the previous note, where interest payments are made in installments during the loan period, here the entire interest amount is paid along with the entire principal amount in one lump sum at the end of the loan term. For more information on this type of payment plan, see "Lump-Sum Repayment With Interest" in Chapter 13.

EXAMPLE:

Rosie borrows $10,000 for three years at 6% interest from her LLC. Multiply 10,000 x .06 x 3 ($1,800) to calculate the total interest owed by Rosie for these funds. At the end of the three-year loan term, Rosie will owe a one-time payment of $11,800 (the $10,000 principal plus the entire $1,800 interest).

CD-ROM

Complete the note following the special instructions below. You'll find this resolution on the CD-ROM and as a tearout form in Appendix C. (See Appendix A for information on selecting and using the CD-ROM files.)

Special Instructions

❶ This paragraph specifies that the loan may be repaid by the borrower at any time without triggering a prepayment penalty. This allows the borrower to pay off the loan at any time. The loan is assumable (meaning another company or person can take over the payment obligation for the borrower) with the permission of the noteholder (the LLC), but it is unlikely that another person will wish to assume payments under the loan. The note is also nontransferable—the LLC may not transfer the note to another company or person to collect payments from the borrower. This provision is customary for loans from a small LLC. You can easily change this sentence to allow transfers if you wish, though it's highly unlikely that anyone would wish to buy this type of note, even at a discount.

❷ The borrower should complete and sign the first set of signature lines. If the borrower is married, the spouse should complete and sign the second set; otherwise, it should be deleted.

Individual Promissory Note:
Lump-Sum Payment of Principal
and Interest On Specified Date

For value received,_____[name of member, manager, officer, employee, or other individual (plus name of spouse if LLC person is married)]_____, the borrower(s), promise(s) to pay to the order of _____[name of LLC]_____ , the noteholder, the principal amount of $_[principal amount of loan]_ , together with simple interest on the unpaid principal balance from the date of this note until the date this note is paid in full, at the annual rate of _[annual rate of interest]_ %. Payments will be made at _____[address of LLC]_____.

The entire principal amount of the loan, together with total accrued but unpaid interest, will be paid by the borrower(s) on _[due date for payment of all principal and interest]_. Any payment made by the borrower(s) prior to the due date specified above will be applied first to accrued but unpaid interest, and the remainder will be applied to unpaid principal.

This note may be prepaid by the borrower(s) in whole or in part at any time without penalty. This note is not assumable without the written consent of the noteholder. Consent will not be unreasonably withheld. This note is nontransferable by the noteholder. ❶

In the event of a default, the borrower(s) is/are responsible for the costs of collection, including, in the event of a lawsuit to collect on this note, the noteholder's reasonable attorney fees as determined by a court hearing the lawsuit.

If two persons sign below, each is jointly and severally liable for repayment of this note.❷

Name of Borrower #1: _____

Signature: _____

Address: _____

City, or County, and State Where Signed: _____

Date of Signing: _____

Name of Borrower #2: _____

Signature: _____

Address: _____

City, or County, and State Where Signed: _____

Date of Signing: _____

Individual Promissory Note: Lump-Sum Payment of Principal and Interest on Demand by Noteholder

Here is a "demand note" that allows the noteholder (LLC) to call the note due at any time. Rather than specifying a particular date in the future for repayment, the LLC can call the loan due and payable by making a written demand for payment. Obviously, you want to be sure the borrower has sufficient cash resources to comply with a demand for repayment prior to making a loan of this sort. Make sure to call any demand loans you make to members within a reasonable period of making the loan. If you don't, and the IRS audits your LLC, it is likely to claim that the demand loans were really a distribution of profits to a member (See "Illegitimate Member Loans Treated as Distributions of Profit," above.)

CD-ROM

Complete the note following the special instructions below. You'll find this resolution on the CD-ROM and as a tearout form in Appendix C. (See Appendix A for information on selecting and using the CD-ROM files.)

Special Instructions

❶ This paragraph specifies that the loan may be repaid by the borrower at any time without triggering a prepayment penalty. This allows the borrower to pay off the loan at any time. The loan is assumable (meaning another company or person can take over the payment obligation for the borrower) with the permission of the noteholder (the LLC), but it is unlikely that another person will wish to assume payments under the loan. The note is also nontransferable—the LLC may not transfer the note to another company or person to collect payments from the borrower. This provision is customary for loans from a small LLC. You can easily change this sentence to allow transfers if you wish, though it's highly unlikely that anyone would wish to buy this type of note, even at a discount.

❷ The borrower should complete and sign the first set of signature lines. If the borrower is married, the spouse should complete and sign the second set; otherwise, it should be deleted.

Individual Promissory Note:
Lump-Sum Payment of Principal and Interest
on Demand by Noteholder

For value received, _____ [name of member, manager, officer, employee, or other individual (plus name of spouse if LLC person is married)]_____ , the borrower(s), promise(s) to pay to the order of _____ [name of LLC]_____ , the noteholder, the principal amount of $_ [principal amount of loan]_ , together with simple interest on the unpaid principal balance from the date of this note until the date this note is paid in full, at the annual rate of _[annual rate of interest]_ %. Payments will be made at _____ [address of LLC]_____ .

The entire principal amount of the loan, together with total accrued but unpaid interest, will be paid within _ [period, for example, "30 days or other period agreeable to the LLC and borrower"]_ of receipt by the borrower(s) of a demand for repayment by the noteholder. A demand for repayment by the noteholder will be made in writing and delivered or mailed to the borrower(s) at the following address: _____ [address of borrower(s)]_____ . If demand for repayment is mailed, it will be considered received by the borrower(s) on the third business day after the date when it was deposited in the U.S. mail as registered or certified mail.

Any payment made by the borrower(s) prior to the due date specified above will be applied first to accrued but unpaid interest, and the remainder will be applied to unpaid principal.

This note may be prepaid by the borrower(s) in whole or in part at any time without penalty. This note is not assumable without the written consent of the noteholder. Consent will not be unreasonably withheld. This note is nontransferable by the noteholder. ❶

In the event of a default, the borrower(s) is/are responsible for the costs of collection, including, in the event of a lawsuit to collect on this note, the noteholder's reasonable attorney fees as determined by a court hearing the lawsuit.

If two persons sign below, each is jointly and severally liable for repayment of this note. ❷

Name of Borrower #1: _____

Signature: _____

Address: _____

City, or County, and State Where Signed: _____

Date of Signing: _____

Name of Borrower #2: _____

Signature: _____

Address: _____

City, or County, and State Where Signed: _____

Date of Signing: _____

Individual Promissory Note: Special Schedule of Payments of Principal and Interest

This promissory note allows you to specify a special (nonuniform) schedule for repayments of principal and interest under the loan. Typically, the schedule will require principal and/or interest payments of unequal amounts and at irregular intervals during the life of the note, ending with a final payment of principal and all accrued and unpaid interest due.

> **! CAUTION**
>
> **Make sure to include interest.** All loans should have provisions for the payment of interest on the borrowed funds, unless, of course, you are purposely setting up a no-interest loan program. If you are, watch out for the below-market loan rules (see "Below-Market Member Loans," above) and check with your tax adviser.

The options here are unlimited; but here's one example.

EXAMPLE:

On July 1, Hamid's LLC lends him $10,000 for five years at 8% interest. They agree that Hamid will not make payments until the end of the second year. Using the amortization table in Chapter 13, Hamid calculates that he'll pay $1,600 in interest-only payments for the first two years of the loan ($10,000 x .08 x 2). Hamid will make an interest-only payment of $800 at the end of the third year. At the end of the fourth year, he will make an $800 interest payment, along with a payment of $4,000 in principal, leaving a principal balance of $6,000. Finally, at the end of the fifth year, Hamid will make his last payment, which consists of the balance of the $6,000 principal along with $480 in interest ($6,000 x .08). Here is the special repayment schedule:

June 31, 2nd year	$1,600	(interest)
June 31, 3rd year	$800	(interest)
June 31, 4th year	$4,800	($4,000 principal; $800 interest)
June 31, 5th year	$6,480	($6,000 principal; $480 interest)
Total Payments	$13,680	($10,000 principal; $3,680 interest)

> **CD-ROM**
>
> Complete the note following the special instructions below. You'll find this resolution on the CD-ROM and as a tearout form in Appendix C. (See Appendix A for information on selecting and using the CD-ROM files.)

Special Instructions

❶ This paragraph specifies that the loan may be repaid by the borrower at any time without triggering a prepayment penalty. This allows the borrower to pay off the loan at any time. The loan is assumable (meaning another company or person can take over the payment obligation for the borrower) with the permission of the noteholder (the LLC), but it is unlikely that another person will wish to assume payments under the loan. The note is also nontransferable—the LLC may not transfer the note to another company or person to collect payments from the borrower. This provision is customary for loans from a small LLC. You can easily change this sentence to allow transfers if you wish, though it's highly unlikely that anyone would wish to buy this type of note, even at a discount.

❷ The borrower should complete and sign the first set of signature lines. If the borrower is married, the spouse should complete and sign the second set; otherwise, it should be deleted.

Individual Promissory Note:
Special Schedule of Payments
of Principal and Interest

For value received,_____[name of member, manager, officer, employee, or other individual (plus name of spouse if LLC person is married)]_____, the borrower(s), promise(s) to pay to the order of _____[name of LLC]_____, the noteholder, the principal amount of $_[principal amount of loan]_, together with simple interest on the unpaid principal balance from the date of this note until the date this note is paid in full, at the annual rate of _[annual rate of interest]_%. Payments will be made at _____[address of LLC]_____.

Principal and interest will be paid as follows:

[Include schedule of payments here. For last payment, you can insert the following: "The borrower(s) will make a final payment in the amount of all remaining principal and all accrued but unpaid interest on (date)."]

This note may be prepaid by the borrower(s) in whole or in part at any time without penalty. This note is not assumable without the written consent of the noteholder. Consent will not be unreasonably withheld. This note is nontransferable by the noteholder. ❶

If any installment payment due under this note is not received by the noteholder within _[number of days]_ of its due date, the entire amount of unpaid principal and accrued but unpaid interest of the loan will, at the option of the noteholder, become immediately due and payable without prior notice by the noteholder to the borrower(s). In the event of a default, the borrower(s) will be responsible for the costs of collection, including, in the event of a lawsuit to collect on this note, the noteholder's reasonable attorney fees as determined by a court hearing the lawsuit.

If two persons sign below, each is jointly and severally liable for repayment of this note. ❷

Name of Borrower #1: _____

Signature: _____

Address: _____

City, or County, and State Where Signed: _____

Date of Signing: _____

Name of Borrower #2: _____

Signature: _____

Address: _____

City, or County, and State Where Signed: _____

Date of Signing: _____

Release of Promissory Note

This form can be used to show that a promissory note has been paid in full. A borrowing member or other LLC insider will usually want the LLC to fill out this release when the final payment has been received. When this occurs, the LLC should fill in and sign and date the form. The promissory note also should be marked "paid in full" by the LLC and attached to the release form. Copies of both should be placed in the LLC records binder. You also should record the release if the loan was secured by property and a security interest document, such as a deed of trust, was recorded for the loan transaction.

CD-ROM

You'll find this resolution on the CD-ROM and as a tearout form in Appendix C. (See Appendix A for information on selecting and using the CD-ROM files.)

Release of Promissory Note

The undersigned noteholder,   [name and address of noteholder]   , in consideration of full payment of the promissory note dated   [date of note]   in the principal amount of $ [principal amount of note] , hereby releases and discharges the borrower(s),   [name of borrower(s)]   ,   [address of borrower(s)]   , from any claims or obligations on account of the note.

Dated: _____

Name of Noteholder: _____

Signature: _____

[If the LLC is the noteholder, use the following signature lines instead:]

Name of Noteholder: _____[name of LLC]_____

By: _____[signature of treasurer]_____, Treasurer

on behalf of _____[name of LLC]_____

Self-Interested Business Dealings Between the LLC and Its Members or Managers

A general principle of LLC law is that LLC members and managers must not advance their own personal interests at the expense of the LLC. This does not mean that a member or manager can't take part in any deal that benefits him or her personally, however. A member or manager who is considering such a deal must disclose all the facts surrounding the deal to LLC comembers and/or managers, who must approve it. This chapter includes a resolution that the members and/or managers can use to approve an LLC business deal that may benefit a particular member or manager.

SKIP AHEAD

Formal approval of this sort is probably not necessary for LLCs with one owner or LLCs owned by spouses. If you have a single-member LLC, you can skip this chapter.

Approval can legally validate LLC business that benefits a member or manager. It can also help head off later conflict by disclosing upfront any personal financial benefit a member or manager stands to gain by doing business with the LLC.

Who Approves Self-Interested Business Resolutions?

As discussed below, the self-interested business resolution presented in this chapter should be approved, if possible, by a disinterested majority of the LLC members (in a member-managed LLC) or a disinterested majority of LLC managers (in a manager-managed LLC). By a "disinterested majority," I mean a majority of the group of members or managers who do not stand to derive a direct personal financial benefit from the business deal in question. If this isn't possible because most or all of the members or managers will benefit from the proposed business deal with the LLC, make sure you can show that the deal is fair and in the best interests of the LLC. The resolution in this chapter helps you make this showing.

For an important or potentially controversial deal, you may wish to seek approval of *all members* (if your LLC is either managed by managers or is member-managed by less than all members).

How to Select and Use LLC Resolutions

- Read the background material that precedes the resolution.

- Follow the instructions included with the sample resolution to complete a draft of the resolution on your computer. If you need guidance on selecting and using the computer disk files, see Appendix A. (You'll have to fill in the tearout resolution included in Appendix C if you aren't using a computer.)

- Complete any needed attachment forms.

- If a resolution involves complex issues that will benefit from expert analysis, have your legal or tax adviser review your paperwork and conclusions.

- Prepare meeting minutes or written consent forms as explained in Chapters 5–7, and insert the completed resolution in the appropriate form.

- Have the LLC secretary sign the printed minutes or have members and/or managers sign the written consent forms and waivers. Then place the signed forms, together with any attachments, in your LLC records binder.

Legal Duties Owed by Members and Managers

LLC members and managers have certain legal obligations to their LLC. These duties apply to members who manage a member-managed LLC or to the managers of a manager-managed LLC. (Note that nonmanaging members of an LLC generally do not owe any statutory duty to their LLC, because they are not responsible for managing the business.)

Duties of Care and Loyalty

State statutes define the duties of "care" or "loyalty" owed by LLC members or managers. These statutes vary from state to state. Most of them are couched in general terms, but their thrust is clear: LLC members and managers must deal honestly with the LLC and not use it as a vehicle to advance their own personal interests over the business interests of the LLC and the other members. Similarly, LLC members and managers must act based on sound business principles and with at least some attention to detail. While honest mistakes in business judgment are legally allowed, extremely sloppy, reckless, or unlawful decision making by a member or manager can result in personal liability.

EXAMPLE:

Ward, in his capacity as LLC manager, receives a call from an executive of an outside company asking about the availability of merchandise sold by the LLC. Rather than pass the request through normal LLC channels, Ward decides to broker the deal personally, giving the client a reduced contract price for the merchandise, with Ward secretly pocketing a 10% commission. Obviously, this deal is shady from a moral and honest-business perspective. It also fails to meet the standard duty of loyalty that a managing LLC member or a manager owes to the company. Ward can be held personally liable to the LLC and its other members for the amount of his commission, plus any additional amount the LLC lost on the deal, and interest.

Here is a typical state statute setting out an LLC member's duties of care and loyalty, taken from the Alabama LLC Act.

Alabama LLC Act, Section 10-12-21

[...]

(e) In a limited liability company managed by its members [...], the only fiduciary duties a member owes to the company or to its other members are the duty of loyalty and the duty of care imposed by sections (f) and (g).

(f) A member's duty of loyalty to a member-managed limited liability company and its members is limited to each of the following:

(1) To account to the limited liability company and to hold as trustee for it any property, profit, or benefit derived by the member in the conduct or winding up of the limited liability company's business or derived from a use by the member of the limited liability company's property, including the appropriation of the limited liability company's opportunity.

(2) To refrain from dealing with the limited liability company in the conduct or winding up of the limited liability company's business as or on behalf of a party having an interest adverse to the limited liability company.

(3) To refrain from competing with the limited liability company in the conduct of the limited liability company's business before the dissolution of the limited liability company.

(g) A member's duty of care to a member-managed limited liability company and its other members in the conduct or winding up of the limited liability company's business is limited to refraining from engaging in grossly negligent or reckless conduct, intentional misconduct, or a knowing violation of law.

Approval of Self-Serving Business by Members or Managers

The duties of care and loyalty owed by a managing LLC member or manager are not necessarily violated if, in the course of managing LLC business, a member or manager approves a business deal that gives him or her a personal financial benefit. For example, Ward in the previous example would not have compromised his duties of care and loyalty to the LLC if he had fully disclosed his proposed commission deal to the exec of the outside company and to his comanagers, who felt that the LLC would benefit in the long term by allowing Ward a personal incentive to broker the deal with the outside company.

In fact, it is common for LLC members and managers to accept an LLC business deal that, as a side effect, produces a personal financial benefit for one or more of the members or managers. Some states (as part of their LLC statutes that define the duties of care and loyalty owed by a member or manager) use the following or similar wording, which makes it clear that members or managers may approve business in which they have a financial stake. (The sample wording, taken from Section 180/15-3 of the Illinois LLC Act, applies to members of a member-managed LLC, but Illinois and other states go on to say in their statutes that the rule also applies to managers of a manager-managed LLC.)

Illinois LLC Act, Section 180/15-3

[...]

(e) A member of a member-managed LLC does not violate a duty or obligation under this Act or under the operating agreement merelybecause the member's conduct furthers the member's own interest.

Other states take a more general approach, as seen in the following statute.

Maryland LLC Act, Section 4A-405

Except as provided in the operating agreement, a member may lend money to and transact other business with the limited liability company and, subject to other applicable law, has the same rights and obligations with respect to the transaction as a person who is not a member.

To help clarify what types of self-interested business transactions are legally permissible, some states list the requirements for their approval. Typically, these state statutes require either of the following:

- A majority of members (or managers) who are not benefited by the business deal approve it, after full disclosure of how the deal will benefit the self-interested member.

- The business deal is fair to the LLC, even if not approved by a disinterested majority of members or managers. After all, in a smaller LLC, there may not be a majority of members who do not benefit from the proposed business deal.

In some states, the statutes make it clear that routine items of business that necessarily benefit a member or manager, such as the setting of salaries of members who work for the LLC, do not require a special vote or validation procedure. Obviously, these laws assume that the members or managers, when approving this type of routine business, will not overreach—that they will set salaries and make other routine decisions in a way that is fair both to the LLC as a whole and to the members and managers personally.

> **CAUTION**
>
> **Fair and honest dealing is required in every state.** Even in states that seem to permit any sort of self-interested business between an LLC and an LLC member or manager, you can expect trouble if a member or manager derives an unfair or secret financial advantage from a transaction, or if a deal benefits a member or manager at the expense of the LLC. In other words, even if the duties of care and loyalty are not spelled out in a state statute, the rules of fair and honest dealing will generally be enforced by any court in the matter of a self-interested business deal between a member or manager and the LLC.

Here is some advice for LLCs in any state when approving self-interested business deals.

- Make sure the transaction is fair. If you are unjustly benefiting members at the expense of the LLC, and you have nonmanager members, you are just asking for trouble.

- Get unanimous approval. If at all possible, have self-interested transactions approved by all disinterested members or managers after full disclosure of the details of the deal and the member's or manager's potential financial interest in it. By taking these steps, you can help avoid future controversy and claims against the LLC and its members and managers.

- If unanimous approval is not possible, get majority approval by the disinterested members and/or managers.

EXAMPLE:

AB LLC is managed by five members. (It also has two nonmanaging member-investors.) The president asks the managing members to approve a contract for supplies with a company in which one member has a part ownership interest. After the disclosure of the interested member's owner-ship interest in the outside company, three of the four disinterested LLC managing members—a majority—vote to approve the transaction (only after making sure that the cost of supplies is at least as good as the lowest price available from independent suppliers). A statement that the member's interest was disclosed and the deal was considered fair is included in the resolution approved at the membership meeting. Because of these precautions, it is unlikely that any member who did not approve the deal will challenge the transaction later.

- If approval by the disinterested members and/or managers is not meaningful, take extra steps. As a practical matter, if yours is a small, closely held LLC, it's possible that a majority of your LLC members or managers will have a financial interest in the transaction. Even though you may be able to get the approval of all disinterested members or managers, their number may not be sufficient to pass the resolution by normal voting rules. In that case, you should have all members (not just disinterested members or managers) formally approve a resolution that states why the deal is fair to the LLC and is comparable to the type of deal that the LLC would make in a transaction with an outside party.
- If your LLC has only one manager (as is common in small LLCs), the manager should get approval of the members before going ahead with a deal that would benefit him or her personally.

EXAMPLE:
The sole manager of Threadbare Sofa Reconditioners, LLC, will benefit financially from a transaction. Obviously, there is no way for the manager alone to approve the deal by a disinterested majority vote. The manager can take two steps:

- formally approve a resolution (by signing it himself or herself) that states why the deal is fair to the LLC and is comparable to the type of deal that the LLC would make in a transaction with any other party, and
- get formal approval from the members by having them sign a resolution or written consents that show their approval after full disclosure of the manager's personal financial interest in the deal.

Resolution for Approval of Member or Manager Self-Interested Business Deals

Here's some practical advice for approving transactions involving the financial interests of members or managers.

When Resolutions Are Necessary

Prepare resolutions whenever a particular member or manager (or two) is singled out. If a member or manager is going to benefit from a business deal that doesn't benefit other members or managers, it's best to prepare a formal resolution that shows you took a few extra precautions before approving the transaction (for example, that you disclosed the member's or manager's interest in the deal and made sure that a majority of the disinterested members or managers approved the deal as fair to the LLC).

In addition, prepare resolutions any time there are secondary benefits to members or managers. This applies if one or more members or managers will clearly receive a significant, collateral financial benefit as a secondary effect of the transaction.

EXAMPLE:

The LLC members approve an across-the-board 10% increase in salary for all LLC employees, but two of the LLC members also work for the LLC. As the highest-paid employees, these two will receive the highest salary increase in terms of actual dollars. A formal resolution will prevent arguments later.

Resolution to Approve Business That Benefits an LLC Member or Manager

Below is a basic resolution you can use to approve an LLC item of business in which one or more members or managers have a personal financial interest. As discussed above, approval should be sought only after a disclosure of the material facts of the transaction, including the financial benefit that will accrue to the interested members or managers.

CD-ROM

Complete the self-interested business resolution following the special instructions provided. You'll find this resolution on the CD-ROM and as a tearout form in Appendix C. (See Appendix A for information on selecting and using the CD-ROM.)

Special Instructions

❶ Describe the business transaction or contract to be approved. If the terms of the transaction are contained in a separate agreement or contract (such as a lease, promissory note, or the like), refer to the agreement or contract (for example, "see attached lease agreement") and attach a copy to the resolution.

EXAMPLE:

Shake and Rake Tree Trimmers, LLC, wishes to obtain full membership approval of a proposed loan by the LLC to a member. Instead of describing the loan and the terms of the note here, the secretary fills in: "proposed loan by LLC to [name of member], with terms as described in a proposed promissory note attached to this resolution." (Chapters 13 and 14 contain promissory note forms.)

❷ As explained above, many self-interested decisions by members or managers do not violate state law, simply because they are also fair to the LLC. To give extra weight to your determination of fairness, insert the explicit reasons why the proposed deal is fair to the LLC (for example, "the rent amount under a lease of property by [name of member] to the LLC is the prevailing commercial rate in the area").

EXAMPLE:

The Shake and Rake Tree Trimmers, LLC secretary inserts the following reason for the fairness of the proposed LLC loan to a member: "The LLC has sufficient cash reserves to make the loan without impeding ongoing LLC business, and the interest rate to be charged on the loan is the current rate charged on commercial loans by commercial lenders."

❸ Insert the names of the members and/or managers asked to approve the self-interested transaction, and show the vote cast by the member or manager—for or against the resolution. As discussed, usually you will seek approval of the managing members or managers of the LLC. But for an important or potentially controversial deal, you may wish to seek approval of all members (if your LLC is either managed by managers or is member-managed by less than all members).

LLC Approval of Transaction Benefiting
a Member or Manager

The members and/or managers of the LLC have considered: __[state nature of transaction or contract]__. ❶ It was understood that the following persons have a material financial interest in this transaction or contract as follows: __[state the name(s) of the member(s) or manager(s) and their personal financial interest in the transaction or contract with the LLC]__.

After discussion, it was agreed that the approval of this business was fair to and in the best interests of the LLC because ____[state why the transaction or contract was determined to be fair]____. ❷ Therefore, it was approved by the votes of the members and/or managers as follows:

Name   Vote ❸

_____   _____

_____   _____

Lawyers, Tax Specialists, and Legal Research

Much of the work required to hold LLC meetings and document decisions is routine. Any knowledgeable and motivated businessperson can do it. But there's no way around it—from time to time you are bound to need help from outside sources. Some LLC decisions involve complex areas of law or taxation. Others involve a mix of business and legal savvy and are likely to be best made with the input of an experienced small-business lawyer.

You may wish to turn to a lawyer for help in drafting resolutions to approve special items of business approved at meetings or with written consents of your members and/or managers. And, of course, there will be important legal consequences associated with ongoing LLC decisions that may require input from an experienced legal professional. One good way to learn more about any legal decision or form is to read up on these areas in a law or business library. (See "How to Do Your Own Legal Research," below.) Or you can decide, as many busy businesspeople do, to pay a lawyer, accountant, or financial adviser (such as a pension plan specialist, bank loan officer, or financial investment adviser) to check your conclusions about tricky legal areas. The sections below provide a few tips to help you in your search for competent expert information, assistance, and advice.

How to Find the Right Lawyer

Most small businesses can't afford to put a lawyer on retainer. Even when consulted on an issue-by-issue basis, lawyer's fees mount up fast—often way too fast to be affordable except for the most pressing problems. Just as with individuals, more and more small businesses are trying to at least partially close this affordability gap by doing as much of their own legal form preparation as possible. Often a knowledgeable self-helper can sensibly accomplish the whole task. Other times, it makes sense to briefly consult with a lawyer at an interim stage, or have the paperwork reviewed on completion.

You already have taken one positive step toward making your legal needs affordable by using this book to prepare standard LLC minutes and written consent forms. Depending on the size of your business and the complexity of your legal needs, your next step is likely to be to find a cooperative lawyer who will help you consider important legal decisions and review or draft specific resolutions you will insert in your minutes.

You obviously don't want a lawyer who is bent on taking over all your legal decision making and form-drafting while running up billable hours as fast as possible. Instead, you need a legal coach—someone who is willing to work *with* you, not just *for* you. Under this model, the lawyer helps you take care of many routine legal matters yourself, while remaining available to consult on more complicated legal issues as the need arises.

TIP

You don't need a big-time LLC lawyer. There is a lawyer surplus these days, and many newer lawyers, especially, are open to nontraditional business arrangements. Look for a lawyer with some small business experience, preferably in your field or area of operations. For the most part, you don't want a lawyer who works primarily with big businesses. Not only will this person deal with issues that are far from your concerns, but he or she is almost sure to charge too much.

Don't Ask a Lawyer for Tax Advice

When it comes to LLC decisions that have tax implications, accountants often have a better grasp of the issues than lawyers. And an added bonus is that although tax advice doesn't come cheap, accountants often charge less than lawyers.

Look and Ask Around

When you go looking for a lawyer, don't start with phone books or advertisements. Lawyer referral services operated by bar associations are equally unhelpful. These simply supply the names of lawyers who have signed on to the service, often accepting the lawyers' own word for what types of skills or experience they have. A better approach is to talk to people in your community who own or operate businesses you respect. Ask them who their lawyer is and what they think of that person's work. If you talk to half a dozen businesspeople, chances are you'll come away with several good leads. Other people, such as your banker, accountant, insurance agent, or real estate broker, may be able to provide the names of lawyers they trust to help them with business matters. Friends, relatives, and business associates within your own company may also have names of possible lawyers.

TIP

Let your legal coach refer you to experts when necessary. What if you have a very technical legal question? Should you start by seeking out a legal specialist? For starters, the answer is probably no. First, find a good business lawyer to act as your coach. Then rely on this person to suggest specialized materials or experts as the need arises.

Talk to the Lawyer Ahead of Time

After you get the names of several good prospects, don't wait until a legal problem arises before contacting a lawyer. Once enmeshed in a crisis, you may not have time to find a lawyer who will work with you at affordable rates. Chances are you'll wind up settling for the first person available at a moment's notice—which all but guarantees you'll pay too much.

When you call a lawyer, announce your intentions in advance—that you are looking for someone who is willing to review your papers from time to time, point you in the right direction as the need arises, serve as a legal adviser as circumstances dictate, and tackle particular legal problems as necessary. In exchange for this, let the lawyer know you are willing to pay promptly and fairly. If the lawyer seems agreeable to this arrangement, ask to come in to meet for a half-hour or so. Although many lawyers will not charge you for this introductory appointment, it's often a good idea to offer to pay for it. You want to establish that while you are looking for someone to help you help yourself, you are able to pay as you go.

At the interview, reemphasize that you are looking for a nontraditional "legal coach" relationship. Many lawyers will find this unappealing—for example, saying they don't feel comfortable reviewing documents you have drafted using self-help materials. If so, thank the person for being frank and keep interviewing other lawyers. You'll also want to discuss other important issues in this initial interview, such as the lawyer's customary charges for services, as explained further below.

Pay particular attention to the rapport between you and your lawyer. Remember: You are looking for a legal coach who will work with you. Trust your instincts and seek a lawyer whose personality and business sense are compatible with your own.

Set the Extent and Cost of Services in Advance

When you hire a lawyer, get a clear understanding about how fees will be computed. For example, if you call the lawyer from time to time for general advice or to be steered to a good information source, how will you be billed? Some lawyers bill a flat amount for a call or a conference; others bill to the nearest six-, ten-, or twenty-minute interval. Whatever the lawyer's system, you need to understand it.

Especially at the beginning of your relationship, when you bring a big job to a lawyer, ask specifically about what it will cost. If you feel it's too much, don't hesitate to negotiate; perhaps you can do some of the routine work yourself, thus reducing the fee.

It's a good idea to get all fee arrangements—especially those for good-sized jobs—in writing. In several states, fee agreements between lawyers and clients must be in writing if the expected fee is $1,000 or more, or is contingent on the outcome of a lawsuit. But whether required or not, it's a good idea to get it in writing.

How Lawyers Charge for Legal Services

There are no across-the-board arrangements on how lawyers' fees are to be charged. Expect to be charged by one of the following methods:

- **By the hour.** In most parts of the United States, you can get competent services for your small business for $150 to $250 an hour. Newer attorneys still in the process of building a practice may be available for paperwork review, legal research, and other types of legal work at lower rates.

- **Flat fee for a specific job.** Under this arrangement, you pay the agreed-upon amount for a given project, regardless of how much or how little time the lawyer spends. Particularly when you first begin working with a lawyer and are worried about hourly costs getting out of control, negotiating a flat fee for a specific job can make sense.

- **Contingent fee based on settlement amounts or winnings.** This type of fee typically occurs in personal injury, products liability, fraud, and discrimination-type cases, where a lawsuit will likely be filed. The lawyer gets a percentage of the recovery (often 33%–40%) if you win and nothing if you lose. A contingency fee can go as high as 50% if the case does not settle and goes to court. Because most small business legal needs involve advice and help with drafting paperwork, a contingency fee approach doesn't normally make sense.

- **Retainer.** Some LLCs can afford to pay relatively modest amounts, perhaps $1,000 to $2,000 a year, to keep a business lawyer on retainer for ongoing phone or in-person consultations, routine premeeting minutes review or resolution preparation, and other business matters during the year. Of course, your retainer won't cover a full-blown legal crisis, but it can help you take care of ongoing minutes and other legal paperwork (for example, contract or special real estate paperwork) when you need a hand.

> **TIP**
>
> **Use nonlawyer professionals to cut down on legal costs.** Often, nonlawyer professionals perform some tasks better and at lower cost than lawyers. For example, look to management consultants for strategic business planning, real estate brokers or appraisers for valuation of properties, financial planners for investment advice, insurance agents and brokers for advice on insurance protection, independent paralegals for routine LLC resolution- or form-drafting, and CPAs for help in setting up and maintaining the LLC's financial records and preparing its tax returns. Each of these matters is likely to have a legal aspect, and you may eventually want to consult your lawyer, but normally you won't need to until you've gathered information on your own.

Confront Any Problems Head-On

If you have any questions about a lawyer's bill or the quality of his or her services, speak up. Buying legal help should be just like purchasing any other consumer service—if you are dissatisfied, seek a reduction in your bill or make it clear that the work needs to be redone properly. If the lawyer runs a decent business, he or she will promptly and positively deal with your concerns. If you don't get an acceptable response, find another lawyer pronto. If you switch lawyers, you are entitled to get your important documents back from the first lawyer.

Even if you fire your lawyer, you may still feel unjustly wronged. If you can't get satisfaction from the lawyer, write to the client grievance office of your state bar association (with a copy to the lawyer, of course). Often, a phone call from this office to your lawyer will bring the desired results.

Finding the Right Tax Adviser

Many resolutions and ongoing LLC decisions involve tax issues and advice. To make good decisions in these and other tax areas, you may need the help of a tax adviser. Depending on the issue before you, this adviser may be a certified public accountant, financial or investment adviser, LLC loan officer at a bank, pension plan specialist, or inside or outside bookkeeper trained in employment and LLC tax reporting and return requirements.

Whatever your arrangement, consider the same issues for finding, choosing, using, and resolving problems with a tax professional as those discussed above for legal services. Shop around for someone recommended by small business people you respect. Again, you may be able to take advantage of the lower rates offered by newer local practitioners or firms. Your tax person should be available over the phone to answer routine questions, or by mail or fax to handle paperwork and correspondence, with a minimum of formality or ritual. It is likely that you will spend much more time dealing with your tax adviser than your legal adviser, so be particularly attentive to the personal side of this relationship.

Tax issues are often cloudy and subject to a range of interpretations and strategies, particularly in the LLC area, so it is absolutely essential that you discuss and agree on the level of tax-aggressiveness you expect from your adviser. Some small business owners want to live on the edge, saving every possible tax dollar, even at the risk that deductions and other tax practices will be challenged by the IRS or state tax agents. Others are willing to pay a bit more in taxes to gain an extra measure of peace of mind. Whatever your tax strategy, make sure you find a tax adviser who feels the same way you do, or is willing to defer to your more liberal or conservative tax tendencies.

As with legal issues that affect your business, it pays to learn as much as you can about LLC taxation. Not only will you have to buy less help from professionals but you'll also be in a better position to make good financial and tax-planning decisions. IRS forms, business and law library publications, trade groups, and countless other sources provide accessible information on LLC tax issues. Your accountant or other tax adviser should be able to help you put your hands on good materials. Banks are an excellent source of financial advice, particularly if they will be LLC creditors—after all, they will have a stake in the success of your LLC. Further, the federal Small Business Administration can be an ideal source of financial and tax information and resources (as well as financing in some cases). Check it out online at www.sba.gov.

How to Do Your Own Legal Research

Law is information, not magic. If you can look up necessary information yourself, you need not purchase it from a lawyer—although, for important issues, you may wish to check your conclusions with a lawyer, or use one as a sounding board for your intended course of action.

Much of the research necessary to understand your state's business LLC law can be done without a lawyer by spending a few minutes online browsing your state LLC act or by visiting a local law or business library. You can find the citations and Web links to each state's LLC act in Appendix B. Even if you need to go to a lawyer for help in preparing an LLC resolution or to discuss the legal ramifications of a proposed LLC transaction, you can give yourself a head start by reading legal manuals prepared for lawyers, which are available at law libraries.

How do you find a law library open to the public? In many states, you need to look only as far as your county courthouse or, failing that, your state capital. In addition, publicly funded law schools generally permit the public to use their libraries, and some private law schools grant limited access to their libraries— sometimes for a modest user's fee. If you're lucky enough to have access to several law libraries, select one that has a reference librarian to assist you. Also look through the business or reference department of a major city or county public library. These often carry LLC statutes as well as books on LLC law and taxation useful to the small business owner.

In doing legal research for an LLC or other type of business, there are a number of sources for legal rules, procedures, and issues that you may wish to examine. Here are a few:

- **LLC Act.** These state statutes should be your primary focus for finding the rules for operating your LLC, including holding meetings and obtaining the approval of members and managers for ongoing legal, tax, business, and financial decisions. Your state LLC act is probably available for browsing and/or downloading from your state-maintained Web page on the Internet. Appendix B includes the URL for each state's LLC laws.

- **Other state laws.** A state's securities, commercial, civil, labor, and revenue codes govern the issuance and transfer of securities; the content, approval, and enforcement of commercial contracts; employment practices and procedures; state tax requirements; and other aspects of doing business in your state. Depending on the type of business you have, you may also want to research statutes and regulations dealing with other legal topics, such as environmental law, product liability, real estate, copyrights, and so on.

- **Federal laws.** These include the tax laws and procedures found in the Internal Revenue Code and Treasury Regulations implementing these code sections; regulations dealing with advertising, warranties, and other consumer matters adopted by the Federal Trade Commission; and equal opportunity statutes such as Title VII of the Civil Rights Act administered by the Equal Employment Opportunities Commission.

- **Administrative rules and regulations.** Issued by federal and state administrative agencies charged with implementing statutes, these regulations clarify the statute and contain rules for an agency to follow in implementing and enforcing the statutes.

- **Case law.** These are decisions of federal and state courts interpreting statutes—and sometimes making law, known as "common law," if the subject isn't covered by a statute. Annotated state LLC codes contain not only the statute itself but also references to any court cases interpreting and implementing specific sections of the law. However, because LLC law is relatively new, there aren't yet many court cases in the codes.

- **Secondary sources.** Also important in researching LLC and business law are sources that provide background information on particular areas of law. One example is this book. Others are commonly found in the business, legal, or reference section of your local bookstore. Also see "Resources From Nolo," below.

TIP

Consider joining a trade group. As a final method of finding legal information, think about joining and participating in one or more trade groups related to your business. These groups often track legislation in particular areas of business and provide sample contracts and other useful legal forms. Some also retain law firms for trade association purposes that may refer you to competent local lawyers.

Resources From Nolo

Below are a few titles published by Nolo with valuable information for the small business person:

- *LLC Maker* (software), by Anthony Mancuso. This interactive program assembles LLC articles and operating agreements for use in each state. Contains built-in links to each state's LLC filing office and LLC act.

- *Form Your Own Limited Liability Company* (book with CD-ROM), by Anthony Mancuso. This national title shows you how to form an LLC under each state's LLC law and the latest federal tax rules.

- *Business Buyout Agreements: A Step-By-Step Guide for Co-Owners* (book with CD-ROM), by Anthony Mancuso and Bethany K. Laurence. This book shows you how to adopt comprehensive buy-sell provisions to handle the purchase and sale of ownership interests in an LLC, partnership, or corporation when an owner withdraws, dies, becomes disabled, or wishes to sell an interest to an outsider. Comes with an easy-to-use agreement as a tearout and on disk.

- *How to Form Your Own California Corporation*, by Anthony Mancuso. This book shows you how to form a corporation under the specific rules for California. Step-by-step instructions for preparing articles, bylaws, and organizational minutes. If you don't live in California, see *Incorporate Your Business: A 50-State Legal Guide to Forming a Corporation*, also by Anthony Mancuso.

- *Legal Guide for Starting & Running a Small Business*, by Fred S. Steingold. This book is an essential resource for every small business owner, whether you are just starting out or are already established. Find out how to form a sole proprietorship, partnership, or LLC; negotiate a favorable lease; hire and fire employees; write contracts; and resolve business disputes.

- *The Employer's Legal Handbook*, by Fred S. Steingold. Employers need legal advice daily—and can get it in this comprehensive resource. The only book that compiles all the basics of employment law in one place, it covers safe hiring practices, wages, hours, tips and commissions, employee benefits, taxes and liability, insurance, discrimination, sexual harassment, and termination.

- *Tax Savvy for Small Business*, by Frederick W. Daily. Gives business owners information about federal taxes and shows them how to make the best tax decisions for their business, maximize profits, and stay out of trouble with the IRS.

- *How to Write a Business Plan*, by Mike McKeever. Whether starting a business or expanding an existing one, this book will show you how to write the business plan and loan package necessary to finance your idea and make it work. Includes up-to-date sources of financing.

- *Patent It Yourself*, by David Pressman. This state-of-the-art guide is a must for any inventor who wants to get a patent—from the patent search to the actual application. Patent attorney and former patent examiner David Pressman covers use and licensing, successful marketing, and infringement. This best-selling book is now available in software as well.

- *The Copyright Handbook: How to Protect & Use Written Works*, by Stephen Fishman. Provides forms and step-by-step instructions for protecting all types of written expression under U.S. and international copyright law. It also explains copyright infringement, fair use, works for hire, and transfers of copyright ownership.

How to Use the CD-ROM

The tearout forms in Appendix C are included on a CD-ROM in the back of the book. This CD-ROM, which can be used with Windows computers, installs files that you use with software programs that are already installed on your computer. It is not a stand-alone software program. Please read this appendix and the README.TXT file included on the CD-ROM for instructions on using the Forms CD.

Note to Mac users: This CD-ROM and its files should also work on Macintosh computers. Please note, however, that Nolo cannot provide technical support for non-Windows users.

How to View the README File

If you do not know how to view the file README.TXT, insert the Forms CD-ROM into your computer's CD-ROM drive and follow these instructions:

- **Windows 2000, XP, and Vista:** (1) On your PC's desktop, double click the My Computer icon; (2) double click the icon for the CD-ROM drive into which the Forms CD-ROM was inserted; (3) double click the file README.TXT.

- **Macintosh:** (1) On your Mac desktop, double click the icon for the CD-ROM that you inserted; (2) double click the file README.TXT.

If the README file is open, print it out by using the Print command in the File menu.

Installing the Form Files Onto Your Computer

Word processing forms that you can open, complete, print, and save with your word

processing program (see "Using the Word Processing Files to Create Documents," below) are contained on the CD-ROM. Before you can do anything with the files on the CD-ROM, you need to install them onto your hard disk. In accordance with U.S. copyright laws, remember that copies of the CD-ROM and its files are for your personal use only.

Insert the Forms CD and do the following:

Windows 2000, XP, and Vista Users

Follow the instructions that appear on the screen. (If nothing happens when you insert the Forms CD-ROM, then (1) double click the My Computer icon; (2) double click the icon for the CD-ROM drive into which the Forms CD-ROM was inserted; and (3) double click the file WELCOME.EXE.)

By default, all the files are installed to the \Limited Liability Company Forms folder in the \Program Files folder of your computer. A folder called "Limited Liability Company Forms" is added to the "Programs" folder of the Start menu.

Macintosh Users

Step 1: If the "LLC Forms CD" window is not open, open it by double clicking the "LLC Forms CD" icon.

Step 2: Select the "Limited Liability Company Forms" folder icon.

Step 3: Drag and drop the folder icon onto the icon of your hard disk.

Using the Word Processing Files to Create Documents

This section concerns the files for forms that can be opened and edited with your word processing program.

All word processing forms come in rich text format. These files have the extension ".RTF." For example, the form for the Meeting Summary Sheet discussed in Chapter 3 is on the file MEETSUM.RTF. All forms, their file names, and file formats are listed in at the end of this appendix.

RTF files can be read by most recent word processing programs including all versions of MS *Word* for Windows and Macintosh, *WordPad* for Windows, and recent versions of *WordPerfect* for Windows and Macintosh.

To use a form from the CD-ROM to create your documents you must: (1) open a file in your word processor or text editor; (2) edit the form by filling in the required information; (3) print it out; and (4) rename and save your revised file.

The following are general instructions. However, each word processor uses different commands to open, format, save, and print documents. Please read your word processor's manual for specific instructions on performing these tasks.

Do not call Nolo's technical support if you have questions on how to use your word processor or your computer.

Step 1: Opening a File

There are three ways to open the word processing files included on the CD-ROM after you have installed them onto your computer.

- Windows users can open a file by selecting its "shortcut" as follows: (1) Click the Windows "Start" button; (2) open the "Programs" folder; (3) open the "Limited Liability Company Forms" subfolder; and (4) click on the shortcut to the form you want to work with.

- Both Windows and Macintosh users can open a file directly by double clicking on it. Use My Computer or Windows Explorer (Windows 2000, XP, and Vista) or the Finder (Macintosh) to go to the folder you installed or copied the CD-ROM's files to. Then, double click on the specific file you want to open.

- You can also open a file from within your word processor. To do this, you must first start your word processor. Then, go to the File menu and choose the "Open" command. This opens a dialog box where you will tell the program (1) the type of file you want to open (*.RTF); and (2) the location and name of the file (you will need to navigate through the directory tree to get to the folder on your hard disk where the CD's files have been installed).

Where Are the Files Installed?

Windows Users

- RTF files are installed by default to a folder named \Limited Liability Company Forms in the \Program Files folder of your computer.

Macintosh Users

- RTF files are located in the "Limited Liability Company Forms" folder.

Step 2: Editing Your Document

Fill in the appropriate information according to the instructions and sample agreements in the book. Underlines are used to indicate where you need to enter your information, frequently followed by instructions in brackets. Be sure to delete the underlines and instructions from your edited document. You will also want to make sure that any signature lines in your completed documents appear on a page with at least some text from the document itself.

Editing Forms That Have Optional or Alternative Text

Some of the forms have check boxes before text. The check boxes indicate:

- optional text, where you choose whether to include or exclude the given text, or

- alternative text, where you select one alternative to include and exclude the other alternatives.

If you are using the tearout forms in Appendix B, you simply mark the appropriate box to make your choice.

If you are using the Forms CD, however, we recommend that instead of marking the check boxes, you do the following:

Optional text

If you don't want to include optional text, just delete it from your document.

If you do want to include optional text, just leave it in your document.

In either case, delete the check box itself as well as the italicized instructions that the text is optional.

Alternative text

First delete all the alternatives that you do not want to include.

Then delete the remaining check boxes, as well as the italicized instructions that you need to select one of the alternatives provided.

Step 3: Printing Out the Document

Use your word processor's or text editor's "Print" command to print out your document.

Step 4: Saving Your Document

After filling in the form, use the "Save As" command to save and rename the file. Because all the files are "read-only," you will not be able to use the "Save" command. This is for your protection. *If you save the file without renaming it, the underlines that indicate where you need to enter your information will be lost, and you will not be able to create a new document with this file without recopying the original file from the CD-ROM.*

Files Included on the Forms CD

File Name	Form Title
MEETSUM.rtf	Meeting Summary Sheet
CALL.rtf	Call of Meeting
MEETLIST.rtf	Meeting Participant List
NOTICE.rtf	Notice of Meeting
ACKREC.rtf	Acknowledgment of Receipt of Notice of Meeting
PROXY.rtf	Membership Voting Proxy
MAILCERT.rtf	Certification of Mailing of Notice
LLCMTG.rtf	Minutes of LLC Meeting
WAIVER.rtf	Waiver of Notice of Meeting
APPROVE.rtf	Approval of LLC Minutes
PAPERLET.rtf	Cover Letter for Approval of Minutes of LLC Meeting
CONSENT.rtf	Written Consent to Action Without Meeting
CH08.rtf	CH08_01 Authorization of Treasurer to Open and Use LLC Accounts
	CH08_02 Authorization of Treasurer to Open and Use Specific LLC Account(s)
	CH08_03 Authorization of LLC Account and Designation of Authorized Signers
	CH08_04 Authorization of Rental of Safe Deposit Box
	CH08_05 Adoption of Assumed LLC Name
	CH08_06 Approval of Contract
	CH08_07 Approval of Lease of Premises by LLC
	CH08_08 Purchase of Real Property by LLC
	CH08_09 Authorization of Sale of Real Property by LLC
	CH08_10 Delegation of LLC Authority
	CH08_11 Ratification of Contract or Transaction
	CH08_12 Rescission of Authority
	CH08_13 Certification of LLC Resolution
	CH08_14 Affidavit of LLC Resolution
	CH08_15 Acknowledgment
CH09.rtf	CH09_01 LLC Election of Corporate Tax Treatment
	CH09_02 Approval of Independent Audit of LLC Financial Records
	CH09_03 Approval of LLC Tax Year
CH10.rtf	CH10_01 Approval of Amendment to Articles of Organization
	CH10_02 Approval of Restatement of Articles of Organization
	CH10_03 Amendment of Articles Form
	CH10_04 Amendment of LLC Operating Agreement
CH11.rtf	CH11_01 Approval of LLC Distribution
	CH11_02 Approval of Additional Contributions of Capital by Members
	CH11_03 Admission of New Member

		CH11_04 Approval of Transfer of Membership
		CH11_05 Approval of LLC Purchase of Interest of Withdrawing Member
CH12.rtf		CH12_01 Approval of LLC Hiring
		CH12_02 Approval of Bonuses and Salary Increases
		CH12_03 Approval of Independent Contractor Services
		CH12_04 Appointment of LLC Officers
		CH12_05 Authorization of Payment for Attending LLC Meetings
		CH12_06 Annual Stipend for Attendance at LLC Meetings
		CH12_07 LLC Indemnification and Insurance
CH13.rtf		CH13_01 Authorization of Loan to LLC at Specific Terms
		CH13_02 Authorization of Maximum Loan Amount to LLC
		CH13_03 Authorization of LLC Representative to Borrow Funds on Behalf of LLC as Needed
		CH13_04 Authorization of Loan Terms Secured by LLC Property
		CH13_05 Authorization of Line of Credit
		CH13_06 Authorization of Line of Credit With Cap on Each Transaction
		CH13_07 Authorization of Line of Credit Secured by LLC Property
		CH13_08 Approval of Loan to the LLC
		CH13_09 LLC Promissory Note: Installment Payments of Principal and Interest (Amortized Loan)
		CH13_10 LLC Promissory Note: Installment Payments of Principal and Interest (Amortized Loan) Secured by LLC Property
		CH13_11 LLC Promissory Note: Installment Payments of Principal and Interest (Amortized Loan) With Balloon Payment
		CH13_12 LLC Promissory Note: Periodic Payments of Interest With Lump-Sum Principal Payment
		CH13_13 LLC Promissory Note: Lump-Sum Payment of Principal and Interest on Specified Date
		CH13_14 LLC Promissory Note: Lump-Sum Payment of Principal and Interest on Demand by Noteholder
		CH13_15 LLC Promissory Note: Special Schedule of Payments of Principal and Interest
CH14.rtf		CH14_01 Approval of LLC Loan to Insider
		CH14_02 Individual Promissory Note: Installment Payments of Principal and Interest (Amortized Loan)
		CH14_03 Individual Promissory Note: Installment Payments of Principal and Interest (Amortized Loan) Secured by Property
		CH14_04 Individual Promissory Note: Installment Payments of Principal and Interest (Amortized Loan) With Balloon Payment
		CH14_05 Individual Promissory Note: Periodic Payments of Interest With Lump-Sum Principal Payment
		CH14_06 Individual Promissory Note: Lump-Sum Payment of Principal and Interest on Specified Date

	CH14_07 Individual Promissory Note: Lump-Sum Payment of Principal and Interest on Demand by Noteholder
	CH14_08 Individual Promissory Note: Special Schedule of Payments of Principal and Interest
	CH14_09 Release of Promissory Note
CH15.rtf	CH15_01 LLC Approval of Transaction Benefiting a Member or Manager

State Information

This appendix provides the basic legal rules for major LLC decisions during the life of an LLC. Because most LLC statutes are flexible, most of the rules shown here are state default rules—that is, in most cases, they apply unless a contrary rule is set out in the LLC articles or operating agreement. (When we can, we'll tell you whether a rule can be changed in the articles, operating agreement, or both.)

Please use this information as a guide. LLC laws constantly change and are subject to different interpretations. Further, other statutes may affect different areas of LLC operations, such as the admission or departure of a member. If any area is particularly important to you, check this information by reading the relevant statute in your state's latest LLC act. (See the state LLC act link in your state sheet, below.)

This state-specific information is organized into different headings, which we summarize here.

LLC Filing Office

Here you'll find the address and phone number (subject to change) of the state office that handles LLC legal filings, such as the filing of the original articles of organization (or the certificate of formation or similar document) to start the legal existence of the LLC. Other filings that typically occur during the life of the LLC are:

- amendments or restatements of articles or certificate

- change of LLC registered agent or registered office, and

- articles or a certificate of dissolution (to dissolve the LLC).

Commonly, the secretary of state or department of state is the office that handles LLC filings, but some states use a different title for this office. Normally this office, or a separate division of this office, handles legal filings for other business entities, such as filings for corporations and limited partnerships.

We also show any Internet Web address currently available for this office. Links from this Web page usually bring you to a page from which you can download official LLC filing forms and instructions.

State LLC Act

Under this heading we list the state LLC act and indicate whether the state provides a link from which you can browse and download sections of your state's LLC act. If the state provides a link, we explain how to use it to locate and research your state's LLC act.

CROSS REFERENCE

For more information on researching your state's LLC act, see Chapter 1.

State Tax Office

We list the city and website address (URL) of your state's revenue and taxation (or similar) office. We recommend that you call this number early on in the life of your LLC and ask for tax forms and other tax materials.

Manager Election

This heading is relevant to manager-managed LLCs—those that have designated one or more managers (who may be members but normally do not need to be) to manage the LLC. We list the basic rules in each state for the election and reelection of managers—the number of members or the percentage of membership voting power that is necessary to elect managers and the managers' terms of office (which determine when they should be reelected). The rules shown here are usually default rules—an LLC often can set its own rules for election and reelection of LLC managers, typically in its operating agreement.

CROSS REFERENCE

For more information, see "How Your Management Structure Affects Decision-Making Requirements" in Chapter 2.

Meeting Requirements

We list the state LLC act requirements for calling, holding, and voting at LLC meetings of members and managers. There is significant variation among the states, particularly with regard to membership meeting rules. Of course, these are mostly state default rules, so you will want to look at your operating agreement first to determine if your LLC has any specific requirements for holding meetings of your LLC members or managers that may override your state's law.

Managers normally vote to approve a resolution or a decision to act at a meeting or by written consent on a one-manager, one-vote basis. Normally a majority of the managers is needed for approval. But pay particular attention to the default membership voting requirements listed here. These vary considerably from state to state. Some states give members per capita (one member, one vote) voting power, while others grant voting rights to members according to the members' current capital account balances. If your operating agreement is silent on how your members vote, you may need to rely on your state's default membership voting rules when seeking the approval of your members for a resolution presented at a members' meeting or contained in a written consent form. For the latest information on these rules, you will want to consult the statute numbers shown in this section.

Regardless of how voting power is measured (per capita or by capital accounts balances), members and managers normally approve resolutions presented at meetings or included in a written consent form by a majority—the vote of a majority of members or managers or the vote of a majority of the capital accounts balances. But keep in mind that special supermajority voting requirements (such as a unanimous vote) may apply to special LLC decisions, particularly those involving structural changes to the LLC or changes in the relative interests of members, such as amendments to the articles or operating agreement or a vote to approve the admission of a member or the continuation of the LLC after a member departs. We cover special matters of this sort under special headings in this appendix (for example, see "Amendments,"

"Admission of Members," "Withdrawal of Members," and "Continuation of the LLC," discussed below).

CROSS REFERENCE

For more information, see "Steps to Prepare for a Meeting" in Chapter 3.

Amendments

In this heading, we list the state requirements for amending the articles of organization (or similar organizing document such as a certificate of formation) and the LLC operating agreement. Note that the members of the LLC are usually required to approve these amendments by a unanimous or majority vote of the entire membership, unless otherwise provided in the LLC articles or operating agreement. Even if not required, we recommend obtaining the approval of all members to all amendments to the articles or operating agreement. These are the essential organizing and operating documents of the LLC, so changes to them can have significant effects on the legal and financial rights and responsibilities of all members.

CROSS REFERENCE

For more information, see Chapter 10.

Admission of Members

This heading contains the state rules for approving the admission of members. We provide two sets of rules for each state if possible. The first states the membership vote necessary for the LLC to issue a membership to a new member. The second shows the requirement for admitting a person who is transferred (sold, given, willed) a membership from a former member. This type of new member is called a transferee or assignee. Typically, all existing members must approve the admission of a new member of either type, unless the articles or operating agreement contain a different approval rule.

TIP

If a transferee is not approved for membership. If a new member who has been transferred a membership interest from a former member is not approved by the required vote, most state statutes give the transferee mere economic rights in the transferred membership. In other words, the new member only receives a right to share in profits and receive any other monetary distributions the former member had a right to receive. The transferee is not given voting rights, management rights, or any other rights associated with the transferred membership. The other members would have to approve the admission of the transferee for such rights to accrue to the new member.

CROSS REFERENCE

For more information, see "Admitting LLC Members" in Chapter 11.

Withdrawal of Members

This heading lists the state rules for the withdrawal of a member from the LLC. Two basic items of information from the state statutes are provided, if available:

- whether a member is allowed to withdraw under the default state rules and, if so, the type and length of notice the member must give the LLC and/or the other members

- the amount the LLC must pay the withdrawing member, if the operating agreement is silent on this issue, and any costs or damages the LLC is entitled to subtract from this amount if the withdrawal violates the operating agreement or is otherwise wrongful.

CROSS REFERENCE

For more information, see "Withdrawal of LLC Members" in Chapter 11.

These rules relate to a member who unilaterally resigns or otherwise withdraws from the LLC and expects payment for his or her membership interest from the LLC. For the rules that cover the withdrawal of a member who has transferred his or her interest to a person who wishes to be admitted as a new member, see "Admission of Members," above.

Continuation of the LLC

Some states require the remaining members to approve the continuation of the LLC after a member:

- withdraws from the LLC
- sells or otherwise transfers an interest
- is expelled, or
- otherwise terminates his or her membership interest in the LLC or has it terminated involuntarily.

Membership-terminating events of this sort are referred to as the dissociation of a member. Some states say that in the absence of a contrary provision in the articles or operating agreement, the LLC is automatically dissolved by the dissociation of a member unless the remaining members formally vote to approve the continuance of the LLC.

This result may seem capricious and harsh. But the reason some states require a vote to continue the LLC is to help it look more like a partnership and less like a corporation under the traditional IRS entity-classification rules. Fortunately, the IRS no longer uses these corporation/partnership classification rules, so many states that used to require a vote to continue the LLC after the dissociation of a member no longer do so. But there are a minority of states that still require this vote, and this heading lists them.

Keep in mind, however, that if your articles or operating agreement say that the LLC continues without the need for a vote after a member is dissociated, you normally don't need to formally approve the continuance of the LLC (unless your state statute says that a continuation vote must be taken in all cases after the dissociation of a member). And if your remaining members must vote to continue your LLC, it's easy to formally approve such a vote by holding a membership meeting or preparing written consents to continue the LLC for the remaining members to sign.

Even if your state is listed as requiring a vote to continue the LLC after a member leaves, it may have repealed this vote requirement, or will soon do so, perhaps by the time a member leaves your LLC. The best way to check is to look up the section of the state LLC act given in this heading to see if it still requires a vote or if it has been changed or repealed.

TIP

It makes sense to review LLC operations after a member leaves. It's always a good idea to review the status of your LLC after a member leaves, to see where the company and the remaining members stand. In most cases, the fact that the LLC should stay in business will be a foregone conclusion, but you may want to discuss the prospect of admitting a new member or reassigning the departing member's management and operational duties.

CROSS REFERENCE

For more information, see Chapter 11.

Special Statutory Rules

This heading lists any special statutory rules that struck our eye as we browsed each state's LLC act. For example, we may list actions that must be approved by a unanimous vote of members under the state LLC act (usually, unless the operating agreement provides otherwise) or a special statutory rule involving the approval of contracts or loans to LLC members or managers. The list here is not exhaustive—your state's LLC act no doubt has other special voting rules for approving special transactions. Again, we list just a few rules that stand out from the rest.

ALABAMA

LLC Filing Office

Secretary of State
Corporate Section
Box 5616
Montgomery, AL 36103
Telephone: 334-242-5324
www.sos.state.al.us/business/corporations.aspx

State LLC Act

The Alabama LLC Act is contained in Title 10, Chapter 12 of the Alabama Statutes and is browseable from the following Web page (select Title 10, then Chapter 12):

www.legislature.state.al.us/CodeofAlabama/1975/coatoc.htm

State Tax Office

Department of Revenue, Montgomery
www.ador.state.al.us

Manager Election

Unless otherwise provided in the operating agreement, managers are elected by at least one-half of the number of members. Managers hold office for an indefinite term unless otherwise provided in the operating agreement. [Section 10-12-22]

Meeting Requirements

Rules for the notice, time, place, quorum, and manner of voting by members or managers at a meeting, or by written consent, are to be specified in the articles or operating agreement. [Section 10-12-22]

Amendments

Unless the articles require a greater vote, amendment to articles must be approved by a majority vote of voting members. [Section 10-12-11] Unless otherwise stated in the operating agreement, the operating agreement must be amended by written consent of all members.

Admission of Members

Unless the operating agreement says otherwise, new members are admitted by written consent of all members. [Section 10-12-31] Unless otherwise provided in the operating agreement, the admission of transferees must be approved by unanimous written consent of all nontransferring members. [Section 10-12-33]

Withdrawal of Members

If not prohibited by the LLC operating agreement, a member can withdraw from the LLC at any time upon 30 days' written notice to the other members. If a member's withdrawal is in violation of the operating agreement or is due to wrongful conduct by the member, the member can be held personally liable for financial damages caused by the withdrawal from the LLC (including the cost of paying another person to perform services promised by the withdrawing member). [Section 10-12-36]

Continuation of the LLC

After the loss of a member, the LLC continues—a vote to continue the LLC is not required. But if the LLC loses its last member, it automatically dissolves unless the LLC's articles or operating agreement contains a provision that continues the existence of the LLC and provides for the appointment of one or more new members (or unless the holders of financial rights in the LLC, such as prior members, agree in writing within 90 days of the loss of the last member to continue the LLC and to appoint one or more new members). [Section 10-12-37]

ALASKA

LLC Filing Office

State of Alaska
Corporations Section
P.O. Box 110808
Juneau, AK 99811
Telephone: 907-465-2530
Anchorage Office: 907-269-8140
www.commerce.state.ak.us/occ/home.htm

State LLC Act

The Alaska LLC Act is contained in Title 10, Chapter 10.50 of the Alaska Statutes, starting at Section 10.50.010, and is browseable online. Go to the Web page listed below (the corporations section home page), select the link to Alaska Statutes and Regulations, then select The Current Alaska Statutes, expand the Title 10 heading and select Chapter 10.50 to view the LLC Act.

www.commerce.state.ak.us/occ/home.htm

State Tax Office

Department of Revenue, Juneau
www.revenue.state.ak.us/

Manager Election

Unless otherwise provided in the operating agreement, managers are elected by at least one-half of the number of members. [Section 10.50.115] Managers hold office for an indefinite term unless otherwise provided in the operating agreement. [Section 10.50.125]

Meeting Requirements

Unless otherwise stated in the operating agreement or articles, members in a member-managed LLC approve LLC management decisions by consent of more than one-half of all of the members. Unless otherwise stated in the operating agreement, the managers of a manager-managed LLC must approve management decisions by more than one-half of the number of managers. [Section 10.50.150]

Amendments

All members must consent in writing to amendments of the articles or operating agreement, but the operating agreement may reduce this level of consent for amendments to a majority of the members (but no less than a majority). [Section 10.50.150]

Admission of Members

Unless the operating agreement says otherwise, new memberships are issued by written consent of all members. [Section 10.50.155] Unless otherwise provided in the operating agreement, the admission of a transferee as a member must be approved by unanimous written consent of nontransferring members. [Section 10.50.165]

Withdrawal of Members

Unless otherwise provided in the operating agreement, if the LLC has a limited term or is formed for a particular undertaking (project), the withdrawal of a member before the end of the term or the accomplishment of the undertaking is a breach of the operating agreement. [Section 10.50.190]

If the voluntary withdrawal of a member with the power to withdraw breaches the operating agreement, or if the withdrawal occurs as a result of otherwise wrongful conduct of the member, the LLC may recover from the withdrawing member damages that result from the breach of the operating agreement or the wrongful conduct, including the reasonable costs of obtaining replacement services the withdrawing member was obligated to perform. The LLC may offset these damages against the amount the withdrawing member is entitled to receive upon the member's withdrawal. [Section 10.50.195]

In addition to a distribution of profits owed to a member who withdraws or whose interest is terminated prior to the dissolution of the LLC (and except for removal of a member under other provisions of the LLC Act), the LLC shall distribute to the member the amount of the member's limited liability company interest. If the operating agreement does not specify the amount of the distribution or a method for determining the amount, the LLC shall make the distribution within a reasonable time after termination, and the amount of the distribution shall be the fair value of the member's interest as of the date of termination based upon the member's right to share in LLC distributions. [Section 10.50.335]

Continuation of the LLC

After the loss of a member, the LLC continues—a vote to continue the LLC is not required. [Section 10.50.400]

Special Statutory Rules

Memberships can be issued to persons in exchange for a promissory note or promise to contribute property or services in the future only if the person has also paid in some property or services to the LLC. [Section 10.50.275]

ARIZONA

LLC Filing Office

Arizona Corporation Commission
Corporation Filing Section
1300 West Washington
Phoenix, AZ 85007-2996
Telephone: 602-542-3026
Tucson Branch Office: 520-628-6560
(accepts LLC filings)
www.cc.state.az.us/corp/index.htm

State LLC Act

The Arizona LLC Act is contained in Title 29, Chapter 4 of the Arizona Statutes, starting at Section 29.601, and is browseable from the following Web page (scroll down to Chapter 4 to begin browsing the LLC Act):

www.azleg.state.az.us/ArizonaRevisedStatutes
.asp?Title=29

State Tax Office

Department of Revenue, Phoenix
www.revenue.state.az.us

Manager Election

Designation, election, replacement, and removal of managers are according to any rules set out in the operating agreement. If all managers resign and the operating agreement is silent on how to elect new ones, a majority of members may elect a new manager or managers. [Section 29-681]

Meeting Requirements

Rules for the notice, time, place, quorum, and manner of voting by members or managers at a meeting, or by written consent, are to be specified in the operating agreement. [Section 29-682]

Amendments

Except as provided in the operating agreement, all members must approve an amendment to articles that changes the LLC from member-managed to manager-managed or from manager-managed to member-managed; otherwise, amendments to the articles must be approved by a majority of members (or majority of managers in a manager-managed

LLC). Amendments to the articles that simply correct information in the articles, however, can be filed by any member or manager. Unless provided otherwise in the operating agreement, all members must approve amendments to the operating agreement. [Section 29-681]

Admission of Members

Except as provided in the operating agreement, new memberships must be issued with the consent of all members. [Section 29-681] Unless otherwise provided in the operating agreement, the admission of a transferee as a member must be approved by consent of all nontransferring members. [Section 29-731]

Withdrawal of Members

A member may withdraw from the LLC at any time by mailing or delivering a written notice of withdrawal to the other members, but, if the withdrawal violates the operating agreement, the LLC may recover from the member damages for breach of the operating agreement and offset the damages against any amount otherwise distributable to the member. [Section 29-734]

On any event of withdrawal of a member (which includes the withdrawal or expulsion of a member), except as otherwise provided in the operating agreement, the member does not have a right to a distribution because of the withdrawal but does have the same right to continued distributions as would an assignee of the interest, and to a distribution when the LLC dissolves (less any amount recoverable from the withdrawing member because the withdrawal violated the operating agreement). [Section 29-707]

Continuation of the LLC

Except as provided in the operating agreement, a membership vote to continue the LLC after withdrawal of a member is not required, and the LLC continues. But if the last remaining member withdraws, unless a transferee of the member admits a new member into the LLC within 90 days, the LLC dissolves. [Section 29-781]

Special Statutory Rules

Except as provided in the operating agreement, under Section 29-681, a majority of members (or, in a manager-managed LLC, a majority of managers) must consent to:

1) settle differences on running the business of the LLC

2) distribute LLC cash or property to members

3) authorize the repurchase by the LLC of a member's interest, and

4) authorize the filing of a notice to wind up the LLC. [Section 29-681]

Except as otherwise provided in the operating agreement, the approval of all members is required to fix or change the amount or type of capital contributions to be made by members. [Section 29-701]

Except as provided in the operating agreement, the approval of more than one-half the members and the member(s) entitled to receive upon dissolution of the LLC more than one-half the value of its assets is required to dissolve the LLC. [Section 29-781]

ARKANSAS

LLC Filing Office

Arkansas Secretary of State
Corporations Division
State Capitol
Little Rock, AR 72201-1094
Telephone: 501-682-3409
Toll-free: 888-233-0325
www.sosweb.state.ar.us/corp_ucc.html

State LLC Act

The Arkansas LLC Act (called the Small Business Entity Tax Pass Through Act) is located in Title 4 (Business and Commercial Law), Subtitle 3 (Corporations and Associations), Chapter 32, starting with Section 4-32-101, and is browseable from the following Web page (choose HTML or Java version, then select Arkansas Code to see a list of title headings; then select Title 4, then Subtitle 3, then Chapter 32):

www.arkleg.state.ar.us/Siteindex.asp?

State Tax Office

Department of Finance & Administration
Revenue Division, Little Rock
www.ark.org/dfa

Manager Election

Unless otherwise provided in the operating agreement, designation, election, replacement, and removal of managers must be by the vote of more than one-half the number of members; terms of managers are indefinite unless otherwise stated in the operating agreement. [Section 4-32-401]

Meeting Requirements

Unless otherwise stated in the operating agreement, approval of more than one-half the members (or managers in a manager-managed LLC) is required to decide LLC business. [Section 4-32-403] We could not find specific rules for notice, time, place, or quorum for membership and management meetings in the LLC Act, so, presumably, any such rules are as provided in the operating agreement.

Amendments

Unless otherwise stated in the operating agreement, amendments to the operating agreement must be approved by all members. [Section 4-32-403] No specific rules for amendments of the articles were found in the LLC Act.

Admission of Members

Except as provided in the operating agreement, new memberships must be issued with the consent of all members. [Section 4-32-801] Unless otherwise stated in the operating agreement, the admission of a transferee as a member must be approved by unanimous written consent of nontransferring members. [Section 4-32-706]

Withdrawal of Members

Unless otherwise provided in the operating agreement, a member may withdraw upon 30 days' written notice to the other members. Exception: Unless otherwise stated in the operating agreement, if the LLC is established for a definite term or project, the member may not withdraw before the completion of the term or project. If a withdrawal is in violation of the operating agreement or due to wrongful conduct, the LLC may offset damages against the amount due a withdrawing member, including the cost of replacement services owed by the member, if the withdrawal was due to the member's wrongful conduct or was a breach of the LLC operating agreement. [Section 4-32-802(c)]

Unless provided otherwise in the operating agreement, and subject to exceptions involving assignments of a withdrawing member's interest, a withdrawing member is entitled to receive the fair value of the member's interest within a reasonable time after withdrawal. [Section 4-32-603]

Continuation of the LLC

After a member withdraws, the LLC continues automatically—a vote to continue the LLC is not required. [Section 4-32-901]

Special Statutory Rules

Default membership approval rule is by a vote of one-half or more of the number of members; the operating agreement may change this requirement, and special statutory rules may require a greater vote in some matters (unanimous membership is the default rule to amend the operating agreement). [Section 4-32-403]

CALIFORNIA

LLC Filing Office

California Secretary of State
Document Filing Support Unit
P.O. Box 944228
Sacramento, CA 94244-2280
Telephone: 916-657-5448

Branch offices of the Secretary of State are located in Fresno, Los Angeles, San Francisco, and San Diego. Currently, branch offices provide LLC forms over the counter only and do not mail out forms or accept LLC filings.

www.ss.ca.gov/business/business.htm

Note for Professionals: Only businesses that render services under nonprofessional, occupational licenses can form an LLC in California.

Professionals who must form a professional corporation if they incorporate (doctors, architects, lawyers, pharmacists, and so on) are the same group of professionals who can't form an LLC in the state. There may be others, however, who fall into this group. If you provide any type of licensed service that may be considered a licensed professional service, contact your state licensing board and ask if you are allowed to form an LLC in California before getting started on the process.

State LLC Act

The California Beverly-Killea Limited Liability Company Act is contained in the California Corporations Code, Title 2.5 (Limited Liability Companies), starting with Section 17000, and is browseable from the following Web page (check the Corporations Code box, then click the search button at the bottom of the page; then scroll down to Section 17000 to find the LLC Act sections):

www.leginfo.ca.gov/calaw.html

State Tax Office

Franchise Tax Board, Sacramento
www.ftb.ca.gov

Manager Election

Unless otherwise stated in the articles or operating agreement, managers are elected and removed by vote of majority in interest of the members (if not defined in the operating agreement, this term means the vote of members who have a right to more than one-half of the current profits of the LLC). Managers are elected for an indefinite term unless otherwise provided in the articles or operating agreement. [Section 17152]

Meeting Requirements

Unless otherwise provided in the articles or operating agreement, members vote in proportion to their right to receive profits of the LLC (according to their profits interests in the LLC). [Section 17103]

Unless otherwise provided in the articles or operating agreement, the following default rules apply to LLC membership meetings:

- Meetings are held at the principal executive office of the LLC.
- Meetings can be called by any manager or by a member or members who hold more than 10% of the membership interests allowed to vote on the matters brought before the meeting.
- Notice of meetings must be given at least ten and no more than 60 days before the date of the meeting, and must state the time, date, place, and purpose of the meeting.
- Members may sign a waiver of notice to validate the actions taken at a meeting, however called and noticed.
- A quorum for a meeting consists of a majority in interest of the members (if not defined in the operating agreement, this term means the vote of members who have a right to more than one-half of the current profits of the LLC). [Section 17103]

Members also may take action by written consent if the number of members signing the consent is at least equal to the number of members who would have been required to approve the action at a membership meeting attended by all voting members. But the written consent of all members is required for special actions, such as the amendment of the LLC's articles or operating agreement or a dissolution of the LLC. [Section 17103]

Except as otherwise stated in the articles or operating agreement, managers approve decisions by a majority vote at a meeting, or by unanimous written consent. [Section 17156] Apparently, meetings of managers may be called, noticed, and held according to rules contained in the articles or operating agreement or as the managers see fit (no statutory rules were found in the LLC Act).

Amendments

Unless otherwise provided in the articles or operating agreement, amendments to the articles or operating agreement must be approved by all members. Note: The LLC articles or operating agreement cannot reduce the membership vote required to amend the articles below a majority in interest of members (if not defined in the operating agreement, this term means the vote of members who have a right to more than one-half of the current profits of the LLC). [Section 17103]

Admission of Members

Except as provided in the articles or operating agreement, new memberships must be issued with the consent of a majority in interest of the members, and only after the new member signs the LLC's operating agreement. [Section 17100] Except as otherwise provided in the articles or operating agreement, the admission of a transferee as a member must be approved by the consent of a majority in interest of nontransferring members. [Section 17303]

Withdrawal of Members

A member may withdraw upon giving notice to the other members. Unless the articles or operating agreement provide otherwise, the member is not entitled to a distribution but shall have the right of a holder of an economic interest in the LLC to receive continuing distributions. The LLC can offset these distributions by any damages recoverable against the member for breach of the LLC operating agreement. [Section 17252]

Continuation of the LLC

After a member withdraws, the LLC continues automatically—a vote to continue the LLC is not required. [Section 17350]

Special Statutory Rules

LLCs may be dissolved by vote of a majority in interest of the members or by any greater percentage of members stated in the articles or operating agreement. [Section 17350]

COLORADO

Secretary of State
Business Division
1700 Broadway, Ste 200
Denver CO 80290
Telephone: 303-894-2200
www.sos.state.co.us/pubs/business/main.htm

State LLC Act

The Colorado LLC Act is contained in Title 7, Article 80 of the Colorado Statutes, starting with Section 7-80-101, and is browseable from the following Web page (select Colorado Statutes in the left pane, then select Title 7, then Limited Liability Companies):

http://198.187.128.12/colorado/lpext.dll?f=templates&fn=fs-main.htm&2.0

State Tax Office

Revenue Department, Denver
www.revenue.state.co.us/main/home.asp

Manager Election

Managers are elected by a majority of the members for a one-year term. [Section 7-80-402] LLCs with six or more managers may elect managers for staggered terms, electing each group of managers for a two- or three-year term—this arrangement is called a classified management scheme. [Section 7-80-403] Managers may be removed by a majority of members, and manager vacancies may be filled by written agreement of a majority of remaining managers. [Sections 7-80-404 and 7-80-405] These manager election, removal, and replacement rules may be overridden in the LLC operating agreement. [Section 7-80-108]

Meeting Requirements

Members and managers vote according to any rules set out in LLC articles or operating agreement. [Sections 7-80-401 and 7-80-706]

Unless otherwise provided in the LLC operating agreement, the following rules apply to membership meetings:

- Meetings of members shall be held at the principal office of the LLC. [Section 7-80-707]
- An annual meeting of members shall be held for the election of managers. [Section 7-80-707]
- Meetings of the members may be called by any manager or by not less than 1/10 of all voting members. [Section 7-80-707]
- A majority of the LLC's voting members make up a quorum for purposes of membership meetings. [Section 7-80-708]

- The yes vote of a majority of members at which a quorum is present is required to approve membership decisions at a meeting. [Section 7-80-708]

- Written notice of regular (annual meetings scheduled in the operating agreement) and special meetings must be given to each voting member. The notice must state the time, date, and place (and, for special meetings, the purpose) of the meeting. It must be distributed no fewer than ten nor more than 50 days before the date of the meeting. [Section 7-80-709]

- Members may waive notice of a meeting by signing a written waiver before or after the membership meeting. [Section 7-80-710]

- Members may take action by unanimous written consent in lieu of a meeting. [Section 7-80-711]

Amendments

Unless otherwise stated in the LLC operating agreement, amendments to the articles must be approved by the written consent of all members. [Sections 7-80-209 and 7-80-108] No statutory rule was found for amendments to the operating agreement, so presumably the members can set their own rule within the agreement.

Admission of Members

Except as provided in the operating agreement, new memberships must be issued with the written consent of all members. [Section 7-80-701] Unless otherwise stated in a written operating agreement, the admission of a transferee as a member must be approved by unanimous written consent of nontransferring members. [Sections 7-80-702 and 7-80-108]

Withdrawal of Members

Unless prohibited in the operating agreement, a member can resign at any time from the LLC. If withdrawal is in violation of the operating agreement, distributions payable to the member may be offset by damages owed because of the breach. [Section 7-80-602]

A member who resigns has no right to participate in management of the LLC, and has a right to receive only that share of profits and distributions that are owed to nonresigning members (presumably, in the absence of a contrary provision in the operating agreement). [Section 7-80-603]

Continuation of the LLC

A membership vote to continue the LLC after dissociation of a member (cessation or termination of a membership interest) is not required under the LLC Act.

Special Statutory Rules

The LLC Act provides for annual meetings of members; if managers are chosen, they are elected or reelected by majority vote of the number of members at each annual meeting of members. [Section 7-80-402] In the absence of a provision in the operating agreement, profits and losses and distributions of capital are allocated and distributed to members according to the value of each member's capital contribution. [Sections 7-80-503 and 7-80-504]

CONNECTICUT

LLC Filing Office
Connecticut Secretary of State
ATTN: Commercial Recording Division
P.O. Box 150470
Hartford, CT 06115-0470
Telephone: 860-509-6002
www.sots.ct.gov/CommercialRecording/Crdindex.html

State LLC Act

The Connecticut LLC Act is contained in Title 34, Chapter 613 of the Connecticut Statutes, starting with Section 34-100, and is browseable from the following Web page (click Browse Statutes, then select Title 34, then Chapter 613):

www.cga.ct.gov/asp/menu/Statutes.asp

State Tax Office

Department of Revenue Services, Hartford
www.ct.gov/drs/site/default.asp

Manager Election

Unless otherwise stated in the operating agreement, managers are elected and removed by majority in interest (presumably, a majority of the profits and capital interests of members—we were unable to find a definition of this term in the Act) of members, and serve for an indefinite term. [Section 34-140]

Meeting Requirements

Except as provided in the articles or operating agreement, or as required under special provision of the LLC Act, members approve action by the vote of a majority in interest of the members (presumably, a majority of the profits and capital interests of members); if the LLC is manager-managed, managers approve decisions by more than one-half the total number of managers. [Section 34-142] The LLC Act seems open-ended with respect to procedures for holding membership and manager meetings—so, notice, time, place, quorum, and manner of voting by members or managers at a meeting or by written consent can be set as desired in the operating agreement. [Section 34-140]

Amendments

Except as otherwise provided in the articles, amendments to the articles must be approved by a vote of a majority in interest of the members (presumably, by members who hold at least a majority of the capital and profits interests in the LLC). Except as otherwise provided in the articles or operating agreement, amendments to the operating agreement must be approved by at least two-thirds in interest of members (presumably, by members who own at least two-thirds of the capital and profits interests in the LLC). [Section 34-142]

Admission of Members

Except as provided in the operating agreement, new memberships must be issued with written consent of a majority in interest of members. [Section 34-179] Unless otherwise provided in the operating agreement, the admission of a transferee as a member must be approved by a majority in interest of the members, not counting the interests of the transferring member, or, if the transferring member

is the only LLC member, if the transferor agrees that the buyer can become a member. [Section 34-172]

Withdrawal of Members

If not prohibited by the LLC operating agreement, a member can withdraw from the LLC at any time upon 30 days' notice to the other members. If the withdrawal is not prohibited by the operating agreement, but is otherwise in violation of the operating agreement, the member can be held personally liable for financial damages caused by the withdrawal from the LLC (including the cost of paying another person to perform services promised by the withdrawing member). [Section 34-180]

Generally, unless otherwise provided in the articles or operating agreement, a member who resigns is not entitled to be paid for his or her interest, but only has a right to receive a share of LLC profits and other distributions that would be paid to an assignee of an economic interest in the LLC (such as ongoing profits and capital distributions on liquidation of the LLC). [Section 34-159]

Continuation of the LLC

A vote to continue the LLC after dissociation of a member (cessation or termination of a membership interest) is not required under the LLC Act.

Special Statutory Rules

If an LLC is member-managed, transfers of LLC property may be transferred by a document signed by a member on behalf of the LLC; if manager-managed, only a manager can execute such a transfer document on behalf of the LLC. [Section 34-168]

DELAWARE

LLC Filing Office

Department of State
Division of Corporations
P.O. Box 898
Dover, DE 19903
Telephone: 302-739-3073
www.state.de.us/corp/default.shtml

State LLC Act

The Delaware LLC Act is contained in Title 6 (Commerce and Trade), Chapter 18 of the Delaware Statutes, starting with Section 18-101, and is browseable from the following Web page (click Chapter 18. Limited Liability Company Act):

www.state.de.us/corp/DElaw.htm

State Tax Office

Division of Revenue, Dover

www.state.de.us/revenue/default.shtml

Manager Election

Election of managers, and managers' terms of office, are as provided in the operating agreement. [Section 18-402]

Meeting Requirements

Members make management decisions by approval of the members owning more than 50% of the current profits interests in the LLC. Manager voting rules are as provided in the operating agreement. [Sections 18-402 and 18-404] Notice, time, place, and quorum requirements for membership and manager meetings are as specified in the operating agreement. Unless otherwise provided in the operating agreement, action by written consent of members or managers must be signed by members or managers having at least the minimum number of votes necessary to approve the action at a meeting. [Sections 18-302 and 18-404]

Amendments

No statutory requirements were found for amending the certificate of formation or operating agreement.

Admission of Members

Except as provided in the operating agreement, new memberships must be issued with written consent of all members and after the admission of the new member is reflected in the LLC records. [Section 18-301] Admission of a transferee as a member must be approved by vote of all nontransferring members of the LLC, or as provided in the LLC operating agreement. [Section 18-704]

Withdrawal of Members

Unless allowed by the LLC operating agreement, a member may not resign prior to the dissolution and winding up of the LLC. [Section 18-603]

Generally, upon resignation authorized by the LLC operating agreement, a resigning member is entitled to receive the fair value of his or her membership interest within a reasonable period after resignation (unless the operating agreement has its own provisions for payments to a resigning member). [Section 18-604]

Continuation of the LLC

Generally, a vote to continue the LLC after dissociation of a member (cessation or termination of a membership interest) is not required. Exception: If the sole remaining member of the LLC is dissociated, the LLC automatically dissolves unless, within 90 days, the personal representative of the last member agrees to continue the LLC and consents to serve as an LLC member or appoints another person in his or her place. [Section 18-801]

Special Statutory Rules

Unlike most other states, the LLC Act says that unless otherwise provided in the operating agreement, both members and managers are agents of the LLC (whether the LLC is manager- or member-managed), and both have the authority to bind the LLC. [Section 18-402]

The operating agreement may prohibit a member assigning his or her membership interest prior to the dissolution of the LLC. [Section 18-603]

DISTRICT OF COLUMBIA

LLC Filing Office

Department of Consumer and Regulatory Affairs
Corporations Division
P.O. Box 92300
Washington, D.C. 20090
Telephone: 202-442-4432
http://mblr.dc.gov/corp/index.shtm

State LLC Act

The D.C. LLC Act is contained in Title 29 (Corporations), Chapter 10 of the D.C. Code, starting with sSection 29-1001, and is browseable from the following Web page (select District of Columbia, District of Columbia Code, then Division 5, then Title 29, then Chapter 10):

www.michie.com

State Tax Office

Office of Tax and Revenue

http://otr.cfo.dc.gov/otr/site/default.asp

Manager Election

Managers are elected by the members (no specific membership voting rules for election are given in the Act). But unless otherwise stated in the articles or operating agreement, the removal of managers and the filling of vacancies in manager positions must be approved by those members owning at least a majority of profits interests in the LLC. [Section 29-1019]

Meeting Requirements

Unless otherwise provided in the articles or operating agreement, members vote in proportion to their profits interests in the LLC, with the vote of members owning at least a majority of the profits interests necessary to take membership action. Rules for notice, time, place, and quorum for membership meetings, or action by written consent of members, are as specified in the articles or operating agreement. [Section 29-1017] Unless otherwise provided in the articles or operating agreement, managers take action by vote of a majority of the managers. [Section 29-1019] Other rules for manager meetings and action by written consent of the managers were not found in the Act, and presumably should be stated in the LLC articles or operating agreement.

Amendments

Unless otherwise provided in the articles or operating agreement, amendments to the articles or operating agreement must be approved by members who own at least a majority of the profits interests in the LLC. [Sections 29-1007 and 29-1018]

Admission of Members

Except as provided in the articles or operating agreement, new memberships must be issued with unanimous consent of the members. [Section 29-1032] Unless otherwise provided (or restricted) by the articles or operating agreement, the admission of a transferee as a member must be approved by consent of the nontransferring members holding a majority of the interests in profits of the LLC. [Section 29-1036] If the articles or operating agreement restricts the rights of members to assign their interests, these restrictions must comply with Section 29-1037 of the LLC Act.

Withdrawal of Members

A member may resign from a limited liability company only at the time or upon the happening of such events as are specified in the articles of organization or the operating agreement. [Section 29-1034]

If not otherwise provided in the operating agreement, a resigning member is entitled to receive the fair value of the membership interest within a reasonable time after resignation. If the resignation is a breach of the operating agreement or the result of wrongful conduct, the LLC may offset the amount paid to the resigning member by the amount of damages caused by the breach or wrongful conduct, including the costs of obtaining replacement services owed by the resigning member. [Section 29-1027]

Continuation of the LLC

Generally, a vote to continue the LLC after dissociation of a member (cessation or termination of a membership interest) is not required. Note: Except as otherwise provided in the operating agreement, the LLC automatically dissolves when the limited liability company has had no members for 90 consecutive days. [Section 29-1047]

FLORIDA

LLC Filing Office

Florida Department of State
Division of Corporations
P.O. Box 6327
Tallahassee, FL 32314
Telephone: 850-245-6051
www.dos.state.fl.us/doc/index.html

State LLC Act

The Florida LLC Act is contained in Title XXXVI (Business Organizations), Chapter 608 of the Florida Statutes, starting with Section 608.401, and is browseable from the following Web page (click Statutes and Constitution tab, then select Title XXXVI, then Chapter 608 from the index):
www.leg.state.fl.us/Welcome/index.cfm

State Tax Office

Revenue Department, Tallahassee
http://sun6.dms.state.fl.us/dor

Manager Election

Managers must be elected for one-year terms according to procedures contained in the articles or operating agreement (the LLC Act refers to the operating agreement as the regulations of the LLC). [Section 608.422]

Meeting Requirements

In a member-managed LLC, members vote according to the relative percentages of their capital accounts (the percentage of each member's capital contribution to all members' contributions, plus any additions and minus any withdrawals made to these accounts during the life of the LLC). If a member's capital account is zero or a negative amount, the member has one vote. Note: Unless otherwise provided in the LLC articles or operating agreement, only managers who are also members are allowed to vote on matters affecting the limited liability company (presumably, the operating agreement of a manager-managed LLC with one or more nonmember managers will give all managers the right to vote on and otherwise manage LLC business). [Sections 608.422 and 608.4231] Rules

for notice, time, place, and quorum for membership and manager meetings and action by written consent by members and managers were not found in the Act and are presumably as specified in the LLC's articles or operating agreement.

Amendments

Unless provided otherwise in the articles or operating agreement, only members of the LLC can amend the operating agreement (but even if not provided in the articles or operating agreement, the managers can adopt emergency regulations to use in a time of catastrophe that prevents members from assembling for a meeting, such as a hurricane or flood). [Section 608.423] Specific rules for amendment of articles were not found in the Act.

Admission of Members

Except as provided in the articles or operating agreement, new memberships must be issued with unanimous written consent of the members. [Section 608.423] Unless otherwise stated in the articles, the admission of a transferee as a member must be approved by unanimous consent of the nontransferring members. [Section 608.433]

Withdrawal of Members

A member may withdraw from an LLC only in accordance with the articles of organization or operating agreement and only at the time or upon the occurrence of an event specified in those documents. Notwithstanding anything to the contrary under applicable law, unless the articles of organization or operating agreement provide otherwise, a member may not resign from an LLC prior to its dissolution and winding up. Notwithstanding anything to the contrary under applicable law, the articles of organization or operating agreement may provide that an LLC interest may not be assigned prior to the LLC's dissolution and winding up. Upon withdrawal, a withdrawing member is entitled to receive any distribution to which the member is entitled under the articles of organization or operating agreement, and, if not otherwise provided in the articles of organization and operating agreement, the withdrawing member is entitled to receive, within a reasonable time after withdrawal, the fair value of his or her interest in the LLC as of the date of resignation based upon the member's right to share in distributions. [Section 608.427]

Continuation of the LLC

Except as may be provided in the articles, a vote to continue the LLC after dissociation of a member (cessation or termination of a membership interest) is not required. [Section 608.441]

GEORGIA

LLC Filing Office

Secretary of State
Corporations Division
Suite 315, West Tower
2 Martin Luther King Jr. Drive
Atlanta, GA 30334
Telephone: 404-656-2817
www.sos.state.ga.us/corporations

State LLC Act

The Georgia LLC Act starts with Section 14-11-100 of the Georgia Code, and is browseable from the following Web page (expand Title 14, then Chapter 11 to start browsing the LLC Act—you may first be asked to acknowledge that you understand the terms of use before being granted free access to the Georgia Code, which is provided by the state of Georgia and LexisNexis):

http://w3.lexis-nexis.com/hottopics/gacode/default.asp

State Tax Office

Department of Revenue, Atlanta
www.etax.dor.ga.gov/index.html

Manager Election

Unless otherwise provided in the articles or operating agreement, managers must be elected and removed by more than one-half the number of members. Managers are elected for an indefinite term unless otherwise stated in the articles or operating agreement. [Section 14-11-304]

Meeting Requirements

Except as provided in the articles or operating agreement, members and managers have one vote each in reaching membership decisions, and, except for special voting rules specified in the LLC Act for special decisions, the approval of a majority of members is required to take membership or manager action. Except as provided in the articles or operating agreement, members or managers may take action by unanimous written consent, or, if allowed by the articles or operating agreement, by the minimum number of votes that would be necessary to approve the action. If not otherwise fixed under the articles or operating agreement, the record date for determining members or managers entitled to take action by written consent is the date the first member or manager signs a consent. If action is taken by members or managers by written consent, unless otherwise provided in the articles or operating agreement, all voting members or managers who did not sign the consent must be given written notice of the action taken by written consent not more than ten days after the date of written consent. [Section 14-11-309]

Except as otherwise provided in the articles or operating agreement, meetings of members and managers shall abide by the following rules. [Section 14-11-310]:

- Membership meetings must be called by at least 25% of the members; manager meetings may be called by any manager.

- The members or managers calling a meeting shall give at least two days' notice of the meeting to the other members or managers.

- A majority of the members or managers constitutes a quorum for membership or manager meetings.

- Members and managers act at a meeting by the approval of a majority of the members or managers present at a meeting at which a quorum has been reached.

- Notice of a meeting should be in writing unless oral notice is reasonable under the circumstances. [Section 14-11-311]

- Members and managers may waive notice by signing a waiver before or after the date of the meeting. [Section 14-11-312]

Amendments

Unless otherwise provided in the articles or operating agreement, the approval of all members is required to amend the LLC's articles or the operating agreement. [Section 14-11-308]

Admission of Members

Unless otherwise provided in the articles or operating agreement, new memberships must be issued with unanimous approval of members. [Section 14-11-308] Except as otherwise stated in the articles or operating agreement, the admission of a transferee as a member must be approved by unanimous consent of the nontransferring members. [Section 14-11-503]

Withdrawal of Members

Specific approval by other members is not required for a member to withdraw. [Section 14-11-601.1] Unless otherwise provided in the articles or operating agreement, the approval of all members is required to approve distributions to members prior to the dissolution of the LLC, to sell all LLC assets, and to voluntarily dissolve the LLC. [Section 14-11-308]

Continuation of the LLC

Except as may be provided in the articles, a vote to continue the LLC after dissociation of a member (cessation or termination of a membership interest) is not required. [Section 14-11-602]

Special Statutory Rules

If LLC articles that contain a limitation on the power of members or managers to convey real property are filed with the clerk of the superior court in a county, they will be effective against a purported grantee of real property owned by the LLC in that county. [Section 14-11-302]

Unless otherwise provided in the LLC articles or operating agreement, a contract or transaction that personally benefits a manager or managing member can be approved by members or managers without a personal interest in the contract or transaction after disclosure of the interest of the member or manager in the contract or transaction. [Section 14-11-307]

HAWAII

LLC Filing Office

Department of Commerce and Consumer Affairs
Business Registration Division
P.O. Box 40
Honolulu, HI 96810
Telephone: 808-586-2744
www.hawaii.gov/dcca/areas/breg

State LLC Act

The Hawaii LLC Act is contained in Chapter 428 of the Hawaii Statutes, starting with Section 428-101, and is browseable from the following Web page. Select Legal Info at the left of the page, click Statutes, then select Uniform Limited Liability Company Act:

www.businessregistrations.com

State Tax Office

Hawaii Tax Department, Honolulu
www.state.hi.us/tax/tax.html

Manager Election

Unless otherwise provided in the articles or operating agreement, managers must be elected and removed by a majority of the members for an indefinite term. [Section 428-404]

Meeting Requirements

Unless otherwise provided in the articles or operating agreement [Sections 428-103 and 428-404]:

- Members and managers have equal voting rights (for example, one vote per member or manager).
- Members and managers approve action by a majority vote.
- Members and managers may take action by unanimous written consent.

Rules for notice, time, place, and quorum for membership and manager meetings were not found in the Act, and presumably may be specified in the LLC's articles or operating agreement.

Amendments

Unless otherwise provided in the articles or operating agreement, all LLC members must approve amendments to its articles and operating agreement. [Section 428-404]

Admission of Members

Unless otherwise provided in the articles or operating agreement, new memberships must be issued with unanimous approval of the members. [Section 428-404] Except as otherwise stated in the operating agreement, the admission of a transferee as a member must be approved by unanimous consent of the nontransferring members. [Section 428-503]

Withdrawal of Members

A member has the power to dissociate (withdraw) from the LLC at any time. If the withdrawal is a breach of the operating agreement or happens before the end of the term of the LLC (if a definite term is set for the existence of the LLC), the LLC may offset the amount paid to the withdrawing member by the amount of damages to the LLC and other members caused by the withdrawal. [Section 428-602]

Unless otherwise provided in the LLC operating agreement, a withdrawing member, generally, is entitled to receive the fair value of his or her membership interest. The LLC must present an offer to purchase the withdrawing member's interest to the member no later than 30 days from the date of withdrawal (but, if the LLC has a specified term, the purchase apparently need not occur until the expiration of the term). Financial statements must be included with the offer. [Section 429-701] The LLC Act also contains provisions allowing a withdrawn member to institute a court action to determine the fair value of a withdrawing member's interest. [Section 428-702]

Continuation of the LLC

A vote to continue the LLC after dissociation (withdrawal or loss) of a member is not required. [Section 428-801]

Special Statutory Rules

Unless otherwise provided in the articles or operating agreement, the approval of all members is required to approve distributions to members prior to the dissolution of the LLC, to sell all LLC assets, or to voluntarily dissolve the LLC. [Section 428-404]

IDAHO

LLC Filing Office

Idaho Secretary of State
Corporations Division
700 West Jefferson
P.O. Box 83720
Boise, ID 83720-0080
Telephone: 208-334-2301
www.idsos.state.id.us/corp/corindex.htm

State LLC Act

The Idaho LLC Act is contained in Title 53 (Partnership), Chapter 6 of the Idaho Statutes, starting with Section 53-601, and is browseable from the following Web page:

www3.state.id.us/idstat/TOC/53006KTOC.html

State Tax Office

State Tax Commission, Boise
http://tax.idaho.gov/

Manager Election

Unless otherwise provided in the operating agreement, managers must be elected, removed, and replaced by a vote of more than one-half the members, and serve for an indefinite term. [Section 53-621]

Meeting Requirements

Unless otherwise provided in the operating agreement, members and managers have one vote each, and the approval of more than one-half of the members or managers is necessary to take action. [Section 53-623] Rules for notice, time, place, quorum, and other aspects of membership and manager meetings or actions by written consent of the members and managers were not found in the Act, and presumably may be specified in the LLC's operating agreement.

Amendments

Unless otherwise provided in a written operating agreement, the approval of all members is required to amend the operating agreement (no statutory rule was found for amendments to articles). [Section 53-623]

Admission of Members

Unless otherwise provided in the articles or operating agreement, new memberships must be issued with the written consent of all members. [Section 53-640] Unless otherwise stated in the operating agreement, the admission of a transferee as a member must be approved by unanimous written consent of the nontransferring members. [Section 53-638]

Withdrawal of Members

Unless the operating agreement prohibits a member from withdrawing, a member may withdraw upon 30 days' notice to the other members. If the withdrawal is a breach of the operating agreement or a result of a member's wrongful conduct, the LLC may offset the amount paid to the withdrawing member by the amount of damages caused by the breach or wrongful conduct, including the cost of obtaining replacement services owed by the member. Unless otherwise provided in the operating agreement, a withdrawal by a member prior to the end of the term of an LLC organized for a specific term is a breach of the agreement. [Section 53-641c]

Unless otherwise provided in the operating agreement, a withdrawing member is treated as an assignee of a membership interest. Generally, this means that the member is only entitled to receive ongoing distributions of LLC profits until the LLC is dissolved, unless the other members unanimously agree otherwise. A member who is removed, however, has a right to receive the fair value of his or her interest within a reasonable time after removal. [Section 53-630]

Continuation of the LLC

Unless otherwise stated in the operating agreement, the dissociation (loss of membership rights) of a member automatically causes the LLC to dissolve unless all its remaining members vote to continue the LLC within 90 days of the dissociation. [Section 53-642]

Special Statutory Rules

If an LLC is member-managed, transfers of LLC property may be transferred by a document signed by a member on behalf of the LLC; if manager-managed, only a manager can execute such a transfer document on behalf of the LLC. [Section 53-634]

ILLINOIS

LLC Filing Office

Illinois Secretary of State
Department of Business Services
Limited Liability Company Division
Michael J. Howlett Bldg.
501 S. 2nd St., Rm 328
Springfield, IL 62756
Telephone: 800-252-8980
Branch office in Chicago: 312-793-3380 (for questions and info only; not LLC filing)
www.cyberdriveillinois.com/departments/business_services/home.html

State LLC Act

The Illinois LLC Act is contained in Chapter 805 (Business Organizations), starting with Section 180/1-1, and is browseable from the following Web page (select Chapter 805, then select 805 ILCS 180/ Limited Liability Company Act):

www.ilga.gov/legislation/ilcs/ilcs.asp

State Tax Office

For annual tax information, contact the Department of Business Services, Springfield

www.cyberdriveillinois.com/departments/business_services/home.html

For other tax information, contact the Department of Revenue, Springfield

www.revenue.state.il.us

Manager Election

Managers are elected, removed, and replaced by consent of a majority of members, and hold office for an indefinite term. [Section 180/15-1]

Meeting Requirements

Unless otherwise provided in the articles or operating agreement [Section 180/15-1]:

- Members and managers have equal voting rights (for example, one vote per member or manager).
- Members and managers approve action by a majority vote.

Rules for notice, time, place, and quorum for membership and manager meetings, and action by written consent of members and managers, were not found in the Act, and presumably may be specified in the LLC's articles or operating agreement.

Amendments

Except as otherwise provided in the LLC's articles or operating agreement, managers may, by a majority vote, amend the articles to remove the name of an initial manager who is no longer a manager, remove the name of the initial registered agent of the LLC, or change the LLC name. Other amendments to the articles or operating agreement require the full membership's approval. [Sections 180/5-15 and 180/15-1]

Admission of Members

Unless otherwise provided in the articles or operating agreement, new memberships must be issued with the written consent of all members. [Section 180/10-1] Unless otherwise stated in the articles or operating agreement, the admission of a transferee as a member must be approved by unanimous consent of the nontransferring members. [Section 180/30-10]

Withdrawal of Members

A member has the power to dissociate (withdraw) at any time by giving the LLC notice of withdrawal, but the member may be liable for financial damages if the withdrawal is in violation of the LLC's operating agreement. The LLC can also offset any distribution owed to the withdrawing member by the amount of the damages. [Sections 180/35-45 and 180/35-50]

Generally, unless the operating agreement provides otherwise, after a member's withdrawal, the member's interest must be purchased for its fair value by the LLC. The LLC must also provide a purchase offer to the withdrawing member 30 days after the withdrawal, as well as financial statements of the LLC. If the LLC and member cannot agree on the value of the interest within 120 days after the member's withdrawal, the member can institute a court action to determine the fair value of the interest. [Section 180/35-60]

Continuation of the LLC

A vote to continue the LLC after the dissociation of a member (cessation or termination of a membership interest) is not required. Unless otherwise stated in the LLC operating agreement, an Illinois LLC continues despite the dissociation of a member. [Section 180/35-1]

Special Statutory Rules

Unless a member's or manager's authority to do so is limited in the articles, in a member-managed LLC, transfers of LLC property may be transferred by a document signed by any member on behalf of the LLC; in a manager-managed LLC, any manager can execute such a transfer document on behalf of the LLC. [Section 180/13-5]

Unless otherwise provided in the articles or operating agreement, the approval of all members is required to approve distributions to members prior to the dissolution of the LLC, to sell all LLC assets, or to voluntarily dissolve the LLC. [Section 180/15-1]

INDIANA

LLC Filing Office

Indiana Secretary of State
Corporations Division
302 W. Washington, Room E018
Indianapolis, IN 46204
Telephone: 317-232-6576
www.in.gov/sos/business/corporations.html

State LLC Act

The Indiana LLC Act (also called the Indiana Business Flexibility Act) is contained in Title 23 (Business and Other Associations), Article 18 of the Indiana Code, starting with Section 23-18-1-1, and is browseable from the following Web page (select Title 23, then Article 18):

www.in.gov/legislative/ic/code

State Tax Office

Department of Revenue, Indianapolis

www.state.in.us/dor

Manager Election

Unless provided otherwise in the articles or operating agreement, managers are elected, removed, and replaced by a majority in interest of members (this means members who have contributed more than 50% of the current capital of the LLC), and serve for an indefinite term. [Sections 23-18-4-1 and 23-18-1-13]

Meeting Requirements

Except as provided in the articles or operating agreement, members must take action by the vote or consent of a majority in interest; managers act by a majority vote of the number of managers. [Section 23-18-4-3]

Rules for notice, time, place, and quorum for membership and manager meetings, and action by written consent of members and managers, were not found in the Act, and presumably may be specified in the LLC's articles or operating agreement.

Amendments

Except as otherwise provided in the articles or operating agreement, amendments to the operating agreement require the approval of all members (no rule was found for amendments to the articles). [Section 23-18-4-3] Also, the initial operating agreement must be signed by all the LLC's current members. [Section 23-18-4-6]

Admission of Members

Unless otherwise provided in the articles or operating agreement, new memberships must be issued with the written consent of all members. [Section 23-18-6-1] Unless otherwise stated in the operating agreement, the admission of a transferee as a member must be approved by unanimous written consent of the nontransferring members. [Section 23-18-6-4]

Withdrawal of Members

Unless the operating agreement prohibits a member from withdrawing, a member may withdraw upon 30 days' notice to the other members. If the withdrawal is a breach of the operating agreement or a result of a member's wrongful conduct, the LLC may offset the amount paid to the withdrawing member by the amount of damages caused by the breach or wrongful conduct, including the cost of obtaining replacement services owed by the member. Unless otherwise provided in the operating agreement, a withdrawal by a member prior to the end of the term of an LLC organized for a specific term is a breach of the agreement. [Section 23-18-6-6]

Generally, unless otherwise provided in the operating agreement, a withdrawing member is entitled to receive the fair value of the member's interest within a reasonable period after withdrawal. [Section 23-15-5-5]

Continuation of the LLC

A membership vote to continue the LLC after dissociation of a member (cessation or termination of a membership interest) is not required. [Section 23-18-9-1.1]

IOWA

LLC Filing Office

Iowa Secretary of State
Corporations Division
Lucas Building, 1st Floor
Des Moines, IA 50319
Telephone: 515-281-5204
www.sos.state.ia.us/business/index.html

State LLC Act

The Iowa LLC Act is contained in Title XII (Business Entities), Chapter 490A of the Iowa Code, starting with Section 490A.100, and is browseable from the following Web page (click Tables and Index to the Code of Iowa under the 2007 Iowa Code heading, then click Skeleton Index, then open the 2007 Iowa Code folder in the left pane, then

Statutes, then select Title XII Business Entities, then open the folder for Subtitle 2, then open the folder for Chapter 490A Limited Liability Companies):
www.legis.state.ia.us/IowaLaw.html

State Tax Office

Department of Revenue and Finance, Des Moines
www.state.ia.us/tax/index.html

Manager Election

Unless otherwise provided in the articles or operating agreement, managers are elected or removed and manager vacancies are filled by a majority vote of the members (membership voting is according to capital account balances unless otherwise provided in the articles or operating agreement). [Sections 490A.705 and 490A.701]

Meeting Requirements

Unless otherwise provided in the articles or operating agreement, members vote according to the current balance in their capital accounts. [Section 490A.701] Rules for notice, time, place, and quorum for membership meetings and action by written consent of the members depend on the LLC's operating agreement. [Section 490A.307]

Unless otherwise provided in the articles or operating agreement, a quorum for managers' meetings is a majority of managers, and managers approvals must be made by a majority vote. [Section 490A.705] Rules for notice, time, and place for managers' meetings and actions by written consent of the managers were not found in the LLC Act, and presumably may be set forth in the LLC's operating agreement.

Amendments

Unless otherwise provided in the articles or operating agreement, a unanimous vote of members is required to amend the articles or operating agreement. [Section 490A.701]

Admission of Members

Unless otherwise provided in the operating agreement, new memberships must be issued with the written consent of all members. [Section 490A.306] Unless otherwise stated in the articles or operating agreement, the admission of a transferee as a

member must be approved by unanimous written consent or a vote at a meeting of nontransferring members. [Section 490A.903]

Withdrawal of Members

Generally, unless otherwise stated in the articles or operating agreement, a member may not withdraw from the LLC prior to its dissolution (but the Act allows a member to resign if certain types of amendments to the articles or operating agreement adversely affect the member). [Section 490A.704A]

Generally, unless otherwise provided in the operating agreement, a withdrawing member is entitled to receive the fair value of the member's interest within a reasonable period after withdrawal. [Section 490A.805]

Continuation of the LLC

A vote to continue the LLC after the termination of a membership is not required.

Special Statutory Rules

Unless otherwise provided in the articles or operating agreement, a majority vote of members (voting is according to capital account balances unless otherwise provided in the articles or operating agreement) is required to dissolve the LLC or sell all its assets. [Section 490A.701]

A contract or transaction that personally benefits a manager can be approved by a majority of managers who have no personal interest in the contract or transaction after disclosure of the interest of the affected member or manager. [Section 490A.708]

KANSAS

LLC Filing Office

Kansas Secretary of State
Corporation Division
First Floor, Memorial Hall
120 S.W. 10th Ave.
Topeka, KS 66612
Telephone: 785-296-4564
www.kssos.org/main.html

State LLC Act

The Kansas LLC Act is contained in Chapter 17 of the Kansas Statutes, Article 76, starting with Section 17-7662 (ignore Sections 17-7601 to 17-7661; this is the prior LLC Act), and is browseable from the Web page listed below (use the arrow keys to highlight Chapter 17, Corporations, in the center box, then press List Articles in Chapter. Then use the arrow keys to highlight Article 76, Limited Liability Companies, and press List Statutes in Article to see a list of the LLC Act statutes):

www.kslegislature.org/legsrv-statutes/index.do

State Tax Office

Department of Revenue, Topeka

www.ksrevenue.org/

Manager Election

Managers are elected by members as set out in the articles or operating agreement. [Section 17-7612]

Meeting Requirements

Unless otherwise provided in the articles or operating agreement, members have one vote each (presumably, managers also have one vote each in a manager-managed LLC). Regular meetings of managers and members are held at times stated in the operating agreement or, if not stated, upon at least ten days' written notice; other meetings of members or managers may be called at any time by members or managers, respectively, who hold at least 1/5 the voting power of the LLC, upon at least ten and not more than 60 days' written notice. Members can take action by written consent by consent of all members. A quorum for LLC meetings is a majority of the voting power. [Section 17-7613] Rules for notice, time, and place for managers' meetings, and action by written consent of managers, were not found in the LLC Act, and presumably may be provided in the LLC operating agreement.

Amendments

Rules for membership approval of amendments to the articles and operating agreement were not found in the LLC Act.

Admission of Members

Unless otherwise provided in the operating agreement, new memberships must be issued with the written consent of all members. Unless otherwise provided in the operating agreement, the admission of a transferee as a member must be approved by majority of the nontransferring members. [Section 17-7618]

Withdrawal of Members

We found no specific provisions on withdrawal of a member; Section 17-7616 says that a member may demand a return of capital (which is, generally, the minimum amount requested by a member upon withdrawal) only on dissolution of the LLC or on a date specified in the articles. [Section 17-7616]

Continuation of the LLC

A vote to continue the LLC after the dissociation of a member (cessation or termination of a membership interest) is not required (but members can vote to dissolve the LLC, if they wish, within 90 days of the dissociation of a member). However, the LLC automatically dissolves if there are no remaining members. [Section 17-7622]

KENTUCKY

LLC Filing Office

Kentucky Secretary of State
Business Filings
P.O. Box 718
Frankfort, KY 40602
Telephone: 502-564-2848
http://sos.ky.gov/business/

State LLC Act

The Kentucky LLC Act is contained in Title XXIII (Private Corporations and Associations), Chapter 275 of the Kentucky Statutes, starting with Section 275.001, and is browseable from the following Web page:

http://162.114.4.13/krs/275-00/CHAPTER.HTM

State Tax Office

Kentucky Revenue Cabinet, Frankfort
http://revenue.ky.gov/

Manager Election

Unless otherwise provided in the articles or operating agreement, managers are to be elected for an indefinite term, and removed or replaced by a majority in interest of members (unless otherwise provided in the operating agreement, this means members who have contributed a majority of the capital to the LLC). [Sections 275.165, 275.015, and 275.175]

Meeting Requirements

Unless otherwise provided in the articles or operating agreement, members vote in proportion to their contributions to the LLC, with a majority vote necessary to take membership action. In other words, the vote of members who have contributed a majority of the capital to the LLC is normally necessary to take membership action. [Section 275.175] Rules for notice, time, place, and quorum for members' and managers' meetings and action by written consent by members and managers were not found in the LLC Act, and presumably may be provided in the LLC operating agreement.

Amendments

Unless otherwise provided in the articles or operating agreement, a majority in interest is required to amend the articles to change management of the LLC from member- to manager-management, or vice versa, or to amend the operating agreement. [Section 275.175]

Admission of Members

Unless otherwise provided in the operating agreement, new memberships must be issued with the written consent of all members. [Section 275.275] Unless otherwise provided in the operating agreement, the admission of a transferee as a member must be approved by written consent of a majority in interest of members (this normally means members who have contributed a majority of the capital to the LLC). [Section 275.265]

Withdrawal of Members

Unless the operating agreement says otherwise, a member can withdraw from the LLC only by obtaining the consent of all other members. [Section 275.280] No specific provision was found in the LLC Act that says how much the member is entitled to receive upon withdrawal in the absence of a provision in the operating agreement.

Continuation of the LLC

A vote to continue the LLC after termination of a membership is not required.

Special Statutory Rules

Unless otherwise provided in the operating agreement, the approval of a majority in interest of members is required to amend the operating agreement or to amend the articles to switch from member- to manager-management (or vice versa). [Section 275.175]

A promise by a member to make contributions to capital is not enforceable unless in writing. [Section 275.200]

In a member-managed LLC, transfers of LLC property may be transferred by a document signed by an authorized member on behalf of the LLC; in a manager-managed LLC, any authorized manager can execute such a transfer document on behalf of the LLC. [Section 275.245]

Unless otherwise provided in the operating agreement, the written consent of a majority in interest of members is required to voluntarily dissolve the LLC. [Section 275.285]

LOUISIANA

LLC Filing Office

Louisiana Secretary of State
Commercial Division
P.O. Box 94125
Baton Rouge, LA 70804
Telephone: 225-925-4704
www.sec.state.la.us/comm/corp-index.htm

State LLC Act

The Louisiana LLC Law is contained in Chapter 22, Title 12 of the Louisiana Statutes, starting with Section 12:1301. See the following Web page to browse the Law (click Louisiana Laws in the left panel, then select the RS check box to search the Revised Statutes, then insert in the search box the section number you wish to view—currently, the law must be browsed section by section):

www.legis.state.la.us

State Tax Office

Department of Revenue and Taxation, Baton Rouge
www.rev.state.la.us

Manager Election

Unless otherwise provided in the articles or operating agreement, vacancies in manager positions must be filled by a plurality vote of the members. Managers can be removed only by a majority of members at a meeting called for that purpose. [Section 1313] Apparently, managers are elected as provided in the operating agreement, and serve for an indefinite term.

Meeting Requirements

Unless otherwise provided in the articles or operating agreement, members and managers each have one vote, and members and manager decisions must be made by a majority of managers. [Sections 1316 and 1318] Rules for notice, time, place, and quorum for members' and managers' meetings, and action by written consent by members and managers, were not found in the LLC Act, and presumably may be provided in the LLC operating agreement.

Amendments

Unless otherwise provided in the articles or operating agreement, amendments to the articles or operating agreement require the approval of a majority of members. [Section 1318]

Admission of Members

No statutory rule was found for membership approval of the issuance of new memberships in the LLC. Unless otherwise stated in the articles or operating agreement, the admission of a transferee as a member must be approved by unanimous written consent of the nontransferring members. [Section 1332]

Withdrawal of Members

A member of an LLC organized for a specific term may withdraw from the LLC only for just cause arising out of the failure of another member to perform an obligation. Unless otherwise provided in the operating agreement, a member of an LLC with an indefinite duration may withdraw upon 30 days' prior written notice to each member and manager (notice must also be given to the LLC's registered office). Unless otherwise provided in the operating agreement (and except as provided in the LLC Act), a withdrawing member is entitled to be paid the fair market value of the member's interest within a reasonable time after withdrawal. [Section 1325]

Continuation of the LLC

A vote to continue the LLC after the termination of a membership is not required. [Section 1334]

Special Statutory Rules

Unless otherwise provided in the articles or operating agreement, the approval of a majority of members is required to voluntarily dissolve the LLC, sell all its assets, or approve a loan not in the ordinary course of business. [Section 1318]

To validate a contract or transaction between the LLC and a member or manager with a personal financial interest in the contract or transaction, approval of a majority of disinterested members after full disclosure should be obtained. [Section 1318]

MAINE

LLC Filing Office

Secretary of State
Corporate Examining Section
101 State House Station
Augusta, ME 04333-0101
Telephone: 207-624-7740
www.state.me.us/sos/cec/corp/corp.htm

State LLC Act

The Maine LLC Act is contained in Title 31 (Partnerships and Associations), Chapter 13 of the Maine Statues, starting with Section 601, and is browseable from the following Web page:

http://janus.state.me.us/legis/statutes/31/title31sec601.html

State Tax Office

Maine Revenue Services, Augusta
www.state.me.us/revenue

Manager Election

Unless otherwise provided in the articles or operating agreement, managers are to be elected for an indefinite term and removed and replaced by a majority (per capita) vote of the members. [Section 651]

Meeting Requirements

Except as provided in the articles or operating agreement, members and managers must make decisions through approval by more than one-half of the members or managers on a per capita basis (one vote per member or manager). [Section 653]

Rules for notice, time, place, and quorum for managers' and members' meetings, and action by written consent by managers, and members, may presumably be provided in the LLC articles or operating agreement. [Section 651]

Amendments

Amendments to articles must be made by a majority in interest of the members (a definition was not found in the LLC Act but, presumably, this means the vote of members owning a majority of the profits and capital interests in the LLC). [Section 623] Note that an amendment to the articles must be filed with the state LLC filing office within 90 days of a:

- change of LLC name

- change in management of the LLC from member-managed to manager-managed, or vice versa, or

- a change in the minimum or maximum number of managers (in a manager-managed LLC).

Except as provided in the articles or operating agreement, amendments to the operating agreement can be made only after approval by all the LLC members. [Section 653]

Admission of Members

Unless otherwise provided in the operating agreement, new memberships must be issued with the written consent of all members. [Section 691] Admission of transferee as a member must be approved by unanimous consent of the nontransferring members and the transferee, and as otherwise provided in the articles or operating agreement. [Section 687]

Withdrawal of Members

Unless otherwise provided in the articles or operating agreement, a member of an LLC may withdraw upon 30 days' prior written notice to the other members. [Section 692(3)]

Upon withdrawal of a member, the member is not entitled to receive a distribution except as may be required under the LLC operating agreement. [Section 672]

Continuation of the LLC

A vote to continue the LLC after withdrawal of a member is not required. [Section 701]

Special Statutory Rules

An LLC may file a statement of authority with the secretary of state, listing the names of managers or members authorized or not authorized to enter into transactions on behalf of the LLC, including the transfer of real estate. This statement also may be recorded in the county where the real property is located. Outside persons dealing with the LLC may rely on filed statements of authority, and the LLC may hold responsible outsiders bound with knowledge of the information contained in these filed statements. See statute for more information. [Section 626]

An LLC must file, upon the request of a third party, a list of the names and addresses of its members with the secretary of state. [Section 647]

In a member-managed LLC, LLC property may be transferred by a document signed by a member on behalf of the LLC; in a manager-managed LLC, any manager can execute such a transfer document. [Section 683]

Written consent of all members is required to voluntarily dissolve the LLC. [Section 701]

MARYLAND

LLC Filing Office

Maryland Department of Assessments and Taxation
Corporate Charter Division
301 West Preston Street, Room 801
Baltimore, MD 21201
Telephone: 410-767-1340
Toll-free: 888-246-5941
www.dat.state.md.us/sdatweb/charter.html

State LLC Act

The Maryland LLC Act is contained in the Corporations and Associations heading, Title 4A, starting with Section 4A-101, and is browseable from the following Web page (select Maryland, then Maryland Code, then Corporations and Associations, then select Title 4A to begin browsing the LLC Act):

http://198.187.128.12/

State Tax Office

Comptroller of Maryland, Revenue Administration Division, Annapolis
www.comp.state.md.us/default.asp

Manager Election

No rules were found in the LLC Act, but the operating agreement is allowed to specify all aspects of LLC management—presumably this includes the manner of election and term for managers in a manager-managed LLC. [Section 4A-402]

Note: Unless otherwise provided in the operating agreement, members manage the LLC. [Section 4A-403] The LLC Act does not mention managers or manager-management, but it allows the operating agreement to delegate management to persons who are not members. In effect, this allows LLCs to elect manager-management, and to assign management

to one or more persons (who may or may not be members). [Section 4A-402]

Meeting Requirements

Unless otherwise provided in the articles or operating agreement, members must vote in proportion to their relative interests in the profits of the LLC. The approval of members owning a majority of such profits interests is required for membership action. [Section 4A-403] Rules for the notice, time, place, and quorum for managers' and members' meetings, and for action by written consent by managers and members, were not found in the Act. Presumably, these may be provided in the LLC articles or operating agreement.

Amendments

Amendments to articles require unanimous consent of LLC members. [Section 4A-204] Except as otherwise stated in the operating agreement, the operating agreement must be amended by consent of all LLC members. If, as authorized in the operating agreement, the agreement is amended without full membership approval, a copy of the amendments to the agreement must be delivered to each nonconsenting member. [Section 4A-402]

Admission of Members

Unless otherwise provided in the operating agreement, new memberships must be issued with the written consent of all LLC members. [Section 4A-601] Admission of a transferee as a member must be approved by unanimous written consent of the nontransferring members, and as otherwise specified in the operating agreement. [Section 4A-604] Also, unless otherwise provided in the operating agreement, if the LLC has no members (that is, the remaining member or members has/have assigned their membership interests), the assignee(s) can elect to become members. [Section 4A-604]

Withdrawal of Members

Unless otherwise provided in the operating agreement, a member can withdraw from the LLC by giving the other members no fewer than six months' prior written notice at the members' addresses shown on the LLC records. [Section 4A-605]

An LLC may elect to pay a withdrawing member or the member's successor in interest the fair value of the member's interest within a reasonable period after withdrawal (payment does not seem to be required; if a liquidating payment is not made, the withdrawing member is treated as an assignee—that is, he or she is entitled to receive a continuing share of profits and other LLC distributions made to all members). [Section 4A.606.1]

Continuation of the LLC

A vote to continue the LLC after termination of a membership interest is not required. But, except as may otherwise be provided in the operating agreement, a Maryland LLC automatically dissolves if it has no members for a period of 90 consecutive days. [Section 4A-902]

MASSACHUSETTS

LLC Filing Office

Commonwealth of Massachusetts
Corporations Division
One Ashburton Place, 17th Floor
Boston, MA 02108
Telephone: 617-727-9640
www.sec.state.ma.us/cor/coridx.htm

State LLC Act

The Massachusetts LLC Act is contained in Title XXII (Corporations), Chapter 156C of the Massachusetts General Laws, starting with Section 1, and is browseable from the following Web page (scroll down to and select Chapter 156C to begin browsing the LLC Act):

www.mass.gov/legis/laws/mgl/gl-pt1-toc.htm

State Tax Office

Department of Revenue, Boston
www.dor.state.ma.us/Dorpg.htm

Manager Election

Managers may be designated, elected, replaced, and removed for a term as provided in the LLC operating agreement. [Sections 2, 23, and 24]

Meeting Requirements

Unless otherwise provided in the operating agreement, the vote of members who own more than 50% of unreturned capital contributions to the LLC is required in order to make decisions. [Section 20] Unless stated in the operating agreement, managers must approve actions by a majority vote (one vote each). [Section 26] Rules for notice, time, place, and quorum for members' and managers' meetings and action by written consent by members and managers may be provided in the LLC operating agreement. [Sections 20 and 26]

Amendments

No voting rules for amendments to the certificate of organization or operating agreement were found in the LLC Act. Presumably, these may be specified in the operating agreement.

Admission of Members

Unless otherwise provided in the operating agreement, new memberships must be issued with the written consent of all members. [Section 19] Admission of a transferee as a member must be approved by unanimous consent of the nontransferring members or as provided in the operating agreement. [Sections 39 and 41]

Withdrawal of Members

A member may resign from an LLC upon at least six months' prior written notice to the LLC and to each member and manager (at their addresses listed in the LLC records). If the resignation is in violation of the operating agreement, the LLC can recover damages for this breach and can offset such damages against any amounts owed by the LLC to the resigning member. [Section 36]

A manager may resign from the LLC at any time upon prior notice to each member and manager. As noted just above, if the resignation is in violation of the operating agreement, the LLC can recover and offset against payouts owed to the manager any damages for breach of the agreement. [Section 37]

If not otherwise specified in an operating agreement, a resigning member is entitled to receive the fair value of the member's interest within a reasonable time after withdrawal. [Section 32]

Continuation of the LLC

A vote to continue the LLC after termination of a membership interest is not required. [Section 43]

Special Statutory Rules

The certificate of organization may list the names of one or more persons authorized to execute and record title documents for real estate. [Section 12]

An LLC manager who votes for or assents to the making of a distribution to members in violation of the LLC operating agreement is personally liable to the LLC for the amount of the unwarranted distribution. [Section 35]

In addition to any event specified in the operating agreement, the approval of all members may voluntarily dissolve the LLC. [Section 43]

MICHIGAN

LLC Filing Office

Bureau of Commercial Services
Corporation Division
P.O. Box 30054
Lansing, MI 48909
Telephone: 517-241-6470
www.michigan.gov/cis

State LLC Act

The Michigan LLC Act is contained in Chapter 450 (Corporations) of the Michigan Compiled Laws, Act 23 of 1993, starting with Section 450.4101, and is browseable from the following Web page (select Chapter Index under Michigan Compiled Laws Information, then select Chapter 450, then select Act 23 of 1993 at the bottom of the page, which is the LLC Act):

www.michiganlegislature.org

State Tax Office

Michigan Department of Treasury, Lansing
www.michigan.gov/treasury

Manager Election

A vote of a majority in interest of the members entitled to vote in accordance with Section 502(1) is required to select managers to fill initial positions or vacancies. The members may remove one or more managers with or without cause unless an operating agreement provides that managers may be removed only for cause. The members may remove a manager for cause only at a meeting called expressly for that purpose, and that manager shall have reasonable advance notice of the allegations against him or her and an opportunity to be heard at the meeting. [Section 450.4403]

Meeting Requirements

Except as provided in the articles or operating agreement, the vote of a majority of managers is required for manager action, with managers given one vote each. [Section 450.4405] Except as provided in the articles or operating agreement, members take action by approval of a majority of all members, with each member having one vote. [Section 450.4502] Rules for notice, time, place, and quorum for members' and managers' meetings, and for action by written consent by members and managers, presumably may be provided in the LLC operating agreement.

Amendments

Only members may amend the articles. [Section 450.4502] Unless the articles or operating agreement allow amendment of articles by majority membership vote, amendments of articles must be approved by all voting members. [Section 450.4603] No statutory rule was found for amending the operating agreement. Presumably these rules may be provided in the operating agreement.

Admission of Members

Unless otherwise provided in the operating agreement, new memberships must be issued with the consent of all voting members. [Section 450.4501] Unless otherwise provided in the operating agreement, in an LLC with more than one member, the admission of a transferee as a member must be approved by unanimous consent of the voting members. An assignee of an LLC with one member may become a member if allowed under the terms of the agreement between the selling member and the assignee. [Section 450.4506]

Withdrawal of Members

A member may withdraw from the LLC only as provided in the LLC's operating agreement. [Section 450.4509] If the LLC operating agreement permits withdrawal, but is silent on the issue of payments to a withdrawing member, a withdrawing member is entitled to receive the fair value of the member's interest within a reasonable time after withdrawal. [Section 450.4305]

Continuation of the LLC

A vote to continue the LLC after termination of a membership is not required.

Special Statutory Rules

Only members may vote to voluntarily dissolve the LLC or, unless otherwise provided in an operating agreement, sell all its assets (presumably by the normal majority voting rule). [Section 450.4502] Unless authorized in advance by an operating agreement, a majority of disinterested members must approve a contract or transaction that personally benefits a manager of the LLC after full disclosure of the facts surrounding the transaction. [Section 450.4502]

MINNESOTA

LLC Filing Office

Minnesota Secretary of State
Business Services Division
180 State Office Building
100 Rev. Dr. Martin Luther King Jr. Blvd.
St. Paul, MN 55155-1299
Telephone: 651-296-2803
Toll-free: 877-551-6767
www.sos.state.mn.us/home/index.asp?page=3

State LLC Act

The Minnesota LLC Act is contained in Chapter 322B of the Minnesota Statutes, starting with Section 322B.01, and is browseable from the following Web page (select Retrieve an entire chapter, then insert 322B in the Chapter box, then click Get Chapter):

www.leg.state.mn.us/leg/statutes.asp

State Tax Office

Department of Revenue, St. Paul
www.taxes.state.mn.us

Manager Election

The Minnesota LLC Act presupposes management by a board of governors (management by governors is similar to the vesting of management power in a corporate board of directors). The law specifies that LLCs must have one or more governors, elected by the members, who serve for an indefinite term of office. Section 322B.606, however, recognizes that LLCs may wish to adopt membership management. That section says that the LLC members may act in the place of the governors as long as they make management decisions by unanimous vote; this is usually easy to achieve in smaller LLCs, and we assume most smaller Minnesota LLCs will opt for membership management, rather than management by a board of governors (governor management is subject to many corporate-type rules and procedures specified in the LLC Act). To reinforce this member-management election, the LLC operating agreement should require a unanimous membership vote for management decisions.

If you decide to go along with the statutory scheme and opt for management by governors, see Sections 322B.60 and following of the LLC Act to learn more about the default statutory management scheme, and special rules that apply to board of governor action.

To make matters more confusing, Minnesota law requires the appointment or election of two persons who function as the LLC president and treasurer but who are called managers (one is called the chief manager, the other is called the treasurer). [Section 322B.67] Don't be confused by this nonstandard nomenclature. Simply decide which of your members (or managers, in a manager-managed LLC) will be chief manager and function as the LLC president, and also pick a member or manager to serve as treasurer.

Board of governors' election procedures are as specified in the articles or operating agreement. [Section 322B.613] Unless a fixed term is provided in the articles or operating agreement, governors serve an indefinite term until the next regular meeting of members; if a fixed term is specified, it cannot exceed five years. [Section 322B.616] Unless otherwise provided in the articles, members vote for governors by cumulative voting (similar to how shareholders vote for directors in larger corporations). [Section 322B.63] Unless otherwise provided in the articles or operating agreement, removal of governors requires the same membership vote as a vote to elect them. [Section 322B.636] Unless otherwise provided in the articles or operating agreement, vacancies on the board of governors may be filled by persons approved by a majority of the remaining governors. [Section 322B.64]

These governor-management rules are complex and riddled with exceptions. If you wish to follow them, see the LLC Act sections noted above. We expect most LLCs will allow management by unanimous vote of members instead. [Section 322B.606]

Meeting Requirements

Unless otherwise provided in the articles, members vote in proportion to the value reflected in the LLC records of each member's capital contribution to the LLC. [Section 322B.356] Unless otherwise provided in the articles, the approval of a majority of the membership voting power present at a meeting is required for membership action. [Section 322B.35] But remember, when members act as managers of the LLC (as is usually the case when members are asked to take action in a smaller LLC that wishes to avoid the governor-management rules), members must act by unanimous approval. [Section 322B.606] Members may take action by unanimous written consent without a meeting (articles may lower this written consent requirement to written consent of the members required to take action at a meeting at which all members were present). [Section 322B.35] Unless otherwise specified in the articles or operating agreement, regular meetings of members need not be held, unless demanded by a member under certain conditions. [Section 322B.333] Special members' meetings may be called by the chief manager (president), treasurer, two or more governors, or members owning 10% or more of the membership voting power. [Section

322B.336] Unless otherwise stated in articles, the operating agreement, or a special LLC Act provision, at least ten days' and no more than 60 days' notice must be given of a members' meeting. [Section 322B.34] Unless otherwise stated in the articles or operating agreement, a quorum for members' meetings is a majority of the membership voting power. [Section 322B.353]

Board of governors' meetings may be held as provided in the articles or operating agreement. [Section 322B.643] Unless otherwise stated in the articles or operating agreement, governors' meetings can be held only after at least ten days' notice. [Section 322B.643] A quorum for governors' meetings is a majority of the number of governors unless otherwise stated in the articles or operating agreement. [Section 322B.65] Generally, governors take action by a majority of those present at a governors' meeting. [Section 322B.653] Unless otherwise provided in the articles, governors may take action by written consent of all governors. [Section 322B.656]

Again, these governor-management rules are complex and riddled with exceptions. If you wish to follow them, see the LLC Act sections noted above. We expect most LLCs will allow management by unanimous vote of members instead. [Section 322B.606]

Amendments

Amendments to articles must be approved by the majority vote of LLC members. Section 322B.15 of the LLC Act has specific rules for calling, noticing, and holding a meeting of members to amend the articles. As an alternative, all members can approve the amendments by written consent. [Section 322B.35]

Amendments to the operating agreement are normally reserved for the governors, but governors are not allowed to make certain decisions (changing qualifications, terms of office, and decreasing number of governors, for example). [Section 322B.603] Again, we assume smaller LLCs will wish to avoid governor-management rules and, instead, will approve amendments to the operating agreement by unanimous consent of members. [Section 322B.606]

Admission of Members

No statutory rule was found regarding issuance of new memberships. Unless otherwise stated in the articles, the admission of a transferee as a member must be approved by unanimous written consent of the nontransferring members. [Section 322B.313]

Withdrawal of Members

A member has the legal power to withdraw at any time from a Minnesota LLC. Also, a member cannot be expelled from the LLC except as provided in the articles of organization. If a member's resignation violates the operating agreement, the member is liable to the LLC for damages caused by the resignation. [Section 322B.306] No specific provision was found in the LLC Act that says how much the member is entitled to receive upon withdrawal in the absence of a provision in the operating agreement. Section 322B.51 simply says that a member is entitled to receive distributions prior to the termination of the LLC only as specified in the LLC operating agreement or by the act of the board of governors (managers) of the LLC.

Continuation of the LLC

The LLC automatically dissolves upon the occurrence of an event that terminates the continued membership of a member, but only if: (A) the articles of organization or a member control agreement specifically provides that the termination causes dissolution, and in that event only as provided in the articles or member control agreement; or (B) if the membership of the last or sole member terminates, and the legal representative of that last or sole member does not cause the LLC to admit at least one member within 180 days after the termination. [Section 322B.80]

Special Statutory Rules

The chief manager of the LLC shall:

1) have general active management of the business of the LLC

2) sign and deliver in the name of the LLC documents related to LLC business, including deeds, mortgages, bonds, and contracts

3) maintain records and certify all proceedings of the board of governors and the members, and

4) preside at meetings of the board of governors, and see that all orders of the board of governors are carried out. [Section 322B.673]

Again, we see the chief manager as the CEO of the LLC. If you have all members make management decisions in place of the board (as we expect most smaller LLCs will do to avoid cumbersome statutory rules), the chief manager's primary responsibilities will be acting as first-in-command in running the LLC and performing the ministerial functions listed in the second and third items above.

MISSISSIPPI

LLC Filing Office

Mississippi Secretary of State
Corporate Division
P.O. Box 136
Jackson, MS 39205-0136
Telephone: 601-359-1633
Toll-free: 800-256-3494
www.sos.state.ms.us/busserv/corp/
jer_corporations.asp

State LLC Act

The Mississippi LLC Act is contained in Title 79 (Corporations, Associations and Partnerships) of the Mississippi Code, Chapter 29, starting with Section 79-29-101, and is browseable from the following Web page (select Mississippi, then Title 79, then Chapter 29 to begin browsing the LLC Act):
www.michie.com

State Tax Office

Mississippi State Tax Commission, Jackson
www.mstc.state.ms.us

Manager Election

Unless otherwise provided by the certificate of formation or operating agreement, managers are elected or removed, and manager vacancies are filled, by members (presumably, by normal membership voting rules). [Section 79-29-401]

Meeting Requirements

Unless otherwise stated in the certificate of formation or operating agreement, members are given one vote each, with a majority vote required to take membership action. Rules for notice, time, place, and quorum for members' meetings and action by written consent by members may be provided in the certificate of formation or the LLC operating agreement. [Section 79-29-304] Managers take action by a majority vote of the managers unless otherwise provided in the certificate of formation or operating agreement. [Section 79-29-401] Rules for notice, time, place, and quorum for managers' meetings, and for action by written consent of the managers, were not found in the Act. Presumably, these may be provided in the certificate of formation or the LLC operating agreement.

Amendments

Unless otherwise provided in the certificate of formation or operating agreement, all members must agree to amend the certificate. [Section 79-29-202] Amendments to the operating agreement must be by approval of all members. [Section 79-29-306]

Admission of Members

Unless otherwise provided in the certificate of formation or operating agreement, new memberships must be issued with the written consent of all members. [Section 79-29-301] Admission of a transferee as a member must be approved by the unanimous consent of all nontransferring members, or as provided in the certificate of formation or operating agreement. [Section 79-29-704]

Withdrawal of Members

If not prohibited by the certificate of formation or operating agreement, a member can withdraw from the LLC at any time upon 30 days' written notice to the other members. If the withdrawal is not prohibited by the operating agreement, but is otherwise in violation of the operating agreement, the member can be held personally liable for financial damages caused by the withdrawal from the LLC. [Section 79-29-307(3)]

Upon dissociation, a dissociating member is entitled to receive any distribution to which he or she is entitled under the certificate of formation or limited liability company agreement and, if not otherwise provided therein, the dissociating member is entitled to receive, within a reasonable time after the dissociation, the fair value of his or her interest in the limited liability company as of the date of dissociation based upon his or her right to share in distributions from the limited liability company. [Section 79-29-602]

Continuation of the LLC

A membership vote to continue the LLC after the dissociation of a member (cessation or termination of a membership interest) is not required. [Section 79-29-801]

MISSOURI

LLC Filing Office

Secretary of State
Corporation Division
P.O. Box 778
Jefferson City, MO 65102
Telephone: 573-751-4153
Toll-free: 866-223-6535
www.sos.mo.gov/business/corporations/Default.asp

State LLC Act

The Missouri LLC Act is contained in Title XXIII (Corporations, Associations, and Partnerships) of the Missouri Statutes, Chapter 347, starting with Section 347.010, and is browseable from the following Web page:

www.moga.state.mo.us/STATUTES/C347.HTM

State Tax Office

Department of Revenue, Jefferson City
http://dor.mo.gov/tax/

Manager Election

Unless otherwise stated in the articles or operating agreement, managers are elected for an indefinite term and are removed and replaced by a majority vote of the members (with members given one vote each). [Section 347.079]

Meeting Requirements

Rules for voting by members and managers, and notice, time, place, and quorum for members' and managers' meetings, are as may be provided in the LLC operating agreement. [Section 347.081] Unless otherwise provided in the articles or operating agreement, action may be taken by unanimous written consent by members or managers in lieu of a meeting. [Section 347.083]

Amendments

Unless otherwise provided in the articles or operating agreement, all members shall approve amendments to the operating agreement or to the articles to change from member-management to manager-management, or vice versa. [Section 347.079]

Admission of Members

Unless otherwise provided in the articles or operating agreement, new memberships must be issued with the approval of all members. [Section 347.079] The admission of a transferee as a member is governed by the operating agreement. [Section 347.113]

Withdrawal of Members

Unless otherwise provided in the articles or operating agreement, a member can withdraw from the LLC at any time upon 90 days' written notice to other members. If the withdrawal is not prohibited by the operating agreement, but is otherwise in violation of the operating agreement, the member can be held personally liable for financial damages caused by the withdrawal. [Section 347.121]

Unless otherwise provided in the operating agreement, generally, a resigned member (except one who assigns his or her interest to another person in violation of the operating agreement or without the consent of all other members) has a right to receive the fair value of the membership interest (the member must demand payment within 180 days of withdrawal). If the withdrawal is a breach of the operating agreement, the value of the goodwill of the business is excluded from the computation of the value of the LLC used to value the resigning member's interest, and the LLC can offset any amount payable to the member by damages caused by the member's withdrawal. [Section 347.103]

Continuation of the LLC

A vote to continue the LLC after the dissociation (cessation or termination of a membership interest) of a member is not required. But, except as provided in the operating agreement, a majority (in number) of the remaining members are allowed to vote to dissolve the LLC within 90 days of the dissociation. [Section 347.137]

Special Statutory Rules

A promise by a member to make a contribution to the LLC must be in writing to be enforceable. [Section 347.099]

The written consent of all members is required to voluntarily dissolve the LLC. [Section 347.137]

MONTANA

LLC Filing Office

Montana Secretary of State
Corporation Bureau
P.O. Box 202801
Helena, MT 59620-2801
Telephone: 406-444-3665
http://sos.state.mt.us/BSB/index.asp

State LLC Act

The Montana LLC Act is contained in Title 35 (Corporations, Partnerships, and Associations) of the Montana Code, Chapter 8, starting with Section 35-8-101, and is browseable from the following Web page (select Title 35, then Chapter 8):
http://data.opi.state.mt.us/bills/mca_toc/index.htm

State Tax Office

Department of Revenue, Helena
http://mt.gov/revenue/default.asp

Manager Election

Unless otherwise provided in the articles or operating agreement, managers are elected for an indefinite term and removed and replaced by the consent of more than one-half the members. [Section 35-8-402]

Meeting Requirements

Unless otherwise provided in the articles or operating agreement, the approval of more than one-half the members (or managers, in a manager-managed LLC) is required for member (or manager) decisions. Presumably, members and managers are given one vote each unless otherwise stated in the articles or operating agreement. [Section 35-8-403] Rules for notice, time, place, and quorum for members' and managers' meetings, and action by written consent by members and managers, were not found in the LLC Act. Presumably, these may be provided in the LLC articles or operating agreement.

Amendments

Unless otherwise stated in the articles or operating agreement, approval of all LLC members is required to amend the articles or the operating agreement. [Section 35-8-403]

Admission of Members

Unless otherwise provided in the articles or operating agreement, new memberships must be issued with the written consent of all members. [Section 35-8-801] Unless otherwise stated in the operating agreement, the admission of a transferee as a member must be approved by unanimous consent of the nontransferring members. [Section 35-8-707]

Withdrawal of Members

Unless otherwise provided in the operating agreement, a member has the power to dissociate from an LLC at any time, rightfully or wrongfully, pursuant to Section 35-8-803(1). A member that wrongfully dissociates is liable to the LLC and the other members for damages caused by the dissociation. The liability is in addition to any other obligation of the member to the LLC or to the other members. If an LLC does not dissolve and wind up its business as a result of a member's wrongful dissociation, damages sustained by the company for the wrongful dissociation must be offset against distributions otherwise due the member after the dissociation. [Section 35-8-804]

Continuation of the LLC

A membership vote to continue the LLC after the dissociation of a member (cessation or termination of a membership interest) is not required. [Section 35-8-901]

Special Statutory Rules

In a member-managed LLC, LLC property may be transferred by a document signed by a member on behalf of the LLC. In a manager-managed LLC, any manager can execute such a transfer document. [Section 35-8-702]

NEBRASKA

LLC Filing Office

Nebraska Secretary of State
Corporate Division
P.O. Box 94608
Lincoln, NE 68509
Telephone: 402-471-4079
www.sos.state.ne.us/business/corp_serv/

State LLC Act

The Nebraska LLC Act is contained in Chapter 21 (Corporations and Other Companies) of the Nebraska Statutes, starting with Section 21-2601, and is browseable from the Web page listed below (click the Statutes tab, select Chapter 21, then scroll down to Section 21-2601 to begin browsing the LLC Act):

http://uniweb.legislature.ne.gov/legaldocs/search.php

State Tax Office

Department of Revenue, Lincoln
www.revenue.state.ne.us/index.html

Manager Election

Managers are elected by members for terms according to rules set out in the LLC operating agreement. [Section 21-2615]

Meeting Requirements

Unless otherwise stated in the articles or operating agreement, management power (voting power) of the members is according to each member's capital account balance in the LLC. [Section 21-2615] No rule is stated for management power of managers (presumably, each manager gets one vote in a manager-managed LLC unless otherwise stated in the articles or operating agreement). Rules for the notice, time, place, and quorum for members' and managers' meetings, and for action by written consent by members and managers, were not found in the LLC Act. Presumably, these may be provided in the LLC articles or operating agreement.

Amendments

No statutory rules were found for amendments to the articles or operating agreement (presumably, voting for amendments is according to provisions in the operating agreement).

Admission of Members

No statutory rule was found for issuance of new memberships (presumably, this can be done according to the operating agreement). Unless otherwise provided in the articles or operating agreement, the admission of a transferee as a member must be approved by written consent of two-thirds of a majority in interest (presumably, a majority of capital and profits interests in the LLC of nontransferring members). [Section 21-2621]

Withdrawal of Members

In the absence of a contrary provision in the articles or operating agreement, unless all members agree otherwise, a withdrawing member has no right to a return of capital upon withdrawal but is granted the status of a transferee of an interest (has a right to a share of continuing profits and distributions made to all members). [Section 21-2619]

Continuation of the LLC

A vote to continue the LLC after the termination of a membership is not required.

Special Statutory Rules

The members (or managers in a manager-managed LLC) of the LLC are liable to the same extent as corporate officers for the LLC's unpaid taxes. [Section 21-2612]

Only members (or managers in a manager-managed LLC) may contract debts or transfer property on behalf of the LLC. [Sections 21-2616 and 21-2617]

NEVADA

LLC Filing Office

Secretary of State
New Filings Section
202 North Carson Street
Carson City, NV 89701
Telephone: 775-684-5708

Filings may also be made at the Secretary of State Satellite Office in Las Vegas: 702-486-2880

http://sos.state.nv.us/comm_rec/index.htm

State LLC Act

The Nevada LLC Act is contained in Title 7 (Business Associations; Securities; Commodities), Chapter 86 of the Nevada Statutes, starting with Section 86.011, and is browseable from the following Web page (select Statutes and Regulations, then click on NRS Chapter 86 Limited Liability Companies).

http://sos.state.nv.us/comm_rec/index.htm

State Tax Office

Department of Taxation, Carson City
http://tax.state.nv.us

Manager Election

Managers are elected by members for terms according to rules set out in the LLC operating agreement. [Section 86.291]

Meeting Requirements

Unless otherwise provided in the articles or operating agreement, management power (voting power) is vested in members according to their current capital account balances. No rule is stated for manager voting. [Section 86.291] Rules for the notice, time, place, and quorum for members' and managers' meetings, and for action by written consent by members and managers, were not found in the LLC Act. Presumably, these may be provided in the LLC articles or operating agreement.

Amendments

Unless otherwise provided in the articles or operating agreement, amendments to the operating agreement must be approved by all members. [Section 86.286]

Admission of Members

No statutory rule was found for issuance of new memberships in the LLC (presumably, according to rules stated in the operating agreement). Unless otherwise provided in the articles or operating agreement, the admission of a transferee as a member must be approved by a majority in interest of the nontransferring members (by nontransferring members owning a majority of the rights to LLC profits). [Sections 86.351 and 86.065]

Withdrawal of Members

Generally, a member may not withdraw until the dissolution of the LLC, unless as otherwise provided by law, the articles, or the operating agreement. Upon withdrawal, unless provided otherwise by law, the articles, or the operating agreement, a member is entitled to receive the fair value of the membership interest within a reasonable time after withdrawal. [Section 86.331]

Continuation of the LLC

A vote to continue the LLC after termination of a membership is not required.

Special Statutory Rules

Only members (or managers in a manager-managed LLC) may contract debts on behalf of the LLC. One or more managers may transfer title to property in a manager-managed LLC. In a member-managed LLC, title to LLC property may be transferred by any member. [Sections 86.301 and 86.311]

NEW HAMPSHIRE

LLC Filing Office

New Hampshire Secretary of State
Corporation Division
Department of State
107 North Main Street
Concord, NH 03301
Telephone: 603-271-3246
www.sos.nh.gov/corporate/

State LLC Act

The New Hampshire LLC Act is contained in Title XXVIII (Partnerships), Chapter 304C of the New Hampshire Statutes, starting with Section 304-C:1, and is browseable from the Web page listed below (select Title XXVIII Partnerships, then click Chapter 304-C to see a listing of the LLC Act sections):

www.gencourt.state.nh.us/rsa/html/nhtoc.htm

State Tax Office

Department of Revenue Administration, Concord
www.nh.gov/revenue/

Manager Election

Election, removal, replacement, and terms of office of managers are as may be provided in the operating agreement. [Section 304-C:31]

Meeting Requirements

Unless otherwise provided in the operating agreement, consent of more than one-half the number of members (or managers in a manager-managed LLC) is required for membership (or manager) action. Rules for notice, time, place, and quorum for members' and managers' meetings, and action by written consent by members or managers, may be provided in the LLC certificate of formation or operating agreement. Unless otherwise provided in the certificate of formation, members and managers may take action without a meeting (presumably, by normal voting rules specified in the agreement or under the default membership voting rule noted above). [Sections 304-C:24 and 304-C:31]

If a member-managed LLC is managed by less than all its members (if one or more members are issued a nonvoting membership interest), and if a meeting of members has not been held during the past 240 days, any member may demand a meeting to be held within 30 days of the demand. Unless otherwise provided in the certificate of formation or operating agreement, notice must be given of the meeting. A quorum for this meeting is one more than one-half the number of all members, unless otherwise provided in the operating agreement or certificate. At the meeting, the members having management of the LLC must report on LLC affairs. [Section 304-C:24]

Amendments

Unless otherwise stated in the certificate of formation or operating agreement, the approval of all members is required to amend the operating agreement. [Section 304-C:24] No statutory voting rule was found for amendment of the certificate of formation.

Admission of Members

New memberships are issued according to provisions in the operating agreement. If the operating agreement does not provide a procedure, the admission of a new member occurs after the consent of all members and when reflected on LLC records. [Section 304-C:23] Unless otherwise stated in the operating agreement, the admission of a transferee must be approved by unanimous consent of the nontransferring members. [Section 304-C:46]

Withdrawal of Members

If not prohibited by the operating agreement, a member can withdraw from the LLC at any time upon 30 days' written notice to the other members. Unless otherwise provided in the operating agreement, if the LLC has a limited term or is formed for a particular undertaking (project), the withdrawal of a member before the end of the term or the accomplishment of the undertaking is a breach of the certificate or operating agreement. If the withdrawal is a breach of the operating agreement or is based upon wrongful conduct of the member, the LLC may offset the amount paid to the withdrawing member by the amount of damages caused by the

breach or wrongful conduct, including the cost of obtaining replacement services owed by the member. [Section 304-C:27(III)]

Unless otherwise provided in the operating agreement, a dissociating (withdrawing) member is not entitled to be paid for the value of the membership interest, but has the status of an assignee of an interest, and is entitled only to the continuing payments of profits and other distributions made to all members. [Section 304-C:41]

Continuation of the LLC

A vote to continue the LLC after the termination of a membership is not required.

NEW JERSEY

LLC Filing Office

New Jersey Department of Treasury
Division of Revenue/Corporate Filing Unit
P.O. Box 308
Trenton, NJ 08646
Telephone: 609-292-9292
www.state.nj.us/njbgs/

State LLC Act

The New Jersey LLC Act is contained in Title 42 (Partnerships and Partnership Associations), Chapter 2B of the New Jersey Statutes, starting with Section 42:2B-1, and is browseable from the following Web page (select Statutes in the left pane, then select Browse by Table of Contents, then expand Title 42, and scroll to Section 42:2B-1):

www.njleg.state.nj.us

State Tax Office

Division of Taxation, Trenton
www.state.nj.us/treasury/taxation

Manager Election

Managers are chosen as provided in the operating agreement. [Section 42:2B-27]

Meeting Requirements

Rules for voting, notice, time, place, and quorum for members' and managers' meetings, and actions by written consent by members or managers, may be provided in the operating agreement. Unless otherwise provided in the operating agreement, members vote in proportion to their current ownership of the profits interests in the LLC, with the approval of members owning more than 50% of profits interests necessary to take membership action. [Sections 42:2B-22, 42:2B-27, and 42:2B-29]

Amendments

Amendments to operating agreements are approved as provided in the operating agreement. [Section 42:2B-22] No statutory rule was found for approval of amendments to the certificate of formation.

Admission of Members

New memberships are issued according to provisions in the operating agreement; if the operating agreement does not provide procedure, admission of a new member occurs after consent of all members and when reflected on LLC records. [Section 42:2B-21] Except as provided in the operating agreement, the admission of a transferee must be approved by all the nontransferring members. [Section 42:2B-46]

Withdrawal of Members

The operating agreement may prohibit a member from resigning from the LLC. If the operating agreement is silent on the issue, a member may resign after a minimum of six months' notice to the LLC and each other member and manager. [Section 42:2B-38] Unless provided otherwise in the operating agreement, a member is entitled to receive the fair value of the membership interest, based upon the net present value of his or her right to share in LLC distributions, less all applicable valuation discounts (due to lack of liquidity, relative size of holding, absence of trading market, and comparable factors), within a reasonable time after resignation. If the resignation is a breach of the agreement, the LLC may offset the amount due to the member by the amount of damages caused by the breach. [Section 42:2B-39]

Continuation of the LLC

A vote to continue the LLC after the termination of a membership is not required. But note that the LLC automatically dissolves 90 days after the date on which the LLC has no remaining members unless a member is admitted within the 90 days. [Section 42:2B-48]

Special Statutory Rules

Except as otherwise provided in the operating agreement, the written consent of all members is required to voluntarily dissolve the LLC. [Section 42:2B-48]

NEW MEXICO

LLC Filing Office

Public Regulation Commission
Corporations Bureau
Chartered Documents Division
P.O. Box 1269
Santa Fe, NM 87504
Telephone: 505-827-4508
Toll-free: 800-947-4722
www.nmprc.state.nm.us/cb.htm

State LLC Act

The New Mexico LLC Act is contained in Chapter 53 (Corporations), Article 19 of the New Mexico Statutes, starting with Section 53-19-1, and is browseable from the following Web page (first select Statues in the left panel, then in the left panel select the folder titled New Mexico Statutes and Court Rules, select Statutory Chapters in New Mexico Statutes Annotated 1978, then scroll down in the right panel and select 53. Corporations, then select 19. Limited Liability Companies, 53-19-1 through 53-19-74 to browse the sections of the Act):
http://legis.state.nm.us/lcs/default.asp

State Tax Office

Taxation and Revenue Department, Santa Fe
www.state.nm.us/tax

Manager Election

Unless otherwise provided in the articles or operating agreement, managers must be elected for an indefinite term and can be removed only by a majority of the voting power of LLC members. [Section 53-19-15]

Meeting Requirements

Except as provided in the articles or operating agreement, members must vote in proportion to their capital account balances in the LLC, with a majority of the voting power necessary to take membership action. Managers can take action by a majority vote of the managers. [Section 53-19-17] Rules for the notice, time, place, and quorum for members' and managers' meetings, and for actions by written consent of the members or managers, were not found in the LLC Act. Presumably, these may be provided in the LLC articles or operating agreement.

Amendments

Unless otherwise provided in the articles or operating agreement, the approval of a majority of the voting power of members is required to amend the articles or operating agreement. [Section 53-19-17]

Admission of Members

Unless otherwise provided in the articles or operating agreement, new memberships must be issued with the written consent of all members. [Section 53-19-36] Unless otherwise stated in the articles or operating agreement, the admission of a transferee as a member must be approved by unanimous consent of the nontransferring members. [Section 53-19-33]

Withdrawal of Members

A member may withdraw from an LLC with a perpetual existence if withdrawal is not prohibited by the articles or operating agreement. A member may withdraw from an LLC with a limited term if allowed to do so in the articles or operating agreement. [Section 53-19-38]

Upon withdrawal, if the articles and operating agreement do not provide for a distribution to a withdrawing member, the member is entitled to receive the fair market value of the interest within a reasonable period after withdrawal. [Section 53-19-24]

Continuation of the LLC

A vote to continue the LLC after the termination of a membership is not required.

Special Statutory Rules

Unless otherwise provided in the articles or operating agreement, a member must be removed by approval of all other members. [Section 53-19-17]

Unless otherwise provided in the articles or operating agreement, the approval of a majority of the voting power of members is required to sell all LLC assets or voluntarily dissolve the LLC. [Sections 53-19-17 and 53-19-39]

In a member-managed LLC, LLC property may be transferred by a document signed by any member on behalf of the LLC. In a manager-managed LLC, any manager can execute such a transfer document. [Section 53-19-30]

NEW YORK

LLC Filing Office

Department of State
Division of Corporations
State Records and Uniform Commercial Code
41 State Street
Albany, NY 12231
Telephone: 518-473-2492
www.dos.state.ny.us/corp/corpwww.html

State LLC Act

The New York LLC Law is contained in Chapter 34 of the New York Consolidated Laws, starting with Section 101, and is browseable from the following Web page (click New York State Laws, then New York State Consolidated Laws, then Limited Liability Company Law, then select Article headings to view each part of the law):

http://assembly.state.ny.us/leg

State Tax Office

Taxation and Finance Department, Albany

www.tax.state.ny.us

Manager Election

Unless otherwise provided in the operating agreement, managers are elected annually by the members. [Section 413] Unless otherwise provided in the operating agreement, managers may be removed or replaced and manager vacancies filled by a vote of members owning a majority of the profits interests in the LLC. [Section 414]

Meeting Requirements

The operating agreement may set rules for notice, time, place, and quorum for members' and managers' meetings and action by written consent by members or managers. [Sections 418 and 419]

Unless otherwise stated in the operating agreement, members vote in proportion to their share in the current profits of the LLC, and the approval of members owning a majority of the profits interests is necessary to take membership action. [Section 402]

Unless otherwise provided in the operating agreement, the following membership rules apply to the LLC:

- Members are required to hold meetings annually at the LLC office; one of the items of business is to elect managers of the LLC. [Sections 403 and 413]

- Members owning a majority of the profits interests in the LLC constitute a quorum for membership meetings. [Section 404]

- Notice of meetings must be given to members no fewer than ten nor more than 60 days prior to the meeting (for a special meeting, it must state the purpose of the meeting). [Section 405]

- Members may sign a waiver of notice prior to or after the date of a membership meeting. [Section 406]

- Members can take action by written consent if the number of members signing would have been sufficient to approve the action at a meeting at which all members were present and voted (generally, this means members owning

a majority of the profits interests must sign a written consent to take action). Notice of action by written consent must be sent to members who did not sign the consent form. [Section 407]

Unless otherwise provided in the operating agreement, managers take action by approval of a majority of the managers or by the written consent of all managers. [Section 408] Quorum, notice, and frequency rules for manager meetings were not found in the Act. Presumably, these may be provided in the operating agreement.

Amendments

Unless otherwise provided in the operating agreement or under the LLC Act for special amendments (see below), amendments to the articles or operating agreement require the approval of at least a majority in interest (that is, a majority of the profits interests in the LLC) of the members. But a majority of the managers of a manager-managed LLC may adopt the following amendments to the articles without membership approval:

1) change of the registered agent name or address

2) change of LLC address for service of process, and

3) correction of an error in the articles. [Sections 213 and 402]

Amendments to the articles or operating agreement that accomplish any of the following purposes must be approved by all members adversely affected by such amendments:

- a change in contributions made by members

- a change in the allocation of tax items, such as allocations of profits or losses, or

- a change in the manner of computing distributions made to members.

Admission of Members

Unless otherwise provided in the operating agreement, new memberships must be issued with the approval of members owning at least a majority of the interests in LLC profits. [Sections 402 and 602] Except as provided in the operating agreement, the admission of a transferee as a member must be approved by the vote or written consent of a majority in interest of nontransferring members (nontransferring members owning more than 50% of the interests in LLC profits). [Section 604]

Notwithstanding anything to the contrary under applicable law, an operating agreement may provide that a membership interest may not be assigned prior to the dissolution and winding up of the LLC. [Section 606]

Withdrawal of Members

A member may withdraw as a member of an LLC only in accordance with the operating agreement, at the time or upon the happening of events specified in the operating agreement. Notwithstanding anything to the contrary under applicable law, unless an operating agreement provides otherwise, a member may not withdraw from an LLC prior to its dissolution and winding up. [Section 606]

If not otherwise provided in the operating agreement, a member is entitled to receive the fair value of the interest within a reasonable period after withdrawing. [Section 509]

Continuation of the LLC

A membership vote to continue the LLC after the dissociation of a member (cessation or termination of a membership interest) is not required. [Section 701]

Special Statutory Rules

Unless otherwise provided in the articles or operating agreement, the approval of members owning at least two-thirds of the interests in the profits of the LLC is required to sell all LLC assets or to voluntarily dissolve the LLC. [Sections 402 and 701]

NORTH CAROLINA

LLC Filing Office

North Carolina Department of the Secretary of State
Corporations Division
P.O. Box 29622
Raleigh, NC 27626-0622
Telephone: 919-807-2225
www.secretary.state.nc.us/corporations

State LLC Act

The North Carolina LLC Act is contained in Chapter 57C of the North Carolina Statutes, starting with Section 57C-1-01, and is browseable from the following Web page (click NC General Statutes at the bottom of the page, then click Table of Contents in the right-hand box, then select Chapter 57C, North Carolina Limited Liability Company Act):
www.secstate.state.nc.us
State Tax Office
Department of Revenue, Raleigh
www.dor.state.nc.us

Manager Election

Managers are designated for an indefinite term as provided in the operating agreement. [Section 57C-3-21]

Meeting Requirements

Except as provided in the articles or operating agreement, members and managers have equal voting rights (presumably, one vote each), and member or manager action requires approval of a majority of the members or managers. [Section 57C-3-21] Rules for the notice, time, place, and quorum for members' and managers' meetings, and for actions by written consent by members or managers, were not found in the LLC Act. Presumably, these may be provided in the articles or operating agreement.

Amendments

Unless the articles or operating agreement state otherwise, amendments to the articles or operating agreement require the approval of all members. [Sections 57C-2-22 and 57C-3-03]

Admission of Members

Unless otherwise provided in the articles or operating agreement, new memberships must be issued with the approval of all members. [Section 57C-3-01] Except as provided in the articles or operating agreement, the admission of a transferee as a member must be approved by the unanimous approval of nontransferring members. [Section 57C-5-04]

Withdrawal of Members

A member may withdraw only at the time or upon the happening of the events specified in the articles of organization or a written operating agreement. [Section 57C-5-06] If not otherwise provided in the operating agreement, a member is entitled to receive the fair value of the interest within a reasonable period after withdrawal. [Section 57C-5-07]

Continuation of the LLC

A membership vote to continue the LLC after the dissociation of a member (cessation or termination of a membership interest) is not required. [Section 57C-6-01]

Special Statutory Rules

Unless otherwise provided in the articles or operating agreement, the approval of all members is required to sell all LLC assets or to voluntarily dissolve the LLC. [Sections 57C-3-03 and 57C-6-01]

The LLC must indemnify (pay back) managers for payments and personal liabilities incurred in carrying out authorized business for the LLC. Unless limited by the articles or operating agreement, a member or manager must be indemnified for expenses (lawyers' fees) incurred in defending any proceeding (lawsuit) based upon the member's or manager's status as a member or manager. [Section 57C-3-31]

NORTH DAKOTA

LLC Filing Office

North Dakota Secretary of State
Corporations Division
600 East Boulevard Avenue
Bismarck, ND 58505-0500
Telephone: 701-328-4284
Toll free: 800-352-0867 ext. 4284
www.nd.gov/sos/businessserv/

State LLC Act

The North Dakota LLC Act is contained in Title 10-32 of the North Dakota Century Code, starting with Section 10-32-01, and is browseable from the Web page listed below (click 10 Corporations, then select Chapter 10-32 in the left-panel table of contents):

www.legis.nd.gov/information/statutes/cent-code.html

State Tax Office

Office of State Tax Commission, Bismarck
www.nd.gov/tax/

Manager Election

The North Dakota LLC Act presupposes management by a board of governors (management by governors is similar to the vesting of management power in a corporate board of directors). The law specifies that LLCs must have one or more governors, elected by the members, who serve until reelection at the next regular meeting of members, or for an indefinite term if no such meeting is scheduled in the operating agreement (alternatively, a fixed term for governors of up to five years may be specified in the operating agreement). [Section 10-32-72] The LLC Act has a slew of corporate-like rules and procedures that divide action and authority between the governors and the members of the LLC, which we believe most smaller LLCs will find unwieldy. Section 10-32-69(2), fortunately, recognizes that LLCs may wish to adopt membership management. That section says that the LLC members may act in the place of the governors as long as they make management decisions by unanimous vote; this is usually easy to achieve in smaller LLCs, and we assume most smaller North Dakota LLCs will opt for membership management under this Section of the Act. To reinforce this member-management election, the LLC operating agreement should require a unanimous membership vote for management decisions by members pursuant to Section 10-32-69(2).

If you decide to go along with the statutory scheme and opt for management by governors, see Sections 10-32-69 and following of the LLC Act to learn more about the default statutory governor-management scheme, and special rules that apply to board of governor action.

To make matters more complicated, North Dakota law requires the appointment or election of two persons who function as the LLC president and treasurer but who are called managers. [Section 10-32-88] Don't be confused by this nonstandard nomenclature; the real managers of your LLC are your governors (in a governor-managed LLC) or your members (in a member-managed LLC where members take action by unanimous agreement as explained above).

Board of governors' election procedures are as specified in the articles or operating agreement. [Section 10-32-71] Unless a fixed term is provided in the articles or operating agreement, governors serve an indefinite term until the next regular meeting of members. If a fixed term is specified, it cannot exceed five years. [Section 10-32-72] Unless otherwise provided in the articles, membership voting for governors is by cumulative voting (similar to how shareholders vote for directors in larger corporations). [Section 10-32-76] Unless otherwise provided in the articles or operating agreement, removal of governors requires the same membership vote as in a vote to elect them. [Section 10-32-78] Unless otherwise provided in the articles or operating agreement, vacancies on the board of governors may be filled by a person approved by a majority of remaining governors. [Section 10-32-79]

These governor-management rules are complex and riddled with exceptions. If you wish to follow them, see the LLC Act sections noted above. We expect most LLCs will allow management by unanimous vote of members instead. [Section 10-32-69(2)]

Meeting Requirements

Unless otherwise provided in the articles, members vote in proportion to the value reflected in the LLC records of each member's capital contribution to the LLC. [Section 10-32-40.1] Unless otherwise provided in the articles, the approval of a majority of the membership voting power present at a meeting (or a majority of a quorum, whichever is greater) is required for membership action. [Section 10-32-42] But remember, when members act as managers (governors) of the LLC (this is usually the case when members are asked to take action in a smaller LLC that wishes to avoid the governor-management

rules), members must act by unanimous approval. [Section 10-32-69(2)] Members may take action by unanimous written consent without a meeting (the articles may lower this written consent requirement to written consent of members required to take action at a meeting at which all members were present). [Section 10-32-43] Unless otherwise specified in the articles or operating agreement, regular meetings of members need not be held, unless demanded by a member under certain conditions. [Section 10-32-38] Special members' meetings may be called by the LLC president, two or more governors, or members owning 10% or more of the membership voting power. [Section 10-32-39] Unless otherwise stated in the articles, the operating agreement, or a special LLC Act provision, at least ten days' and no more than 50 days' notice must be given of a members' meeting. [Section 10-32-40] Unless otherwise stated in the articles or operating agreement, a quorum for members' meetings is a majority of the membership voting power. [Section 10-32-44]

Board of governors' meetings are to be held as provided in the LLC articles or operating agreement. Unless these state otherwise, governors' meetings are to be held on at least ten days' notice. [Section 10-32-80] A quorum for governors' meetings is a majority of the number of governors unless otherwise stated in the articles or operating agreement. [Section 10-32-82] Generally, governors take action by a majority of those present at a governors' meeting (or a majority of a quorum if greater). [Section 10-32-83] Unless otherwise provided in the articles, governors may take action by the written consent of all governors. [Section 10-32-84]

Again, these governor-management rules are complex. If you wish to follow them, see the LLC Act sections noted above. We expect most LLCs will allow management by unanimous vote of members instead. [Section 10-32-69(2)]

Amendments

Amendments to articles must be approved by a majority vote of the members present at the meeting (at which a quorum is present). Section 10-32-16 of the LLC Act has specific rules for calling, noticing, and holding a meeting of the members to amend the articles. As an alternative, have all members approve amendments by written consent. [Section 10-32-43]

Amendments to the operating agreement are normally reserved to the governors, but governors are not allowed to make certain decisions (changing qualifications, terms of office, and decreasing number of governors for example). [Section 10-32-68] Again, we assume smaller LLCs will wish to avoid governor-management rules and, instead, will approve amendments to the operating agreement by unanimous consent of members. [Section 10-32-69(2)]

Admission of Members

No statutory rule was found regarding issuance of new memberships. Unless otherwise stated in the LLC's articles, the admission of a transferee as a member must be approved by the unanimous written consent of nontransferring members (but a member may assign full membership rights to another member without the consent of remaining members). [Section 10-32-32]

Withdrawal of Members

A member has the power, though not necessarily the right, to withdraw from the LLC at any time. The withdrawn member is given the status of an assignee of an interest, with the right to receive ongoing profits and other distributions along with the other members (presumably, unless the operating agreement provides otherwise—for example, the operating agreement may specify that the member shall be paid the value of his membership interest upon withdrawal). [Section 10-32-30] If a member withdraws in violation of the articles or operating agreement, the LLC may deduct damages caused by the wrongful withdrawal from the amount paid the member for the interest (this payment occurs on dissolution of the LLC unless provided otherwise in the articles or operating agreement). [Section 10-32-131]

Continuation of the LLC

Except as otherwise provided in the articles, a vote to continue the LLC after termination of a membership is not required. [Section 10-32-109]

Note: This section requires dissolution when the LLC has no remaining members unless the last member or his or her legal representation admits a member within 180 days after the last member's termination.

Special Statutory Rules

The LLC president shall:

1) have general active management of the business of the LLC

2) sign and deliver in the name of the LLC documents related to the business of the LLC, including deeds, mortgages, bonds, and contracts

3) maintain records and certify all proceedings of the board of governors and the members, and

4) preside at meetings of the board of governors, and see that all orders of the board of governors are carried out. [Section 10-32-89]

If you have all members make management decisions in place of the board (as we expect most smaller LLCs will to avoid statutory rules for implementing governor management), the president's primary responsibilities will be acting as first-in-command in running the LLC, and performing the ministerial functions listed in the second and third items above.

Members can vote to voluntarily dissolve the LLC at a meeting called for that purpose by approval of a majority of members. [Section 10-32-111]

OHIO

LLC Filing Office

Ohio Secretary of State
Business Services Division
P.O. Box 670
Columbus, OH 43216
Telephone: 614-466-3910
Toll-free: 1-877-SOS-FILE (1-877-767-3453)
www.sos.state.oh.us/sos/businessservices/corp.aspx

State LLC Act

The Ohio LLC Act is contained in Title XVII (Corporations-Partnerships), Chapter 1705 of the Ohio Statutes, starting with Section 1705.01, and is browseable from the following Web page (click Revised Code, select Title 17 in the left pane, click Chapter 1705, then select each section of the Act you wish to view):

http://onlinedocs.andersonpublishing.com

State Tax Office

Taxation Department, Columbus
http://tax.ohio.gov/

Manager Election

No statutory rules were found. Presumably, managers may be elected, removed, and replaced, and their terms set, according to the LLC articles or operating agreement.

Meeting Requirements

Unless otherwise stated in the LLC operating agreement, membership voting is according to the current capital account balances of each member. [Section 1705.24] Rules for notice, time, place, and quorum for members' and managers' meetings, and action by written consent by members or managers, were not found in the LLC Act. The Act allows members or managers to adopt bylaws to regulate LLC affairs, including rules for members' and managers' meetings (as long as the bylaws are consistent with the articles and operating agreement). [Section 1705.27] We expect most LLCs to adopt these rules as part of their operating agreement, rather than to adopt a separate set of bylaws.

Amendments

No statutory rules for approving amendments were found in the LLC Act. Presumably, the LLC articles and operating agreement may be amended as provided in the articles or operating agreement.

Admission of Members

Unless otherwise provided in the operating agreement, new memberships must be issued with the written consent of all members. [Section 1705.14] Admission of a transferee as a member must be approved by unanimous consent of the nontransferring members, and as may be provided in the LLC operating agreement. [Section 1705.20]

Withdrawal of Members

A member may withdraw only at the time or upon the occurrence of an event specified in the LLC articles or operating agreement. [Section 1705.16]

Continuation of the LLC

A vote to continue the LLC after withdrawal of a membership is not required. [Section 1705.43]

OKLAHOMA

LLC Filing Office

Oklahoma Secretary of State
Business Filing Department
2300 N. Lincoln Blvd., Room 101
Oklahoma City, OK 73105-4897
Telephone: 405-521-3912
www.sos.state.ok.us/business/business_filing.htm

State LLC Act

The Oklahoma LLC Act is contained in Title 18 (Corporations) Oklahoma Statutes, Chapter 32, starting with Section 18-2000. It is browseable from the Web page listed below. First, click Links to Statutes in the left margin. Then click the Expand link for Title 18, Corporations. Finally, scroll down the chapter index to Chapter 32, the Oklahoma LLC Act.

www.sos.state.ok.us/exec_legis/exec_leg_home.htm

State Tax Office

Tax Commission, Oklahoma City
www.oktax.state.ok.us

Manager Election

Unless otherwise provided in the articles or operating agreement, managers are elected by a majority vote (presumably one vote each) of members, and managers are removed by written consent of (presumably all) the members. [Section 2014]

Note: An Oklahoma LLC is managed by its managers unless the articles or operating agreement vest management in its members. [Section 2013] Also, if the articles or operating agreement say that the LLC will be managed without designated managers, members are considered managers under the LLC Act. [Section 2015] Note that this scheme is the reverse of most states, where member-management, rather than manager-management, is the default management scheme. We expect the articles or operating agreement of most smaller LLCs to specifically vest management in the members of the LLC.

Meeting Requirements

Unless otherwise stated in the articles or operating agreement, members vote in proportion to their capital interests in the LLC, with the approval of members owning a majority of the capital interests necessary in order to take membership action. Membership approval by majority voting may be at a meeting or through signed written consents. [Section 2020] Unless otherwise stated in the articles or operating agreement, managers must take action by majority vote. [Section 2018] Rules for notice, time, place, and quorum for members' and managers' meetings were not found in the LLC Act. Presumably, these may be provided in the LLC articles or operating agreement.

Amendments

Unless otherwise provided in the articles or operating agreement, amendments to the articles or operating agreement require approval by a majority vote of the members (presumably, with each member being given one vote). [Section 2020] But note that all members must approve amendments to the articles or operating agreement that:

- reduce the LLC's term of existence
- reduce the vote necessary to dissolve the LLC or sell all its assets
- permit a member to voluntarily withdraw from the LLC, or
- reduce the vote required to amend the articles or operating agreement. [Section 2020]

Admission of Members

No statutory rule was found regarding issuance of new memberships in an LLC. Admission of a transferee as a member must be approved either as stated in the LLC operating agreement or by written consent of the members who hold a majority of capital interests in the LLC (not counting the capital interests being transferred to the new member). [Section 2035]

Withdrawal of Members

Unless specifically permitted by operating agreement, a member may not voluntarily withdraw from the LLC. If the withdrawal is a breach of the operating agreement or is based upon wrongful conduct of the member, the LLC may offset the amount paid to the withdrawing member by the amount of damages caused by the breach or wrongful conduct, including the cost of obtaining replacement services owed by the member. [Section 2036]

If not otherwise provided in the operating agreement, a member is entitled to receive the fair market value of the interest within a reasonable period after withdrawal. Fair market value is defined along standard legal lines as the amount that a willing buyer would pay a willing seller, neither being under a compulsion to buy or sell, and both being cognizant of all relevant facts concerning the value of the dissociating (withdrawing) member's interest. [Section 2027]

Continuation of the LLC

A vote to continue the LLC after the termination of a membership is not required. [Section 2037]

OREGON

LLC Filing Office

Oregon Secretary of State
Corporation Division
Business Registry Section
Public Service Building, Suite 151
255 Capitol Street NE
Salem, OR 97310-1327
Telephone: 503-986-2200
www.filinginoregon.com

State LLC Act

The Oregon LLC Act is contained in Chapter 63 of the Oregon Statutes, starting with Section 63.001, and is browseable from the following Web page:
www.leg.state.or.us/ors/063.html

State Tax Office

Department of Revenue, Salem
http://egov.oregon.gov/DOR/

Manager Election

Unless otherwise provided in the articles or operating agreement, the election and filling of manager positions and removal of managers must be made by a majority vote of the members (with each member given one vote). [Sections 63.145 and 63.150]

Meeting Requirements

Unless otherwise provided in the articles or operating agreement, managers and members have one vote each, with a majority vote necessary to take action by members or managers. Members and managers may take action by unanimous written consent, unless the articles or operating agreement permit written consent approval by a lesser vote of managers or members. [Section 63.150] Rules for the notice, time, place and quorum for members' and managers' meetings were not found in the LLC Act. Presumably, these may be provided in the articles or operating agreement.

Amendments

Unless otherwise provided in the articles or operating agreement, these can only be amended by approval of all LLC members. [Section 63.444]. (But note that Section 63.150 allows amendments to the articles and operating agreement by just a majority of the members—we assume that the unanimous vote requirement, which is typical of many LLC Acts, is the intended requirement.) Managers may make nonsubstantive, technical changes to the articles, as allowed under Section 63.441, without membership approval.

Admission of Members

Unless otherwise provided in the operating agreement, new memberships must be issued with the consent of a majority of members. [Section 63.245] Unless otherwise provided in the articles or operating agreement, a transferee does not become a member until approved by a majority of the nontransferring members. Exception: The transferee of the last remaining membership interest in an Oregon LLC automatically becomes a member. [Section 63.245]

Withdrawal of Members

Unless the articles or operating agreement say that a member cannot withdraw or otherwise limit or restrict a member's power to do so, a member may withdraw upon six months' written notice to the LLC. The articles or operating agreement also may specify an alternate withdrawal procedure. If the withdrawal is a breach of the articles or operating agreement, the LLC may offset the amount paid to the withdrawing member by the amount of damages caused by the breach. Unless otherwise provided in the articles or operating agreement, if the LLC has a limited term or is formed for a particular undertaking (project), the withdrawal of a member before the end of the term or the accomplishment of the undertaking is a breach of the articles or operating agreement. [Section 63.205]

If not otherwise provided in the articles or operating agreement, a member is entitled to receive the fair value of the interest within a reasonable period after withdrawal. [Section 63.215]

Continuation of the LLC

A vote to continue the LLC after the termination of a membership is not required.

Special Statutory Rules

A majority vote of the members is required to sell all LLC assets or approve a transaction in which a member or manager has a personal financial interest. [Section 63.150]

PENNSYLVANIA

LLC Filing Office

Commonwealth of Pennsylvania
Department of State
Corporation Bureau
P.O. Box 8722
Harrisburg, PA 17105-8722
Telephone: 717-787-1057
Toll-free: 888-659-9962
www.dos.state.pa.us/corps/site/default.asp

State LLC Act

The Pennsylvania LLC Act is contained in Title 15 (Corporations and Business Associations), Chapter 89 of the Pennsylvania Statutes, starting with Section 8901. Chapter 89 (the LLC Act) is not posted on a state website as of the date of our research. Please check the state filing office Web page to see if the Pennsylvania LLC Act has been linked to the website. A copy of the LLC Act can be obtained upon request from The Agricultural Law Research and Education Center website listed below (or call the Pennsylvania State Bookstore in Harrisburg—look under state of Pennsylvania listings in directory assistance—and ask about purchasing a copy of the Associations Code that contains the LLC Act):

http://www.dsl.psu.edu/centers/aglawpubs/llc.html

State Tax Office

Department of Revenue, Harrisburg
www.revenue.state.pa.us

Manager Election

Managers are elected as provided in the operating agreement, and, except as provided in the operating agreement, serve for one-year terms (or until a successor is elected). [Sections 8941 and 8903]

Meeting Requirements

Except as provided in the operating agreement, the approval by a majority of the members or managers is necessary to take action on any matter submitted to the members or managers for approval. Rules for the notice, time, place, and quorum for members' and managers' meetings, and actions by written consent of the members or managers, may be provided in the operating agreement. [Section 8942] Presumably, in a manager-managed LLC, members will meet at least once each year to elect managers, unless the operating agreement makes managers' terms indefinite.

Amendments

Except as provided in the operating agreement, amendments to the articles or operating agreement require approval of all LLC members. [Section 8942]

Admission of Members

No statutory rule was found regarding the issuance of new LLC memberships. Unless otherwise stated in the operating agreement, the admission of a transferee as a member must be approved by unanimous written consent of the nontransferring members. [Section 8924]

Withdrawal of Members

An operating agreement may prohibit a member from withdrawing prior to the dissolution of the LLC; if it does and a member attempts to withdraw, the withdrawal is ineffective. [Section 8948]

A member who withdraws is entitled to receive the fair value of the interest within a reasonable period after withdrawal. [Section 8933]

Continuation of the LLC

Except as otherwise provided in the operating agreement, the LLC automatically dissolves after the dissociation of a member (cessation or termination of a membership interest) unless all remaining members vote to continue the LLC within 90 days of the dissociation event. [Section 8971]

RHODE ISLAND

LLC Filing Office

Rhode Island Secretary of State
Corporations Division
148 W. River Street
Providence, RI 02904-2615
Telephone: 401-222-3040
http://www3.sec.state.ri.us/divs/corps

State LLC Act

The Rhode Island LLC Act is contained in Title
7 (Corporations, Associations, and Partnerships),
Chapter 7-16 of the Rhode Island General Laws,
starting with Section 7-16-1, and is browseable from
the following Web page:

www.rilin.state.ri.us/Statutes/TITLE7/7-16/
INDEX.HTM

State Tax Office

Division of Taxation, Providence
www.tax.state.ri.us

Manager Election

Unless otherwise provided in the articles or
operating agreement, managers are to be elected
and removed by a majority vote of LLC members.
[Section 7-16-16]

Meeting Requirements

Unless otherwise provided in the articles or operating agreement, members must vote in proportion
to the value of capital each has contributed to the
LLC. A default voting rule for membership action
at a meeting is not given (presumably, as specified
in the operating agreement), but the Act specifically
requires approval of a majority of capital interests of
all members to approve certain substantial actions,
such as the dissolution of the LLC. Members and
managers may take action by unanimous written
consent, and, if not provided otherwise in the
articles or operating agreement, members can
take action by written consent of the number of
members who would be necessary to approve action
at a meeting at which all members were present; all
nonconsenting members must be given notice of the
approval by less than unanimous written consent of
members. [Section 7-16-21]

Unless otherwise stated in the articles or operating
agreement, managers take action by majority vote,
with each manager given one vote. [Section 7-16-
19]

Rules for notice, time, place, and quorum for
members' and managers' meetings were not found
in the LLC Act. Presumably, these may be provided
in the articles or operating agreement.

Amendments

Unless otherwise provided in the articles or
operating agreement, members owning a majority
of the value of capital contributions made to the
LLC must approve amendments to the articles or
operating agreement. [Section 7-16-21]

Admission of Members

No statutory rule was found regarding issuance of
new memberships in an LLC. Unless otherwise
stated in the operating agreement, the admission
of a transferee as a member must be approved by
unanimous written consent of nontransferring
members. [Section 7-16-36]

Withdrawal of Members

A member may withdraw upon six months'
written notice to the LLC and to each member
and manager. If the withdrawal is a breach of
the operating agreement, the LLC may offset the
amount paid to the withdrawing member by the
amount of damages caused by the breach. [Section
7-16-28.1]

Except as otherwise provided in the operating
agreement, the withdrawal of a member does
not entitle the member to payment for his or
her interest; instead, the member is treated as an
assignee of an interest, with the right to share
ongoing profits and distributions along with the
other members. [Section 7-16-29]

Continuation of the LLC

A vote to continue the LLC after the termination of
a membership is not required. But unless otherwise
provided in the articles or operating agreement,
the LLC automatically dissolves when the last
remaining member loses his or her interest unless
the successor(s) or assignee(s) of the last member
or members agree(s) in writing within 90 days to

admit a new member into the LLC to continue its business. [Section 7-16-39]

Special Statutory Rules

Unless otherwise provided in the articles or operating agreement, members owning a majority of the value of capital contributions made to the LLC must approve a decision to voluntarily dissolve the LLC, sell all its assets, or approve a transaction in which a manager has a personal financial interest. [Section 7-16-21]

SOUTH CAROLINA

LLC Filing Office

South Carolina Secretary of State
Corporations Department
P.O. Box 11350
Columbia, SC 29211
Telephone: 803-734-2158
www.scsos.com/Corporations.htm

State LLC Act

The South Carolina Uniform Limited Liability Company Act of 1996 is contained in Title 33 (Corporations, Partnerships and Associations), Chapter 44 of the South Carolina Code, starting with Section 33-44-101, and is browseable from the Web page listed below (click on Title 33, then select Chapter 44 from the list—chapter numbers are referenced in the right margin; click on the leftmost HTML link to open the chapter as an html page in your browser). Note that the prior LLC Act (Chapter 43) also is available for downloading (repealed January 1, 2001).

http://www.scstatehouse.net/code/statmast.htm

State Tax Office

Department of Revenue, Columbia
www.sctax.org/default.htm

Manager Election

Unless otherwise stated in the articles or operating agreement, managers must be elected, removed, and replaced by the consent of a majority of members. Managers hold office for an indefinite term. [Section 33-44-404]

Meeting Requirements

Unless otherwise stated in the LLC articles or operating agreement, members and managers must approve action by a majority vote. Members and managers may take action by written consent (presumably, by normal voting rules). [Section 33-44-404] Rules for the notice, time, place, and quorum for members' and managers' meetings were not found in the LLC Act. Presumably, these may be provided in the LLC articles or operating agreement.

Amendments

Unless otherwise provided in the articles or operating agreement, consent of all members is required to amend the articles or operating agreement. [Section 33-44-404]

Admission of Members

Unless otherwise provided in the articles or operating agreement, new memberships must be issued with the consent of all members. [Section 33-44-404] Admission of transferee as a member must be approved by unanimous consent of the nontransferring members, and as may be provided in the LLC operating agreement. [Section 33-44-503]

Withdrawal of Members

A member may withdraw upon notice to the LLC. If the withdrawal violates the operating agreement or is prior to the end of a specified term established for the LLC, the LLC may offset the amount paid the withdrawing member by the amount of damages caused by the breach or early withdrawal. [Sections 33-44-601 and 33-44-602]

Generally, a member is entitled to the fair value of the member's interest (different valuation dates are used, depending on whether the LLC has a specified term or a perpetual existence). The LLC must deliver an offer to purchase the interest of the withdrawing member and financial statements to the member within 30 days of the date of withdrawal. The member has a right to bring a court action to determine the fair value of the member's interest if the member and the LLC cannot agree. [Section 33-44-701]

Continuation of the LLC

A membership vote to continue the LLC after the dissociation of a member (cessation or termination of a membership interest) is not required. [Section 33-44-801]

Special Statutory Rules

Unless otherwise provided in the articles or operating agreement, consent of all members is required to authorize transactions that personally benefit managers of the LLC, make interim distributions to members (prior to departure of a member or winding up of the LLC), sell all LLC assets, or voluntarily dissolve the LLC. [Section 33-44-404]

SOUTH DAKOTA

LLC Filing Office

South Dakota Secretary of State
State Capitol
500 East Capitol Ave.
Pierre, SD 57501
Telephone: 605-773-4845
www.sdsos.gov/businessservices/corporations.shtm

State LLC Act

The South Dakota LLC Act is contained in Title 47 (Corporations), Chapter 34 of the South Dakota Codified Laws, starting with Section 47-34-1, and is browseable from the following Web page (click South Dakota, drill down through the links in the left pane, as follows: South Dakota Codified Laws, Title 47, Chapter 47-34):

www.michie.com

State Tax Office

Department of Revenue, Pierre
www.state.sd.us/drr2/revenue.html

Manager Election

Managers are elected for an indefinite term by a majority of members, unless the operating agreement provides otherwise. [Sections 47-34A-103 and 47-34A-404.1]

Meeting Requirements

Generally, unless the operating agreement provides otherwise, each member (and in a manager-managed LLC, each manager) has equal voting and management rights, and a majority of members (or managers) must vote to approve an act or decision. But special matters, such as the amendment of the articles or operating agreement, the admission of new members, or the dissolution of the LLC, must be approved by all members. Managers and members may take action by written consent without a meeting. [Section 47-34A-404.1] Rules for notice, time, place, and quorum for members' and managers' meetings were not found in the LLC Act. Presumably, these may be provided in the LLC articles or operating agreement.

Amendments

Unless otherwise provided in the operating agreement, amendments of the articles or operating agreement must be approved by all members. [Section 47-34A-404.1]

Admission of Members

Unless otherwise provided in the operating agreement, the admission of a new member must be approved by all members. [Section 47-34A-404.1]

Withdrawal of Members

A member may withdraw upon notice to the LLC. If the withdrawal violates the operating agreement or is prior to the end of a specified term established for the LLC, the member is liable to the LLC and the other members for the amount of damages caused by the breach or early withdrawal. [Sections 47-34A-601(1) and 602]

Apparently, unless the operating agreement provides otherwise, a member who withdraws is treated as a transferee, with the right to share ongoing profits and distributions along with the other members prior to the dissolution of the LLC. [Section 47-34A-603]

Continuation of the LLC

A vote to continue the LLC after the termination of a membership is not required. [Section 47-34A-801]

TENNESSEE

LLC Filing Office

Tennessee Department of State
Business Services Division
312 8th Avenue North
6th Floor, Snodgrass Tower
Nashville, TN 37243
Telephone: 615-741-2286
www.state.tn.us/sos/bus_svc/corporations.htm

State LLC Act

The Tennessee Revised Limited Liability Company Act, effective January 1, 2006, is contained in Title 48 (Corporations and Associations), Chapter 249 of the Tennessee Code Annotated, starting with Section 48-249-101, and is browseable from the following Web page (select the link to the Tennessee Revised Limited Liability Company Act at the bottom of the page):

www.state.tn.us/sos/bus_svc/index.htm

State Tax Office

Department of Revenue, Nashville
www.state.tn.us/revenue

Manager Election

The manager (and member) formality rules in the Act appear to be very flexible. Managers hold office until their successors are elected, and both manager and member meetings are called, noticed, and held as may be provided in the LLC documents (articles or operating agreement). The default voting rule for both managers and members in the Act is per-capita (one person, one vote) voting. [Section 405(a) and (b)]

Meeting Requirements

The member (and manager) formality rules in the Act appear to be very flexible. Member (and manager) meetings are called, noticed, and held as may be provided in the LLC documents (articles or operating agreement). The default voting rule for both members and managers in Act is per-capita (one person, one vote) voting. [Section 405(a) and (b)]

Amendments

Generally, amendments to the LLC's articles must be approved by all of the members; but some actions (specified in Section 204(c)) may be approved by a majority vote of the members. Amendment to the LLC's operating agreement can be approved by the method provided in its LLC documents. If the LLC documents do not provide a method of approval, all of the members must approve any amendment to the operating agreement. [Section 204(c)]

Admission of Members

After an LLC is formed, all members must approve the admission of a new person as a member, the membership interest of such person, and the contribution of such person. Such approvals may be unreasonably withheld, and are in the sole discretion of the members. [Section 501(b)] Generally, transfer of governance rights attached to a membership is effective only if all of the members, other than the member seeking to make the transfer, approve the transfer by unanimous consent. [Section 508(b)(3)] Apparently, this restriction can be waived or altered in the LLC operating agreement. [Section 205] Check with a lawyer for help in altering your operating agreement.

Withdrawal of Members

A member has the power to withdraw by giving notice to the LLC. [Section 503] If the membership interest of a member is terminated by the member in contravention of the LLC documents, the member forfeits all the member's governance rights in the LLC (including in the winding up and termination process of the LLC) and the member is liable for damages incurred by all the other members and the LLC due to the wrongful termination. Such damages and all other amounts owing to the LLC, whether or not currently due, arising from the wrongful termination may be offset against any amount owing from the LLC to the wrongfully terminating member. [Section 504]

Continuation of the LLC

A vote to continue the LLC after termination of a membership is not required. [Section 601(b)] Note however, that the LLC may continue despite the dissociation of the last remaining LLC member. [Section 601(a)(7)]

Special Statutory Rules

Section 401(c) of the Tennessee Revised Limited Liability Company Act provides for a third type of LLC management in addition to the two standard types of member-management and manager-management. This third type is called "director management" and allows an LLC to be managed by an elected board of directors, much like a corporation. If you wish to learn more about the special type of director management in Tennessee, see Section 401(c) of the Tennessee Revised Limited Liability Company Act (click the State LLC Act button at the bottom of the LLC Maker State Info screen).

If the LLC documents do not provide for allocations of profits and losses, profits and losses shall be allocated among the members and holders of financial rights in equal shares. [Section 304]

Professional LLCs: See Sections 1101 and following of the Tennessee Revised Limited Liability Company Act, the state filing office website, and contact your state licensing board for information on the special requirements that apply to forming and operating a Tennessee professional LLC.

TEXAS

LLC Filing Office

Texas Secretary of State
Statutory Filings Division
Corporations Section
P.O. Box 13697
Austin, TX 78711
Telephone: 512-463-5583
www.sos.state.tx.us/corp/index.shtml

State LLC Act

The Texas Limited Liability Company Law, effective January 1, 2006, is contained in Title 3, Chapter 101 of the Texas Business Organizations Code (BOC). General provisions that apply to LLCs and other business entities are contained in Title 1 of the Code. The LLC Law can be browsed from the following Web page (scroll down to Title 3, and expand the link to Chapter 101 to browse the LLC Law):

http://tlo2.tlc.state.tx.us/statutes/bo.toc.htm

State Tax Office

Comptroller of Public Accounts, Austin
www.window.state.tx.us

Manager Election

A manager of a limited liability company serves for the term, if any, for which the manager is elected and until the manager's successor is elected. [Section 101.303] Subject to Section 101.306(a), a manager of a limited liability company may be removed, with or without cause, at a meeting of the company's members called for that purpose. [Section 101.304]

Meeting Requirements

Except as provided by Subsection (b) (discussed in the next paragraph), notice of a regular or special meeting of the governing authority or members of a limited liability company, or a committee of the company's governing authority, shall be given in writing to each governing person, member, or committee member, as appropriate, and as provided by Section 6.051. [Section 101.352 (a)]

If the members of a limited liability company do not constitute the governing authority of the company (in other words, if the LLC is manager-managed) notice shall be given by or at the direction of the governing authority not later than the 10th day or earlier than the 60th day before the date of the meeting. Notice of a meeting required under this subsection must state the business to be transacted at the meeting or the purpose of the meeting if: (1) the meeting is a special meeting; or (2) a purpose of the meeting is to consider a matter described by Section 101.356. [Section 101.352 (b)]

A majority of all of the governing persons (managers), members, or committee members of a limited liability company constitutes a quorum for the purpose of transacting business at a meeting of the governing authority, members, or committee of the company, as appropriate. [Section 101.353] Each governing person (manager), member, or committee member of a limited liability company has an equal vote at a meeting of the governing authority, members, or committee of the company, as appropriate. [Section 101.354] Generally, the affirmative vote of the majority of the governing persons (managers), members, or committee members of a limited liability company present at a meeting at which a quorum is present constitutes an act of the governing authority, members, or committee of the company, as appropriate. [Section 101.355]

Amendments

Note: The Texas LLC Law refers to operating provisions adopted by an LLC as the "company agreement." Wide latitude is given to each LLC to construct its own rules—in effect, many of the default rules in the law (including those cited here) are suggestions only. See Sections 101.052 and 101.054 for more information.

Generally, an amendment to the LLC certificate of formation must be approved by all members. [Section 101.356] The company (operating) agreement of a limited liability company may be amended only if each member of the company consents to the amendment. [Section 101.053]

Admission of Members

A limited liability company, after the formation of the company, may issue membership interests with the approval of all of the members of the company. [Section 101.105] An assignee of a membership interest in a limited liability company is entitled to become a member of the company on the approval of all of the company's members. [Sections 101.103(c) and 101.109(b)]

Withdrawal of Members

As a default rule, a member of a limited liability company may not withdraw or be expelled from the company. [Section 101.107] A member of a limited liability company who validly exercises the member's right to withdraw from the company granted under the company agreement is entitled to receive, within a reasonable time after the date of withdrawal, the fair value of the member's interest in the company as determined as of the date of withdrawal. [Section 101.205]

Continuation of the LLC

A vote to continue the LLC after termination of a membership is not required, but the termination of the continued membership of the last remaining member of a limited liability company is an event requiring a winding up unless, not later than the 90th day after the date of the termination, the legal representative or successor of the last remaining member agrees: (1) to continue the company; and (2) to become a member of the company effective as of the date of the termination or to designate another person who agrees to become a member of the company effective as of the date of the termination. [Sections 11.051 and 11.056]

Special Statutory Rules

The profits and losses of a limited liability company are, as a default rule, allocated to each member of the company on the basis of the agreed value of the contributions made by each member, as stated in the company's records. [Section 101.201]

UTAH

LLC Filing Office

Utah Division of Corporations & Commercial Code
Box 146705
Salt Lake City, UT 84114-6705
Telephone: 801-530-4849
Toll-free: 877-526-3994
http://corporations.utah.gov/index.html

State LLC Act

The Utah Revised LLC Act is contained in Title 48 (Partnership), Chapter 2c of the Utah Code, starting with Section 48-2c-101, and is browseable from the Web page listed below (Select Code/Constitution—Keyword search, then expand the Utah Code and Constitution folder, Title 48, Chapter 2c to begin selecting and reading sections of the LLC Act):
http://www.le.state.ut.us/

State Tax Office

Utah State Tax Commission, Salt Lake City
http://tax.utah.gov/

Manager Election

Except for the initial managers, each manager shall be elected at any time by the members holding at least a majority of the profits interests in the company, and any vacancy occurring in the position of manager shall be filled in the same manner. [Section 48-2c-804(6)(a)]

Except as provided in the operating agreement, any manager may be removed with or without cause by the members, at any time, by the decision of members owning a majority of the profits interests in the company. [Section 48-2c-804(6)(e)]

Meeting Requirements

Unless otherwise provided in the articles of organization or operating agreement, no meetings need to be held for actions taken by members. If meetings of members are allowed or required under the articles of organization or operating agreement, then, unless otherwise provided in the articles of organization or operating agreement: a meeting of members may be called by any manager in a manager-managed company or by members in any company holding at least 25% interest in profits of the company; any business may be transacted at any meeting of members which is properly called; notice of a meeting of members must be given to each member at least five days prior to the meeting and shall give the date, place, and time of the meeting; a quorum must be present in person or by proxy at a meeting of members for any business to be transacted and a quorum shall consist of members holding at least 51% interest in profits of the company; voting at a meeting shall be determined by percentage interests in the profits of the company. [Section 48-2c-704]

Amendments

Generally, the affirmative vote, approval, or consent of all members shall be required to amend the articles of organization, except to make certain ministerial amendments. [Section 48-2c-803] An operating agreement may be altered, amended, or repealed as provided in the operating agreement. If an operating agreement does not provide for a procedure for altering, amending, or repealing the operating agreement, the operating agreement may be altered, amended, or repealed only by the written consent of all members. [Section 48-2c-506]

Admission of Members

Generally, new memberships can be issued with the written consent of all members. [Section 48-2c-703] Except as otherwise provided in the articles or operating agreement, admission of transferee as a member must be approved by consent of all members. [Section 48-2c-1104]

Withdrawal of Members

A member may withdraw from a company at the time or upon the happening of events specified in and in accordance with the articles of organization or operating agreement. If the articles of organization or operating agreement do not specify the time or the events upon the happening of which a member may withdraw, a member may not withdraw prior to the dissolution and completion of winding up of the company, without the written consent of all other members at the time. [Section 48-2c-709]

Continuation of the LLC

A vote to continue the LLC after termination of a membership is not required. [Section 48-2c-1201]

Special Statutory Rules

For the purpose of determining compliance with a provision of the LLC Act that requires the votes of members holding a certain percentage of the company's profits interests, unless otherwise provided in the articles of organization or the operating agreement, each member's profits interest shall be determined based on the member's capital account balance on the date on which compliance is measured. [Section 48-2c-803.1]

VERMONT

LLC Filing Office

Vermont Secretary of State
Corporations Division
81 River Street, Drawer 09
Montpelier, VT 05609-1104
Telephone: 802-828-2386
www.sec.state.vt.us/corps/corpindex.htm

State LLC Act

The Vermont LLC Act is contained in Title 11 (Corporations, Partnerships, and Associations), Chapter 21 of the Vermont Statutes, starting with Section 3001, and is browseable from the following Web page (select Vermont Statutes Online in the left panel, then scroll down to select Title 11, then Chapter 21):

www.leg.state.vt.us

State Tax Office

Vermont Department of Taxes, Montpelier
www.state.vt.us/tax/index.shtml

Manager Election

Except as provided in the operating agreement, managers are elected for an indefinite term and can be replaced and removed with the approval of a majority of members. [Section 3054]

Meeting Requirements

Unless otherwise provided in the operating agreement:

- Members have equal voting power (presumably, one vote each), and must take action by majority vote.

- Managers can approve decisions by majority vote. [Section 3054]

Rules for the notice, time, place, and quorum for members' and managers' meetings, and for actions by written consent by members and managers, were not found in the LLC Act. Presumably, these may be provided in the articles or operating agreement.

Amendments

Unless otherwise stated in the operating agreement, the articles and operating agreement can be amended with the consent of all members. [Section 3054]

Admission of Members

Unless otherwise provided in the operating agreement, new memberships must be issued with the approval of all members. [Section 3054] Admission of transferee as a member must be approved by unanimous consent of the nontransferring members, and as may also be provided in the LLC operating agreement. [Section 3073]

Withdrawal of Members

A member may withdraw upon notice to the LLC (in an LLC with a perpetual duration, notice must be in writing to the LLC and other members, and be given 90 days in advance of the withdrawal). If the withdrawal violates the articles or operating agreement or is prior to the end of a specified term established for the LLC, the member is liable to the LLC and the other members for the amount of damages caused by the breach or early withdrawal. [Sections 3081(1) and 3082]

Generally, a member is entitled to the fair value of the member's interest (different valuation dates are used, depending on whether the LLC has a specified term or a perpetual existence). The LLC must deliver an offer to purchase the interest of the withdrawing member and financial statements to the member within 30 days of the date of the withdrawal. The member has a right to bring a court action to determine the fair value of the member's interest if the member and the LLC cannot agree. [Section 3091]

Continuation of the LLC

Unless otherwise provided in the operating agreement, the LLC automatically dissolves upon the dissociation (cessation of membership rights) of a member (or a member-manager in a manager-managed LLC) unless a majority in interest of the remaining members (presumably, remaining members holding a majority of both the capital and profits interests in the LLC) consent to the continuance of the LLC within 90 days of the dissociation event. [Section 3101]

Note: The dissociation events that trigger dissolution (or a vote to avoid dissolution) differ for at-will and term LLCs (a term LLC is one whose articles specify a date for dissolution of the LLC; an at-will LLC is one that continues perpetually until dissolved). For an at-will LLC, the normal dissociation events apply: that is, the expulsion, withdrawal, death, bankruptcy, and so on, of a member. For a term LLC, only death, bankruptcy, or certain other events that occur prior to the date of dissolution of the term LLC as stated in the articles apply. For additional information, see Sections 3101(3) and 3081 of the LLC Act.

Special Statutory Rules

The operating agreement may vary any provision of the LLC Act, except certain nonwaivable provisions listed in Section 3003 (mostly dealing with duties of care and loyalty owed by members and managers, rights to inspect records, the right of a member to withdraw, and the right of the members to dissolve the LLC in special cases).

LLC property can be transferred on behalf of the LLC by any member (in a member-managed LLC) or by any manager (in a manager-managed LLC). [Section 3041]

Unless otherwise provided in the operating agreement, all members must consent to making distributions prior to the departure of a member or the winding up of the LLC, selling all its assets and voluntarily dissolving the LLC. [Section 3054]

VIRGINIA

LLC Filing Office

Clerk of the State Corporation Commission
P.O. Box 1197
First Floor
Richmond, VA 23218
Telephone: 804-371-9733
Toll-free: 866-SCC-CLK1
http://www.scc.virginia.gov/division/clk/index.htm

State LLC Act

The Virginia LLC Act is contained in Title 13.1 (Corporations) of the Virginia Code, Chapter 12, starting with Section 13.1-1000, and is browseable from the following Web page (click Code of Virginia, then click Table of Contents on the search page; then select the Title 13.1 heading, then click Chapter 12, Virginia Limited Liability Company Act to see a list of the sections in the LLC Act):
http://legis.state.va.us/codecomm/codehome.htm

State Tax Office

Department of Taxation, Richmond
www.tax.virginia.gov/

Manager Election

Unless otherwise provided in the articles or operating agreement, managers are to be elected by the members, and managers can be removed and vacancies filled by a majority vote of the members (members vote according to their capital account balances with the LLC). [Section 13.1-1024]

Meeting Requirements

Unless otherwise provided in the articles or operating agreement, members must vote in proportion to their capital account balances with the LLC, with the approval of members holding a majority share of capital account balances necessary to take membership action. Unless otherwise provided in the articles or operating agreement, managers can take action by a majority vote (presumably, with each manager entitled to one vote). Members and managers may take action by written consent without a meeting by obtaining signatures from the members or managers who would be sufficient to approve the matter at a meeting of members or managers. [Sections 13.1-1022 and 13.1-1024] Rules for the notice, time, place, and quorum for members' and managers' meetings were not found in the LLC Act. Presumably, these may be provided in the articles or operating agreement.

Amendments

Unless the articles provide for a greater vote, amendments to the articles require the approval of a majority of the members (who vote according to capital account balances with LLC). [Sections 13.1-1014 and 13.1-1022] Unless otherwise provided in the articles or operating agreement, amendments to the operating agreement must be approved by all members. [Section 13.1-1023]

Admission of Members

Unless otherwise provided in the operating agreement, new memberships must be issued with the consent of all members. [Section 13.1-1038.1]

Except as provided in the articles or LLC operating agreement, the admission of a transferee as a member must be approved by consent of a majority in interest (majority of profits and capital interests in the LLC) of the nontransferring members. [Sections 13.1-1040 and 13.1-1002]

Withdrawal of Members

A member may resign from the LLC only if and as provided in the articles or operating agreement. [Section 13.1-1032] No specific provision for distributions to resigning member was found in the Act; Section 13.1-1031 generally provides that distributions prior to the dissolution of the LLC are to be made according to the articles or operating agreement.

Continuation of the LLC

A membership vote to continue the LLC after the dissociation of a member (cessation or termination of a membership interest) is not required. [Section 13.1-1046]

WASHINGTON

LLC Filing Office

Washington Secretary of State
Corporations Division
P.O. Box 40234
Olympia, WA 98504-0234
Telephone: 360-753-7115
www.secstate.wa.gov/corps

State LLC Act

The Washington LLC Act is contained in Title 25.15 (Partnerships), of the Washington Code, starting with Section 25.15.005, and is browseable from the following Web page (insert 25.15 in the Search Legislative Documents box, check the RCW & Dispositions checkbox, then click Search. You will see a listing of related links. Select the link that says Chapter 25.15 RCW LIMITED LIABILITY COMPANIES, which will list the sections of the LLC Act):

http://search.leg.wa.gov/pub/textsearch/default.asp

State Tax Office

Department of Revenue, Olympia
http://dor.wa.gov

Manager Election

Except as provided in the operating agreement, the approval of members who contribute more than 50% of the value of capital to the LLC is necessary to elect, remove, and replace managers. Managers hold office for an indefinite term unless otherwise provided in the operating agreement. [Section 25.15.150]

Meeting Requirements

Except as provided in the operating agreement, the approval of members who contribute more than 50% of the value of the LLC's capital is necessary for membership action. Rules for the notice, time, place, and quorum for members' meetings, or for actions by written consent of members without a meeting, may be provided in the operating agreement. [Section 25.15.120] Unless otherwise provided in the operating agreement, managers can take action by approval of more than one-half the number of managers. Rules for the notice, time, place, and quorum for managers' meetings, or for actions by written consent of managers without a meeting, may be provided in the operating agreement. [Section 25.15.165]

Amendments

Unless otherwise provided in the operating agreement, approval of all members is required in order to amend the operating agreement. [Section 25.15.120] No statutory rule was found for voting to amend the certificate of formation.

Admission of Members

Unless otherwise provided in the operating agreement, new memberships must be issued with the consent of all members. [Section 25.15.115] Admission of a transferee as a member must be approved by unanimous consent of the nontransferring members, and as may be provided in the LLC operating agreement. [Section 25.15.250]

Withdrawal of Members

A member may withdraw from an LLC at the time or upon the happening of events specified in and in accordance with the LLC agreement. If the agreement does not specify when a member may withdraw, a member may not withdraw prior to the time for the LLC's dissolution and commencement of its winding up, unless the member obtains the written consent of all other members at the time. [Section 25.15.130(3)]

Continuation of the LLC

A membership vote to continue the LLC after the dissociation of a member (cessation or termination of a membership interest) is not required. [Section 25.15.270]

WEST VIRGINIA

LLC Filing Office

West Virginia Secretary of State
Corporations Division
Bldg. 1, Suite 157-K
1900 Kanawha Blvd. East
Charleston, WV 25305-0770
Telephone: 304-558-8000
www.wvsos.com

State LLC Act

The West Virginia LLC Act is contained in Chapter 31B of the West Virginia Code, starting with Section 31B-1-101, and is browseable from the following Web page (select WV Code at the top of the page, then select Limited Liability Companies): www.wvsos.com/business

State Tax Office

Department of Tax and Revenue, Charleston
www.state.wv.us/taxdiv

Manager Election

Except as may be provided in the operating agreement, managers are to be elected, removed, and replaced by a majority of members and hold office for an indefinite term. [Section 31B-4-404]

Meeting Requirements

Except as otherwise provided in the operating agreement, members and managers have equal management rights (presumably, this means equal voting power, such as one vote per member or manager), with a majority vote necessary to take membership or manager action. Members and managers may take action by written consent without a meeting (presumably, by normal member or manager voting rules). [Section 31B-4-404] Rules for the notice, time, place, and quorum for members' and managers' meetings, and for actions by written consent of members or managers without a meeting, were not found in the Act. Presumably, these may be provided in the operating agreement.

Amendments

Unless otherwise provided in the operating agreement, approval of all members is required in order to amend operating agreement. [Section 31B-4-404] No statutory rule was found for amendment of articles.

Admission of Members

No statutory rule was found regarding issuance of new memberships in an LLC. Except as may be provided in the operating agreement, the admission of a transferee as a member must be approved by unanimous consent of the nontransferring members. [Section 31B-5-503]

Withdrawal of Members

A member may withdraw upon notice to the LLC. If the withdrawal violates the operating agreement or is prior to the end of a specified term established for the LLC, the member is liable to the LLC and the other members for the amount of damages caused by the breach or early withdrawal, and the LLC must offset any amount paid to the withdrawing member by the amount of the damages. [Sections 31B-6-601(1) and 602]

Generally, a member is entitled to the fair value of the member's interest (different valuation dates are used, depending on whether the LLC has a specified term or has a perpetual existence). The LLC must deliver an offer to purchase the interest of the withdrawing member and financial statements to the member within 30 days of the date of withdrawal. The member has a right to bring a court action to determine the fair value of the member's interest if the member and the LLC cannot agree. [Section 31B-7-701]

Continuation of the LLC

Except as otherwise provided in the operating agreement, the LLC automatically dissolves upon the dissociation of a member (cessation of membership) unless the members who are entitled to receive a majority of current or future distributions vote to continue the LLC within 90 days of the dissociation event. Note: This statutory majority-of-distributions voting rule to continue the LLC applies in manager-managed LLCs only when a member who is also a manager is dissociated—a vote to avoid dissolution is not required when a nonmanaging member's interest is terminated in a manager-managed LLC (of course, the operating agreement can provide otherwise). [Section 31B-8-801]

Also note: The dissociation events that trigger dissolution (or a vote to avoid dissolution) differ for at-will and term LLCs (a term LLC is one whose articles specify a date for dissolution of the LLC; an at-will LLC is one that continues perpetually until dissolved). For an at-will LLC, the normal dissociation events apply: that is, the expulsion, withdrawal, death, bankruptcy, and so on, of a member. For a term LLC, only death, bankruptcy, or certain other events that occur prior to the date of dissolution of the term LLC as stated in the articles apply. For additional information see Sections 31B-8-801(b)(3) and 31B-6-601.

Special Statutory Rules

The operating agreement may vary any provision of the LLC Act, except certain nonwaivable provisions listed in Section 31B-1-103 (mostly dealing with duties of care and loyalty owed by members and managers, rights to inspect records, right of member to withdraw, and right of members to dissolve the LLC in special cases).

Unless otherwise provided in the operating agreement, approval of all members is required to make distributions prior to the departure of a member or the winding up of the LLC, sell all LLC assets, and voluntarily dissolve the LLC. [Section 31B-4-404]

WISCONSIN

LLC Filing Office

Department of Financial Institutions
Division of Corporate and Consumer Services
Corporations Section, 3rd Floor
P.O. Box 7846
Madison, WI 53707-7846
Telephone: 608-261-7577
www.wdfi.org/corporations/

State LLC Act

The Wisconsin LLC Act is contained in Chapter 183 of the Wisconsin Statutes, starting with Section 183.0102, and is browseable from the following Web page (click Statutes Related, then Statutes, then scroll down and select Chapter 183):

http://folio.legis.state.wi.us

State Tax Office

Department of Revenue, Madison
www.dor.state.wi.us

Manager Election

Except as provided in the operating agreement, the approval of members who contribute more than 50% of the value of capital to the LLC is necessary to elect, remove, and replace a manager. Managers hold office for an indefinite term unless otherwise provided in the operating agreement. [Section 183.0401]

Meeting Requirements

Except as provided in the operating agreement, the approval of members who contribute more than 50% of the value of capital to the LLC is necessary for membership action. Unless otherwise provided in the operating agreement, managers take action by approval of more than one-half the number of managers. [Section 183.0404] Rules for the notice, time, place, and quorum for members' and managers' meetings, and for action by written consent of the members and managers without a meeting, were not found in the Act. Presumably, these may be provided in the operating agreement.

Amendments

Unless otherwise provided in the operating agreement, the approval of all members is required to amend the articles or operating agreement. [Section 183.0404]

Admission of Members

Unless otherwise provided in the operating agreement, new memberships must be issued with the consent of all members. [Sections 183.0404 and 183.0801] Unless otherwise stated in the operating agreement, the admission of a transferee as a member must be approved by unanimous written consent of the nontransferring members. [Section 183.0706]

Withdrawal of Members

Unless the operating agreement prohibits withdrawals, a member may withdraw by giving written notice to the other members. If the withdrawal is a breach of the operating agreement or is otherwise based upon wrongful conduct, the LLC may offset the amount paid to the withdrawing member by the amount of damages caused by the breach or wrongful conduct. Unless otherwise provided in the operating agreement, if the LLC has a limited term or is formed for a particular undertaking (project), the withdrawal of a member before the end of the term or the accomplishment of the undertaking is a breach of the operating agreement. [Section 183.0802(3)]

If not otherwise provided in the operating agreement, a retiring member is entitled to receive the fair value of his or her interest within a reasonable time after resignation. [Section 183.0604]

Continuation of the LLC

A membership vote to continue the LLC after the dissociation of a member (cessation or termination of membership) is not required. [Section 183.0901]

Special Statutory Rules

LLC property may be transferred on behalf of the LLC by any member (in a member-managed LLC) or by any manager (in a manager-managed LLC). [Section 183.0702]

WYOMING

LLC Filing Office

Secretary of State's Office
Corporations Division
The State Capitol Building, Room 110
Cheyenne, WY 82002-0020
Telephone: 307-777-7311
http://soswy.state.wy.us/corporat/corporat.htm

State LLC Act

The Wyoming LLC Act is contained in Title 17 of the Wyoming Statutes, Chapter 15, starting with Section 17-15-101, and is browseable from the following Web page (click the link to the Limited Liability Company Act):

http://soswy.state.wy.us/corporat/statutes.htm

State Tax Office

Department of Revenue, Cheyenne
http://revenue.state.wy.us

Manager Election

Unless expressly dispensed with or overridden in the operating agreement, managers are to be elected annually by members in the manner specified in the operating agreement. [Section 17-15-117]

Meeting Requirements

Unless otherwise stated in the operating agreement, members vote in proportion to their capital account balances with the LLC. [Section 17-15-116] Rules for the notice, time, place, and quorum for members' and managers' meetings, and for actions by written consent of the members and managers without a meeting, were not found in the Act. Presumably, these may be provided in the operating agreement. (But Section 17-15-131 says that members and managers can waive notice in writing if notice is required under the Act or the articles or operating agreement.)

Amendments

No statutory rules for amendments to the articles or operating agreement were found in the Act.

Admission of Members

Admission of a transferee as a member must be approved by unanimous written consent of the nontransferring members. (But an LLC that has elected flexible LLC status in its articles can state its own admission rule for transferees in the LLC operating agreement.) [Sections 17-15-122 and 17-15-144]

Withdrawal of Members

Unless otherwise prohibited or restricted in the operating agreement, a member may withdraw and demand a return of his or her capital contribution upon six months' prior written notice to the other members. [Section 17-15-120(b)]

Continuation of the LLC

The LLC automatically dissolves upon the dissociation of a member (cessation of membership) unless the remaining members vote to continue the LLC by unanimous consent under a right to do so stated in the articles of organization. (But an LLC that has elected flexible LLC status in its articles can state its continuance rule or procedure in the LLC operating agreement.) [Sections 17-15-123 and 17-15-144]

Special Statutory Rules

Section 17-15-144 of the LLC Act allows the articles to contain a provision that elects flexible limited liability company status. In addition to allowing an LLC to have one member, rather than the default minimum of two members specified under the Act, this status allows the LLC to adopt its own operating agreement provisions for the approval of assignment of membership interests and for continuance of the LLC after a member is dissociated; without electing this status, the voting rules for admission of members and continuance of the LLC after the dissociation must be stated in the articles.

Only members, or managers in a manager-managed LLC, can contract debts, incur liabilities, or transfer property on behalf of the LLC. [Sections 17-15-117 and 17-15-118]

Forms

Title of Form	Chapter

Title of Form	Chapter

Meeting Summary Sheet

Name of LLC:

_____

Year of Meeting: _____

Type of Meeting: ☐ Annual/Regular or ☐ Special

Meeting of: ☐ Managers and/or ☐ Members

Date: _____, 20_____ Time: _____: _____ _____.M.

Place: _____

Meeting Called by: _____

Purpose: _____

_____

Committee or Other Reports or Presentations: _____

Other Reminders or Notes: _____

Notice Required: ☐ Written ☐ Verbal ☐ None

Notice Must Be Given by Date: _____

Notice of Meeting Given to:

Name	Type of Notice*	Date Notice Given	How and Where Communicated	Date of Acknowledgment
_____	_____	_____	_____	_____
_____	_____	_____	_____	_____
_____	_____	_____	_____	_____
_____	_____	_____	_____	_____
_____	_____	_____	_____	_____
_____	_____	_____	_____	_____

*Types of Notice: Written (mailed, hand-delivered); Verbal (in-person, telephone conversation, answering machine, voice mail); email; Fax.

Call of Meeting

Secretary: _____

Name of LLC: _____

LLC Address: _____

_____

The following person(s):

Name	Title	Membership Interest (if any)
_____	_____	_____
_____	_____	_____
_____	_____	_____

authorized under provisions of the operating agreement of the LLC and/or provisions of state law, hereby make(s) a call and request to hold a meeting of _____ of the LLC for the purpose(s) of: _____
_____.

The requested date and time of the meeting is: _____
_____.

The requested location for the meeting is: _____
_____.

The following LLC officers and other individuals are expected to attend to present reports or otherwise contribute to the meeting, and, in addition to managers and/or members, should be included in those who receive notice of the meeting:

Name	Address
_____	_____
_____	_____
_____	_____

The secretary is requested to provide all proper notices as required by the operating agreement of the LLC and state law to all persons entitled or asked to attend the meeting, and to include with the notice any other materials necessary or helpful to the holding of the upcoming meeting. If possible, the secretary is requested to provide at least _____ notice of the meeting to all meeting participants.

Date: _____

Signed: _____

Signed: _____

Meeting Participant List

Name of LLC:

_____

Type of Meeting: ☐ Regular (_____) or ☐ Special

Meeting of: ☐ Managers and/or ☐ Members

Date: _____, 20_____ Time: _____ : _____ _____.M.

Meeting Participants (*list names in alphabetical order*):

Name: _____

Address: _____

_____ Telephone: _____

☐ Manager: _____

☐ Member: Number or Percentage of Voting Power (per capita or according to percentage of capital, profits, or capital and profits interests as specified in operating agreement): _____

_____

☐ Officer: Title _____

☐ Other (Position and reason for attendance): _____

Name: _____

Address: _____

_____ Telephone: _____

☐ Manager: _____

☐ Member: Number or Percentage of Voting Power (per capita or according to percentage of capital, profits, or capital and profits interests as specified in operating agreement): _____

_____

☐ Officer: Title _____

☐ Other (Position and reason for attendance): _____

Notice of Meeting

Name of LLC: _____

A meeting of _____ of the LLC will be held at _____

_____, on _____ at _____.

The purpose(s) of the meeting is/are as follows:

_____

_____

_____

_____.

_____, LLC Secretary

Signature of Secretary

Acknowledgment of Receipt of Notice of Meeting

LLC Name: _____

(Recipient of Notice: In paragraph 1, please fill in the date on which you received notice of the meeting; in paragraph 2, review for accuracy the type of notice checked, making and initialing corrections as appropriate; in paragraph 3, date and sign your name; and mail or deliver a completed copy to the LLC officer listed in paragraph 4.)

1. I received notice of a meeting of the _____ of the LLC on

   _____. The notice of meeting stated the date, time, place, and purpose of

   the upcoming _____ meeting.

2. The notice of meeting was:

   ☐ received by fax, telephone number_____

   ☐ delivered orally to me in person at _____

   ☐ delivered orally to me by phone call, telephone number _____

   ☐ left verbally in a message on an answering machine or on voice mail, telephone number

   _____

   ☐ delivered by mail to _____

   ☐ delivered via email, email address: _____

   ☐ other: _____

3. Dated: _____

   Signed: _____

   Printed Name: _____

4. Please return to:

   Name of LLC Officer: _____

   Name of LLC: _____

   Address: _____

   Phone: _____

   Fax: _____

Membership Voting Proxy

(Member: Insert name of proxyholder—the person you are authorizing to vote in your place—in first paragraph, then date, sign, and return by the date indicated to LLC officer at address listed below.)

The undersigned member of _____, a limited liability company, authorizes _____ to act as his or her proxy and to represent and vote his/her LLC membership at a meeting of:

(Check one or both boxes)

☐ managers

☐ members

to be held on _____.

This proxy is effective for all items of business brought before the meeting.

Date: _____

Signature of Member: _____

Printed Name of Member: _____

Please return proxy by _____ to:

Name of LLC Officer: _____

Name of LLC: _____

Address: _____

Phone: _____ Fax: _____

Certification of Mailing of Notice

I, the undersigned acting secretary of _____,

a limited liability company, certify that I caused notice of the _____

meeting of the LLC to be held on _____ to be deposited in the United

States mail, postage prepaid, on _____, addressed to the

following persons at their most recent addresses as shown on the books of this LLC:

_____

_____

_____

_____

A true and correct copy of such notice is attached to this certificate.

Dated: _____

Signed: _____, Secretary

Printed Name: _____

Minutes of LLC Meeting

LLC Name: _____

1. A meeting of the _____ of the LLC was held on _____ at _____
   at _____ , for the transaction of all business
   that may properly be brought by participants before the meeting, including any of the special purposes
   listed below:

   (If applicable, check one or more boxes below, and supply additional information as appropriate.)

   ☐ Election of LLC manager(s) by LLC members

   ☐ Review of past LLC business and discussion of future operations

   ☐ The approval of one or more resolutions as follows:

                       [If this box is checked, insert summaries of resolutions.]

2. _____ acted as chairperson, and _____ acted as
   secretary of the meeting.

3. The chairperson called the meeting to order.

4. The secretary announced that the meeting was:

   [Check one of the boxes below and supply additional information.]

   ☐ a regular meeting scheduled to be held _____ under provisions
      in the LLC operating agreement

      (or)

   ☐ a special meeting called by the following person(s):

   _____   ☐ Manager ☐ Member ☐ Other: _____

   _____   ☐ Manager ☐ Member ☐ Other: _____

   _____   ☐ Manager ☐ Member ☐ Other: _____

5. The secretary announced that the meeting was held pursuant to notice, if required and as required under the operating agreement of this LLC, or that notice had been waived by all participants entitled to receive notice under the operating agreement. Copies of any certificates of mailing of notice prepared by the secretary of the LLC and any written waivers signed by participants entitled to receive notice of this meeting were attached to these minutes by the secretary.

6. ☐ **Members Voting.** (Check if members will vote at the meeting, and supply information below.)

The secretary announced that an alphabetical list of the names and interests held by all members of the LLC was available and open to inspection by any person in attendance at the meeting. The secretary announced that there were present, in person or by proxy, the following voting power of the members of the LLC, representing a quorum of the members. (The secretary attached written proxy statements, executed by the appropriate members, to these minutes for any membership voting power listed below as held by a proxyholder.)

Name of Member   Member's Voting Power

_____   _____

_____   _____

_____   _____

_____   _____

7. ☐ **Managers Voting.** (Check if managers will vote at the meeting, and supply information below.)

The secretary announced that an alphabetical list of the names of the managers of the LLC was available and open to inspection by any person in attendance at the meeting. The secretary announced that the following managers of the LLC were present, representing a quorum of the managers:

Name of Manager

_____

_____

_____

_____

8. The secretary announced that the following persons were also present at the meeting in the following capacities:

Name   Title

_____   _____

_____   _____

_____   _____

_____   _____

9. ☐ **Previous Meeting Minutes.** (Check if previous meeting minutes will be approved at this meeting, and supply information, checking one or both additional boxes below.)

The secretary announced that the minutes of the LLC meeting held on _____

☐ had been distributed prior to the meeting, and the secretary was in receipt of any written approval of minutes forms signed and returned by persons who had read and approved the minutes.

☐ were distributed at the meeting, then read by the secretary.

After counting any written approvals, and, if necessary, taking the voice vote of _____ at the meeting, the secretary announced that the minutes as distributed, read, and corrected, as appropriate, were approved. The secretary attached a copy of the approved minutes together with any signed approvals of minutes forms to these minutes.

10. The following reports were presented at the meeting by the following persons:

_____

_____

_____

11. ☐ **Election of Managers.** (Check if managers will be elected, and supply information below.)

The chairperson announced that the next item of business was the nomination and election of the managers for another _____ term. The following nominations were made and seconded:

Names of Manager Nominee(s):

_____

_____

_____

The secretary next took the votes of members entitled to vote for the election of managers at the meeting, and, after counting the votes, announced that the following persons were elected to serve as managers of this LLC:

Names of Elected Manager(s):

_____

_____

_____

☐ **Managers' Acceptance.** (Check if managers accepted positions.)

The above managers, having been elected, accepted their management positions. The secretary announced that the presence of current managers of the LLC at the meeting represented a quorum of managers of the LLC.

12. ☐ **Resolutions.** (Check if resolutions will be passed, and supply information below.)

After discussion, on motion duly made and carried by the affirmative vote of (check one or more boxes and supply any required information):

☐ a majority of the membership voting power in attendance

☐ a majority of the managers in attendance

☐ other, as follows:

_____

_____

_____

The following resolution(s) was(were) approved at the meeting:

_____

_____

_____

☐ **Additional Resolutions.** (Check if additional resolutions will be passed, and supply information below.)

After discussion, on motion duly made and carried by the affirmative vote of (check one or more boxes and supply any required information):

☐ a majority of the membership voting power in attendance

☐ a majority of the managers in attendance

☐ other, as follows:

_____

_____

_____

The following resolution(s) was(were) approved at the meeting:

_____

_____

_____

There being no further business to come before the meeting, it was adjourned on motion duly made and carried.

The above minutes were completed in final form on the date shown below by the undersigned secretary of the meeting:

Date: _____

Signature: _____

Title: _____

Waiver of Notice of Meeting

Name of LLC: _____

The undersigned waive(s) notice of and consent to the holding of the meeting of the LLC held at

_____ on _____, 20____

at ____:____ __.M. The purposes of the meeting are as follows: _____

_____

_____

_____

_____

_____

_____.

Dated: _____

Signature   Printed Name

_____   _____

_____   _____

_____   _____

_____   _____

_____   _____

Approval of LLC Minutes

Name of LLC: _____

The undersigned consent(s) to the minutes of the LLC meeting held at _____

_____ on _____, 20_____

at _____:_____ ___.M., and attached to this form, and accept(s) the resolutions passed and decisions made

at such meeting as valid and binding.

Dated: _____

Signature   Printed Name

_____   _____

_____   _____

_____   _____

_____   _____

_____   _____

_____   _____

_____   _____

_____   _____

Cover Letter for Approval of Minutes of LLC Meeting

Date: _____

Name: _____

Mailing Address: _____

City, State, Zip: _____

Re: Approval of LLC Minutes

Dear _____:

I am enclosing minutes of a meeting of _____ that show

approval of one or more specific resolutions.

Because these items were agreeable to the members and/or manager entitled to vote on them, we did not

hold a formal meeting to approve these decisions. We are now preparing formal minutes that reflect prior

LLC decisions.

To confirm that these minutes accurately reflect the past decisions of the LLC and to formally signify your

agreement to them, please date and sign the enclosed Approval of LLC Minutes form and mail it to me

at the address below. If you have corrections or additions to suggest, please contact me so we can hold a

meeting or make other arrangements to finalize and document these changes.

Sincerely,

_____

Enclosures: Minutes and Approval of LLC Minutes Form

Please return to:

Name: _____

LLC: _____

Mailing Address: _____

City, State, Zip: _____

Phone: _____   Fax: _____

Written Consent to Action Without Meeting

Name of LLC: _____

The undersigned hereby consent(s) as follows:

_____

_____

_____

_____

_____

_____

_____

Dated: _____

Signature   Printed Name

_____   _____

_____   _____

_____   _____

_____   _____

Authorization of Treasurer to Open and Use LLC Accounts

The treasurer of the LLC is authorized to select one or more banks, trust companies, brokerage companies, or other depositories, and to establish financial accounts in the name of this LLC. The treasurer and other persons designated by the treasurer are authorized to deposit LLC funds in these accounts. However, only the treasurer is authorized to withdraw funds from these accounts on behalf of the LLC.

The treasurer is further authorized to sign appropriate account authorization forms as may be required by financial institutions to establish and maintain LLC accounts. The treasurer shall submit a copy of any completed account authorization forms to the secretary of the LLC, who shall attach the forms to this resolution and place them in the LLC records binder.

Authorization of Treasurer to Open
and Use Specific LLC Account(s)

The treasurer of this LLC is authorized to open the following account(s) in the name of the LLC, with the following depositories:

Type of account: _____

Name, branch, and address of financial institution:

_____

_____

_____

Type of account: _____

Name, branch, and address of financial institution:

_____

_____

_____

The treasurer and other persons authorized by the treasurer shall deposit the funds of the LLC in this account. Funds may be withdrawn from this account only upon the signature of the treasurer.

The treasurer is authorized to complete and sign standard authorization forms for the purpose of establishing the account(s) according to the terms of this resolution. A copy of any completed account authorization form(s) shall be submitted by the treasurer to the secretary of the LLC, who will attach the form(s) to this resolution and place them in the LLC records binder.

Authorization of LLC Account and
Designation of Authorized Signers

The treasurer of this LLC is authorized to open a _____ account

in the name of the LLC with _____.

Any officer, employee, or agent of this LLC is authorized to endorse checks, drafts, or other

evidences of indebtedness made payable to this LLC, but only for the purpose of deposit.

All checks, drafts, and other instruments obligating this LLC to pay money must be signed on

behalf of this LLC by _____ of the following: _____

_____

_____.

The above institution is authorized to honor and pay any and all checks and drafts of this LLC

signed as provided herein.

The persons designated above are authorized to complete and sign standard account authorization

forms for the purpose of establishing the account(s), provided that the forms do not vary materially from

the terms of this resolution. The treasurer shall submit a copy of any completed account authorization

forms to the secretary of the LLC, who will attach the forms to this resolution and place them in the LLC

records binder.

Authorization of Rental of Safe Deposit Box

The treasurer of the LLC is authorized to rent a safe deposit box in the name of the LLC with an appropriate bank, trust company, or other suitable financial institution, and to deposit in this box any securities, books, records, reports, or other material or property of the LLC that he or she decides is appropriate for storage and safekeeping in this box.

Adoption of Assumed LLC Name

It was decided that the LLC will do business under a name that is different from the formal name of the LLC stated in its articles of organization (or similar organization document that was filed with the state to commence the legal existence of the LLC). The assumed name selected for the LLC is

_____.

The secretary of the LLC was instructed to register the assumed LLC name as required by law.

Approval of Contract

The _____ were presented a proposed contract to be

entered into between the LLC and _____ for the

purpose of _____, together with

the following attachments:

_____

_____.

    Next, a report on the proposed contract was given by_____

_____, who made the following major points and concluded with

the following recommendation: _____

_____.

    After discussion, _____

_____,

it was decided that the transaction of the business covered by the contract was in the best interests of the

LLC, and the proposed contract and attachments were approved.

    The _____ was instructed to execute the contract

submitted to the meeting in the name of and on behalf of the LLC, and to see to it that a copy of the

contract executed by all parties, together with all attachments, be placed in the records of the LLC.

Approval of Lease of Premises by LLC

A proposed lease agreement between _____ and

_____ for the premises known as

_____

was presented to the board for approval. The lease covered a period of _____,

with _____ rental payments payable of the LLC of _____.

     After discussion, it was decided that the lease terms were commercially reasonable and fair to the LLC and that it was in the best interests of the LLC to enter into the lease.

     The lease and all the terms contained in it were approved, and the secretary of the LLC was instructed to see to it that the appropriate officers of the LLC execute the lease on behalf of the LLC, and that a copy of the executed lease agreement be attached to this resolution and filed in the LLC records binder.

Purchase of Real Property by LLC

The purchase by the LLC of real property commonly known as _____

_____

was discussed. The president announced that the property had been offered to the LLC for sale by the

owner at a price of $_____. After discussing the value of the property to the LLC

and comparable prices for similar properties, it was agreed that the LLC should _____

_____.

It was also agreed that the LLC will seek financing for the purchase of the property on the following

terms: _____

_____

_____.

The president was instructed to see to it that the appropriate LLC officers prepare all financial and

legal documents necessary to submit the offer or counteroffer to the seller and to seek financing for the

purchase of the property according to the terms discussed and agreed to in this resolution.

Authorization of Sale of Real Property by LLC

After discussion, it was agreed that the president of the LLC is authorized to contract to sell real property

of the LLC commonly known as _____

on the following general conditions and terms: _____

_____

_____ .

     The president of the LLC and any other officers of the LLC authorized by the president can execute

all instruments on behalf of the LLC necessary to effectuate and record a sale of the above property

according to the above terms.

Delegation of LLC Authority

After discussion, it was agreed that the following individual, whose LLC title is indicated below, is granted authority to perform the tasks or transact business by and on behalf of the LLC, or to see to it that such tasks are performed for the LLC under his or her supervision as follows:

_____

_____.

    This person is also granted the power to perform any and all incidental tasks and transact incidental business necessary to accomplish the primary tasks and business described above.

Ratification of Contract or Transaction

After discussion, it was agreed that the following contract or other business transaction undertaken on behalf of the LLC by the following individual whose title appears below is hereby adopted, ratified, and approved as the act of the LLC and is accepted as having been done by, on behalf of, and in the best interests of the LLC:

_____

_____

_____.

Rescission of Authority

After discussion, it was agreed that prior authority granted to _____

on _____ for the purpose of _____

_____

is no longer necessary to the interests of the LLC and that any and all authority granted under this prior

approval of authority is hereby rescinded and no longer in effect.

Certification of LLC Resolution

The undersigned, duly elected and acting _____ of

_____, certifies that the attached resolution was

adopted by the _____

    [ ] at a duly held meeting at which a quorum was present, held on _____

    or,

    [ ] by written consent(s) dated on or after _____

    and that it is a true and accurate copy of the resolution, and that the resolution has not been

    rescinded or modified as of the date of this certification.

Date: _____

_____

_____, Secretary [or other title]

Affidavit of LLC Resolution

STATE OF _____

COUNTY OF _____

Before me, a Notary Public in and for the above state and county, personally appeared

_____ who, being duly sworn, says:

   1. That he/she is the duly elected and acting _____ of

_____, a _____ LLC.

   2. That the following is a true and correct copy of a resolution duly approved by the

_____ of the LLC _____

_____:

_____

_____

_____

   3. That the above resolution has not been rescinded or modified as of the date of this affidavit.

_____

_____, Secretary

Sworn to and subscribed before me this _____ day of _____, 20__.

Notary Public: _____

My commission expires: _____

NOTARY SEAL

Acknowledgment

STATE OF _____

COUNTY OF _____

I hereby certify that on _____, before me, a Notary Public in and for the

above state and county, personally appeared _____, who

acknowledged himself/herself to be the _____

of _____ and that he/she, having been authorized to do so, executed

the above document for the purposes contained therein by signing his/her name as _____

_____ of _____.

Notary Public: _____

My commission expires: _____

NOTARY SEAL

LLC Election of Corporate Tax Treatment

After consultation with the LLC's tax adviser, the LLC treasurer recommended that the LLC elect to be taxed as a corporation, starting _____. After discussion, all members agreed that this election should be made, and the treasurer was authorized by the members to complete IRS Form 8832, "Entity Classification Election," to accomplish this election, and to sign the form on behalf of each of the members of this LLC, and to file it with the IRS.

It was also agreed that, if applicable, the treasurer file any additional forms necessary to elect corporate tax treatment of the LLC for state income tax purposes.

Approval of Independent Audit of
LLC Financial Records

After discussion, it was agreed that the accounting firm of _____

was selected to perform an independent audit of the financial records of the LLC for the _____ fiscal

year and to prepare all necessary financial statements for the LLC as part of its independent audit.

    The LLC treasurer was instructed to work with the auditors to provide all records of LLC finances

and transactions that may be requested by them, and to report to the LLC on the results of the audit upon

its completion.

Approval of LLC Tax Year

After discussion and a report from the treasurer, which included advice obtained from the LLC's accountant, it was resolved that the accounting period of the LLC will end on _____ of each year. The treasurer was appointed to file the necessary tax forms on behalf of the LLC to adopt or change the tax year of the LLC with the IRS [add, if applicable, "and the appropriate state tax agency"].

Approval of Amendment to Articles of Organization

RESOLVED, that Article _____ of the articles of organization of this LLC be _____

as follows:

_____

_____

_____

_____ .

Approval of Restatement of Articles of Organization

RESOLVED, that the articles of organization be amended and restated to read in full as follows:

_____

_____

_____

_____

_____

_____

_____

_____

_____.

Amendment of Articles Form

To: _____

Articles of Amendment

of

_____

One: The name of the LLC is _____.

Two: The following amendment to the articles of organization was approved by the members on
_____:

_____

_____

_____

_____

_____

_____

_____

_____.

Three: The number of members required to approve the amendment was _____,
and the number of members that voted to approve the amendment was _____.

Date: _____

By:

_____

_____, President

_____

_____, Secretary

Amendment of LLC Operating Agreement

RESOLVED, that _____ of the operating agreement of the LLC is

_____ as follows:

_____

_____

_____

_____

_____.

Approval of LLC Distribution

The LLC resolves that the LLC will make the following distribution of profits of the LLC to the following members:

Name of Member	Amount
_____	$_____
_____	$_____
_____	$_____
_____	$_____
_____	$_____

It was announced that the above distribution of LLC profits was in accordance with the requirements for the allocation of distributions to members as set out in the LLC operating agreement, or as required under state law. The treasurer presented a current balance sheet of the LLC at the meeting for review by the attendees, and announced that he/she had consulted the LLC's tax adviser. It was agreed that, after giving effect to the distribution, the LLC would continue to be able to pay its obligations as they become due in the normal course of its operations, and that the LLC would meet any applicable financial and legal tests under state law for making distributions to members. The treasurer was instructed to attach a copy of the balance sheet to this resolution for inclusion in the LLC's records binder.

The treasurer of the LLC is instructed to prepare and deliver or mail a check drawn on the LLC's account in the appropriate amount to each member entitled to the distribution no later than _____.

Approval of Additional Contributions of Capital by Members

It was agreed that the following members will make the following contributions of capital to the LLC, on or by _____:

Name of Member   Amount

_____ $_____

_____ $_____

_____ $_____

_____ $_____

_____ $_____

☐ It was agreed that the operating agreement of the LLC will be amended, if necessary, to reflect the capital, profits, voting, and other interests of all members of the LLC as a result of the making of the above capital contributions.

☐ It was agreed that the LLC will pay interest at the rate of _____% per year on the above capital contributions, subject to the following terms: _____

_____.

Admission of New Member

After discussion, it was agreed that the LLC will issue the following membership interest to the following person for the following payment or transfer of property to the LLC:

Name   Payment

_____   _____

      It was agreed that the operating agreement of the LLC will be amended, if necessary, to reflect the capital, profits, voting, and other interests of all members of the LLC as a result of the admission of the person named above. It was also agreed that, as a condition to being formally accepted as a member of this LLC, the new member agrees to the rights and responsibilities associated with membership by signing the most current LLC operating agreement or by signing a statement, attached to the most current LLC operating agreement, in which the new member agrees to be bound by the terms of the agreement.

Approval of Transfer of Membership

After discussion, it was agreed that the LLC approves the transfer of the membership interest of _____, "former member," to _____, "new member." The new member is admitted as a full member of this LLC, with all economic, management, voting, and any other rights associated with the membership interest of the former member.

It was agreed that the books of this LLC will be adjusted to show the termination of membership rights of the former member and the establishment of membership rights of the new member.

The operating agreement of the LLC will be amended, if necessary, to reflect the capital, profits, voting, and other interests of all members of the LLC as a result of the admission of the new member named above. It was also agreed that, as a condition to being formally accepted as a member of this LLC, the new member must agree to the rights and responsibilities associated with membership by signing the most current LLC operating agreement or by signing a statement, which will be attached to the most current LLC operating agreement, agreeing to be bound by the terms of the agreement.

It was further resolved that the nontransferring members of the LLC, whose signatures appear below, consent to the continuance of the business and legal existence of the LLC following the withdrawal of the former member and the admission of the new member.

Date: _____

Signature: _____

Signature: _____

Signature: _____

Signature: _____

Approval of LLC Purchase of Interest of Withdrawing Member

The LLC resolves that the LLC will purchase the entire membership interest of _____ , a member of this LLC, on the terms specified below. It was agreed that the purchase of the membership interest will terminate all capital, profits, loss, and, voting, and all other management, ownership, and economic interests of the member in this LLC.

The date of purchase is: _____ .

The terms of the purchase are as follows: _____
_____ .

After a report of the treasurer, which included an analysis of the most recently prepared balance sheet of the LLC and LLC operations since its preparation, it was agreed that the LLC was able financially and in accordance with any applicable state legal requirements to purchase the withdrawing member's interest according to the terms set out above.

The treasurer was instructed to prepare a balance sheet of the LLC as of the date set for purchase of the withdrawing member's interest, and to see to it that a copy of the balance sheet, plus any additional supporting documentation, be given to the member prior to the date of purchase for the member's review and, if appropriate, signature. A copy of the balance sheet and any supporting documentation, signed by the withdrawing member if appropriate, will be attached to this resolution and placed in the LLC records binder.

On completion of the necessary paperwork, the treasurer will pay, or make appropriate arrangements for payment, on behalf of the LLC to purchase the withdrawing member's interest on the terms specified above.

It was further resolved that the remaining members of the LLC, whose signatures appear below, consent to the continuance of the business and legal existence of the LLC following the withdrawal of the member named above.

Date: _____

Signature: _____

Signature: _____

Signature: _____

Signature: _____

Approval of LLC Hiring

After discussion, the hiring of _____ to the position of
_____ was approved.

It was agreed that the duties of this position and compensation for performing these services will be
as follows: _____
_____.

Approval of Bonuses and Salary Increases

The LLC considered the question of salary increases and bonuses to persons who performed compensated services for the LLC. After discussion, the LLC approved the following salary increases and bonuses, to be paid for the upcoming fiscal year to the following persons:

Name and Title	Amount	Type	
_____	$_____	☐ Salary Increase	☐ Bonus
_____	$_____	☐ Salary Increase	☐ Bonus
_____	$_____	☐ Salary Increase	☐ Bonus
_____	$_____	☐ Salary Increase	☐ Bonus
_____	$_____	☐ Salary Increase	☐ Bonus
_____	$_____	☐ Salary Increase	☐ Bonus
_____	$_____	☐ Salary Increase	☐ Bonus

The above salary amounts or bonuses shall be paid as follows:

_____

_____

_____.

Approval of Independent Contractor Services

After discussion, the following independent contractor services were approved to be performed by

_____:

_____

_____

_____

_____

_____

_____.

Appointment of LLC Officers

After discussion, the following individuals were appointed to serve in the following LLC officer positions. Any annual salary to be paid to any officer and approved is shown next to the name of the officer:

TItle of Officer	Name	Compensation, if any
_____:	_____	$_____
_____:	_____	$_____
_____:	_____	$_____
_____:	_____	$_____

Each officer shall have such duties as are specified in the operating agreement of the LLC and as may be designated from time to time by the LLC management. An officer shall serve until his or her successor is elected and qualified to replace the officer.

Authorization of Payment for Attending LLC Meetings

After discussion, it was agreed that all of the following persons will be paid the following amounts for each day, or fraction of a day, during which they attend a meeting of the LLC

Name and Title	Per Diem Amount
_____	$_____
_____	$_____
_____	$_____
_____	$_____
_____	$_____

It was also discussed and agreed that the following persons will be _____ the following reasonable and necessary travel expenses incurred to attend meetings of the managers and/or members of the LLC:

Name and Title	Per Meeting Travel Allotment
_____	$_____
_____	$_____
_____	$_____
_____	$_____
_____	$_____

Annual Stipend for Attendance at LLC Meetings

After discussion, it was agreed that, on or by _____ of each year,

the following persons will be paid the following annual amounts, which comprise a yearly travel allotment,

for traveling to and attending regular and special meetings of the LLC:

Name and Title   Annual Stipend and Travel Allotment

_____ $_____

_____ $_____

_____ $_____

_____ $_____

_____ $_____

LLC Indemnification and Insurance

The LLC will indemnify its current and former _____

to the fullest extent permitted under the laws of this state. Such indemnification shall not be deemed to

be exclusive of any other rights to which the indemnified person is entitled, consistent with law, under

any provision of the LLC articles of organization (or similar organizing document of this LLC) or the LLC

operating agreement; as a result of any general or specific action of the members or managers of this LLC;

under the terms of any contract; or as may be permitted or required by law.

The LLC may purchase and maintain insurance or provide another arrangement on behalf of any

person who is or was a _____ of this LLC

against any liability asserted against him or her and incurred by him or her in such a capacity or arising out

of his or her official capacity with this LLC, whether or not the LLC would have the power to indemnify

him or her against that liability under the laws of this state.

Authorization of Loan to LLC at Specific Terms

It was announced that the officers of the LLC have received a loan commitment from the following bank, trust company, or other financial institution on the following terms:

Name of Lender: _____

Loan Amount: $_____

Terms of the Loan:

_____

_____

_____.

It was resolved that the proposed terms of the loan are fair and reasonable to the LLC and that it is in the best interests of the LLC to borrow the funds on the terms stated above.

It was further resolved that the following member, manager, or officer is authorized to execute the notes and documents necessary to make the above loan on behalf of the LLC:

Name   Title

_____   _____

_____   _____

Authorization of Maximum Loan Amount to LLC

It was resolved that it was in the best interests of the LLC to borrow up to the following amount from the following bank, trust company, or other financial institution:

Name of Lender: _____

Loan Amount: $_____

On behalf of the LLC, the following member, manager, or officer is authorized to sign the appropriate notes and documents necessary to borrow an amount that does not exceed the amount noted above, on terms commercialy reasonable to the LLC:

Name   Title

_____   _____

_____   _____

Authorization of LLC Representative to Borrow Funds
on Behalf of LLC as Needed

It was resolved that the following member, manager, or officer of the LLC is authorized to borrow funds on behalf of the LLC from one or more banks or other financial institutions in the amounts he or she decides are reasonably necessary to meet the business needs of the LLC:

Name   Title

_____   _____

_____   _____

_____   _____

Authorization of Loan Terms Secured
by LLC Property

It was resolved that the following LLC member, manager, or officer is authorized to borrow the sum of

$_____ on behalf of the corporation from _____:

Name   Title

_____   _____

_____   _____

_____   _____

The person named above is authorized to execute a promissory note for the principal amount shown above, together with a mortgage, deed of trust, or security agreement and any other documents necessary to secure payment of the note with the pledge of the following LLC property:

Property Used as Security for Note:

_____

The terms for repayment of the note will be as follows:

Terms of Note:

_____

Authorization of Line of Credit

It was resolved that it would be in the best interests of the LLC to obtain a line of credit for borrowing funds from _____.

The following LLC member, manager, or officer is authorized to complete all necessary forms, documents, and notes, and to pledge as security for the loan any LLC assets necessary to obtain and use the line of credit:

Name   Title

_____   _____

_____   _____

_____   _____

It was further decided that the authority granted by this resolution be limited and that the person named above not be allowed to establish a line of credit that exceeds _____.

Authorization of Line of Credit With Cap
on Each Transaction

It was resolved that it is in the best interests of the LLC to obtain a line of credit from

_____.

    The following LLC member, manager, or officer was authorized to complete all necessary forms, documents, and notes necessary to obtain and utilize the line of credit to allow borrowing by the LLC in an aggregate amount that does not exceed $_____.

Name   Title

_____   _____

_____   _____

_____   _____

    It was further resolved that the amount borrowed under the line of credit in one transaction will not exceed $_____ unless any excess amount is specifically approved by further resolution of the LLC.

Authorization of Line of Credit
Secured by LLC Property

It was resolved it is in the best interests of the LLC to obtain a line of credit for borrowing funds from

_____.

The following LLC member, manager, or officer is authorized to complete all necessary forms, documents, and notes and to pledge as security for the loan any LLC assets necessary to obtain and utilize the line of credit:

Name   Title

_____   _____

_____   _____

_____   _____

The person named above is authorized to execute a promissory note for the line of credit amount shown above, together with a mortgage, deed of trust, or security agreement and any other documents necessary to secure payment of the note with the pledge of the following LLC property:

Property Used as Security for Note:

_____

The terms for repayment of the note will be as follows:

Terms of Note:

_____

Approval of Loan to the LLC

It was resolved it is in the best interests of the LLC to borrow the following amounts from the following individuals:

Name of Lender   Amount

_____ $_____

_____ $_____

_____ $_____

    The terms of each loan were included in a proposed promissory note presented for approval at the meeting. The LLC determined that these terms were commercially reasonable. The LLC also determined that LLC earnings should be sufficient to pay back the loan(s) to the lender(s) according to the terms in the note(s), and that such repayment would not jeopardize the financial status of the LLC.

    Therefore, the LLC approved the terms of each note and directed the treasurer to sign each note on behalf of the LLC. The secretary was directed to attach a copy of each note, signed by the treasurer, to this resolution and to place the resolution and the attachment(s) in the LLC records binder.

LLC Promissory Note:
Installment Payments of Principal and Interest
(Amortized Loan)

For Value Received, _____, the borrower, promises to pay to

the order of _____, the noteholder, the principal amount

of $_____, together with simple interest on the unpaid principal balance from the date

of this note until the date this note is paid in full, at the annual rate of _____%. Payments shall be

made at _____

_____.

    Principal and interest shall be paid in equal installments of $_____,

beginning on _____, 20___ and continuing on _____

until the principal and interest are paid in full. Each payment made by the borrower shall be applied first

to accrued but unpaid interest, and the remainder shall be applied to unpaid principal.

    This note may be prepaid by the borrower in whole or in part at any time without penalty. This

note is not assumable without the written consent of the noteholder. Consent will not be unreasonably

withheld. This note is nontransferable by the noteholder.

    If any installment payment due under this note is not received by the noteholder within

_____ of its due date, the entire amount of unpaid principal

and accrued but unpaid interest due under this note will, at the option of the noteholder, become

immediately due and payable without prior notice by the noteholder to the borrower. In the event of

a default, the borrower is responsible for the costs of collection, including, in the event of a lawsuit to

collect on this note, the noteholder's reasonable attorney fees as determined by a court hearing the

lawsuit.

Date of Signing: _____

Name of Borrower: _____

Address of Borrower: _____

City or County and State Where Signed: _____

Signature of Borrower: _____, Treasurer on Behalf of _____

LLC Promissory Note:
Installment Payments of Principal and Interest
(Amortized Loan) Secured by LLC Property

For Value Received, _____, the borrower, promises to pay to the

order of _____, the noteholder, the principal amount of

$_____, together with simple interest on the unpaid principal balance from the date of this

note until the date this note is paid in full, at the annual rate of _____%. Payments will be made at

_____.

Principal and interest will be paid in equal installments of $_____, beginning

on _____, 20___ and continuing on _____ until the

principal and interest are paid in full. Each payment made by the borrower will be applied first to accrued

but unpaid interest, and the remainder will be applied to unpaid principal.

This note may be prepaid by the borrower in whole or in part at any time without penalty. This

note is not assumable without the written consent of the noteholder. Consent will not be unreasonably

withheld. This note is nontransferable by the noteholder.

If any installment payment due under this note is not received by the noteholder within

_____ of its due date, the entire amount of unpaid principal and accrued but

unpaid interest due under this note will, at the option of the noteholder, become immediately due and

payable without prior notice from the noteholder to the borrower. In the event of a default, the borrower

is responsible for the costs of collection, including, in the event of a lawsuit to collect on this note, the

noteholder's reasonable attorney fees as determined by a court hearing the lawsuit.

Borrower agrees that until such time as the principal and interest owed under this note are paid in

full, the note is secured by the following described mortgage, deed of trust, or security agreement:

_____

_____.

Date of Signing: _____

Name of Borrower: _____

Address of Borrower: _____

City or County and State Where Signed: _____

Signature of Borrower: _____, Treasurer on Behalf of _____

LLC Promissory Note:
Installment Payments of Principal and Interest
(Amortized Loan) With Balloon Payment

For Value Received, _____, the borrower, promises to pay to the order of _____, the noteholder, the principal amount of $_____, together with simple interest on the unpaid principal balance from the date of this note until the date this note is paid in full, at the annual rate of _____%. Payments will be made at _____.

    Principal and interest will be paid in equal installments of $_____, beginning _____, 20____, and continuing on _____. On the installment payment date on _____, a balloon payment of _____ will be added to the installment amount paid by the borrower in order to pay off this note in its entirety on this final installment payment date. Each payment made by the borrower will be applied first to accrued but unpaid interest, and the remainder will be applied to unpaid principal.

    This note may be prepaid by the borrower in whole or in part at any time without penalty. This note is not assumable without the written consent of the noteholder. Consent will not be unreasonably withheld. This note is nontransferable by the noteholder.

    If any installment payment due under this note is not received by the noteholder within _____ of its due date, the entire amount of unpaid principal and accrued but unpaid interest due under this note will, at the option of the noteholder, become immediately due and payable without prior notice from the noteholder to the borrower. In the event of a default, the borrower is responsible for the costs of collection, including, in the event of a lawsuit to collect on this note, the noteholder's reasonable attorney fees as determined by a court hearing the lawsuit.

Date of Signing: _____

Name of Borrower: _____

Address of Borrower: _____

City or County and State Where Signed: _____

Signature of Borrower: _____, Treasurer on Behalf of _____

LLC Promissory Note:
Periodic Payments of Interest
with Lump-Sum Principal Payment

For Value Received, _____, the borrower, promises to pay to the order of _____, the noteholder, the principal amount of $_____, together with simple interest on the unpaid principal balance from the date of this note until the date this note is paid in full, at the annual rate of _____%. Payments will be made at _____.

Interest will be paid in equal installments of $_____, beginning on _____, and continuing on the _____ until _____, on which date the entire principal amount, together with total accrued but unpaid interest, will be paid by the borrower.

This note may be prepaid by the borrower in whole or in part at any time without penalty. This note is not assumable without the written consent of the noteholder. Consent will not be unreasonably withheld. This note is nontransferable by the noteholder.

If any installment payment due under this note is not received by the noteholder within _____ of its due date, the entire amount of unpaid principal and accrued but unpaid interest due under this note will, at the option of the noteholder, become immediately due and payable without prior notice from the noteholder to the borrower. In the event of a default, the borrower is responsible for the costs of collection, including, in the event of a lawsuit to collect on this note, the noteholder's reasonable attorney fees as determined by a court hearing the lawsuit.

Date of Signing: _____

Name of Borrower: _____

Address of Borrower: _____

City or County and State Where Signed: _____

Signature of Borrower: _____, Treasurer on Behalf of _____

LLC Promissory Note:
Lump-Sum Payment of Principal and Interest
on Specified Date

For Value Received, _____, the borrower, promises to pay to the order of _____, the noteholder, the principal amount of $_____, together with simple interest on the unpaid principal balance from the date of this note until the date this note is paid in full, at the annual rate of _____%. Payments will be made at _____.

The entire principal amount of the loan, together with total accrued but unpaid interest, will be paid by the borrower on _____. Any payment made by the borrower prior to the due date specified above will be applied first to accrued but unpaid interest, and the remainder will be applied to unpaid principal.

This note may be prepaid by the borrower in whole or in part at any time without penalty. This note is not assumable without the written consent of the noteholder. Consent will not be unreasonably withheld. This note is nontransferable by the noteholder.

In the event of a default, the borrower is responsible for the costs of collection, including, in the event of a lawsuit to collect on this note, the noteholder's reasonable attorney fees as determined by a court hearing the lawsuit.

Date of Signing: _____

Name of Borrower: _____

Address of Borrower: _____

City or County and State Where Signed: _____

Signature of Borrower: _____, Treasurer on Behalf of _____

LLC Promissory Note:
Lump-Sum Payment of Principal and Interest
on Demand by Noteholder

For Value Received, _____, the borrower, promises to pay to the order of _____, the noteholder, the principal amount of $_____, together with simple interest on the unpaid principal balance from the date of this note until the date this note is paid in full, at the annual rate of _____%. Payments will be made at _____.

The entire principal amount of the loan, together with total accrued but unpaid interest, will be paid within _____ of receipt by the LLC of a demand for repayment by the noteholder. A demand for repayment by the noteholder will be made in writing and will be delivered or mailed to the borrower at the following address: _____ _____. If demand for repayment is mailed, it will be considered received by the borrower on the third business day after the date when it was deposited in the U.S. mail as registered or certified mail.

Any payment made by the borrower prior to the due date specified above will be applied first to accrued but unpaid interest, and the remainder will be aplied to unpaid principal.

This note may be prepaid by the borrower in whole or in part at any time without penalty. This note is not assumable without the written consent of the noteholder. Consent will not be unreasonably withheld. This note is nontransferable by the noteholder.

In the event of a default, the borrower is responsible for the costs of collection, including, in the event of a lawsuit to collect on this note, the noteholder's reasonable attorney fees as determined by a court hearing the lawsuit.

Date of Signing: _____

Name of Borrower: _____

Address of Borrower: _____

City or County and State Where Signed: _____

Signature of Borrower: _____, Treasurer on Behalf of _____

LLC Promissory Note:
Special Schedule of Payments
of Principal and Interest

For Value Received, _____, the borrower, promises to pay to the order of _____, the noteholder, the principal amount of $_____, together with simple interest on the unpaid principal balance from the date of this note until the date this note is paid in full, at the annual rate of _____%. Payments will be made at _____.

Principal and interest will be paid as follows:

_____

_____

_____.

This note may be prepaid by the borrower in whole or in part at any time without penalty. This note is not assumable without the written consent of the noteholder. Consent will not be unreasonably withheld. This note is nontransferable by the noteholder.

If any installment payment due under this note is not received by the noteholder within _____ of its due date, the entire amount of unpaid principal and accrued but unpaid interest due under this note will, at the option of the noteholder, become immediately due and payable without prior notice from the noteholder to the borrower. In the event of a default, the borrower is responsible for the costs of collection, including, in the event of a lawsuit to collect on this note, the noteholder's reasonable attorney fees as determined by a court hearing the lawsuit.

Date of Signing: _____

Name of Borrower: _____

Address of Borrower: _____

City or County and State Where Signed: _____

Signature of Borrower: _____, Treasurer on Behalf of _____

Approval of LLC Loan to Insider

It was resolved it is in the best interests of the LLC to make the following loan to the following person under the following terms:

Name and Title of Borrower: _____

Principal Amount of Loan: $_____

Rate of Interest: _____%

Term of Loan: _____

Payment Schedule:

_____

_____

It was further resolved that the above loan could reasonably be expected to benefit the LLC and that the LLC would be able to make the loan payments without jeopardizing its financial position, including its ability to pay its bills as they become due.

Therefore, the LLC approved the terms of the note and directed the borrower to sign the note. The secretary was directed to attach a copy of the note, signed by the borrower, to this resolution and to place the resolution and the attachment(s) in the LLC records binder.

Individual Promissory Note:
Installment Payments of Principal and Interest
(Amortized Loan)

For Value Received, _____, the borrower(s), promise(s) to pay to the order of _____, the noteholder, the principal amount of $_____, together with simple interest on the unpaid principal balance from the date of this note until the date this note is paid in full, at the annual rate of _____%. Payments will be made at _____.

Principal and interest will be paid in equal installments of $_____, beginning on _____, 20____ and continuing on _____ until the principal and interest are paid in full. Each payment made by the borrower(s) will be applied first to accrued but unpaid interest, and the remainder will be applied to unpaid principal.

This note may be prepaid by the borrower(s) in whole or in part at any time without penalty. This note is not assumable without the written consent of the noteholder. Consent will not be unreasonably withheld. This note is nontransferable by the noteholder.

If any installment payment due under this note is not received by the noteholder within _____ of its due date, the entire amount of unpaid principal and accrued but unpaid interest of the loan will, at the option of the noteholder, become immediately due and payable without prior notice by the noteholder to the borrower(s). In the event of a default, the borrower(s) is/are responsible for the costs of collection, including, in the event of a lawsuit to collect on this note, the noteholder's reasonable attorney fees as determined by a court hearing the lawsuit.

If two persons sign below, each is jointly and severally liable for repayment of this note.

Signature of Borrower #1: _____

Name of Borrower #1: _____

Address: _____

City or County, State Where Signed: _____

Date of Signing: _____

Signature of Borrower #2: _____

Name of Borrower #2: _____

Address: _____

City or County, State Where Signed: _____

Date of Signing: _____

Individual Promissory Note:
Installment Payments of Principal and Interest
(Amortized Loan) Secured by Property

For Value Received, _____, the borrower(s),
promise(s) to pay to the order of _____, the noteholder, the
principal amount of $_____, together with simple interest on the unpaid principal balance from
the date of this note until the date this note is paid in full, at the annual rate of _____%. Payments
will be made at _____.

Principal and interest will be paid in equal installments of $_____, beginning on
_____, 20____ and continuing on _____ until
the principal and interest are paid in full. Each payment made by the borrower(s) will be applied first to
accrued but unpaid interest, and the remainder will be applied to unpaid principal.

This note may be prepaid by the borrower(s) in whole or in part at any time without penalty. This
note is not assumable without the written consent of the noteholder. Consent will not be unreasonably
withheld. This note is nontransferable by the noteholder.

If any installment payment due under this note is not received by the noteholder within
_____ of its due date, the entire amount of unpaid principal and accrued but unpaid
interest of the loan shall, at the option of the noteholder, become immediately due and payable without
prior notice by the noteholder to the borrower(s). In the event of a default, the borrower(s) is/are
responsible for the costs of collection, including, in the event of a lawsuit to collect on this note, the
noteholder's reasonable attorney fees as determined by a court hearing the lawsuit.

Borrower(s) agree(s) that until such time as the principal and interest owed under this note are
paid in full, the note will be secured by the following described mortgage, deed of trust, or security
agreement: _____.

If two persons sign below, each is jointly and severally liable for repayment of this note.

Signature of Borrower #1: _____

Name of Borrower #1: _____

Address: _____

City or County, State Where Signed: _____

Date of Signing: _____

Signature of Borrower #2: _____

Name of Borrower #2: _____

Address: _____

City or County, State Where Signed: _____

Date of Signing: _____

Individual Promissory Note:
Installment Payments of Principal and Interest
(Amortized Loan) With Balloon Payment

For Value Received, _____,
the borrower(s), promise(s) to pay to the order of _____,
the noteholder, the principal amount of $_____, together with simple interest on the unpaid
principal balance from the date of this note until the date this note is paid in full, at the annual rate of
_____%. Payments will be made at _____.

    Principal and interest will be paid in equal installments of $_____, beginning on
_____, 20____ and continuing on _____. On
the installment payment date on _____, a balloon payment of $_____
will be added to the installment amount paid by the borrower in order to pay off this note in its entirety
on this final installment payment date. Each payment on this note will be applied first to accrued but
unpaid interest, and the remainder will be applied to unpaid principal.

    This note may be prepaid by the borrower(s) in whole or in part at any time without penalty. This
note is not assumable without the written consent of the noteholder. Consent will not be unreasonably
withheld. This note is nontransferable by the noteholder.

    If any installment payment due under this note is not received by the noteholder within
_____ of its due date, the entire amount of unpaid principal and accrued but unpaid
interest of the loan will, at the option of the noteholder, become immediately due and payable without
prior notice by the noteholder to the borrower(s). In the event of a default, the borrower(s) is/are
responsible for the costs of collection, including, in the event of a lawsuit to collect on this note, the
noteholder's reasonable attorney fees as determined by a court hearing the lawsuit.

    If two persons sign below, each is jointly and severally liable for repayment of this note.

Signature of Borrower #1: _____

Name of Borrower #1: _____

Address: _____

City or County, State Where Signed: _____

Date of Signing: _____

Signature of Borrower #2: _____

Name of Borrower #2: _____

Address: _____

City or County, State Where Signed: _____

Date of Signing: _____

Individual Promissory Note:
Periodic Payments of Interest
With Lump-Sum Principal Payment

For Value Received, _____,
the borrower(s), promise(s) to pay to the order of _____,
the noteholder, the principal amount of $_____, together with simple interest on the unpaid
principal balance from the date of this note until the date this note is paid in full, at the annual rate of
_____%. Payments will be made at _____.

Interest will be paid in equal installments of $_____, beginning on
_____, 20____ and continuing on _____
until _____, on which date the entire principal amount, together with
total accrued but unpaid interest, will be paid by the borrower(s).

This note may be prepaid by the borrower(s) in whole or in part at any time without penalty. This
note is not assumable without the written consent of the noteholder. Consent will not be unreasonably
withheld. This note is nontransferable by the noteholder.

If any installment payment due under this note is not received by the noteholder within
_____ of its due date, the entire amount of unpaid principal and accrued but unpaid
interest of the loan will, at the option of the noteholder, become immediately due and payable without
prior notice by the noteholder to the borrower(s). In the event of a default, the borrower(s) shall be
responsible for the costs of collection, including, in the event of a lawsuit to collect on this note, the
noteholder's reasonable attorney fees as determined by a court hearing the lawsuit.

If two persons sign below, each is jointly and severally liable for repayment of this note.

Signature of Borrower #1: _____

Name of Borrower #1: _____

Address: _____

City or County, State Where Signed: _____

Date of Signing: _____

Signature of Borrower #2: _____

Name of Borrower #2: _____

Address: _____

City or County, State Where Signed: _____

Date of Signing: _____

Individual Promissory Note:
Lump-Sum Payment of Principal and Interest
on Specified Date

For Value Received, _____ ,
the borrower(s), promise(s) to pay to the order of _____ ,
the noteholder, the principal amount of $_____ , together with simple interest on the unpaid
principal balance from the date of this note until the date this note is paid in full, at the annual rate of
_____%. Payments will be made at _____ .

The entire principal amount of the loan, together with total accrued but unpaid interest, will
be paid by the borrower(s) on _____ . Any payment made by the
borrower(s) prior to the due date specified above will be applied first to accrued but unpaid interest, and
the remainder will be applied to unpaid principal.

This note may be prepaid by the borrower(s) in whole or in part at any time without penalty. This
note is not assumable without the written consent of the noteholder. Consent will not be unreasonably
withheld. This note is nontransferable by the noteholder.

In the event of a default, the borrower(s) is/are responsible for the costs of collection, including, in
the event of a lawsuit to collect on this note, the noteholder's reasonable attorney fees as determined by a
court hearing the lawsuit.

If two persons sign below, each is jointly and severally liable for repayment of this note.

Signature of Borrower #1: _____

Name of Borrower #1: _____

Address: _____

City or County, State Where Signed: _____

Date of Signing: _____

Signature of Borrower #2: _____

Name of Borrower #2: _____

Address: _____

City or County, State Where Signed: _____

Date of Signing: _____

Individual Promissory Note:
Lump-Sum Payment of Principal and Interest
on Demand by Noteholder

For Value Received, _____,

the borrower(s), promise(s) to pay to the order of _____,

the noteholder, the principal amount of $_____, together with simple interest on the unpaid

principal balance from the date of this note until the date this note is paid in full, at the annual rate of

_____%. Payments will be made at _____.

The entire principal amount of the loan, together with total accrued but unpaid interest, will be

paid within _____ of receipt by the borrower(s) of demand for repayment by the

noteholder. A demand for repayment by the noteholder will be made in writing and will be delivered or

mailed to the borrower(s) at the following address: _____

_____. If demand for repayment is mailed, it will be considered received by the

borrower(s) on the third business day after the date when it was deposited in the U.S. mail as registered or

certified mail.

Any payment made by the borrower(s) prior to the due date specified above will be applied first to

accrued but unpaid interest, and the remainder will be applied to unpaid principal.

This note may be prepaid by the borrower(s) in whole or in part at any time without penalty. This

note is not assumable without the written consent of the noteholder. Consent will not be unreasonably

withheld. This note is nontransferable by the noteholder.

In the event of a default, the borrower(s) is/are responsible for the costs of collection, including, in

the event of a lawsuit to collect on this note, the noteholder's reasonable attorney fees as determined by a

court hearing the lawsuit.

If two persons sign below, each is jointly and severally liable for repayment of this note.

Signature of Borrower #1: _____

Name of Borrower #1: _____

Address: _____

City or County, State Where Signed: _____

Date of Signing: _____

Signature of Borrower #2: _____

Name of Borrower #2: _____

Address: _____

City or County, State Where Signed: _____

Date of Signing: _____

Individual Promissory Note:
Special Schedule of Payments of
Principal and Interest

For Value Received, _____,

the borrower(s), promise(s) to pay to the order of _____, the

noteholder, the principal amount of $_____, together with simple interest on the unpaid

principal balance from the date of this note until the date this note is paid in full, at the annual rate of

_____%. Payments will be made at _____.

Principal and interest will be paid as follows:

_____

_____

_____.

This note may be prepaid by the borrower(s) in whole or in part at any time without penalty. This note is not assumable without the written consent of the noteholder. Consent will not be unreasonably withheld. This note is nontransferable by the noteholder.

If any installment payment due under this note is not received by the noteholder within _____ of its due date, the entire amount of unpaid principal and accrued but unpaid interest of the loan will, at the option of the noteholder, become immediately due and payable without prior notice by the noteholder to the borrower(s). In the event of a default, the borrower(s) is/are responsible for the costs of collection, including, in the event of a lawsuit to collect on this note, the noteholder's reasonable attorney fees as determined by a court hearing the lawsuit.

If two persons sign below, each is jointly and severally liable for repayment of this note.

Signature of Borrower #1: _____

Name of Borrower #1: _____

Address: _____

City or County, State Where Signed: _____

Date of Signing: _____

Signature of Borrower #2: _____

Name of Borrower #2: _____

Address: _____

City or County, State Where Signed: _____

Date of Signing: _____

Release of Promissory Note

The undersigned noteholder, _____ , in consideration

of full payment of the promissory note dated _____ in the principal amount of

$_____ , hereby releases and discharges the borrower(s), _____ ,

_____ from any claims or obligations on account of the note.

Date: _____

Name of Noteholder: _____

Signature: _____

[If the LLC is the noteholder, use the following signature lines instead:]

By: _____ , Treasurer

on behalf of: _____

LLC Approval of Transaction Benefiting
a Member or Manager

The members and/or managers of the LLC have considered: _____

_____. It was understood that the following persons

have a material financial interest in this transaction or contract as follows: _____

_____

_____.

      After discussion, it was agreed that the approval of this business was fair to and in the best interests

of the LLC because _____

_____.

Therefore, it was approved by the votes of the members and/or managers as follows:

Name   Vote

_____   _____

_____   _____

_____   _____

Index

Q

T

Protecting your family
has never been easier

...make your will online *now*

Nolo Now lets you create a legal will from the comfort of your home computer. Complete a quick step-by-step interview, print your document, get witnesses, sign it – and you're done! Best of all, you don't pay until you're ready to click "print."

Nolo Now is simple, straightforward and completely legal. Providing your loved ones with the safety and security of a will is so easy, anyone can do it!

Find out more and get a free eBook!
http://nolonow.nolo.com/book

Get the Latest in the Law

 Nolo's Legal Updater
We'll send you an email whenever a new edition of your book is published!
Sign up at **www.nolo.com/legalupdater**.

 Updates at Nolo.com
Check **www.nolo.com/update** to find recent changes in the law that
affect the current edition of your book.

 Nolo Customer Service
To make sure that this edition of the book is the most recent one, call us at
800-728-3555 and ask one of our friendly customer service representatives
(7:00 am to 6:00 pm PST, weekdays only). Or find out at **www.nolo.com**.

4 **Complete the Registration & Comment Card ...**
... and we'll do the work for you! Just indicate your preferences below:

- -

Registration & Comment Card

NAME _____ DATE _____

ADDRESS _____

CITY _____ STATE _____ ZIP _____

PHONE _____ EMAIL _____

COMMENTS _____

WAS THIS BOOK EASY TO USE?   (VERY EASY)   5   4   3   2   1   (VERY DIFFICULT)

☐ Yes, you can quote me in future Nolo promotional materials. *Please include phone number above.*

☐ Yes, send me **Nolo's Legal Updater** via email when a new edition of this book is available.

Yes, I want to sign up for the following email newsletters:

    ☐ **NoloBriefs** (monthly)
    ☐ **Nolo's Special Offer** (monthly)
    ☐ **Nolo's BizBriefs** (monthly)
    ☐ **Every Landlord's Quarterly** (four times a year)

☐ Yes, you can give my contact info to carefully selected
partners whose products may be of interest to me.

LOP 5.0

Nolo
950 Parker Street
Berkeley, CA 94710-9867
www.nolo.com